D1357988

THE AMERICAN REGIONAL COOKBOOK

THE AMERICAN REGIONAL COOKBOOK

RECIPES FROM
YESTERDAY AND TODAY
FOR THE MODERN COOK

NANCY & ARTHUR HAWKINS

GREENWICH HOUSE
Distributed by Crown Publishers, Inc.
New York

Copyright © MCMLXXVI by Nancy and Arthur Hawkins.
All rights reserved.

This 1984 edition is published by Greenwich House,
a division of Arlington House, Inc.,
distributed by Crown Publishers, Inc.
by arrangement with the authors.

Manufactured in the United States of America

Library of Congress Cataloging in Publication Data

Hawkins, Nancy.
    The American regional cookbook.
    Reprint. Originally published: Englewood Cliffs,
N.J. : Prentice-Hall, c1976.
    Includes index.
    1. Cookery, American.   I. Hawkins, Arthur.
II. Title.
TX715.H3918 1984   641.5973   83-25468

ISBN: 0-517-43122X
h g f e d c b a

To All Those Who Have Shared in the
Creation and Development of American Cooking:

WAGON TRAIN WOMAN

NEW ENGLAND SETTLER

PLANTATION WORKER

ALASKAN PROSPECTOR

MIGRANT FARMWORKER

NORTHWEST EXPLORER

NEW YORK IMMIGRANT

FRANCISCAN PADRE

INDIAN WOMAN

PENNSYLVANIA FARMER

FRENCH MISSIONARY

NEW ORLEANS CHEF

CALIFORNIA FISHERMAN

CHUCK WAGON COOK

CHARLESTON CHEF

RAILROAD PIONEER

NATIVE HAWAIIAN

PRAIRIE TRAPPER

COUNTRY STOREKEEPER

BIG CITY RESTAURANTEUR

RIVERBOAT CHEF

SPANISH CONQUISTADOR

MIDWEST HOMESTEADER

LUMBER CAMP COOK

TEXAS RANCHER

MAINE GUIDE

KENTUCKY MOUNTAINEER

BOOKS BY NANCY AND ARTHUR HAWKINS

The American Regional Cookbook,
The Shellfish Cookbook, Nantucket and
Other New England Cooking, The Low
Cost Meat Book, Chef's Magic,
Chef's Special.

By Nancy Hawkins
Let's Cook

By Arthur Hawkins
The Steak Book, Who Needs A Cookbook,
Cook it Quick, The Complete Seafood
Cookbook, The Architectural Cookbook
The Antisocial Cookbook, Kids Cooking (in collaboration)
and Candies, Cookies, Cakes (in collaboration)

CONTENTS

PREFACE

William Penn, who founded Pennsylvania, had a great interest in eating—and in cooking. (It was he who introduced coffee to Philadelphia—the doughnuts for dunking followed later). He also had a great interest in writing and publishing and it was during these pursuits that he ran across a cookbook that commanded his attention. He reviewed the book for his newspaper and was so impressed that he wrote in effect: This book is so complete and so full of fine instructions for preparing food of all kinds that there seems no reason for writing another book on cookery. What Penn didn't know was that curiosity about cooking is insatiable and each new generation has its own changes in style which have to be written about and learned.

William Penn's pronouncement must have been made around 1690 when he was a middle-aged man. By that time Americans could have been exposed to a number of cookbooks, among them: *The Compleat Cook's Guide*, *The Frugal Housewife*, *The Accomplished Cook* and *The Cook's Oracle*, all written and published in England and brought to these shores by the early settlers. There are diaries and lists of supplies but no cookbooks written by the monks who settled the West Coast.

The first cookbook to be written by an American and published in America did not appear until almost eighty years after Penn's death. *American Cookery* written by Amelia Simmons, was printed and issued in 1796 by a firm known as Hudson and Goodwin of Hartford, Connecticut. *American Cookery* was a plain folksy book that spoke the language and described the dishes of the New England farmer.

A more sophisticated cookbook written by Mary Randolph appeared at a later date. *The Virginia Housewife* contained many of the recipes that gourmet Thomas Jefferson, then the first American Minister to France, brought to Virginia from Paris.

The recipes in these early books were stated in indisputably vague language. Follow along, for example, with Amelia Simmons' recipe for roast beef:

The general rules are, to have a brifk hot fire, to hang down rather than to fpit, to bafte with falt and water, and one quarter of an hour to every pound of beef, tho' tender beef will require lefs, while old tough beef will require more roafting; pricking with a fork will determine you whether done or not; rare done is the healthieft and the tafte of this age.

Or consider for a moment the recipe for Thomas Jefferson's favorite dish, boeuf à la mode, as served at Monticello:

Take a fleshy piece; (piece de tranche) beat it & lard it & season it with the ingredients below mentioned: salt, pepper, laurel leaf & green lemons; put all in a pot together & shut it perfectly close; cook it by a slow fire & when the juice is well out, put in a glass of wine; let it boil and when it is pretty near dry, serve it up with lemon juice.

Perhaps these old recipes were loosely recorded because measurements were not precise—"Take a good handful of raisins" is an example. Experienced cooks can read method into a recipe, and although cooks were skillful then, they had minimal education and gave little thought to the ignorance of the amateur. Also open hearth cooking provided only a crude means of temperature control. To slow the cooking the pot was removed from the fire or pulled aside, or in the case of a roast, a baffle was put between it and the fire. All this required more experience on the part of the cook than do the present day methods and equipment.

What William Penn also failed to realize, was our cooking methods, equipment, and utensils were to change by leaps and bounds from generation to generation—open-hearth to wood stove to coal range to gas range to electrical units to microwave. Refrigeration has developed from the old icehouse to the modern freezer. Food once bought at the corner grocery store in quantities enough to last a few days, is now bought by the cart load at shopping centers, where each year greater varieties of foods—fresh, canned, and frozen—crowd the shelves. And customs for preparing food have changed as well.

In short, there has been such a need for cookbooks, such a demand for old, traditional recipes clearly and accurately stated, and for new and different recipes, that there is scarcely a town in the country that has not produced its own share. These local cookbooks—books produced in towns from Great Falls to Charleston and from Nantucket to New Orleans—have been a valuable resource and an aid in the discovery that the cooking in America varies, not so much from city to city and state to state, as from region to region.

In the course of our work in compiling a contemporary regional cookbook we settled on nine regions, which in a way chose themselves, often because of comparable history, ethnic migration, similar crops, climate, pattern of living.

For each of these regions, we have tried to select recipes that are regional but not trite. (Our criteria were that the recipe be characteristic or representative of the region and still be in general use in some form or another.) Old favorites have been included because they are typical and reflect American variations of ethnic importations. We have reproduced or adapted heirloom regional recipes handed down to us by our families and the families of friends across the country. It was necessary to test and translate many of them into contemporary form, and we have quoted cookbooks from Colonial days as well as from the recent past and the present.

All this was done in the effort to bring forth a book revealing the rich harvest of American cooking: 300 years ago, today, and the years in between; simple American cooking as practiced in the farmlands and sophisticated cooking in the cities. Most of all, we have endeavored to produce a book of interesting, workable recipes you can follow without effort in your own kitchen.

THE ROOTS OF AMERICAN COOKERY

The Bicentennial celebrated only the 200th year of political independence from Great Britain. America's cooking began to evolve long before 1776.

The roots of American cookery go as deep as the recurrent migrations that swept into the vast territories of the North American continent. First came the tribes across the Siberian ice bridge, later called Indians, who developed

in the varied regions of America their own distinct gastronomies, commingled in the course of time by tribal wars and travels. Much later, came the first whites, sailors or fishermen marooned on beaches by shipwreck. Small parties of adventurers cast off from Iceland, Norway, Ireland, England—and sometimes they landed and stayed. Then companies of people from Holland, Sweden, Spain and

England came to settle here. When these colonies had established a foothold, more people came until it was a flood of the poor, the persecuted, the ambitious—anyone who was in search of a better life or freedom. Each brought an ethnic treasury of recipes from the homeland kitchen, specialties that have enriched the table of American cookery.

They came in small boats, then larger ships. They came as patroons, servants, slaves, governors, soldiers, housewives, artisans, and indentured servants (three to seven years servitude to pay their passage). Most were farm families with a knowledge of animal husbandry and crops. How they came is not as important to cookery as what they brought with them in their hearts and memories of the home hearth. From Maine to Florida and westward they adapted old methods to new foods and new foods to old methods.

The hearth for many centuries meant home. The hearth was first of all warmth, and in most of America wood was plentiful. It was also the kitchen stove. Up until the middle of the nineteenth century all cooking was open-hearth cookery. This was so, whether in a log cabin or a Philadelphia mansion, a Spanish hacienda or a New England keeping room. Later, when the open fire was replaced by the wood stove, it, too, became a symbol of warmth—a hearth.

The fire burned all day and all night in winter to warm the family. Chairs and settles were built with high backs to retain the warmth within the magic circle of the fire. Because the fire was always there, many foods could be cooked over low heat for a long time without inconvenience. A soup pot was kept at the back to simmer slowly into flavorful lusciousness. This method was not only good, but practical. A woman could work all day in the fields, or go to market, and return to a meal that required only dishing up.

For cooking, the fire was burned down to coals. It was covered with ashes at night to keep it dormant, and replenished each morning. Elaborate utensils were devised to ease the cooking process over the centuries. Rings were built into the mortar of the fireplace. Into these rings cast-iron arms were fitted. Pots were hung from the arms by a chain, and the links in that chain controlled the desired distance from the fire. Frying pans called spiders had long handles and three legs to hold them above the coals. Dutch ovens had tops grooved to hold coals to make a small bake-oven. Grills and waffle irons from Flanders had very long handles to protect the cook from the fire. The spit, an indispensable adjunct to open-hearth cookery, went into disuse with the advent of the wood-coal stove in the middle nineteenth century, only to be revived in our own time, turned by electricity.

The settlers brought with them apples, pears, quinces, currants, and potatoes which had been discovered earlier in South America by explorers. They brought wheat, domestic rice, buckwheat, rye, swine, cattle, coffee, tea, oats, barley, cabbage, turnips, carrots, and green peas. The Indians introduced them to corn, and they discovered unbelievable bounty—venison, rabbit, turkey, duck, and other wild fowl and seafood—on which they flourished.

Daily or weekly markets were the centers for the exchange of goods of all kinds. They were also social centers where people met friends and heard the latest news and gossip. Market day was exciting and pleasurable, an important and integral part of the life of the Colonial period and into the present century.

A good eye for freshness was essential in the days when there was no refrigeration. Dr. Thomas Cooper's "Domestic Cookery," published in *Old Time Cookery*, by Monroe Aurendote, Jr., in Reading, Pennsylvania, in 1824, advised as much on healthful eating as on culinary excellence and gave good advice in both instances. Dr. M. Appert of Reading, Pennsylvania, writing in the same publication, was very precise when he set down guiding principles for the purchase of meat.

He began with venison:

If the fat be clear, bright, thick, and the cleft part smooth and close, it is young; but if the cleft is wide and tough, it is old. To judge of its sweetness, run a very sharp narrow knife into the haunch and you will know by its scent. The sooner venison is eaten after being killed, the better.

He went on:

Beef—If the flesh of the ox-beef is young it will have a fine smooth open grain, be of a good red and feel tender. The fat should look white rather than yellow; for when it is of deep color the meat is seldom good. Lamb—Observe the neck of the forequarter; if the vein is bluish, it is fresh; if it has a green yellow cast it is stale. Pork—Pinch the lean, and if it is young, it will break. If the rind is tough, thick, and cannot easily be impressed by the finger, it is old. A thin rind is always a good sign on pork.

The book has sixteen pages, closely printed, on how to preserve, dress, and cook meats, game, and poultry, and how to choose fish and shellfish.

It is interesting to discover in reading early cookbooks that in the seventeenth century it was the custom to season food well and with great variety. Garlic was used in many meat dishes, and herbs of all kinds had many uses in cooking. These books also recommend a large selection of *salatts* dressed with *oyl* and vinegar and herbs. The recipes resemble the gourmet cooking of the present day. Somewhere between the seventeenth and twentieth centuries the use of many seasonings was almost lost. It is possible that when people lost faith in herbs as medicines, they no longer needed to plant them and so the kitchen lost their use as well.

The American Revolution lasted five years and stopped commerce with Europe, except for that of blockade runners. The custom of drinking tea in the morning never did recover from that "unhappy affair," as Englishmen of that generation referred to the Revolution. The fashionable dinners with many courses had succumbed to food shortages, anti-royalism and other austerities. Plump colonists had become slender Americans.

Restaurants and caterers in the American cities flourished during the Colonial period. Samuel Fraunces, a free mulatto who had come from the West Indies, was the best caterer in New York. Washington hired him as his official caterer when the city became the national capital in 1789. Shocked by the size of the bill for his establishment Washington asked Fraunces how he had spent so much. Fraunces, who loved good food, had not discriminated; the domestics, the staff, everyone had been served the same elaborate food that the General and his distinguished guests had been served. Washington regretfully let him go. Fraunces

Tavern still stands and bears his name in downtown New York.

Benjamin Franklin and Thomas Jefferson brought French recipes and wines back to this country from their ambassadorial assignments, though neither were strangers to good food and wines in Philadelphia and Williamsburg. French refugees, fleeing their Revolution, settled in Baltimore and other places on the Eastern Seaboard. Their classic French cooking came with them.

In 1744 Benjamin Franklin had invented what he called a Pennsylvania fireplace made of cast iron. Later called the Franklin stove, it was, in actuality, a free standing fireplace—warming stoves had come out from the hearth and into the rooms. This development led eventually to square, 10-plate cook stoves; perfected by Baron Stiegal, a German-American iron and glass manufacturer (1729-1785), these stoves came into general use much later.

All this time people had been moving westward. After the Revolution the lands were opened to the west because the treaties with the Indians had been with the defeated English. Toll roads were opened which carried traffic into Kentucky, Ohio, and West Virginia. A traveler in New England said with a certain sadness, "Everyone yearns for this land, farmers send half of their sons so far away that here, parts of a family may live six or eight hundred, even up to a thousand miles from each other, and one may never hear anything of the other."

Later the Louisiana Purchase opened even more lands. After the Battle of New Orleans Creole cuisine, so called from the word *Criolla* (which the Spanish settlers on the Gulf had called themselves), became another element of American Cookery.

The thirteen original states had evolved from the northern colonies, the middle colonies, and the Carolinas, or southern colonies, and in a way those regional divisions still existed. With the advent of the Civil War, or War Between the States as it was called in the South, the country split in two, and loyalties to one side or another firmed into partisan action. Pride in all that was northern or southern—including their cooking—flared and has continued to the present, buffered again by the eastern states between Connecticut and Virginia.

When the war was over and the period of Reconstruction began, many southerners found themselves deprived of their lands and living in the aftermath of the Civil War. They migrated to the Southwest, and took their culinary customs with them. There they combined them with the earlier Spanish and Mexican-Indian cookery, to the advantage of both.

Wagon trains were on the trails to California and Oregon as early as 1844, but after the war and when gold was discovered in California, the influx of people into that territory was so large that the population doubled, tripled, and then quadrupled in just a few years. Eggs were $12.00 a dozen, milk $55.00 a quart, if they were to be had at all. Ships brought Chinese to work from the Hawaiian Islands and the Orient. San Francisco's reputation for fine food grew, encouraged by the gold and shipping millionaires.

The flow of wagon trains continued through the '60s and '70s even as the railroads were being built across the prairie. For a long time the Western Frontier had been like a blockade to be run. It was Indian Territory. The trails ran from river to river because people and animals needed water. Their fuel was buffalo chips, the droppings of the thousands of buffalo over the years, sun-dried to hard mats of grass—in a treeless wilderness a valuable commodity. The women at first did not want to pick them up, but soon of necessity lost their repugnance. Sometimes the wagon trains stopped and stayed where they were, because the settlers liked the land or were tired of travel. There they built sod houses. Around these places towns grew, and were often later abandoned for better locations.

Except in the established city and town kitchens, at this time only the simplest dishes were cooked from recipes passed down from mother to daughter, and crossed the country with them to California and Oregon. On the wagon train the evening's dinner was cooked at the *nooning* for no fires were allowed at night in Indian territory. After the U. S. Cavalry had driven the tribes into reservations, Indian lands were open to homesteading. Recipes in Army manuals of the time are in quantities "enough for 24 men"—the number of a Cavalry patrol. These were substantial recipes, heavy on starch and gravy, and staples such as apples, sugar, cinnamon. Before the land was settled, ranchers had begun to repopulate the plains with cattle after the slaughter of the buffalo.

In the winter of 1865-1866, a cattle drive moved up from the southwest to Sedalia, Missouri, to feed the rising population in the East. Others followed on the Sedalia, Chisholm, and Western Trails. The reason was the difference in the price of beef in Texas and at the railheads—seven to eight dollars a head in Texas, forty to fifty dollars in Missouri. The Cattle Kingdom was to last twenty years. Companies and combines formed to invest in cattle ranches in the American West. British and French noblemen plunged heavily into these companies and often went West for the "shooting" as well as for business reasons bringing their chefs with them.

The food of the trail hand was different. Here the chuck wagon, always at the head of the drive, came into its own. The cook's pay was $32.50 per month, just under the $43.20 paid to top hands. He made stew with beans, beef, and chili peppers—Texas chili. He made hash of beef, potatoes, and onions, and he roasted beef ribs over a fire. Salads were wild greens, and pies, wild blackberries. Altogether he made the hard cowboy life palatable. The overpopulated ranges were struck first with drought, and then in the 1886 blizzards, fifty to ninety percent of the herds was lost. The Cattle Kingdom was over, but the trail foods remain in the Southwest, the Prairies, and the Northwest.

Back East, massive immigration from Ireland, and eastern and southern Europe was in progress. New industries needed workers. There was a potato famine in Ireland, Poles fled oppression, and Jews pogroms. Prolific Italy sent families fleeing hunger. In America's cities—New York, New Orleans, St. Louis, Chicago, San Francisco—one could find the cooking of almost any nation or ethnic group in the world.

Before America had an income tax, millionaires mushroomed in the burgeoning economy. Money was lavished in restaurants and hotels and town houses and palatial country "cottages." Debutante parties and weddings were so extravagant the purpose of the celebration was often lost in ostentation. Each millionaire tried to outdo the other in foods served and gifts given to their wealthy and noble guests. In one instance a pretentious father gave his daughter a party in a coal mine complete with white damask tablecloths, crystal, silver and wine. Elaborate bouquets of flowers decorated these elegant tables. Cakes were adorned with sugar roses, violets, and lilies, upon which the sugar cook had lavished hours of preparation. Swans and fishes carved from ice served as containers for lobster salad, mousses, and ices. Chefs were imported from France to prepare these extravagances and European nobility discovered American heiresses and married them. Pictures of European royalty graced the rotogravure sections of American newspapers beside those of American society belles, whose delicate necks supported coiffures almost as big as the swirls of tulle, feathers, and flowers that were their hats.

Even middle-class families had a "hired girl" who did the cooking and cleaning. She was called a "maid of all work." The working class was offered "free lunch" with the purchase of drinks in saloons. One end of the bar was laden with such foods as sausages, cheeses, cold cuts, sliced breads, crackers, sardines, cole slaw, and steamed pig's head (in higher-priced bars this was almost a smorgasbord). It was customary too, at that time, to take "Mother" out to dinner on Sunday, a custom that is still followed in parts of America. Restaurants catered to this custom by serving "Sunday dinner."

World War I burst upon this established order with sudden reality. Food shortages developed quickly, with much of America's food production going to hungry Europe. Victory gardens were planted, and Salvation Army girls served doughnuts at Army Camps, at War Bond Rallies, and to men waiting to board troopships for Europe. Our boys went off to fight for democracy and apple pie, while at home suffragettes starved for the vote.

The Volstead Act prohibited the drinking, the sale, and the production of alcoholic beverages. This law was to have a profound effect on America's eating habits. Hotels failed, and so did restaurants, because now Americans went where they could drink, regardless of the quality of the food.

Free lunches disappeared, no longer needed to lure customers into saloons that were closed. Speakeasies served bad food and "mixed" drinks to hide the taste of the "gin" or "whiskey" made the night before in a bathtub. This unpopular law was finally repealed in 1934, and good food returned to public dining. Some of the first and best restaurants to open were former speakeasies. Jack and Charlie's, now the 21 Club, was one.

Meanwhile the country had slipped into the depths of the Depression. Unable to get a price for their produce, farmers destroyed meat animals and crops, while people starved in the cities. Prices were so low by the mid-thirties that an excellent restaurant dinner could be bought for $2.75, and men and women stood on breadlines by the thousands at food kitchens set up to feed the hungry. Farm families migrated from the dust bowl to the Pacific Coast to work picking crops for as little as five cents an hour, to stay alive. Tomatoes sold for ten cents a basket. The New Deal developed food programs to assist those in distress and food surpluses were later distributed to the poor. Farmers were given subsidies for their crops to raise their living standard and to prevent the desertion of their farmland. Unemployment insurance and Social Security brought a certain stability to the ravaged country.

Despite the Depression, the success of the Century of Progress Exposition in Chicago which opened in May 1933, prompted New York City to promote the 1939 New York World's Fair, with its hundreds of good restaurants of many nationalities, where Americans were introduced to new and exciting foods. Some of the chefs imported for the Fair opened restaurants here when their countries were overrun by Hitler's armies. Refugees from Europe and Asia came here, too, swelling the ranks of foreign restaurateurs on both coasts.

World War II continued to broaden American tastes. Our soldiers returned from all over the world with a knowledge of exotic and foreign foods. At the same time their wives had learned to cook. There were no surplus cooks to be had when everyone was at work in the war effort. With the lady of the house in the kitchen, the kitchen blossomed into an attractive room, utensils burst into color, and television experts, beginning with Dione Lucas, brought real gourmet cooking into every home. Although more viewed than copied, they united the country in cooking experience.

In each region's cooking are the traces of its history. New England's Indian, English, Irish, and Canadian migrations, and the East's Dutch, Quaker, Scotch-Irish, German influence, are now almost lost in their large cities crowded with descendants of immigrants from every nation on earth. The South, with its Anglo-Saxon and African heritage; the Gulf Coast Creole tradition of good cooking; the Midwest's pioneer, Middle-European, corn-bowl bounty; the Prairie's Scandinavian kitchen delicacy; the Southwest's Mexican-Indian beginnings; the Northwest's frontier freedom, including the Alaskan frontier, game, game birds, fish, and beef; and finally the Pacific Coast's Spanish-American, Oriental heritage and its abundance of fruits and vegetables—these are America's regions, the geography and customs ill-defined at times, and at others as clear in demarcation as the regional face of New England.

Mobility—jet travel, the automobile, trains, fast cross-country trucks—carry the good of one region to another, causing confusion, sparking creativity, eventually broadening the base of regional cookery. The packaging of regional specialties speeds the spread of regional food lore. Odd ethnic combinations show up everywhere—frankfurter on roll with chili, turkey with sauerkraut, oriental goulash, Swedish meatballs and lasagne, venison salami; also new and different ways of preparation—macaroni salad, fried bologna sausage, cheese waffles, shrimp parmesan, hamburger quiche. All this is as much due to the enterprise of diner and luncheonette cooks, as to women's magazines and TV commercials, in which fantastic mixtures are concocted before one's eyes, with suitable groans of delight at ever-mounting calories and condiments.

Roadside eating, once the glory and despair of regional cooking, has undergone a metamorphosis. Part of the joy of travel once was the change from region to region—though sometimes for the worse, there was a certain adventure and anticipation when one sat down to table. Today fast-food enterprises serve up food quickly, cleanly, expertly though starchily, to the traveler. The uniformity is such that one can be three thousand miles away and eat exactly what could be bought at the highway complex around the corner from home. A successful formula for a restaurant is sold throughout the country. As a result it is possible to land in a small airport and find that instead of a pork chop dinner, there is a choice of chicken kiev or boeuf bourguignonne, imported wine, French bread and tossed salad. Or in an Arizona highway town to find on the menu a 1½-pound Snake River rainbow trout with tartar sauce, and to have it served broiled to perfection. It is also possible to go off the Ohio Turnpike a mile and find a perfect regional restaurant with a choice of chicken fricassee with dumplings or hot biscuits, country baked ham and corn bread, homemade apple pie and ice cream. There is a restaurant in Montana where a standing rib roast as big around as a service plate is served with crusted ribs eighteen inches long; another in New Jersey serving planked shad right out of the Hudson River, roasted in front of a wood fire and basted with butter; another in Maryland serving crab cakes from the Chesapeake Bay, rich and peppery; another in California that serves a whole avocado filled with dressed crabmeat with sourdough French bread; and so on throughout the country.

The food industry has done much to equalize the distribution of food across America. Quality is uniform. The fresh vegetables, meats, and dairy products that travel from the warmer regions in refrigerator cars permit year-round enjoyment of seasonal foods.

Our kitchens are efficient and comfortable, often the gathering place of the family, like an old New England keeping room, where good cooking flourishes.

Often the hardships of our forebears are stressed to show how well off we are now. There were many hardships, but it is a pleasure to turn back the years and see how well they managed without the conveniences of today. It is also interesting to discover that a dish that would have required a day's work to prepare then can now be put together in, perhaps, an hour and still be as good as it ever was. This book is a journey into American kitchens in all regions, with their differences and similarities, their histories and their pleasures. It offers indisputable evidence that the best experiences in American eating have not been lost to the present.

NEW ENGLAND
COOKING

SOUPS AND CHOWDERS

New England Clam Chowder
Baked Bean Soup
Cream of Turkey Soup
Potato Soup
Boston Fish Chowder
Maine French Pea Soup
Alsatian Soup

PASTA, EGG, AND CHEESE DISHES

Rinktum Ditty
Baked Eggs
Welsh Rabbit
Quiche Lorraine
Cheese Soufflé

FISH AND SHELLFISH

Boiled Lobster, Drawn Butter
Stuffed Lobster Barbecue
Bar Harbor Lobster Salad
Scalloped Oysters
New England Clam Bake
Clam Fritters
Clams Casino
Old-fashioned Scallop Broil
Baked Scallops with Mushrooms
Down East Mussel Pie
Salt Codfish Dinner
Stewed Cod
Codfish Balls
Baked Haddock with Cheese
Broiled Salmon

MEATS

Old Colony Succotash
Yankee Pot Roast with Cranberries
Nantucket Squantum
Mulligan Stew with Dumplings
Portuguese Pot Roast
Rabbit Stew
Corned Beef
New England Boiled Dinner
Glazed Corned Beef
Corned Beef Hash

POULTRY AND GAME BIRDS

Roast Stuffed Turkey with Cranberry
   Sauce and Corn Bread Stuffing
Turkey Pie
New England Barbecued Chicken
Chicken Croquettes
Braised Pheasant
Chicken Curry

VEGETABLES AND SIDE DISHES

Boston Baked Beans
Harvard Beets
Fiddleheads
Bubble and Squeak
Corn Pudding
New Potatoes in Jackets
Scalloped Potatoes, Maine Style
Braised Celery
Fried Apples
Grape Ketchup

SALADS AND DRESSINGS

Dandelion Salad
Cranberry Turkey Mold
New England Coleslaw
Boiled Salad Dressing

BREADS AND BATTERCAKES

Cornmeal Mush
Fried Mush
Old Johnnycake
Hasty Pudding
Yankee Cornmeal Flapjacks
Raised Buckwheat Cakes
Doughnuts
Blueberry Griddle Cakes
Soda Biscuits
Boston Brown Bread

DESSERTS

Indian Pudding
Butternut Cake
Strawberry Shortcake (Biscuit)
Blueberry/Huckleberry Pie
Blueberry Flummery
Gingerbread
Brown Betty with Hard Sauce
Pumpkin Pie
Rhode Island Cob-Apple Pie
Vinegar Pie
Chocolate Cornstarch Pudding
Maple Mousse
Hyannis Molasses Sauce
Nutmeg Sauce

BEVERAGES

Mint Tea
Spruce Beer
Hot Buttered Rum
Grog
Tom and Jerry

NEW ENGLAND COOKING

The early New England kitchen was as simple and disciplined as the Puritan and Quaker religious practices of the settlers themselves, who migrated from England by way of Holland.

All the East Coast at the time was called Virginia, but the Pilgrims landed six hundred miles north of their goal, the place presently called by that name. Having left their homeland in protest, they brought relatively little in the way of worldly goods and their food stores had been depleted by the delays caused by severe storms at sea. After searching several days a landing at the base of Cape Cod was decided upon.

Although Cape Cod had been many times visited by Europeans—explorers and fishermen—the *Mayflower*'s people found few traces of these predecessors. To quote from William Bradford's and Edward Winslow's diaries, November 16, 1620:

Also we found a great kettle which had been some ship's kettle and brought out of Europe. There was a heap of sand, which we digged up and in it found a little old basket full of fair Indian corn, and digged furthur and found a fine great new basket full of very fair corn of this year, with some thirty-six goodly ears of corn, some yellow and some red, and others mixed with blue, which was a very goodly sight.

Notwithstanding this discovery, and others like it, 50 of the 102 passengers of the *Mayflower* died that winter, most of them from exposure.

Along with the settlers had come their knowledge of accustomed dishes—sausages, roasts, puddings, and pasties and their cereals, oats, wheat, rye. But conditions and foods in the strange land were not the same, and they had to learn to live on foods newly available—wild turkey and duck, wild goose and pigeon. They were taught by the Indians to hunt and eat bear and moose, and to use cranberries, beach plums, and wild grapes. The Indians gave them corn and other foods, and taught a new means of cultivation to the Europeans whose custom had been to broadcast seed in plowed fields and let nature do the rest. Corn, tobacco, and bean crops required tillage between sowing and reaping to produce larger and better plants. The better part of the world's farmers now "cultivate" after planting.

The Indians taught them to fertilize corn by putting a fish in each hill (this supplied nitrogen); to clear land by girdling large trees; and to practice a crude land, or crop, rotation by moving away from a used unfertile field to a new one.

The settlers in Vermont and New Hampshire also learned to process the sap of certain trees indigenous to the area, which they boiled down to make maple syrup.

The Pilgrims improved on their teachers when it came to beans. They baked the beans for six hours in their slow brick ovens, with salt pork, onions, and molasses. The long cooking made the beans digestible; and they kept without spoiling, providing there were any left to keep. Boston brown bread often accompanied the beans, steamed in tins on a rack set in a large kettle.

For a long time their meals did not vary much from one day to another, although an interesting custom of adhering to a rigid weekly menu developed later in some areas. Every Monday, washday, was boiled-dinner day, and the meat for the boiled dinner was set to cook before the washing was begun. Friday was—and still is—chowder day, and Saturday was the day for baked beans, as sure as warmth in summer and cold in winter, for as leftovers they were good cold and no work could be done on Sunday.

In spring there were fiddleheads (shoots of a native fern), which taste something like asparagus, a rare treat after the long winter's diet of cabbage, turnips, beets, and parsnips. In summer there were blueberries for pies and pancakes, eaten with rich butter, powdered sugar, or warm maple syrup. They made butternut cake with maple syrup, and cob-apple pie. They made corn scallop and dozens of bread and dessert dishes with stone-ground cornmeal—Indian pudding, johnnycake, and hasty pudding, to name a few—which became standard fixtures in the early New England menu, and remain so to this day.

Seafood, they soon discovered, was not only plentiful but abundant. The waters along the shore yielded lobsters, clams, oysters, mussels, and scallops. The deeper waters brought forth haddock, flounder, mackerel, halibut, salmon, and cod, and the river herring and shad in spring. The settlers salted down the cod and haddock for use during the winter months, and feasted on broiled, baked, and fried fresh fish in season. Chowders of all sorts were made the year round. Haddock chowder and clam chowder were the two choices Ishmael of *Moby-Dick* had for breakfast, lunch, and dinner when he went to Nantucket to seek work as a whaler. Soups as old as Europe itself were brought by the Portuguese sailors who fished the Grand Banks.

New England lobster (*Homarus americanus*) quickly achieved fame as the most tender and juicy of all lobsters, and is today one of the world's most prized shellfish. Broiled, boiled, baked, stuffed or used as the mainstay of the clambake, lobster is the aristocrat of all seafood. The cod, and young cod called scrod, though not as glamorous, became such a profitable export commodity that it was said Boston merchants regularly offered the famous toast, "To the health of codfish and Catholic countries." The diary of a traveler from Boston in 1797 reveals the importance of codfish to the towns north of that city: "In Ipswitch we changed horses. . . . Here on top of the . . . fences were spread out thousands of

codfish. I have even seen instead of grain, stocks of this dried fish in the barns."

From very early times, trade with the West Indies had been brisk. Sugar cane was shipped to Boston to be processed into molasses, then into sugar. Molasses was also distilled into rum. When the British put a tax on imports, Massachusetts men, undaunted, smuggled in molasses for rum until it was no longer necessary.

One of the glories of New England are the many varieties of apples grown there. Apple epicures make their own cider from their own apple mix, often a secret one. McIntosh, Delicious, and Winesap apples we see in the city markets, but varieties like Northern Spy, Sweet Rhode Island Greening, Baldwin, Rome Beauty, Pippin, Pound Sweet, are rare. In those times all of the varieties had their favored uses. They were baked and made into cobblers, dumplings, pies, and apple sauce. John Chapman, the legendary Johnny Appleseed was from Loeminster, Massachusetts. He traveled as far west as Iowa planting orchards and handing out packages of seeds.

In the 1850s Irish foods—potatoes, corned beef and cabbage, kippers, finnan haddie, soda bread—were added to the New England menu when the potato famine forced immigrants into the new land.

It was said that on Sunday between twelve noon and two P.M. in a good part of Boston the aroma of cooking cabbage and turnips was heavy in the air, for the American institution, Sunday dinner.

After the Irish the Italians migrated in thousands, to work in the factories along with Ukrainians, Poles, and Russians. The factories of New England prospered, and so did the kitchens of the country thereabouts. Many new foods were introduced—and mixed with the old. Oysters were baked with macaroni, bluefish made with Italian sauce, dandelions sold in markets in the spring.

All these New England refugees—the original settlers, together with the French, Irish, Italian, Greeks, Poles, Portuguese, Armenians and others who populated the ports and cities—gradually but undeniably created a cooking style and a fund of good dishes they could rightly call their own, which they have proudly handed down to their descendants— and to all America.

SOUPS AND CHOWDERS

BAKED BEAN SOUP

Rarely found in cookbooks, this dish has served as lunch or supper to many generations of New Englanders.

    3 cups cold baked beans
    6 cups water
    2 slices onion
    2 stalks celery
 1½ cups canned tomatoes, chopped
    1 tablespoon chili sauce
    2 tablespoons butter
    2 tablespoons flour
    1 teaspoon salt
    ¼ teaspoon pepper

Put beans, water, onion, and celery in saucepan; bring to boiling point and simmer 30 minutes.
Add tomatoes, chili sauce, and seasonings.
Mix flour and butter into a roux and add to soup. Simmer 10 minutes and serve with crackers or Johnnycake.* (8 servings)

POTATO SOUP

In open-hearth cooking there was usually a pot of meat, chicken, or fish stock hanging in the back of the fireplace. An easy way to cook up a good nourishing soup was to add some peeled and sliced potatoes (and perhaps other vegetables) to some of the stock. The following recipe is a modern-day adaptation.

    4 large potatoes, peeled and thinly
        sliced
    3 stalks celery, chopped
 1-½ quarts chicken stock (broth or
        bouillon)
    1 teaspoon salt
    ½ teaspoon pepper
    1 cup stale bread crumbs

Place all the ingredients except the bread crumbs into a large pot and cover. Simmer slowly about 30 minutes or until vegetables have disintegrated, forming a puree.
Add the bread crumbs, cook 10 minutes longer, and serve. (about 6 servings)

ALSATIAN SOUP

This unusual soup has a little of the French— not surprising when you consider its source, the state of Maine, near the Canadian border.

    2 tablespoons bacon fat
    3 scallions, chopped
    3 tablespoons flour
    6 cups chicken broth
    1 cup sauerkraut, rinsed
    ½ carrot
    1 whole onion
      pinch thyme
    1 whole clove
      few peppercorns
    1 teaspoon salt
    ½ cup light cream
    1 teaspoon sugar

Heat the bacon fat in a heavy pot, add the scallions, and cook until golden.
Blend in the flour, pour in the broth, cover, and simmer over low heat for 20 minutes.
Meanwhile put the sauerkraut into a saucepan, cover with water, add the vegetables and seasonings, and cook, covered, for 1 hour.
Remove and discard the carrot, onion, and clove.
Chop the sauerkraut fine and add to the broth mixture. Add the cream and sugar, cook for 2 minutes, check seasoning, and serve. (4 servings)

CREAM OF TURKEY SOUP

This soup is as old as Plymouth. Turkey has plenty of meat left after carving. Here's a way to make use of it.

    1 cooked turkey carcass
    2 onions, sliced
    1 carrot, sliced
    1 tomato, chopped
    2 stalks celery, chopped
    2 sprigs parsley, chopped
    1 bay leaf or bayberry leaf
    1 teaspoon Worcestershire sauce
      (optional)
    1 teaspoon salt
    ½ teaspoon pepper
    2 tablespoons butter
    2 tablespoons flour
    1 cup heavy cream or evaporated milk

Remove stuffing from the carcass and discard. Put broken-up carcass, vegetables, and seasonings into a large pot or kettle with enough water to cover; bring to a boil. Cover and simmer 2 hours.
Strain, and skim the fat.
In a separate pan or skillet melt the butter, stir in the flour until brown, then add a little of the soup and stir until smooth. Add to the pot and cook until thickened.
Add the cream, stir, and serve. (*4 to 6 servings*)

MAINE FRENCH PEA SOUP

In early times this soup was frozen in large iron pots in the snow, then used as needed. It sounds familiar to us now, but our ancestors had to defrost foods too.

    1 ham bone with meat on it
    ¼ pound salami or spiced sausage
    2 cups yellow split peas
    2 cups green split peas
    2 onions, peeled and cut lengthwise
    2 tablespoons bacon fat or cooking oil
    1 cup cream, milk, or evaporated milk
    1 tablespoon flour mixed with 1
      tablespoon butter to form a roux
    ¼ pound American cheese, grated
      bread, toasted

Wash and pick over peas. Cover with water and bring to boil with ham bone and salami or sausage.
Cut onions lengthwise and fry in fat or oil over medium heat until very brown, even slightly burned. Add to soup. Simmer 1 hour.
Put soup through a sieve. Chop ham and salami. Return to soup. Add cream or milk and the flour and butter roux. Simmer 10 minutes. Serve in soup plates. Put a slice of toast in each plate with grated cheese on top. Ladle soup over all to melt cheese. (*6 to 8 servings*)

BOSTON FISH CHOWDER

One of the standard ingredients of Boston chowder is milk, but some recipes we have found use 1 cup of dry white wine diluted with 2 cups water in place of the milk. One recipe even called for 2 cups tomatoes, but we could hardly believe it because to the best of our knowledge, New Englanders have avoided tomatoes in chowders.

    4 pounds cod, haddock, or other firm
      fish, cleaned
    2 cups water
    ½ pound salt pork, cubed
    2 medium onions, peeled and sliced
    4 medium potatoes, peeled and sliced
    2 cups hot water
    4 cups milk, scalded
    4 tablespoons butter
    1 teaspoon salt
    ½ teaspoon pepper
    8 unsalted pilot crackers, soaked in milk
    ½ cup chopped parsley

Remove the head and tail from the fish, skin it, bone it, and cut it into 2-inch pieces. Set aside. Put the head, tail, and bones into a stew pot with 2 cups water, simmer 15 minutes, and strain, saving the fish stock.
Sauté the salt pork in a skillet for 5 minutes, until brown; add the onion and cook 5 minutes longer. Then add the potatoes and 2 cups hot water. Simmer 5 minutes.
Add the strained fish stock and the fish pieces. Cover and cook 15 minutes.
Add the milk, butter, seasonings, and crackers. Stir and serve garnished with parsley.
If desired, chowder may be thickened by adding 2 tablespoons flour creamed with a little butter. (*6 to 8 servings*)

NEW ENGLAND CLAM CHOWDER

Chowder is known the world over as a New England dish. But what about the name? The dictionary defines *chowder* (U. S.) as a kind of soup or stew made from clams, fish, or vegetables, with potatoes, onions, and other ingredients and seasonings. The name probably stems from the French word *chaudière*, meaning caldron, a large cooking kettle used by the French for making soups or stews.

Regardless of its French name, chowder as a soup originated in New England with the earliest settlers, who simply tossed into the caldron the things they had on hand: potatoes, onions, milk, and seafood (usually clams, cod, or haddock). Later, a restaurateur on the boardwalk at Coney Island added tomatoes and eliminated the milk, to create Manhattan clam chowder.

There are many variations in the recipe for chowder, depending upon the ingredients at hand. The following old recipe, although authentic, has been altered to yield a smaller quantity of soup.

½ pound salt pork, diced
2 onions, peeled and chopped
2 cups peeled cubed potatoes
2 cups of clam liquor
2 pints chowder clams (quahogs), finely chopped
1 teaspoon salt
dash pepper
4 cups milk
minced parsley
thyme (optional)

Place the salt pork in a deep saucepan and cook slowly until fat melts and the pork is brown. Add the onion, potatoes, and clam liquor; simmer 15 minutes, or until potatoes are just cooked.

Add the clams and the seasonings.

Pour in the milk and heat, stirring. Serve garnished with minced parsley. Present-day cooks serve it also with a sprinkling of thyme. (*8 servings*)

PASTA, EGG, AND CHEESE DISHES

CHEESE SOUFFLÉ

4 tablespoons butter
4 tablespoons flour
1 cup milk, scalded
½ teaspoon salt
few grains cayenne
1 cup grated Cheddar-type cheese
4 egg yolks, beaten until light
4 egg whites, beaten until stiff

Preheat oven to 375 degrees.

Melt the butter, stir in the flour, add the milk gradually. Stir until thick and smooth.

Stir in the seasonings and cheese. Stir until smooth, and remove from the heat.

Cool, then stir in the egg yolks. Stir in a tablespoon of egg whites, then fold in the rest. Spoon into an unbuttered 1½-quart soufflé dish (straight sides), and set into a pan of hot water. Bake 25 minutes (or longer for a firm soufflé).

Serve immediately. (*4 servings*)

QUICHE LORRAINE

This pie must have come across the border from Canada. It is of Swiss, German, French, and Hungarian origin, but those of French descent here have most kept its use.

      1 cup flour
      1 egg yolk
      ½ cup butter, softened
        pinch salt
        flour
      ½ pound sliced bacon, cooked until
        crisp, then crumbled
    1½ cups grated Gruyère cheese
      4 eggs, beaten
      2 cups heavy cream
      ¼ teaspoon salt
      ¼ teaspoon dry mustard
        dash nutmeg
        dash cayenne

Crumble together 1 cup flour, egg yolk, butter, and salt until well mixed. Chill for half an hour, then roll out on a floured board into a thin pie shell.
Preheat the oven to 400 degrees.
Place the pie shell into a 9-inch pie pan, trim the edges, cover them with wax paper, and bake for 10 minutes. Remove from the oven. Reduce oven heat to 325 degrees.
Sprinkle the bacon bits onto the partially baked pie shell, then add the cheese.
Beat together lightly the remaining ingredients, pour into the pie shell and bake about half an hour or until golden and firm. Cut into 12 slices for canapés or 6 for a luncheon dish; serve hot.

RINKTUM DITTY

Also called rum-tum-tiddy and other equally odd names, this early American version of Welsh rabbit was a great favorite of the young people.

      1 tablespoon butter
      1 medium onion, finely chopped
      2 cups cooked tomatoes
      1 teaspoon salt
      ¼ teaspoon pepper
      2 teaspoons sugar
      ½ pound American cheese, grated
      1 egg, beaten
    12 half-slices buttered toast

Cook the onion in butter until soft but not browned. Add the tomatoes, seasonings, and sugar.
Cook 2 minutes, then add the cheese and cook, stirring constantly, until thoroughly melted and blended.
Stir in the egg gradually, cook 1 minute longer, and serve on buttered toast. (*4 servings*)

BAKED EGGS

This dish is said to have found its way to these shores from Belgium.

      6 hard-cooked eggs, shelled and finely
        chopped
      2 tablespoons butter, melted
      ½ teaspoon dried chervil
      ½ teaspoon dried parsley
      ¼ teaspoon dry mustard
      1 teaspoon salt
      ½ teaspoon pepper
      ½ cup chopped cooked shrimp
      1 cup heavy cream
        grated cheese
        butter

Preheat oven to 400 degrees.
Put the eggs and shrimp into 4 buttered baking dishes. Mix seasonings with cream and spoon over them. Sprinkle with grated cheese, dot with butter, and bake until cheese melts and turns golden brown. (*4 servings*)

WELSH RABBIT

      ½ pound Cheddar cheese (either mild or
        sharp, as preferred) cut into bits
      1 tablespoon butter
      ½ teaspoon dry mustard
        dash Worcestershire sauce
        dash Tabasco sauce
        pinch salt
      ½ cup beer
      1 egg, lightly beaten
      6 slices toast, cut diagonally

Mix together the cheese, butter, and seasonings; cook, stirring, in a saucepan over low heat until cheese melts.
Add the beer and egg, and continue cooking and stirring until just thickened.
Serve on toast. (*4 servings*)

FISH AND SHELLFISH

BOILED LOBSTER

Take them alive or dead, lay them in cold water to make the claws tuff, and keep them from breaking off; then have a kettle over the fire with fair water, put in it as much bay ſalt as will make it a good ſtrong brine, when it boils ſcum it, and put in the lobſters, let them boil leaſurely the ſpace of half an hour or more, according to the bigneſs of them, being well boild take them up, waſh them, and then wipe them with beer and butter, and keep them for your uſe.

The foregoing recipe has been taken verbatim from *The Accomplished Cook: Or the Art and Mystery of Cooking*, first published in England in 1664. The book is believed to have been rewritten for publication in Boston around 1712 to include dishes like this one, indigenous to the New England area.

The following recipe will no doubt be considerably easier for present-day cooks to follow:

- 4 quarts water
- 4 tablespoons salt
- 1 large onion, sliced
- 2 stalks celery, with tops
- 2 bay leaves
- 6 peppercorns
- 4 live 2-pound lobsters

Put the water into a large kettle, add salt, onions, celery, bay leaves, and peppercorns. Cover and boil 10 minutes.
Put 2 of the lobsters in headfirst (the hot water kills them instantly), and when boiling begins again, cook for 10 minutes (7 minutes, if less than 2 pounds each).
Remove, then cook the remaining lobsters in the same manner. Serve with drawn butter. (*4 servings*)

DRAWN BUTTER

- ⅓ cup butter
- 3 tablespoons flour
- ½ teaspoon salt
- ⅛ teaspoon pepper
- 1-½ cups hot water

Melt half the butter; add the flour, stirring to prevent lumps; add the water gradually. Add salt and pepper. Simmer five minutes, then piece by piece add the remaining butter. Serve in individual cups with the lobster.

CLAMS CASINO

Here is a delicious first cousin of oysters Rockefeller. In Boston it is made with Dijon mustard, chili sauce, horseradish, Worcestershire sauce, and chopped chives. In New York they use cayenne, chopped green pepper, chopped pimiento, a piece of bacon cut the size of the clam, butter, and a little clam liquor to keep them moist. There is an endless number of variations.

- 6 slices bacon
- ½ cup minced shallots (or scallions)
- ¼ cup minced green pepper
- ¼ cup minced celery
- few drops Worcestershire sauce
- few drops Tabasco sauce
- 24 medium clams on the half shell

Preheat oven to 450 degrees.
Cook the bacon until crisp. Drain, dry, and set aside.
To the bacon fat add the shallots, minced pepper, celery, Worcestershire, and Tabasco. Cook for a minute or two.
Spoon this sauce over the half-shell clams, top with bacon, and bake until the sauce bubbles (4 or 5 minutes). Serve at once. (*4 servings as a main dish, 8 as an appetizer*)

CODFISH BALLS

This dish, dating from the earliest times, is very popular with New Englanders. Fresh-caught codfish, dried and salted, served faithfully as a nourishing and dependable food throughout the long winter months. The Pilgrims learned to mix this salt cod with mashed potatoes, and to this day codfish balls are a popular regional dish. In some recipes grated raw potatoes are used instead of mashed potatoes and the mixture is dropped by spoonfuls onto a hot griddle well greased with bacon fat.

    ½ pound salt codfish
  2½ cups peeled and cubed potatoes
    ½ tablespoon butter
    1 egg, well beaten
    ¼ teaspoon pepper
       flour
       cooking fat

Soak the salt cod overnight, drain, remove the skin and bones, and flake with a fork.
Place the cod and the potatoes into a saucepan, cover with boiling water and cook until potatoes are soft.
Drain thoroughly and mash well. Add the butter, egg, and pepper. Beat with a fork until light and smooth. Form into balls, roll in flour, and put into a heavy skillet containing ½ inch of hot cooking oil. Fry about a minute or until golden. Serve with fried salt pork, bacon, or sausages. (6 servings)

NEW ENGLAND CLAMBAKE

The open hearth was a great place to gather during chilly winter days, but when warmer weather came the early settlers liked to get outdoors and cook. Community cookouts were popular, especially on festive occasions, and along the shore these often took the form of clambakes.
Here is an old Cape Cod recipe passed down through generations. It serves one hundred hungry people.

It is essential to have the necessary equipment before making plans for the food.
This is what you'll need to serve one hundred people:

Dig a shallow pit about five feet by ten feet and fill with rocks about a foot above ground. Upon this pile of rocks, good dry cordwood should be stacked to make a fast-burning fire; the more wood the better, so the rocks will be extremely hot when the fire burns down.
When the fire burns to ashes, add the first layer of rockweed, which must be fresh and soaking wet. Then put the food on, spreading it out over the rockweed.
We use flat wire baskets to hold the fish, corn, potatoes, and sausages. We put the lobsters directly on the rockweed and also pour the clams loosely over the rockweed. Then another layer of rockweed is spread over the entire bake; the more you use, the better, so that it will create plenty of steam.
Over all this spread burlap bags which have been wet down, and then completely cover it all with canvas, making sure the canvas is wet and held down tight around the entire bake so no steam escapes.
Let bake at least 3 hours, preferably 3½ hours.
The following is needed for such a bake:
    5 bushels clams
  200 ears corn
   20 pounds sausage
       brown bread
    1 bushel white potatoes
    1 bushel sweet potatoes
  100 lobsters—1½ pounds each
  100 small mackerel or 50 large, cleaned and cut in half
Corn should have husks removed, leaving only the inner layer on. Sausage and fish are wrapped individually in wax paper. Watermelon and coffee are served for dessert.

Clambakes are still held much as they were in earlier days, but frequently today a large metal drum or trash can takes the place of a hole in the sand. Hot rocks are placed into the bottom of the drum; wet seaweed goes on top of the rocks, followed by the food. Another layer of seaweed is added, and a canvas tarpaulin is tied tightly over the opening so that the steam cannot escape.

DOWN EAST MUSSEL PIE

To the early American settlers, mussels were far from a new taste experience, and the profusion of the little mollusks along the inlets and bays of the East Coast demanded that they be put to culinary use. We offer the following old recipe brought along from England in evidence:

To make a Muskle Pye: Take a peck of muskles, wafh them clean, and fet them a boiling in a kettle of fair water, (but firft let the water boil) then put them into it, give them a walm, and as foon as they are opened, take them out of the fhells, ftone them, and mince them with fome fweet herbs, fome leeks, pepper, and nutmeg; mince fix hard eggs and put to them, put fome butter in the pye, clofe it up and bake it, being baked liquor it with fome butter, white-wine, and flices of orange.

Here is a more modern version of the same recipe which we are sure you will find easier to follow.

    4 dozen mussels, well scrubbed—
        discard open-shelled mussels
    6 or 8 small white onions
    2 tablespoons butter
    ¼ teaspoon nutmeg
    ¼ teaspoon pepper
    1 teaspoon salt
        pinch thyme
    2 unbaked pie crusts
    2 hard-cooked eggs, quartered

Place the mussels in a saucepan, cover with water, bring to a boil, and cook until shells open.
Remove the mussels from the shells and set aside. (Some recipes we have found call for grinding or chopping the mussels.)
Strain the liquid; add the onions, butter, and seasonings; and simmer until the onions are soft but not mushy.
Preheat oven to 400 degrees.
Line a pie pan with a pie crust, add the onions in their liquid, the mussels, and the eggs. Cover with second crust and prick well.
Bake about 20 minutes or until brown. Serve hot. (*4 servings*)

OLD-FASHIONED SCALLOP BROIL

    1 pound scallops
    1 clove garlic, cut
    6 tablespoons butter, melted
    ½ teaspoon salt
    ½ teaspoon white pepper
        few grains cayenne
        flour
    1 teaspoon paprika
        lemon slices

Rub the bottom and sides of a shallow baking dish or pie pan with the garlic; add half the melted butter, and swish around
Arrange the scallops in the dish; season with salt, pepper, and a little cayenne; dust lightly with four and paprika; and pour on the remaining butter.
Slide under the broiler, cook 10 minutes or until golden, and serve with lemon slices. (*4 servings*)

STEWED COD

This dish was originally made along coastal New England from freshly caught cod or dried salt cod, depending upon the season of the year. Today you can prepare it by simply opening packages of frozen cod fillets.

    2 packages (12 ounces each) frozen cod
        fillets (or 2 pounds fresh cod)
    1 teaspoon salt
    ½ teaspoon ground nutmeg
    ½ teaspoon freshly ground pepper
        pinch dried basil
    1 cup dry white wine
    ½ cup water
    4 tablespoons butter
    4 tablespoons flour
    2 tablespoons chopped parsley

Place all the ingredients except the butter, flour, and parsley into a large heavy skillet, cover, and cook about 8 minutes or until fish flakes when fork-tested. Remove the fish to a heated bowl.
Make a roux of the butter and flour (mix flour and butter until smooth), add it to the sauce, and cook, stirring, until smooth and bubbling.
Pour the thickened sauce over the fish and serve garnished with chopped parsley. (*4 servings*)

BROILED SALMON

Here's the recipe as printed in 1664 in *The Accomplished Cook:*

> *Take a whole ſalmon, a jole, rand, chine, or ſlices cut round it the thickneſs of an inch, ſteep theſe in wine vinegar, good ſweet ſallet oyl and ſalt, broil them on a faſt fire, and baſte them with the ſame ſauce they were ſteeped in, with ſome ſtreight ſprigs of roſemary, ſweet marjoram, tyme, and parſley; the fiſh being broild, boil up the gravy and oyſter liquor, diſh up the fiſh, pour on the ſauce, and lay the herbs about it.*

Now here is a modern version of the same recipe, which you might find easier to follow:

    4 pound salmon, cleaned and split
    ½ cup wine vinegar
    ½ cup olive oil
    1 teaspoon salt
      pinch rosemary
      pinch thyme
    1 cup oyster liquor
    1 tablespoon chopped parsley

Place the fish into a shallow glass or porcelain dish; cover with the vinegar and oil; sprinkle with salt, rosemary, and thyme; and marinate 30 minutes.
Preheat the broiler compartment to 550 degrees.
Remove fish from marinade, pat dry with a paper towel, place onto an oiled broiler rack, and slide into the broiler compartment 2 inches from the heat.
Broil for 10 minutes, basting several times with the marinade; remove to a heated platter.
Stir the oyster liquor into the pan drippings, pour over the fish, and garnish with chopped parsley. (*4 servings*)

STUFFED LOBSTER BARBECUE

A great way to entertain—and a lot easier and quicker than a clambake. How could you serve anything more delicious than fresh lobster grilled over live coals?

First make a barbecue pit. You can do this by digging a hole three feet by three feet by eight inches deep. Or construct an eight-inch-high stone or brick wall around a three-foot-square area.
Fill the pit with charcoal (two bags should do it), and ignite. When the charcoals have attained a coating of white ash, place a grill on top and you are ready to start cooking.

    8 live 1½-pound lobsters
    4 cups cracker crumbs
    1 cup melted butter
    ½ cup mayonnaise
    1 tablespoon Worcestershire sauce

Kill the lobsters by inserting a sharp knife between the body and tail (this will sever the spinal cord and kill the lobster instantly and without pain). Place them on their backs and cut from head to tail without cutting through the top shell. Remove spongy lungs.
Prepare stuffing by mixing together the crackers, butter, mayonnaise, and Worcestershire.
Stuff this mixture into the cut part of the lobsters and cover with aluminum foil to hold the stuffing when the lobster is turned. Place stuffing side up onto the grill. Broil 15 minutes.
Turn carefully (so that stuffing does not fall out), and broil 5 to 10 minutes longer. (*8 servings*)
Serve with roasted corn on the cob, baked potatoes, and other cookout-type foods—and lots of cold beer.

SALT CODFISH DINNER

There are a dozen versions of this early New England dinner. This is probably the purest.

    1 large salt cod
    4 medium potatoes, scrubbed and
      boiled
    ¼ pound salt pork, cubed and fried until
      crisp
    1 can (16 ounces) pickled beets

Break cod into pieces, cover with water, and bring almost to a boil. Pour off the water. Repeat twice more until saltiness has been dissipated. Do not boil or cod will be tough. Serve cod on a heated platter with potatoes, salt pork, and beets on the side. (*4 servings*)

BAR HARBOR LOBSTER SALAD

2 cups cooked lobster meat, cut into
  small pieces
½ cup diced celery
½ teaspoon salt
⅛ teaspoon paprika
1 tablespoon French dressing
  lettuce
  mayonnaise
1 hard-cooked egg, sliced
  capers
  stuffed olives

Mix together the lobster, celery, salt, paprika, and French dressing.
Arrange on lettuce leaves; top with mayonnaise; and garnish with egg, capers, and olives. (*4 servings*)

SCALLOPED OYSTERS

½ cup butter, melted
2 cups sea-biscuit crumbs
1 quart shucked oysters with liquor
1 cup light cream
½ teaspoon salt
¼ teaspoon cayenne
¼ teaspoon nutmeg

Preheat oven to 400 degrees.
Butter a 1 ½ quart baking dish or pie plate.
Mix remaining butter with cracker crumbs.
Put a layer of ⅓ the cracker-crumb mixture on bottom of dish; a layer of oysters over this; a sprinkle of salt, pepper, nutmeg, and cream. Another layer of crumb mixture and oysters; another sprinkle of salt, pepper, nutmeg, and cream. Cover all with last layer of crumbs. Add remaining cream.
Bake 25 to 30 minutes. (*6 servings*)

CLAM FRITTERS

2 cups flour
2 teaspoons baking powder
½ teaspoon salt
2 eggs, well beaten
½ cup clam juice
1 cup milk
1 pint freshly opened clams, finely
  chopped

Sift together flour, baking powder, and salt. Add eggs, clam juice, and milk. Stir well to make a batter.
Stir in the chopped clams, and drop by the spoonful onto a hot greased griddle.
Cook about 6 minutes on each side or until golden. (*6 servings*)

BAKED SCALLOPS WITH MUSHROOMS

4 tablespoons butter
1 cup sliced mushrooms
2 stalks celery, chopped
½ green pepper, chopped
1 small onion, chopped
  pinch basil
1 pound bay scallops (or sea scallops,
  cut up)
½ teaspoon salt
2 cups cream sauce (see below)
½ cup cracker crumbs
½ cup grated cheese

Preheat oven to 325 degrees.
Melt the butter in a saucepan; add the mushrooms, celery, pepper, onion, and basil. Simmer gently 5 minutes.
Add the scallops and cream sauce. Mix well and pour into a buttered casserole, sprinkle with cracker crumbs and cheese.
Dot with butter and bake 30 minutes.
To make cream sauce: Melt 4 tablespoons butter over low heat in a saucepan, stir in 4 tablespoons flour, ½ teaspoon salt, and a pinch pepper. Slowly stir in 2 cups milk until sauce is smooth and creamy. (*4 servings*)

BAKED HADDOCK WITH CHEESE

½ cup flour
4 tablespoons butter
1 tablespoon dry mustard
1 cup milk
½ pound American cheese, diced
2 pounds haddock fillets (fresh or frozen)

Preheat oven to 350 degrees.

Make a roux of the flour, butter, and mustard.

Heat the milk in a saucepan and stir in the roux, continuing to stir until thickened.

Add the cheese and continue stirring until cheese is melted and well blended.

Arrange the fillets and cheese sauce in a casserole in alternate layers; bake for ½ hour. Serve from the casserole. (*4 servings*)

MEATS

MULLIGAN STEW WITH DUMPLINGS

Mulligan stew differs from most other stews in that the meat is never floured or browned before cooking, and the gravy is not thickened. For the latter reason, the stew is often served with dumplings. Here is a very old recipe, which calls for the use of venison. Lamb, or even beef, will serve as well.

2 pounds venison, cubed
⅛ pound salt pork, cubed
½ cup diced carrots
½ cup diced turnip
½ cup chopped celery
½ cup sliced onion
4 potatoes, peeled and quartered
1 teaspoon salt
½ teaspoon whole peppercorns
1 cup flour
2 teaspoons baking powder
½ teaspoon salt
½ cup milk

Simmer the meat and salt pork 30 minutes in 2 cups water.

Add the vegetables, 1 teaspoon salt, and peppercorns; simmer slowly for 1 hour.

Mix together the flour, baking powder, ½ teaspoon salt, and milk, and drop by the spoonful onto the boiling stew. Cover tightly and cook for about 20 minutes without lifting cover, to allow dumplings to rise. (*4 servings*)

RABBIT STEW

Although wild rabbit can still be found in season, as of old, these days rabbits are cultivated for sale in city markets—or sold, dressed and frozen, in convenient packages. Wild rabbit requires soaking for 2 hours in salted, vinegared water before cooking.

3 pounds rabbit, fresh or frozen
flour
2 tablespoons bacon fat
1 onion, sliced
1 cup water
1 cup dry white wine
½ teaspoon salt
¼ teaspoon pepper
pinch sweet basil
pinch marjoram
chopped parsley

Have the rabbit dressed and cut up.

Dredge the parts in flour, and brown them on all sides in hot bacon fat, using a heavy skillet.

Add the onion, water, wine, and seasonings (except parsley).

Cover and simmer about 1 hour or until rabbit is tender when fork-tested.

Thicken the sauce, if desired, with 1 tablespoon flour dissolved in ½ cup water. Cook until thickened.

Sprinkle with chopped parsley and serve. (*4 servings*)

CORNED BEEF

In prerefrigeration days, something had to be done to foods to make them last through the winter months. Many vegetables were dried; fish were salted or smoked; and meats were given a wide variety of treatments, from smoking to drying to salting. In New England one of the favorite ways to preserve pork or beef was to corn it. So popular was corned beef that it has lasted down through generations, and is available today in every market in the country.

We quote an early recipe:

> 8 pounds salt
> 2 ounces saltpeter
> 1 quart molasses
> 1 ounce cayenne pepper
> 8 gallons soft water or clean rainwater
> 100 pounds beef

> Dissolve the salt, saltpeter, molasses, cayenne pepper into the 8 gallons of water. Heat.
> Pack beef pieces in a stone crock.
> Pour on the cure hot. Cover, weigh down the cover after cure has been poured over it. Can be used as needed. Remaining meat can be left in cure until it is to be used. The meat will be saltier the later it is used.

Four pounds of beef can be corned in a crock or large pot in your own kitchen.

Here is a modern recipe based upon the traditional early American method:

> 4 to 5-pound piece of beef, preferably brisket
> 2 cups coarse salt, or enough to float an egg or a raw potato
> 3 teaspoons saltpeter (sodium nitrate), optional—is used for color only
> 2 cups brown sugar
> 4 tablespoons whole peppercorns.

Wash and dry the meat and pierce it generously and deeply with a kitchen fork so that the corning liquids will penetrate.

Place the meat into an earthenware crock (or enameled bowl) with all the other ingredients. Pour in a gallon of lukewarm water. Stir. Weight the beef down with a heavy nonmetallic object so that it is immersed in the liquid, and cover.

Marinate for from two to five days. Some like it less salty than others; the longer you corn the beef the saltier it will become, so let your personal taste be your guide.

Remove and rinse with cold water, and cook as you would boiled beef.

NEW ENGLAND BOILED DINNER

This dish is the natural result of having on hand a corned beef and a plentiful supply of fresh vegetables. A New England dish, it has in time been adopted by the entire nation.

> 4 to 5-pound piece of corned beef
> 5 or 6 onions
> 4 or 5 turnips, peeled
> 6 or 7 potatoes, peeled
> 5 or 6 carrots
> 1 head cabbage, quartered
> 6 or 8 cooked beets

Wash the meat, place it in a large pot of cold water and bring to a slow boil. Simmer for 2-½ to 3 hours.

The vegetables are added progressively so that all are properly cooked when the meat is tender. Here is the order: first, the onions and turnips; 30 minutes later, the carrots and potatoes; 15 minutes later, the cabbage. Cook 20 minutes longer and the dinner is done.

Serve on a heated platter with the meat in the center, surrounded by the vegetables.

Serve with mustard and horseradish. (*8 to 10 servings*)

GLAZED CORNED BEEF

Stud a hot piece of cooked corned beef with cloves, pour on enough maple syrup to cover and place in a 350-degree oven for 25 to 30 minutes.

(In other parts of the country, brown sugar and mustard are substituted for the maple syrup.)

CORNED BEEF HASH

The best thing about corned beef is that you usually have enough left over for hash. This popular dish can, of course, be made with leftover roast beef as well. The best hash is made of meat chopped very fine with a sharp knife.

    1½ pounds corned beef
      5 cold boiled potatoes
      4 tablespoons water
      1 onion
      ½ teaspoon pepper
        bacon grease or cooking oil
      4 eggs, poached

Chop beef, potatoes, and onion finely with a knife, or turn them through coarse blade of a meat grinder. Add water and pepper and mix together thoroughly.

Put enough bacon grease into a hot heavy skillet to cover the bottom, add the hash, and form into a firm thin loaf. Cook slowly without stirring.

When a crust has begun to form, turn and re-form into a neat loaf.

When crust has developed completely, loosen with a spatula, fold over, and slide onto a heated platter.

Cut into four portions and serve with a poached egg on top of each. (*4 servings*)

OLD COLONY SUCCOTASH

"Succototh is corn and beans boiled together with bear's flesh," said Captain Jonathan Carver, who had traveled "through the interior parts of North America" on his way to meet Roger Williams in 1643. The dish is served, even today, on Forefathers' Day, which is celebrated in Plymouth, Massachusetts on December 21. First comes the meeting of the Pilgrim Society; then a Church service to commemorate the service held in Scrooby, England, in 1602 before they left for the New World; and then comes dinner, at which only succotash and pumpkin pie are served.

The following recipe is a composite of all the many original recipes the Indians taught the colonists.

      2 fowl
      4 pounds corned beef
      ½ pound lean pork
      2 quarts white pea beans
      4 quarts hulled corn, cornmeal, or
        hominy
      ½ yellow turnip (rutabaga), cut into
        small pieces
    4 to 6 potatoes, thinly sliced

Using a large kettle, cook the fowl with the corned beef in water enough to cover 2 ½ to 3 hours, or until tender.

In a second kettle boil the pork and beans with water to cover 2 ½ to 3 hours, or until soupy. Add more water as needed.

In a third kettle, cook the hominy with water to cover 2 to 3 hours, or until very tender. If canned hominy is used, heat and cook until very tender.

Skim fat from the large kettle with fowl in it and add potatoes and turnip.

Remove one fowl from water when cooked, cut up, and return to succotash. Put other fowl on platter with corned beef and salt pork. Put the beans and hominy into the pot with the potatoes and turnips. Cook all together to blend.

Serve each person with a piece of fowl, corned beef, pork, and succotash.

Some people cook the fowl, beef, and pork together, and then all the other ingredients. (*24 servings*)

YANKEE POT ROAST WITH CRANBERRIES

This satisfying dish is made everywhere in New England where cranberries are abundant.

    3 to 4-pound piece of rump, top or
      bottom round roast
      3 tablespoons flour
      2 tablespoons bacon fat
      3 cups water
      2 cups fresh cranberries, washed and
        picked over
      1 teaspoon salt
      ¼ teaspoon pepper

Roll roast in flour and brown on all sides in bacon fat. Put in deep pot with a cover.
Deglaze browning pan with 3 cups of water and pour over roast. Add cranberries.
Cook over low heat 3 hours or until tender. Turn roast from time to time. Add salt and pepper in last 30 minutes of cooking. Dumplings can be added to this the last 20 minutes of cooking. (*6 to 8 servings*)

NANTUCKET SQUANTUM

This is what we (like many people) thought a squantum was: a sort of super chowder containing chicken, prepared and eaten at public gatherings—religious, social, or political.
We also thought the dish was named after an old Indian chief, and was perhaps made from almost any ingredients that happened to be on hand, which would explain why there did not seem to be in existence a definitive recipe.
We discovered that squantum wasn't the food but the celebration—an outdoor gathering like a clambake, to which everyone brought food, already cooked or to be cooked. The word "squantum" is perhaps a Narragansett Indian word for picnic.

PORTUGUESE POT ROAST

Portugal contributed both manpower for fishing boats, and spice to New England cooking.

      5 pounds rump roast
      2 cups red wine
      2 large onions, chopped
      1 clove garlic, chopped
      1 teaspoon salt
      ¼ teaspoon pepper
      4 tablespoons fat or oil
      1 onion, sliced
      3 tomatoes, sliced thick
      8 medium potatoes, peeled and boiled

Put the meat, wine, onions, garlic, salt, and pepper into a dish, cover, and marinate in the refrigerator for 24 hours. Turn the meat several times.
Heat the fat in a heavy pot large enough to hold the meat. Wipe the meat dry, and brown on all sides in the hot fat.
Brown the sliced onion in the pot with the meat, add the marinade, and cover tightly. Simmer over low heat 3½ hours or until meat is very tender.
Add the tomatoes and cook another 30 minutes. Serve with boiled potatoes. (*8 servings*)

POULTRY
AND GAME BIRDS

BRAISED PHEASANT

      2 young pheasants, dressed and washed
      1 teaspoon salt
      ½ teaspoon pepper
        flour
      2 tablespoons butter
      ½ cup water

Preheat oven to 350 degrees.
Split the pheasants down the middle of the back. Season with salt and pepper, dredge with flour, place into a roasting pan, and dot with butter. Add ½ cup water.
Bake 1½ hours or until tender, basting occasionally. (*4 to 6 servings*)

ROAST STUFFED TURKEY WITH CRANBERRY SAUCE

Everyone knows how to roast a turkey—if you don't, simply read the instructions on the wrapper your turkey came in.

Our own method for preparing a 15-pound turkey is to stuff it, rub it well with butter, and roast it in an open pan in a 325 degree oven for about 3 hours, basting it several times during the cooking.

But we thought you would like to know how Mrs. Simmons in *American Cookery* (1796) advised her readers to tackle the problem. Follow along:

To Stuff and Roaſt a Turkey or Fowl
One pound ſoft wheat bread
3 ounces beef ſuet
3 eggs
a little ſweet thyme, ſweet marjoram
pepper and ſalt
a gill of wine

Fill the bird therewith and ſew up, hang down to a ſteady ſolid fire [turkeys were hung by strings from a crossbar over the fire], baſting frequently with ſalt and water and roaſt until a ſteam emits from the breaſt, put one third of a pound of butter into the gravy, duſt flour over the bird and baſte with the gravy; ſerve up with boiled onions and cranberry ſauce, mangoes, pickles or celery.

2. Others omit the ſweet herbs, and add parſley done with potatoes.

3. Boil and maſh 3 pints potatoes, wet them with butter, add ſweet herbs, pepper, ſalt, fill and roaſt as above.

All one needs to go with Amelia Simmons's almost three-hundred-year-old recipe for roast turkey is the cranberry sauce.

CRANBERRY SAUCE

4 cups cranberries
2 cups water
2 cups sugar

Put all into a saucepan, bring to a boil, and cook until thick. Cool, then refrigerate until ready to serve.

There were those who rejected Miss Simmons's stuffing of "foft wheat bread" in favor of a stuffing of corn bread. Following is a famous early American recipe that seems to have disappeared from recent cookbooks.

CORN BREAD STUFFING (15- to 20-pound turkey)

2 cups rice, cooked
6 seaman's biscuits (or saltines), rolled to crumbs
1 large onion, finely chopped
1 teaspoon parsley, minced
1½ tablespoons butter
2 cups chicken broth
2 eggs, beaten
1 recipe corn bread, crumbled (Old Johnnycake*)

Preheat oven to 325 degrees.

Mix all ingredients together and stuff turkey loosely. Roast 2½ to 3½ hours, depending on size, until the skin on the drumstick pulls back from the bone, or the juice runs clear of pink color when the area between the thigh and drumstick is pricked with a fork.

NEW ENGLAND BARBECUED CHICKEN

Chicken dipped in butter and vinegar is also a part of a New England clambake. Early barbecue sauce like the one below was simply made with butter and vinegar; later recipes include as many as twelve ingredients (see Harlem Barbecue Sauce*).

½ cup butter
1 teaspoon salt
¼ teaspoon pepper
¼ cup vinegar
1 frying chicken, cut in four pieces

Prepare charcoal fire 1 hour before, or preheat oven to 400 degrees.

Melt butter; add salt, pepper, vinegar. Brush chicken with butter mixture and set on grill about 15 inches above the coals. Brush with butter again in 10 minutes and turn; repeat this until the chicken is done. It takes 45 minutes to 1 hour depending on the size of the chicken. The chicken can be roasted in the oven as well, basting occasionally with the butter mixture. 35 to 45 minutes. (*4 servings*)

TURKEY PIE

    2 uncooked pie crusts
    1 cup potatoes, peeled, boiled, and
        diced
    2 cups or 1 package frozen peas and
        carrots, cooked and drained
    2 tablespoons butter
    1 onion, chopped
    2 cups turkey, cooked and diced
    2 tablespoons flour
 1½ cups milk
    ½ teaspoon salt
    ¼ teaspoon pepper
    ⅛ teaspoon cayenne
    2 tablespoons parsley, chopped
    1 pimento, chopped (optional)

Preheat oven to 400 degrees.

Put one of the pie crusts into a 2-quart baking dish. Mix potatoes with peas and carrots, and put into dish.

Melt butter in frying pan, sauté onion until brown. Add turkey, sauté until lightly brown. Sprinkle flour on meat. Stir. Add milk, and stir again until thick. Lower heat, add salt, pepper, cayenne, parsley, and pimento. Stir gently and add this to the vegetables. Cover the dish with top crust. Cut 3 slits in top of crust. Bake 25 to 30 minutes or until brown. (*6 to 8 servings*)

CHICKEN CURRY

New England sailing ships brought exotic spices from the Far East to their home ports. Curry from India was one of these.

    2 broilers, disjointed
    2 tablespoons butter
    2 onions, sliced
    3 teaspoons (or less) curry powder
    1 cup canned tomatoes or 2 fresh
        tomatoes, chopped
    ½ teaspoon cayenne
    1 cup milk

Brown the chicken in butter; add the onions and sprinkle with curry powder. Stir and cook over low heat for 15 or 20 minutes. Turn chicken during this cooking.

Add cayenne and tomatoes. Stir. Cover the pan and simmer for 1 hour.

Add the milk, stir, and heat through. Serve with rice. (*6 to 8 servings*)

CHICKEN CROQUETTES

    2 tablespoons butter
    4 tablespoons flour
    1 cup milk
    2 teaspoons salt
    ⅛ teaspoon pepper
    1 teaspoon Worcestershire sauce
    2 cups cooked chicken, chopped
    2 eggs, lightly beaten
        cracker crumbs
        bread crumbs

Melt butter over low heat; stir in flour until smooth. Add milk gradually, stir until smooth; add salt, pepper, Worcestershire, chopped chicken. Cool.

When cold, mold into balls. Roll in cracker crumbs, roll in beaten egg, and then in bread crumbs. Fry in deep fat at 370 degrees until golden brown. (*4 servings*)

VEGETABLES
AND SIDE DISHES

HARVARD BEETS

8 medium beets, cooked and skinned,
  or 1 can (16 ounces) beets with juice
¼ cup water
2 tablespoons butter
1 tablespoon cornstarch
1 tablespoon sugar
¼ cup vinegar

Put beets into a saucepan with other ingredients, bring to a boil and cook over low heat
until thickened.
Young beets cook tender in 15 to 20 minutes.
Old beets take much longer, and are sometimes
good only as cattle feed. (*4 servings*)

FIDDLEHEADS

Fiddleheads are the young shoots of bracken
and ostrich ferns that grow wild in parts of
New England and in Canada, and are eaten the
way we eat asparagus. Pick when 4 to 6 inches
tall in the very early spring. Take only the part
that snaps easily in your fingers but do not take
all the shoots from one plant. The shoots are
tightly coiled ("fiddlehead") with a white or
brown fuzz.

1 pound fiddleheads, fuzz removed
2 cups water
1 tablespoon vinegar
2 tablespoons butter
½ teaspoon salt

Wash fiddleheads. Bring water to a boil, drop
in fiddleheads, and cook, uncovered, until
tender, about 30 minutes.
Drain, add vinegar, butter, and salt. Shake
saucepan to distribute butter and salt. Cover to
keep warm until ready to serve. (*4 servings*)

FRIED APPLES

For many years lard and bacon fat were used
for deep frying. It wasn't until the turn of the
century that vegetable oils and fats were
processed and cheap enough for the everyday
cook. Butter burns at high temperatures and
was used only in combination with other fats.

2 eggs, beaten
1 tablespoon sugar
3 tablespoons flour
4 apples, peeled and sliced
  bacon fat or lard

Make a batter of the eggs, sugar, and flour.
Dip the apple slices into the batter and fry in
hot cooking oil.
Dust with powdered sugar and serve as a side
dish with meats. (*4 servings*)

SCALLOPED POTATOES, MAINE STYLE

4 potatoes, peeled and thinly sliced
4 teaspoons minced onion
2 tablespoons butter
1 teaspoon salt
½ teaspoon pepper
½ cup flour
  milk

Preheat oven to 350 degrees.
Put a layer of potatoes into a buttered baking
dish. Sprinkle with onion, salt, pepper, and
flour. Dot with butter.
Repeat, making 3 layers. Add enough milk to
be visible through top layer.
Bake 1¼ hours or until tender. (*4 to 6
servings*)

BOSTON BAKED BEANS

Baked beans, one of the prime inventions of the early New England settlers, have spread to all corners of America. Originally made with maple syrup, they later were made with rum, and finally with molasses. Nowadays there is almost no end to the different recipes found in the various sections of the country: recipes with molasses and brown sugar, recipes without molasses (New York baked beans), recipes with tomatoes, with and without onions, with and without mustard. And the beans themselves vary, from the small "white" pea beans—also called navy beans, the larger variety from the Northern Central States—to kidney beans from the South, even mixtures of beans in some western baked-bean concoctions.

    2 pounds navy or pea beans, *"the Small
        White Beans is beft for winter ufe and
        excellent."*
    ½-pound piece salt pork with rind
    1 cup molasses
    2 teaspoons salt
    1 teaspoon dry mustard

Soak the beans overnight in 2 quarts water, using a large saucepan.
Without draining, cook about an hour or until the skins start to burst. Drain, reserving the liquid, and transfer to a bean pot.
Preheat oven to 250 degrees.
Add the molasses, salt, and mustard to 1 cup of the reserved liquid; mix well and pour over the beans.
Cut 1-inch gashes every ½ inch into the salt pork (but do not cut through the rind), and push down into the beans until all but the rind is submerged.
Cover the pot and bake 6 to 8 hours, adding additional reserved liquid as needed to keep beans moist. Uncover the last hour so that the rind will become brown and crisp. The long cooking is necessary to prevent the aftereffects associated with beans. (*10 servings*)

BRAISED CELERY

    2 bunches celery
    1 cup consommé
    1 teaspoon salt
    ½ cup cream

Wash the celery, trim off the leaves, split the stalks in half, and cut each into even lengths. Place stalks into skillet, cover with consommé, season, cover, and cook 15 to 20 minutes or until tender.
Remove the celery, stir the cream into the pan juices, and pour over the celery. This can also be baked in a 350-degree oven. (*4 servings*)

GRAPE KETCHUP

What would New England dinners have been without the spicy ketchup which, before the art of canning was perfected, was a way of preserving the warmth of summer during the long winters. This one is particularly good with fish.

    5 pounds grapes, any kind
    2 ½ pounds sugar
    ½ tablespoon salt
    1 tablespoon pepper
    1 tablespoon cinnamon, cloves, allspice
    1 pint vinegar

Pick over grapes, remove stems, and wash. Put in saucepan with only the water that clings to them. Cook until grapes burst. (If seeded grapes are used, press through sieve or food mill after cooking to remove seeds.)
Add remaining ingredients and boil until the ketchup is the consistency desired. Pour into 6 or 7 pint jars or bottles that have been sterilized in boiling water. Cool, then seal. Keep in a cool place and refrigerate after opening.
This recipe can be used with tomatoes too. (*6 to 7 pints*)

BUBBLE AND SQUEAK

This dish was often served the day after a New England boiled dinner.

    3 tablespoons butter
    2 cups cold boiled cabbage
    2 cups boiled yellow turnips (rutabagas)
    2 cups cold boiled potatoes
    ½ teaspoon salt
    ½ teaspoon pepper

Chop vegetables coarsely. Melt butter in frying pan and brown vegetables lightly. Add salt and pepper. Serve. (*6 servings*)

CORN PUDDING

Without corn, some "found" in an Indian cache and some contributed by the Indians, it is doubtful that the early Colonial settlers in New England could have survived their first grueling winter at Plymouth. They cooked it in every conceivable manner and used it in soup and bread, as a main dish, vegetable, and dessert.

The following supper dish was a favorite—and it's just as good today.

    2 eggs
    1 teaspoon salt
    ½ teaspoon pepper
    ½ teaspoon nutmeg
    1 tablespoon grated onion
    2 tablespoons butter
    2 cups milk
    2 cups cooked corn kernels

Preheat oven to 325 degrees.
Beat the eggs with the salt, pepper, nutmeg, and onion.
Melt the butter, stir in the milk, heat, and fold into the egg mixture.
Stir in the corn, pour into a casserole, and bake for about 1 hour. Serve hot. (*4 servings*)

NEW POTATOES IN JACKETS

New potatoes begin to come to market in the early spring. They have thin skins, fresh flavor, and texture more like a vegetable than a potato. When new, nutritionists tell us, they *are* a vegetable, and not a starch as they are when they age. The more simply cooked, the better to appreciate the light sweetness of taste, like a forerunner of an April day.

    2 pounds new potatoes
      water to cover
    1 teaspoon salt
    1 teaspoon lemon juice
    6 tablespoons butter
    ½ teaspoon salt
    ¼ teaspoon pepper
    3 tablespoons chopped parsley

Wash potatoes well, particularly if they have red dye on the skins.
Put in water and bring to a boil. Add lemon juice and salt. Boil gently for 20 to 30 minutes, until tender when pierced with a fork.
Drain and wrap in napkin, and put in serving dish.
Melt butter; add salt, pepper, chopped parsley. Serve in bowl, pass with potatoes. (*6 servings*)

SALADS
AND DRESSINGS

DANDELION SALAD

Dandelions are tender enough to eat only when very young—before the yellow blossoms have formed. Mix them in with chicory, lettuce, and other greens; serve with oil and vinegar mixed 3 to 1, or with any other dressing.

    1½ pounds young dandelion greens
     3 tablespoons olive oil
     1 tablespoon vinegar
     ½ teaspoon salt
     ⅛ teaspoon pepper

Wash and pick over greens, dry, roll in towel, and chill 30 minutes.
Arrange in salad bowl, add all ingredients and toss. Serve with garlic bread.

CRANBERRY TURKEY MOLD

At last the turkey and the cranberries have come together in this colorful salad, which is good winter or summer.

  2 cups cranberry juice
  ¼ cup water
  1 package unflavored gelatin
  2 teaspoons lemon juice
  1 cup celery, diced
  ½ cup apple, peeled and diced
1½ cups cooked turkey, diced
  ½ teaspoon salt
  2 teaspoons cooking oil
     mayonnaise

Put cranberry juice on stove to heat. Stir gelatin into ¼ cup water, then dissolve in hot cranberry juice. Stir in lemon juice, and cool until partly jelled.
Add the celery, apple, turkey and salt. Turn into a 1-½ quart oiled mold. Chill until set.
Unmold on lettuce and serve with a bowl of mayonnaise. (*4 servings*)

NEW ENGLAND COLESLAW

  1 small head cabbage, shredded fine
  ½ cup heavy cream, whipped
  ½ cup sugar
  ½ cup vinegar
  ½ teaspoon salt
  ¼ teaspoon pepper

Beat sugar into whipped cream, then beat in vinegar. Pour over shredded cabbage. Season, stir well, and chill until ready to serve. (*8 servings*)

BOILED SALAD DRESSING

Before the advent of store-bought salad dressing and mayonnaise, this dressing in one of its many forms was used throughout the country to dress coleslaw, potato salad, and other salads.

  1 cup vinegar
  ½ cup water
  ½ cup sugar
  ⅛ teaspoon salt
  2 tablespoons butter
  2 tablespoons flour
  1 egg, beaten
  ¾ cup milk (or heavy cream, whipped)

Mix vinegar, water, sugar, salt.
Melt butter over low heat, stir in flour. Stir, gradually adding vinegar mixture to butter mixture until smooth.
Remove from heat and stir in beaten egg; add milk, little by little. Cook a few minutes more until thick.
If cream is used, whip the cream. Cool the sauce after the egg is added and then fold in the whipped cream.

BREADS
AND BATTERCAKES

INDIAN MEAL

In the early times cornmeal was always called Indian meal. The dried corn was ground at the local mill. The millstones gave it the name of stone-ground in New England; farther south, the designation became water-ground (water turned the mill wheel). These names came into use when machine-ground meal came on the market; its texture and quality are different, and it cannot be used for these old recipes. Further, in the South there is white water-ground cornmeal and yellow water-ground cornmeal. The white is considered the more delicate.

CORNMEAL MUSH

The following recipe, from a cookbook we have been unable to identify by name, is dated 1887, but the dish actually was among the earliest-known American concoctions.

Put two quarts of water into a clean dinner pot or stewpan, cover and let it become boiling hot over the fire; then a tablespoon of salt, take off the light scum from the top, have sweet, fresh yellow or white corn meal; take a handful of the meal with the left hand and a pudding stick in the right, then with the stick, stir the water around and by degrees let fall the meal; when one handful is exhausted, refill it; continue to stir and add meal until it is as thick as you can stir easily, or until the stick will stand in it; stir it awhile longer; let the fire be gentle; when it is sufficiently cooked, which will be in half an hour, it will bubble or puff up; turn it into a deep basin. This is good eaten cold or hot, with milk or with butter and syrup or sugar, or with meat and gravy, the same as potatoes or rice.

FRIED MUSH

Turn the above recipe of hot mush into bread tins. When cold, cut in slices, and dip each slice in flour; fry it in lard and butter mixed in the frying pan, turning to brown well on both sides. Must be served hot. A good breakfast or supper dish with syrup.

OLD JOHNNYCAKE

    1 cup stone-ground cornmeal
    2 cups boiling water (or hot milk)
    ½ teaspoon salt
    1 tablespoon bacon fat or lard

Preheat oven to 350 degrees.
Scald by pouring boiling water or milk into the cornmeal. Stir and beat to prevent lumps. Add salt and bacon fat.
Spread on a cookie sheet into a round shape or cake ½ inch thick; and bake 35 to 40 minutes, until crisp. (*4 servings*)

HASTY PUDDING

Hasty pudding can be made in a hurry . . . if you have a supply of cornmeal mush on hand, as the early settlers usually did. Generations of children accepted this nutritious and easy-to-prepare dish as a quick supper. Hence its name. To make it, fill individual bowls half-full of milk, add hot cornmeal mush, a lump of butter, and brown sugar, maple syrup, or molasses to each.
Mrs. Beeton's *Book of Household Management*, 1868, has a recipe for hasty pudding (French *poudinge à la minute*) in which the ingredients are milk, sugar, flour, sago or tapioca, and salt. All the ingredients were trickled slowly into boiling water until thickened, then it was cooked for 10 minutes, stirring all the time. The pudding was served with cream and sugar, jam, or treacle (molasses). The name "hasty pudding" was easily transferred to cornmeal pudding in the new country.

YANKEE CORNMEAL FLAPJACKS

    1 cup milk
    ½ cup stone-ground yellow cornmeal
    ½ cup flour
    ½ teaspoon salt
    1 egg, well beaten

Combine all the ingredients and stir until well mixed.
Drop by the spoonful onto a hot, greased griddle. Cook on one side until bubbles form, turn and cook on other side.
Serve with maple syrup or molasses. (*4 servings*)

SODA BISCUITS

    2 cups flour, sifted
    ½ teaspoon baking soda
    ½ teaspoon salt
    4 tablespoons shortening
    ¾ cup buttermilk

Preheat oven to 375 degrees.
Sift together all dry ingredients. Cut in shortening with knives or cutter. Add buttermilk to make a soft dough.
Knead one minute. Pick off biscuit-size pieces and flatten and mold with hands.
Bake 12 to 15 minutes. (*8 biscuits*)

BOSTON BROWN BREAD

This is called "Thirded" Bread in parts of New England. (⅓ rye or graham flour, ⅓ cornmeal, and ⅓ wheat flour)

- ½ cup rye or graham flour
- ½ cup corn meal
- ½ cup all-purpose flour
- ½ teaspoon baking soda
- ½ teaspoon salt
- ½ cup molasses
- 1 cup sour milk or buttermilk

Mix dry ingredients, then stir in molasses and sour milk.

Grease a 1½-quart mold, put in the mixture, and cover.

Place on a rack in a deep pot, and add enough boiling water to reach halfway up around the mold.

Cover the pot, place over low heat, and steam 3½ hours, keeping the water at a slow boil. (Add more water to keep at the proper level.) Preheat oven to 300 degrees. Remove mold from water, uncover, and bake for 15 minutes. Cut into slices and serve with baked beans.

DOUGHNUTS

There was a sea captain in Camden, Maine, named Hanson Crockett Gregory, who said that one day six of his men were eating doughnuts and fell overboard and sank like plummets, so he took a belaying pin and punched a hole in the doughnuts and after that he never lost a man.

- ⅞ cup milk
- ⅓ cup sugar
- 1 egg
- 4 tablespoons butter
- ½ teaspoon baking powder
- 1 to 1½ cups flour
  lard for frying

Mix all ingredients together well, knead gently 8 times, and roll out. Cut with doughnut cutter.

Heat fat to 370 degrees.

Fry doughnuts until brown and light. Drain on brown paper; sprinkle with sugar if desired. (*6 to 8 doughnuts*)

RAISED BUCKWHEAT CAKES

We've never heard of anyone making a summertime breakfast of buckwheat cakes, but when winter comes there's nothing quite like a hearty stack of buckwheats to start the day right. These cakes were *the* breakfast on ships and in logging camps.

- 2 cups buckwheat flour
- ½ cup wheat flour
- 1 teaspoon sugar
- 1 teaspoon salt
- ¼ yeast cake or ½ package dry yeast dissolved in warm water
- 2 cups lukewarm water
- ¼ teaspoon baking soda in 1 cup lukewarm water
- 2 tablespoons molasses or maple syrup

Mix and sift the flours, sugar, and salt into a large bowl. Stir in the yeast and warm water. Cover with a cloth and let stand in a warm place overnight to rise.

When ready to cook, stir in the soda solution and the molasses. Cook on a hot, well-greased griddle. (*4 to 6 servings*)

Note: ½ cup of the above batter may be reserved as "seed." Keep in a cool place and use instead of yeast in making subsequent batches of batter.

BLUEBERRY GRIDDLE CAKES

- 1½ cups milk, buttermilk, or sour milk
- 2 eggs
- ½ teaspoon salt
- 1 cup flour
- 1 teaspoon sugar
- ¾ cup blueberries or huckleberries
- (½ teaspoon baking soda, if sour milk is used)
- 1½ tablespoons melted butter

Mix milk, eggs, salt; add flour, sugar, blueberries, soda, butter. Beat to mix.

Test griddle with a few drops of water; if they dance, griddle is hot enough. Pour or spoon cakes onto griddle. Bake on one side until top is bubbled. Turn and bake on the other side until brown. Serve with maple syrup. (*4 servings*)

DESSERTS

INDIAN PUDDING

The classic New England Indian pudding is made from cornmeal, milk, and molasses, and is cooked very slowly. The following is a very old recipe which has changed very little down through the years. (If you want the pudding to "whey"—have a light custardy top—scald the meal with 3 cups of milk and pour last cup over pudding in baking dish. Do not stir.)
In the old days, Indian pudding was frequently baked in the same oven with baked beans, both required 5½ to 6 hours to cook.

    1 egg, beaten (optional)
    ½ cup molasses
    1 cup cornmeal
    1 quart milk
      butter

Preheat oven to 250 degrees.
Mix together the beaten egg, molasses, and the meal.
Scald the milk and gradually add to the above ingredients. Pour into a well-buttered baking dish and bake 5 to 7 hours (if quicker baking is desired, the mixture can be cooked in a double boiler for 20 minutes before baking).
Serve with butter or Hard Sauce.* (*4 to 6 servings*)

BUTTERNUT CAKE

Butternuts and maple sugar spell Vermont to most people. This cake is why most Vermonters go home to die.

    ½ cup butter
    ½ cup sugar
    1 cup maple syrup
    2 eggs
    2½ cups flour
    2 teaspoons baking powder
    ½ teaspoon baking soda
    ⅛ teaspoon ginger
    ½ cup hot water
    ½ cup butternut meats

Preheat oven to 350 degrees.
Cream butter and sugar until lemon-colored. Add syrup and beat. Add eggs and beat again. Sift together the flour, baking powder, soda, and ginger. Add to butter mixture alternately with the hot water; beat well after each addition. Add the butternut meats last.
Butter a loaf pan and fill with the cake batter. Bake 45 minutes, until the center of the cake springs back when touched. Cool. Frost with Maple Sugar Frosting:

    2 cups maple sugar
    ⅛ teaspoon salt
    1 cup light cream or milk
    ½ cup butternut meats, chopped

Boil sugar, salt, and cream until it forms a soft ball when dropped into a cup of cold water. Add nuts and beat until creamy and thick enough to spread.

MAPLE MOUSSE

While cooks in other parts of the country were using chocolate to make a mousse, New Englanders—especially Vermonters—were, quite understandably, using the pride of their land, maple syrup.

    ⅔ cup milk
    4 egg yolks, beaten
    1 cup maple syrup
    2 cups heavy cream, whipped
    2 teaspoons cooking oil

Mix egg yolks and milk and put in double boiler. Put over boiling water and slowly add the maple syrup. Stir until thick.
Cool, stirring every so often to prevent the formation of a crust.
Fold the whipped cream into the custard. Pour into a 2-quart oiled mold and freeze 4 hours or until ready to use. Unmold by dipping mold in hot water for 30 seconds. (*4 to 6 servings*)

STRAWBERRY SHORTCAKE (BISCUIT)

Strawberry shortcake is found throughout the country, made in some localities of biscuit and in others of cake. It seems incontestable that the original and true strawberry shortcake, however, was borrowed from the English, who used biscuit to make it.

An English cookbook, Mrs. Beeton's *Household Management* (1915 edition), includes a very old recipe that seems to prove the point. We quote Mrs. Beeton:

INGREDIENTS: *1 cup of sour or butter-milk, ⅓ teaspoonful soda, ¼ teaspoonful salt, 2 tablespoonsful butter, 1 cup flour.* METHOD: *Mix the soda, butter and salt into the flour, and wet it up into a nice free paste with the milk. Divide it into four, roll it up round under the hand, and flatten out with a rolling pin; place it on a suitable-sized tin (baking tin), dock or prick it all over with a fork or skewer, and bake in a quick oven. While baking take 1-½ pints of strawberries and mash them fine. When the cakes are baked, allow them to get cold, spread them over with butter, dredge on a layer of sugar, then strawberries, then sugar, and place another cake on top, the buttered side downwards; dredge the top with sugar and serve.* TIME: *10 to 15 minutes. Average cost, 1 s. Sufficient for 2 cakes. Seasonable in June and July.*

The following recipe from Nantucket, dated 1874, is quite similar to that of Mrs. Beeton. We quote the recipe verbatim:

Rub ½ cup butter into 1 quart flour. Mix 1 teaspoon soda, 2 teaspoons cream of tartar and 1 tablespoon white sugar with 1 pint milk and add. An egg may be beaten into sugar and worked into flour if desired. Roll out lightly and bake in 2 round pans. When done, split cakes and lightly butter lower half of each, add a thick layer of strawberries, sprinkle with sugar and pour on a little cream. Replace top crust and serve while hot with a pitcher of heavy cream. Keep second cake to send in after the first.

GINGERBREAD

½ cup butter
½ cup brown sugar or maple sugar
1 tablespoon ginger
½ teaspoon powdered cinnamon
½ teaspoon powdered cloves
2 cups molasses
3 cups flour
3 eggs, well beaten
1 cup milk
½ teaspoon baking soda

Preheat oven to 350 degrees.
Cream the butter and sugar until smooth. Stir in the ginger, cinnamon, and cloves.
Add the remaining ingredients, mixing thoroughly.
Pour into a buttered 9-inch-square baking pan and bake for 1 hour, or until cake tester inserted into cake comes out dry.
Cool a while before removing from pan. Serve with Nutmeg Sauce* or Hard Sauce.* (*6 servings*)

BROWN BETTY

Here is a recipe that came in with the early eastern settlers, traveled all over in the sailing ships that traded along the coast, and then went westward. Travel by ship was easy then, and because of this Boston and Baltimore by sea were closer than Boston and Baltimore by land.

8 slices toast, crumbled
sugar
cinnamon
butter
6 apples, peeled and sliced
½ cup molasses
½ cup water

Preheat oven to 400 degrees.
Butter a baking pan and put in a layer of bread crumbs. Sprinkle with sugar and cinnamon, and dab with butter.
Put in a layer of sliced apple. Repeat, ending with bread crumbs, until all the crumbs and apple have been used up.
Pour in the molasses and water, set into a pan containing boiling water and cook in the oven for 45 minutes. Serve hot or cold with Hard Sauce (recipe follows). (*4 servings*)

HARD SAUCE

A New England Christmas was not complete without this sauce, served with mince pie or Indian pudding.

    ½ cup butter at room temperature
    2 cups powdered sugar
    3 tablespoons rum, bourbon, or brandy
      nutmeg

Beat butter until creamy and lemon-colored. Add sugar gradually, beating after each addition, until all the sugar is used and the sauce is fluffy and cream-colored. Add the rum gradually, beating as it is added to prevent curdling. Spoon the sauce into a serving dish, sprinkle with nutmeg and refrigerate until ready to serve. (*1 cup sauce*)

BLUEBERRY FLUMMERY

The same desserts, or ones very similar, have a way of showing up in different places with totally different names. Blueberry grunt, blueberry slump, and blueberry flummery are all puddings of a sort, served with or without biscuit or dumplings. Grunt, slump, and flummery are supposed to have come with the English settlers, but are not in the English cookbooks we have consulted. We found a Dutch flummery made with cream, eggs, sherry, and gelatin. What the recipes do attest to is that the settlers put the abundant berries to good use.

    1½ pints blueberries, picked over and
        washed
    2 cups sugar
    1 cup water
    ½ lemon, sliced
    ¼ teaspoon powdered cinnamon
      heavy cream

Heat the water, dissolve the sugar, and add the lemon slices and cinnamon. Bring to a boil and cook a few minutes.
Add the berries, simmer for 5 minutes, remove from the heat, and allow to cool in the syrup. Serve hot or cold with cream. Baking powder biscuit dough can be dropped in the boiling berries. Simmer in covered saucepan 15 minutes. (*4 to 6 servings*)

BLUEBERRY/HUCKLEBERRY PIE

Blueberries and huckleberries are so similar that not only are the names interchangeable in the common usage, but the berries themselves are also interchangeable in cooking. The term *blueberry* seems to be used more in the eastern part of the country, while *huckleberry* seems more colloquial in the Midwest and Prairie states. Dictionaries tell us that the name changed from the English *whortleberry*, or *hurtleberry*, to *huckleberry* in early America. Technically blueberries belong to the genus *Vaccinium*; huckleberries belong to the genus *Gaylussacia* of the heath family. Blueberries have been cultivated since 1911; true huckleberries are still harvested only from the wild. Both berries are native American, and the shrubs grow wild on seaside moors, in mountain pastures, and on the wide prairies. There are few dishes as American as blueberry (huckleberry?) pie.

    2 pie crusts (see Plain Pastry*)
    4 cups berries
    ¾ cup sugar
    1 teaspoon ginger

Preheat oven to 400 degrees.
Roll one crust larger than the other to fit a 1-quart, deep pie dish. Put wider crust in dish. Pick over, wash, and stem berries if necessary. Drain well and put in the pie crust. Sprinkle sugar and ginger over all.
Cover with top crust. Crimp the edges by pushing right forefinger into V formed by left forefinger and thumb, held against outside of lower crust. Cut two or three air vents in top crust.
Bake for 5 minutes at 400 degrees, then lower heat to 350 degrees. Cook 35 to 40 minutes, until juice comes through vents. (*6 servings*)

HYANNIS MOLASSES SAUCE

    1 cup molasses
    1 tablespoon butter
    1 tablespoon vinegar

Cook molasses and butter together over low heat for 5 minutes. Add vinegar.
Serve hot over dumplings, puddings, brown betty, Indian pudding.

NUTMEG SAUCE

1 cup sugar
¼ teaspoon salt
1 tablespoon butter
2 cups boiling water
½ whole nutmeg, grated

Mix together the sugar, salt, butter, and water; boil 5 minutes.
Remove from heat. Stir in nutmeg. Serve with cake, dumplings, puddings, or your favorite dessert.

PUMPKIN PIE

In the days of the early settlers, pumpkin was available the year round. Pumpkins were harvested in the fall, cut into strips, and hung up to dry, ready for use when needed.
Often the dried strips were boiled down with spices and cider and put away in sealed jars. Jack-o-lantern pumpkins can be peeled and stewed to make pumpkin pie, but the specially developed creamy orange "pie" pumpkins make better pies.

1 ½ cups cooked pumpkin, mashed (or canned pumpkin)
½ cup brown sugar
1 teaspoon cinnamon
½ teaspoon ginger
¼ teaspoon nutmeg
½ teaspoon salt
2 eggs, slightly beaten
1 ½ cups milk
½ cup cream

Mix together all the ingredients and cook in a double boiler until thickened. Set aside and cool.
Line a 9-inch pie pan with pastry; chill.
Preheat oven to 450 degrees.
Pour the pumpkin filling into the pie crust and bake until done (when a knife inserted into the middle comes out clean). (*8 servings*)
Note: The ingredients can be mixed and put directly into a pastry shell which has been brushed with egg white. In this case, preheat oven to 400 degrees and lower heat after 20 minutes to 325 degrees. Knife-test for doneness.

VINEGAR PIE

An early visitor to this country once remarked, "They make pies out of everything!"

1 cup sugar
1½ cups water
3 tablespoons cornstarch dissolved in ½ cup water
2 tablespoons butter
3 eggs, separated
3 tablespoons cider vinegar
⅛ tablespoon salt
1 teaspoon lemon extract
1 unbaked 8- or 9-inch pie shell (see Plain Pastry*)
9 tablespoons sugar

Preheat oven to 300 degrees.
Put sugar and 1-½ cups water on to boil.
Mix cornstarch with remaining water and stir into boiling sugar and water. Boil until clear. Remove from stove.
Add the butter, the beaten yolks of eggs, vinegar, lemon extract, and salt. Stir well and pour into unbaked pie shell. Bake 20 minutes.
Beat egg whites until stiff, add sugar gradually, spread this meringue over the pie and bake another 15 to 20 minutes to brown. (*6 servings*)

CHOCOLATE CORNSTARCH PUDDING

Irish moss, blancmange, and arrowroot pudding were English. In New England cornstarch was far more plentiful and was at first a substitution in puddings, and then became custom. With time, more chocolate was added, which improved the pudding. This is the way it was made before packaged puddings existed.

2 cups milk
4 squares unsweetened chocolate
4 tablespoons cornstarch
4 tablespoons sugar
¼ teaspoon salt
2 eggs, beaten
1 teaspoon vanilla

Heat milk in double boiler with the chocolate. Mix cornstarch, sugar, and salt. When the chocolate has melted stir in the cornstarch-sugar mixture. Stir until thick. Beat in eggs. Add vanilla.
Spoon into dessert dishes. Serve with gingersnaps or whipped cream. (*4 servings*)

RHODE ISLAND COB-APPLE PIE

How the New Englanders managed to vary their many apple, pastry, sugar, cinnamon, and molasses recipes is a wonder. Here's one that's truly ingenious.

Pastry:

    2 cups flour
    ½ cup butter or lard
    4 tablespoons water
    ½ teaspoon salt

Filling:

    8 large apples, peeled and sliced
    1 cup molasses
    1 teaspoon cinnamon
    4 tablespoons butter

Preheat oven to 250 degrees.

Cut butter into flour, moisten enough to roll out. Make two pie crusts. Line a 9-inch pie pan with one crust.

Alternate layers of apples with molasses, cinnamon, and bits of butter, ending with molasses.

Cover with second crust; pinch the edges. Slit crust 3 times. Put in oven and bake about 2 hours. Turn out in dish upside down.

BEVERAGES

TOM AND JERRY

In the early 1900s the punch bowl on the barroom counter was a common sight around Christmas time. The bowl contained an egg-milk batter with which rum and brandy were mixed.

    1 egg, separated
      powdered sugar
      pinch baking soda
    ¼ ounce rum
      hot milk
      rum
      brandy
      grated nutmeg

Beat the white and yolk of the egg separately, combine in a mixing bowl, and add enough sugar to stiffen. Add the soda and rum to preserve the batter.

To serve, put 1 tablespoon of the batter in an ironstone Tom and Jerry mug, stir in 3 tablespoons hot milk and 1½ ounces rum. Nearly fill mug with hot milk, top with ½ ounce of brandy and grate a little nutmeg on top.

HOT BUTTERED RUM

In Colonial taverns they used a hot poker to heat this drink, and it was recommended as a cold cure.

    2 teaspoons sugar
    1 gill (½ cup) rum
    ½ cup hot water
    ½ teaspoon butter

Put sugar in mug, cover with rum, add hot water, then butter; stir.

GROG

    1 gill (½ cup) dark rum
    1 teaspoon sugar syrup
    1 cup hot tea
    ½ teaspoon nutmeg
    1 strip lemon zest (rind)

Put sugar syrup and rum in a mug or large cup, pour in cup of hot tea, sprinkle with nutmeg and add lemon zest. Stir.

SPRUCE BEER

Here is Amelia Simmons's recipe (written in 1796) for spruce beer:

> *Take four ounces of hops, let them boil half an hour in one gallon of water. Strain the hop water then add sixteen gallons of warm water, two gallons of molasses, eight ounces of essence of spruce, dissolved in one quart of water, put it in a clean cask, then shake it well together, add half a pint of emptins [yeast], then let stand and work one week, if very warm weather less time will do, when it is drawn off to bottle, add one spoonful of molasses to every bottle.*

Below is a more manageable recipe.

   3 pounds sugar
   5 gallons water
   1 cup yeast (1 cake, 1 package)
   1 small piece lemon peel
 2½ ounces essence of spruce

Mix all together and when fermentation stops, bottle. (Make sure the beer has stopped working before it is bottled or the bottles will explode.)
Note: Essence of spruce can be made by boiling ½ pound of spruce twigs in 3-½ pints of water until reduced by half, then strain and continue to boil until the juice is as thick as molasses.

MINT TEA

Throughout New England, mint leaves were used as a substitute for imported tea. Mint tea has a delicate flavor and is a pleasure to drink. The Pennsylvania Dutch drink it plain. In New England a teaspoon or two of tea leaves is added.

   1 cup water
   1 cup sugar
   2 teaspoons black tea
   ½ cup chopped mint leaves
   1 cup lemon juice
   2 quarts boiling water

Boil 1 cup water and sugar together 5 minutes, add tea and mint leaves.
Allow to steep 10 minutes. Strain, add lemon juice and boiling water. Heat and serve. (*12 servings*)

If you'd like to try it plain:

   2 cups water
   ¼ cup mint leaves

Wash mint leaves and put in teapot.
Pour boiling water over leaves. Let steep 3 to 5 minutes.
Serve with sugar and lemon. (*2 servings*)

EASTERN
COOKING

MEATS

Hot Dogs
Schnitz und Knepp with Dumplings
Goulash
American Sauerbraten
Italian Sausage and Peppers
Hero Sandwiches
Hog Jowls and Black-eyed Peas
Sausages with Chocolate
Hungarian Stuffed Cabbage
Dutch Pork Pie
Pork Liver Pudding
Greek Pot Roast with Olives
Roast Beef with Yorkshire Pudding
Umble Pies
Beefsteak and Oyster Pie
Harlem Barbecue Sauce
Hamburgers

POULTRY AND GAME BIRDS

Chopped Chicken Hors d'Oeuvres
Sixth Avenue Chopped Chicken Livers
Puerto Rican Pollo en Mole
Club Sandwich
Maryland Fried Chicken I
Maryland Fried Chicken II
Roast Wild Duck, Maryland Ruddy Duck

VEGETABLES AND SIDE DISHES

New York Baked Beans
Fried Tomatoes
Buttered Brussels Sprouts
Red Cabbage and Apples
Glazed Carrots
Irish Colcannon
Potato Kugel
Dutch Potato Pancake
Hopping John
Broiled Mushrooms

SALADS AND DRESSINGS

Tuna Fish Salad
Iceberg Lettuce with Thousand Island
    Dressing
Waldorf Salad
Chicken in Aspic
Crab Salad, Delaware
Chef's Salad

BREADS AND BATTERCAKES

Ole Kooks
Waffles
Apple Dumplings
Bran Muffins
Cinnamon Buns
Italian Bread
Cracklin' Bread
Cornmeal Battercakes
Beaten Biscuits

DESSERTS

Mincemeat for Pies
Shoofly Pie
Dutch Custard Pie
Cheesecake
Strawberry Shortcake (Cake)
Pears Hélène
Chocolate Mousse
Rice Pudding
Spice Cake with
    Caramel Frosting
Christmas Fruitcake

BEVERAGES

Syllabub
Christmas Eggnog
Black Velvet
Bloody Mary
Mead
Irish Coffee

EASTERN COOKING

Even before formal settlements were established, small groups of peoples began to come to the East Coast of the United States—the Swedes in New Jersey; the English in Maryland; the Dutch in New York, which was a trading post for furs. Refugees from religious and political persecution began to arrive: Huguenots, Quakers, Scotch-Irish Presbyterians, Dutch Jews, and English and French Catholics in Baltimore and other ports. Some, like the Africans, came as slaves. Later, hunger and enterprise drove more people to brave the seas: Irish, Poles, Armenians, Italians, Lithuanians, Latvians, and Russians. Each tyranny swelled the number of nationalities on the East Coast and does so still, among the latest being the Chinese, Haitians, Hungarians, Greeks, South Africans, Indonesians, and East Indians. They all bring their native cuisines with them.

Little is left of the recipes of the early Swedish settlers. There are traces of Dutch influence still, as well as early German influence on the cooking of the New York-New Jersey area.

In New Amsterdam a Dutch yeoman's table was set "with solid substantial food: poultry, eggs, cheese . . . hot breads. . . . Shortcakes, made with buttermilk and baked on a griddle, were in daily demand; and pies, doughnuts, *olekokes* were features even of the morning meal. *Soupann*—well-salted Indian mush eaten with milk and molasses—was the standard Sunday supper, though occasionally a raised biscuit called *zweibak*, or twice-baked, took the place of mush; this biscuit was made in large quantities, bushels at a time, and then dried in the oven until as hard as a rock; in a bowl of rich milk it made a toothsome dish. . . ."

Andrew Mellick wrote in *The Old Farm* of the kitchen of his youth in Peapack, New Jersey,

with its sanded floor for easier cleaning and the large cool cellar, where are firm yellow pats of butter and pans of rich cream, where stone crocks stand on the earthen floor filled with moist pot cheeses, nut cakes, and all manner of good things, while corpulent jars distended with sweets and rows of pies stuffed with lusciousness adorn wooden shelves hanging from the ceiling. Hams and bacon hung in rows in the cool cellar, and a big crock of sauerkraut was always ready and waiting.

From cabbage they also made *Kohl-salat* (German), and *Kohl-sla* (Dutch), perhaps converted to cole slaw by time. "Fresh meat was to be had only when a farmer slaughtered a 'critter' and distributed joints and pieces among the neighbors, relying for pay on return courtesy."

There was ample food, then, at a dinner in New Brunswick in 1797 when Julian Niemcewitz, a Pole, visited the young United States and reported after a rich repast:

The first course, two or three roast capons with a sauce of butter, cooked oysters, etc. a roast beef, some boiled mutton, some fish or ham. The second course a Pouding *or tart or custards or blanc-manger and some preserves. The tablecloth is removed and fruits, almonds, grapes, chestnuts and wine are then served. One drinks the health of the President, the Vice President and Congress at the end of each dinner.*

He also reported that even plain Quakers ate delicious food.

Philadelphia was the port that saw the entry of thousands of Germans and Swiss migrating to America in the early 1700s, beginning very soon after William Penn established the Colony. It was a small town then, and a State house had been completed where newcomers had to register as soon as they landed. Indians still walked the streets, members of the Lenilenape, a tribe of the Algonquian clan known as Delawares, who cultivated pumpkins, corn, and beans. A Quaker city then, except for Germantown, immigrants from everywhere were accepted. Whether Philadelphia pepper pot soup was brought there by a French immigrant after the French Revolution, or had evolved from the thrifty Quaker habits, we don't know. We do know that in New Orleans this same soup is served with croutons, and sounds very French. It could have come in with a black sold in Philadelphia, from Martinique, or refugees from the French Revolution.

Cinnamon buns were taken to market in Philadelphia by women from Germantown, along with fruit pies, cup cheese, and other specialties.

North and west of Philadelphia, several religious sects had settled who had a very different heritage. Some were Germans from a province on the Rhine called the Palatinate. Probably because the German word for German is *Deutsch*, they became known as Pennsylvania Dutch. The most numerous sects were the Moravians, the Mennonites, and the Amish. They adapted the cooking of their native province to the new country. Rhineland's sauerbraten was made with cider vinegar instead of wine; potato pancakes, called *reibe kutchen* (grated cakes), which on the Rhine are still served with lingonberry preserves, are served here with whole cranberry sauce. They make hot potato salad; *schnitz und knepp*; and sausages of all kinds, including the frankfurter sausage. Early versions of macaroni and cheese may have been adapted from a dish of homemade noodles, sour cream, and cheese baked in their ovens.

Delaware and Eastern Maryland became famous for what has come to be known as Eastern Shore cooking. They take pride in crab dishes (and all kinds of seafoods), beaten biscuit, batter bread, ruddy duck, terrapin, (a salt water turtle which is cooked in a stew with heavy cream, eggs, and sherry), and recently chicken and turkey dishes. Western Maryland is known for its pancakes, pies, breads, apples and peaches, and maple syrup. Baltimore is famous for crab cakes, imperial crab, and turkey with sauerkraut (a Baltimore German dish).

With the opening of several great restaurants such as Delmonico's, Rectors, the Waldorf-Astoria and Plaza Hotels, and others in the midnineteenth century, New York became a center of international cookery. Such restaurants were founded usually by great chefs or restaurateurs, who named their creations after celebrities of the day, or the wealthy families of the city—Melba, Caruso, Duveen, Benedick, Waterbury, Vanderbilt, Astor—a custom that seems to have died out. Presently New York has over six thousand restaurants, and one can find almost any kind of food available in the civilized world in them or in the city's food shops.

The influx of Italian immigrants in the late 1900s and early years of this century up to the present has produced a popularity of Italian dishes, both northern and southern Italian in character, so much so that there is a New York Italian cuisine. Some of the changes are unknown in Italy, but are still rooted in its tradition. A multitude of Jewish restaurants and delicatessens are crowded by patrons who have acquired a taste for lox, pastrami, knishes, kosher frankfurters, potato kugel, and other delicacies. There are Chinese restaurants serving foods from all parts of China—North, South, East, and West. In addition to the more prevalent Cantonese cooking, there are also Shanghai, Mandarin, Szechwan, Hunan, Hangchow, Hankow, and Pekingese dishes. There are Japanese and Korean restaurants as well. (In one part of central New Jersey, near Freehold, there are large farms run by Japanese- and Chinese-American farmers who cater to their ethnic restaurants in and around New York City.) Vietnamese food can be had, with its delightful combination of French and Oriental flavors. There are Greek, Armenian, Turkish, Indian and Pakistani restaurants. Millions of Puerto Ricans and other Spanish-Americans live in New York, and some markets seem like those of a Latin city. Interest in African dishes has been stimulated by black Americans in search of their ethnic origins, and African diplomats at the United Nations in search of a bit of home. In Harlem soul-food restaurants flourish.

The culinary riches of this metropolitan city, its markets and the nearby playgrounds at the seashore and in the mountains would take a lifetime to explore. The millions of people in the city and surrounding towns and communities create an enormous market for the excellent, the varied, and the new. All this can only be touched upon in a book of this kind and these recipes are only a sample of the great wealth of eastern cooking.

SOUPS AND CHOWDERS

PHILADELPHIA PEPPER POT SOUP

This is an old recipe modified for preparation in the modern home kitchen. Tripe can be cooked the day before needed.

- 1 pound honeycomb tripe and
- 1 pound plain tripe, cooked 8 hours in water to cover (reserve cooking liquid)
- 1 veal knuckle, with some meat on it, cooked in 3 quarts water
- 1 large onion, chopped
- 1 bay leaf
- 2 medium potatoes, peeled and diced
- 1 teaspoon sweet marjoram
- 1 teaspoon fresh parsley, chopped
- 1 sprig thyme, or ½ teaspoon dried thyme
- 1 teaspoon salt
- ½ teaspoon pepper
- ¼ teaspoon cayenne pepper

Dumplings:

- ½ cup beef suet (or lard), chopped fine
- 1 cup flour
- ¼ cup water

Cut cooked tripe into ½-inch squares.

Cook veal knuckle in water 3 to 4 hours, skim as necessary. Remove meat and chop into ½-inch pieces. Strain broth. Combine with tripe and tripe broth, return all to stove, add onion and bay leaf, and simmer 1 hour. Add potatoes, sweet marjoram, thyme, parsley, salt, pepper, and cayenne. Continue to simmer.

Make dumplings by combining suet and flour; mix well, add enough water to make dough. Roll the dough on a board to ¼-inch thickness and cut into squares the size of the tripe. Roll them in flour and drop into the soup. Cook 15 minutes longer. (*6 to 8 servings*)

MARYLAND CRAB SOUP, SHORE STYLE

The Old Hotel Rennert in Baltimore was a consistent center for unexcelled eating around the turn of the century—and before that. The Rennert family insisted upon the strictest culinary standards. It was said that during the last years of the hotel's existence, when good help was hard to find, Mrs. Rennert herself would don an apron, go into the kitchen, and take charge.

Crab soup, like most other fish soups, varies a great deal from region to region, and even within a given region. The only strictly indispensable ingredients are crab meat, chopped onion, and tomatoes. Almost any additional seasonal vegetables are acceptable: corn, green peppers, okra, lima beans, carrots. The recipe below came from the Old Hotel Rennert in Baltimore, but we suspect even this was not inviolate.

- 4 tablespoons butter
- 1 onion, chopped
- 1 green pepper, chopped
- 2 quarts fish stock (or clam broth)
- ½ cup raw rice
- 3 tomatoes, peeled and diced
- 1 teaspoon Worcestershire sauce meat of 2 large steamed crabs
- 1 pound or 1 can okra, cut into 1-inch pieces; or 1 package of frozen okra salt pepper chopped parsley

Using a large pot, sauté the onion and pepper in the butter for 10 minutes.

Add the fish stock and rice; simmer 15 minutes.

Add the tomatoes, Worcestershire, crab meat, and okra; simmer 20 minutes longer.

Season to taste and serve, sprinkled with chopped parsley. (*4 to 6 servings*)

MANHATTAN CLAM CHOWDER

According to legend, this chowder was invented on the Coney Island boardwalk, and the traditional spice is caraway seed. Many recipes call for the use of thyme.

    ¼ pound salt pork, sliced
    1 onion, chopped
    1 cup diced potatoes
    2 cups canned tomatoes, or 4 medium
      fresh tomatoes
    1 pint chowder clams (quahogs), hard
      parts chopped
    1 pint fish broth, strained (made from
      heads and trimmings)
    1 teaspoon caraway seed
    ¼ teaspoon pepper
    ⅛ teaspoon cayenne
      chowder crackers or sea biscuit

Cook salt pork until brown. Add onion, brown, then add potatoes and tomatoes. Simmer 15 or 20 minutes.
Add the clams, broth, caraway seed, pepper, and cayenne. Simmer 5 minutes and serve with crackers or sea biscuit. (*4 to 6 servings*)

CLAM BELLY SOUP

Here is a superb soup we found at Gage & Tollner, a gaslight restaurant that has been on Fulton Street in Brooklyn since 1879. The soup is made from the round soft parts—the bellies—of soft clams, and is delicately subtle in flavor and texture.

    2 dozen soft clams (steamers)
    2 cups light cream
    2 tablespoons butter
      pinch nutmeg
      pinch salt
    1 teaspoon sherry

Scrub the clams and steam them, covered, in a little water until they open.
Remove the bellies, saving the necks and other parts for use in another dish.
Strain the broth and add ½ cup to the cream, butter, and seasonings. Simmer a few minutes, add the bellies and sherry, and simmer 1 minute longer. (*2 servings*)

SNAPPER SOUP

The snapping turtle, an agressive but flavorsome creature that weighs from ten to thirtyfive pounds wild, is plentiful along the Eastern Seaboard in freshwater bays, inlets, streams, and ponds. Generations of snappers have been netted and trapped to serve in snapper soup.
Snapping turtles have come onto hard times because of water pollution. However, they can still be found in some of the larger fish markets. Care should be taken that they come from a reputable dealer. Frozen turtle and canned snapper soup can sometimes be found in specialty food shops.
Snapper soup originated in the tidal lowlands of the Delaware River and has long been a favorite dish in Philadelphia and parts of Wilmington and Trenton, where it is traditionally served with a pitcher of sherry for those who want more sherry than is already in the soup. The recipe that follows is the best and simplest we have been able to find.

    1¾ pounds veal knuckle, broken
     ½ cup veal fat, cut up
    1½ onions, chopped fine
     1 stalk celery, chopped
     1 carrot, diced
     ½ teaspoon marjoram
     2 cloves
     ½ bay leaf
     ½ teaspoon pepper
     ½ cup flour
    1½ to 2 quarts beef broth
     1 cup steamed tomatoes
       the meat of 1 snapping turtle, cut
       small
     1 cup sherry
     1 teaspoon salt
     1 teaspoon Tabasco sauce
     2 slices of lemon
     1 hard-cooked egg

Preheat oven to 400 degrees.
Put veal-knuckle pieces and fat in a roasting pan. Distribute onion, celery, carrots, and spices around and over it. Put in oven and brown.
Remove and sprinkle flour over all and stir well. Return to oven 30 minutes longer.
Pour this mixture into a large pot, add the broth and tomatoes. Simmer 3½ hours.
Add turtle meat with sherry, salt, Tabasco, and lemon. Simmer 10 minutes. Add chopped egg and serve with a small pitcher of sherry. (*6 servings*)

JERSEY SOUR BEER AND BROWN BREAD SOUP

In Germany there is a dark-bread soup and a beer soup. The following appears to be a combination of the two. The recipe calls for draft beer, since most bottled beer has been pasteurized and will not sour.

This recipe is from *The Old Farm*, written by Andrew Mellick in the late 1800s, remembering the customs of the early German settlers in New Jersey.

    1 quart sour beer, draft
       crusts of a loaf of brown bread
    ½ cup molasses

Simmer beer over medium heat. Add the crusts, sweeten with molasses. (*4 servings*)

VICHYSSOISE

Vichyssoise is a comparatively new addition to American fare. It was created less than fifty years ago by Louis Diat when he was the head chef at the then-famous Ritz-Carlton Hotel in New York. Vichyssoise is always served in chilled cups with a sprinkling of finely chopped chives on top.

    5 leeks, white parts only, thinly sliced
    3 tablespoons butter
    4 cups diced raw potatoes
    4 cups chicken broth
 1½ teaspoons salt
    ½ teaspoon celery salt
       pinch cayenne
    1 cup heavy cream
    ½ teaspoon Worcestershire sauce
       dash nutmeg
       chopped chives

Using a medium saucepan, sauté leeks in butter for 5 minutes, or until soft but not brown.
Add the potatoes, broth, salt, celery salt, and cayenne; cook for 15 minutes or until potatoes are soft.
Remove from heat, mash with a potato masher, and strain.
Chill; stir in the cream, nutmeg, Worcestershire sauce. Pour into chilled cups, top with chopped chives, and serve cold. (*6 to 8 servings*)

SOPA DE PAPAS

From the island of Puerto Rico via New York comes this simple yet interesting potato soup.

    1 cup mashed potatoes
    1 tablespoon flour
    1 cup chicken, veal, or beef broth
    1 cup milk
    1 tablespoon butter
    ½ teaspoon salt
    1 bay leaf

Garnish:

       thinly sliced bread
    ½ cup mild cheese, grated
    1 tablespoon diced sweet red pepper
    1 tablespoon chopped parsley

Mix potatoes, flour, broth, milk, butter, salt, and bay leaf. Bring to boil, lower heat, and simmer 15 minutes. Strain.
Toast bread, cut into nickel-sized rounds. On each piece put a little pile of cheese, a piece of red pepper and a sprinkle of parsley. Float a few of these on each dish of soup. (*4 servings*)

CRÈME WATERBURY

The recipe for this soup, named for a prominent New York family of the early 1900s was given to us by a member of that family. Then of course it was not made with condensed consommé, but with a double consommé.

    1 can condensed consommé or chicken
       broth
    1 can water
    ½ teaspoon curry powder, mixed with a
       little broth
    1 tablespoon onion, chopped fine
    ½ cup heavy cream
    1 apple, peeled and diced, sprinkled
       with lemon juice*

Put consommé, water, curry, and onion on stove and cook for 20 minutes.
Strain. Add cream, heat through. Serve with diced apples on each serving. (*4 servings*)
*Sprinkle with lemon juice to keep the apple from turning brown.

PASTA, EGG,
AND CHEESE DISHES

HOMEMADE NOODLES AND CHEESE

    2 tablespoons butter
    2 tablespoons flour
    1 cup milk
    1 teaspoon salt
    1 cup grated mild cheese
    ½ cup bread crumbs
    2 tablespoons butter

Melt the butter over low heat and stir in the flour. Add the milk and salt. Blend well with a fork or wire whisk until smooth. Cook this cream sauce 2 minutes, set aside.

Noodles:

    3 eggs
    1½ to 2 cups sifted flour
    1 teaspoon salt
    1 or 2 tablespoons water

Beat eggs, salt, and water together. Add flour gradually and knead until the dough is very stiff, 15 to 20 minutes.
Roll out on a floured board. Keep rolling until the dough is very thin, ⅛ inch or thinner. Dust with flour as you roll.
When the dough is as thin as possible, roll the dough up like a newspaper, loosely, and set aside to dry for 30 minutes.
Slice noodle dough crosswise with a sharp knife into noodles ¼-inch wide. Let strips dry again for 30 minutes before cooking; then drop into slowly boiling water, 3 to 5 minutes, until they test done to the tooth.
Preheat the oven to 400 degrees.
Put half the noodles into a buttered baking dish and cover with half the cheese.
Put in the remaining noodles, the remaining cheese, and pour the cream sauce over all. Sprinkle with bread crumbs, dot with butter, and bake 20 to 25 minutes until brown. (4 servings)

EGGS BENEDICK

    4 slices cooked ham or Virginia ham, ¼ inch thick
    2 tablespoons melted butter
    8 eggs
    4 English muffins, split and lightly toasted
    salt and pepper
    hollandaise sauce

Sauté the ham in the butter 2 to 3 minutes, place a slice on each half of the toasted muffins. Poach the eggs and place one on each of the muffin halves. Season, spoon on the hollandaise and serve immediately.

HOLLANDAISE SAUCE

    4 egg yolks
    ½ pound butter, cut into pieces
    salt and pepper
    juice of 2 lemons

Put egg yolks into the top part of a double boiler (water should not touch top pan) and beat with a wire whisk, adding butter piece by piece. Continue beating until sauce thickens. Season to taste, add the lemon juice, and stir. Remove from heat and keep warm over hot water until ready to use. (4 servings)

ROQUEFORT BALLS

    ½ cup butter
    ¼ pound Roquefort cheese or blue cheese
    1 teaspoon paprika
    1 teaspoon minced chives
    2 tablespoons sherry

Cream all the ingredients together and roll with the hands into 1-inch balls. Chill and serve with cocktails or after dinner.

SPAGHETTI (MACARONI) WITH SAUCE

In the nineteenth century Italians migrated by the thousands to the United States in search of work, bringing with them the foods of every province of Italy. In particular, they introduced to their new country the pastas of their native land. They brought their fierce native pride as well, and whenever three Italians meet, talk will often turn to argument when it comes to the preparation of pasta and sauce. There is agreement that pasta should not be cooked too much, only to the point where it is cooked through and firm. It is agreed that pasta should be mixed (condita) with butter and grated cheese before the sauce is added and before the pasta is served.

Enrico Caruso taught Americans to eat spaghetti by twirling it against a spoon, even though many Italians do not eat it that way. Three twirls of the fork are allowed in mannerly circles. The secret is not to take too many strands on the fork to begin with.

Sauces for the many interesting forms of pasta vary a great deal. Italian-Americans from southern Italy prefer a lot of garlic and onion cooked in olive oil, and sweet basil for flavoring. Those from central Italy like onions, parsley, and carrot sautéed in half-oil-half-butter, and sometimes a clove of garlic sautéed and then removed from the pot, with sage and summer savory for flavor. The northern Italians like garlic and onions sautéed in butter, with mushrooms, chicken livers, and rosemary to flavor the tomatoes. There is also a meat sauce made from Italian pot roast with tomatoes, simmered for 3 to 4 hours. The meat is then ground up and returned to the sauce. All the sauces are very good to eat with pasta. They are all made con amore.

Many Americans, whose first taste of spaghetti was canned spaghetti, thought that was the way it should taste. Now, though more people know better, spaghetti is often served "cold"—white, overcooked, partially drained strands of spaghetti in a soup dish with a watery cup of tomato sauce poured over it, with no butter or cheese mixed with it. Perhaps a bowl of cheese is on the table.

There is a better way. Recipes for some typical Italian-American sauces follow.

TOMATO SAUCE (CENTRAL ITALY)

    1½ tablespoons butter
    1½ tablespoons oil
     1 small onion, finely chopped
    1½ tablespoons carrot, finely chopped
    1½ tablespoons parsley, finely chopped
     5 tomatoes, chopped, or 1 can (number
       2) tomatoes
    ⅜ cup beef broth or water
     1 teaspoon sage
     1 teaspoon summer savory
     1 teaspoon salt
    ¼ teaspoon pepper

Sauté onion, carrot, and parsley in butter and oil very slowly until golden brown. Add tomatoes (if canned tomatoes are used, reduce the salt to ¼ teaspoon), broth, sage, savory, salt, and pepper. Simmer slowly. Stir from time to time, and if sauce boils down too much add more water. Cook 1 hour slowly and stir every so often until thick.

TOMATO SAUCE (SOUTHERN ITALY)

    ¾ cup olive oil
     6 cloves garlic, chopped
     1 medium onion, chopped
     1 can (number 2) Italian tomatoes
       (Italian tomatoes have basil cooked
       with them in the can) or 6 medium
       tomatoes, chopped
     3 cans Italian tomato paste
     2 bay leaves
     3 tomato-paste cans water
    ½ teaspoon salt
    ¼ teaspoon pepper

Sauté garlic and onion slowly in olive oil until golden brown.

Meanwhile put tomatoes, tomato paste, 3 cans water, bay leaves, salt, and pepper in saucepan and bring to a boil.

Strain the olive oil from the onion and garlic. Then add onion and garlic to the tomatoes; simmer slowly for 1½ hours. Strain again.

SPAGHETTI SAUCE (NORTHERN ITALY)

3 tablespoons butter
2 medium onions, finely chopped
1 clove garlic, whole
2 chicken livers, chopped
6 mushrooms, chopped (if Italian dried, they should be soaked in water till soft)
¼ teaspoon rosemary
1 large can or 8 fresh plum tomatoes
½ teaspoon salt (if necessary)
¼ teaspoon pepper

Melt butter, sauté the onions and garlic until golden, remove garlic.
Add chicken livers, mushrooms and rosemary, and sauté until golden, then add the tomatoes.
Taste, and if necessary, add salt. Add pepper.
Cook over low heat 45 minutes to 1 hour until thick.

SPAGHETTI (MACARONI) WITH BUTTER

Once in a restaurant in Naples I ordered *Spaghetti al Burro*. About twenty minutes later the waiter returned with a napkin-covered plate. The spaghetti was on the napkin—it had been drained of *all* water, mixed with sweet butter and freshly grated Parmesan cheese, and had been cooked exactly *al dente* (to the tooth), which means just cooked through, not too soft but without a hard center. Italian spaghetti used to be the only kind made with hard durum wheat but now imported and domestic hard-wheat (chewy) spaghettis are available. This dish can be had in the United States in the best Italian restaurants, though I have never seen it served on a napkin in New York.

4 quarts water, boiling
1 teaspoon salt
1 pound spaghetti
6 tablespoons butter
⅜ cup grated Parmesan

Have water at rolling boil. Add salt. Put spaghetti in whole; it will sink slowly into the water. When it is almost down, give it a good whirl in the water to be sure all the strands are separated. Cook 15 minutes; stir again, then test one strand for doneness.
Drain in colander and run cold water through spaghetti briefly. Drain again and return to pot. Put over low heat to evaporate any remaining water.
Add butter and ⅓ cup Parmesan cheese. Toss well.
Sauce should be added at this time when making spaghetti with sauce. Serve with the rest of the cheese in a bowl or sprinkled on top. (*6 servings*)

PIZZA

As far as we know, pizza, a Neopolitan specialty, was first introduced in 1939 when an Italian restaurateur opened the first pizza parlor in New York. Many well-known American Italians were invited, including Mayor La Guardia, and though the pizzas were cooked in special ovens and were delicious, the parlor did not succeed. It took World War II and the American GI's returning home from Italy to make this specialty a national snack. In addition to the ever-present pizza parlors (featuring pizzas with every imaginable topping), pizzas can now be found in fast-food restaurants and, frozen in handy packages, in supermarkets.

Should you want to make a pizza from scratch, try the one below.

2½ cups flour
    pinch salt
1 package yeast, softened in ½ cup lukewarm water
1½ tablespoons olive oil
2 pounds tomatoes, peeled, cored, and cut up (or tomato sauce)
    pinch salt
½ pound Italian sausage, thinly sliced
2 tablespoons olive oil
1½ teaspoons dried orégano
1 teaspoon dried basil
1 pound mozzarella cheese, sliced
1 can flat anchovies, drained

Sift together the flour and salt, add the yeast and oil, and make into a soft (but not sticky) dough. Place on a floured board and knead until smooth. Transfer to a bowl, cover with a towel, and allow to rise about 2 hours in a warm place until double in size.

Simmer the tomatoes in salted water about 10 minutes or until soft. Drain and reserve.

Simmer the sausage in a little water about 5 minutes. Drain and reserve.

Preheat oven to 500 degrees.

Grease a pizza pan or similar large, flat pan. Shape the risen dough into a ball and roll out on a floured board to fit the pan. Place the pastry into the pan and stretch out to the edges. Spread the tomatoes over the pastry; sprinkle with olive oil, orégano, and basil. Spread the cheese slices evenly on top, and arrange anchovies over half the pizza and sausage over the other half.

Bake in the oven about 20 minutes, or until crust is brown and cheese has melted. Slice and serve hot with plenty of napkins. (*6 to 8 servings*)

CHEESE TRIANGLES

This is an American version of a famous Middle Eastern appetizer, *tiropetes, tiropitakia,* or *boereg.* Phyllo can be bought in Greek or Armenian delicatessens; feta is available in many cheese stores as well.

½ pound feta cheese
½ pound dry cottage cheese
1 package (3 ounces) cream cheese
3 eggs, beaten
1 cup butter, melted
½ pound phyllo (pastry)

Filling:
Mix cheeses and eggs together until well blended. Set aside.

Unfold carefully the roll of paper-thin sheets of pastry. Remove one sheet at a time, working quickly. Put damp cloth over remaining sheets until ready for use.

Cut each sheet in 3 strips, lengthwise, brush each strip with butter. Put a teaspoon of filling on end of each strip. Fold corner over the filling in a triangular shape. Continue folding in a triangle until rest of strip is used, forming a triangular-shaped package.

Place triangles under a damp cloth on a buttered cookie sheet. Continue until all the filling is used.

Preheat oven to 375 degrees.

When cookie sheet is filled, bake triangles for 25 to 30 minutes or until golden brown.

Triangles not needed may be frozen and used at a later time. Phyllo is usually sold in 1-pound packages, so freeze the remaining ½ pound and use for another batch, but be sure to defrost before using. (*100 triangles*)

FISH AND SHELLFISH

FRIED WHITEBAIT

These are the tiny young of the common herring, measuring 2 to 3 inches in length. Translucent and pale green in color, they have a subtle and delicate flavor. The season for whitebait, when available, is April to November.

At the Hotel Barclay in Philadelphia whitebait were once a famous dish served with oyster crabs, the little fingernail-size crabs that live with oysters, sharing the hospitality of their shells and food. But the dish appeared on the menu only at such rare times as both ingredients were in season.

To cook whitebait (with or without oyster crabs), carefully pat them dry with a cloth, dust lightly with rice flour and pan-fry in peanut oil and butter until golden. Serve garnished with chopped parsley and a slice of lemon.

CHESAPEAKE BAY CRAB FEAST

On almost any summer weekend in the Chesapeake Bay region of Maryland, Delaware, or Virginia, if you look carefully, you are likely to find a crab feast in session. And, if you can succeed in getting yourself included, you'll never forget the experience.

Great washtubs of hard crabs are steamed and consumed, usually at picnic-type tables covered with newspapers. The dainty utensils employed are wooden clubs or mallets (for cracking claws) and sharply pointed knives. Since the sweet crab meat that is extracted from the shell is most often laced with cayenne and other nice spices, a plentiful supply of cold beer is essential.

If you are a crab fancier, you will find it hard to stop eating—and before you have finished, you might discover that you have put away six or eight crabs, or even more.

The crab feast has been going on for a long time. Marylanders claim that it is as old as the New England clambake.

If you would like to cook up a modest little feast of your own, in kitchen or back yard, here's how you go about it:

Take a large pot or kettle and arrange somehow to fit a grill into it a few inches from the bottom. Pour in 1 cup vinegar, 2 cups water, 1 tablespoon black pepper, 1 tablespoon dry mustard, 1 teaspoon cayenne, and 1 teaspoon curry, mace, or coriander.

Turn the heat up; when the steam begins to rise, toss in 2 dozen crabs one at a time (so that you can be sure they are all alive), and clamp the lid on tightly. The crabs will cook in about 10 minutes—they are done when they are pink. The grill will keep them from becoming waterlogged in their own juices.

To eat, follow this time-honored procedure:
1. Break off the claws and legs, crack, remove the meat.
2. Remove and discard the "apron" from the bottom of the crab.
3. Remove and discard the top shell.
4. Remove and discard the spongy digestive organs called "devil fingers" and the lungs.
5. Break body in two along the central crease.
6. Remove meat with the sharp point of a knife.

Enjoy yourself—and don't forget the beer!

CHESAPEAKE BAY CRAB CAKES

    1 pound cooked blue-claw crab meat
    ½ teaspoon (dry) mustard
    2 tablespoons mayonnaise
    1 egg, beaten
    ½ teaspoon salt
    1 teaspoon Worcestershire sauce
      (optional)
      dash cayenne pepper
    1 slice bread, wet, squeezed out, and
      crumbled
      dry bread crumbs

Combine the crab meat with the mustard, mayonnaise, egg, salt, Worcestershire, cayenne, and bread. Shape into 8 cakes and roll in bread crumbs.

In a heavy frying pan heat the oil until barely smoking and cook cakes at moderate heat until brown on one side, then turn carefully and brown the other side. (*4 servings*)

BALTIMORE CRAB IMPERIAL

We found a recipe for Imperial Crab attributed to an Eastern Shore hotel at the turn of the century. Directions called for steaming hard crabs, removing the meat, combining it with other ingredients, and stuffing the mixture back into the shells. The old recipe did not quite check out when we tested it, so we present the following slightly modernized version below. Today's pure-food laws do not permit the reuse of crab shells. Instead, fake shells of plastic or aluminum are commonly used.

    4 to 6 blue-claw crabs (depending upon
      size), or ¾ pound fresh lump or back-
      fin crab meat
    4 shells, real or fake
    ½ onion, chopped
    2 tablespoons butter
    ½ teaspoon salt
    ½ teaspoon cayenne pepper
      dash Worcestershire sauce
    1 teaspoon English (dry) mustard
    2 tablespoons chopped green pepper
    1 cup cream sauce
    2 egg yolks
      dry bread crumbs
      butter

Preheat oven to 350 degrees
Sauté the onion in the butter, add the crab meat, seasonings, green pepper, and cream sauce. Mix well.
Bind with egg yolk, pile into shells, sprinkle with bread crumbs, dot with butter, and brown in the oven 25 minutes. (*4 servings*)

DEVILED CRABS

    1 pound blue-claw crab meat
    ¼ teaspoon (dry) mustard
    ¼ teaspoon mace
      dash cayenne pepper
    1 tablespoon parsley, finely chopped
    1 teaspoon Worcestershire sauce
    3 tablespoons butter, melted
    1 tablespoon lemon juice
    1 egg, beaten
    ¼ cup dry bread crumbs

Preheat oven to 350 degrees.
Add the seasonings to the crab meat; add the melted butter, lemon juice, and beaten egg; stir gently.
Place into 4 well-buttered "shells" or ramekins, sprinkle with bread crumbs, and bake 15 minutes or until golden. (*4 servings*)

OYSTER ROAST

Since early colonial days, oyster roasts have been a traditional gustatory activity along the Eastern Seaboard, especially on the Delmarva Peninsula, which hems in the Chesapeake Bay. The popularity of the oyster roast, however, has never quite approached that of the clambake or the crab feast, simply because oysters are not eaten during the warm and festive summer months. Oyster roasts in the fall, however, are still events of considerable social importance.
A bed of white-hot coals is built and covered over with a large grill or grating. The oysters, well scrubbed, are simply dumped onto the grill and roasted until they open.
The hungry guests gather about, spear the oysters with forks, and dip them into melted butter or a hot cocktail sauce made of horseradish, ketchup, Worcestershire, and Tabasco. Corn on the cob, sliced tomatoes, and baked potatoes accompany the oysters, and all is washed down with mugs of cold beer.

FRIED OYSTERS

Fried oysters have been a top favorite along the Eastern Seaboard since the earliest Colonial days, and there have been many recipes for preparing them. An English cookbook, *The Accomplished Cook*, published in 1664, gave the following recipe:

Take two quarts of great oyſters being parboiled in their own liquor, and waſhed in warm water, bread them, dry them, and flour them, fry them in unclarified butter criſp and white, then have butter'd prawns or ſhrimps, butter'd with cream and ſweet butter, lay them in the bottom of a clean diſh, and lay the fried oyſters round about them, run them over with beaten butter, juyce of oranges, bay-leaves ſtuck round the oyſters, and ſlices of oranges or lemons.

My own love affair with fried oysters started in 1917 when my father first took me to the Hotel Rennert in Baltimore. The Rennert had begun to decline even then, but the kitchen continued for years to turn out some of the best seafood in America. The following recipe for fried oysters, dating from pre-deep-fat days, follows closely that of the Rennert.

    1 quart shucked oysters
      salt
      pepper
    2 eggs, lightly beaten
    2 tablespoons milk or cream
    1 cup bread crumbs, cracker crumbs, or
      cornmeal
      bacon fat or lard
      butter

Drain the oysters, pat them dry with a napkin, and season with salt and pepper.
Mix the eggs and milk or cream, dip the oysters into this mixture, and roll in crumbs.
Fry in a fifty-fifty mixture of butter and fat for about 5 minutes or until golden brown on both sides. (Fat must be heated to the smoking point.)
If you wish to deep-fat fry oysters, refrigerate them for several hours and place them a few at a time in fat heated to 365 degrees for 2 to 4 minutes or until golden. (*4 to 6 servings*)

GRAND CENTRAL OYSTER STEW

The famous Oyster Bar located in the lower levels of Grand Central Station in New York has been a landmark for oyster stews since the early 1900s. Successive generations of chefs have officiated at the Oyster Bar without once changing the world-famous recipe for stewing an oyster. The stew I had when I first arrived in New York in 1925, I honestly believe, is the same stew I had there last week. This can be made into a clam stew by substituting cherry-stone clams for oysters.

       2 tablespoons butter
       1 teaspoon Worcestershire sauce
       1 teaspoon paprika
       ½ teaspoon pepper
       ½ teaspoon celery salt
       1 dozen medium-sized oysters
       1 cup oyster liquor and clam juice
         combined
       2 cups milk, half-and-half, or cream, as
         desired
         butter
         paprika

Get the top of a double boiler as hot as possible without letting the top pan touch the water in the bottom pan. Put in the butter, Worcestershire, paprika, pepper, and celery salt.
Stir in the oysters or clams, let them froth for half a minute, then pour in the clam broth and boil hard for half a minute longer.
Add the milk, half-and-half, or cream, and bring to the boiling point. Pour into bowls, add a pat of butter and a dash of paprika, and serve. (*2 servings*)

GRAND CENTRAL CLAM PAN ROAST

This is made into an oyster pan roast by substituting oysters for clams.

       2 tablespoons butter
       1 teaspoon Worcestershire sauce
       1 teaspoon paprika
       1 dozen cherrystone clams or 1 dozen
         medium-size oysters
       ½ cup clam juice
       2 tablespoons chili sauce
       1 cup light cream
       1 teaspoon lemon juice
       2 slices dry toast

Get the top of a double boiler as hot as possible without letting the top pan touch the water in the bottom pan. Put in the butter, Worcestershire, paprika, and clams or oysters, and let froth for half a minute.
Pour in the clam broth, add the chili sauce, boil and stir for half a minute.
Add the cream and then the lemon juice. Stir for half a minute more, and serve on dry toast. (*2 servings*)

FILLETS OF SOLE MARGUÉRY

This dish was invented by the chef of the once very fashionable Hotel Marguéry on Park Avenue in New York. You can make it in your own kitchen at home. It is something of a work-out, but well worth the effort.

First, make a court bouillon:

         fish heads and bones
       ½ cup sliced carrots
       1 leek (white part only), cut in chunks
       2 sprigs parsley
      10 peppercorns
       1 bay leaf
       2 quarts cold water

Cook fish heads, vegetables, and seasonings in 2 quarts cold water. Simmer until this stock is reduced to 1 pint, strain.

Second, cook the fish:

       4 large lemon sole or flounder, filleted
      12 small shucked oysters
      12 fresh shrimp, cleaned
       2 tablespoons butter

Preheat oven to 350 degrees.
Place fillets in a buttered baking dish with oysters and shrimp. Pour a cup of the fish stock around them, cover with foil and poach for 15 or 20 minutes.
Carefully transfer the fillets to a warm oven-proof platter, arrange the oysters and shrimp around the fish.

Third, make the sauce:

       1 cup fish stock
       ¼ cup white wine
       ½ cup butter
       4 egg yolks, beaten

Pour the remaining cup of stock into a saucepan and simmer until the quantity of liquid is reduced to 3 tablespoons.

Strain this into a double boiler, add the wine and the butter. Stir over boiling water until butter melts.

Add the well-beaten egg yolks, holding the pan off the heat. Return to boiler and stir constantly until the sauce is as thick as cream sauce.

Pour the sauce over the fillets, oysters, and shrimp; put in oven until the sauce is lightly browned. (*4 servings*)

LOBSTER À L'AMERICAINE

There is a mystery about the origin of this dish. Some say it was originally *Amoricaine*, an ancient word for Brittany, and that perhaps a chef, to compliment an American guest, changed its spelling. Others say that there is a dish very much like it in Provence in southern France, and that perhaps a chef in New York adapted this to American lobster. Since there are so many good chefs in New York who are, or have become, Americans, it is easy to believe whichever story most suits one's fancy. It doesn't matter because the proof is in the eating, which is superb.

2½ pound live female lobster, cut in 1½-inch pieces (save the coral or roe)
¼ cup olive oil
1 onion, chopped fine
1 clove garlic, chopped fine
4 tomatoes, quartered
4 tablespoons brandy
½ cup fish consommé
½ cup dry white wine
⅛ teaspoon thyme or tarragon
1 bay leaf
1 tablespoon butter
4 tablespoons sherry

Kill lobster by cutting quickly between the head and the tail. Cut lobster into 1-½-inch pieces, shell and all. Heat olive oil in large skillet. Add the lobster pieces, turn and brown quickly on both sides. Remove to platter. Lower heat.

Cook onion in oil until almost done. Add garlic, tomatoes, lobster pieces, brandy, thyme or tarragon, bay leaf, consommé, and white wine. Bring the mixture to a boil, lower heat, and cover. Cook 20 minutes, add butter and sherry, and serve in soup plates. (*2 servings*)

LOBSTER NEWBURG

Lobster Newburg was introduced at Delmonico's in New York around 1890. The famous dish was originally called Lobster à la Wenburg after Ben Wenburg, a sea captain and gourmet, who took most of his meals at Delmonico's when not at sea. It was Wenburg who invented this method of preparing lobster. In time, Charles Delmonico and Ben had a falling-out and Delmonico changed the name of the dish on his menu to Newburg (*new* being *wen* spelled backwards).

At the New York World's Fair in 1939, we watched George Rector make Lobster Newburg. Here's the great man's recipe verbatim:

Select a live lobster weighing about 2 pounds and plunge it into boiling salted water to cook for 10 or 20 minutes, according to size. Remove from the water and when cool cut and break open the shell and remove the lobster meat and cut it into pieces about the size of a small walnut. Now melt 2 tablespoons of fresh butter and cook the pieces of lobster in it for several minutes then season with salt and a few grains of cayenne pepper and 4 tablespoons of sherry wine. . . . Cook 1 minute, add 1 cup of heavy cream and the yolks of 2 eggs slightly beaten (or 2 tablespoons hollandaise). Stir gently but do not allow to boil after cream and yolks have been added. Serve with triangles of fresh toast.

Translated into modern-day recipe form, Mr. Rector's Lobster Newburg is made this way:

1 lobster (2 pounds), boiled, cut in pieces the size of a walnut
2 tablespoons butter
¼ teaspoon salt
⅛ teaspoon cayenne
4 tablespoons sherry
1 cup heavy cream
2 egg yolks slightly beaten, or 2 tablespoons hollandaise sauce
2 pieces fresh toast

Melt butter in frying pan over low heat. Add lobster meat, heat a few minutes, then add salt, pepper and sherry. Cook 1 minute.

Add heavy cream and egg yolks or hollandaise; stir and heat, but do not boil. Serve on toast. (*2 servings*)

ANNAPOLIS ROCKFISH

In the Northeast they are striped bass, but Baltimoreans and Washingtonians insist that they are rockfish.

One day when I was eating at Harvey's, a traditional old seafood restaurant in Washington, I found both fish listed and asked the waiter the difference between the two. "They's both the same fish," he replied. "Then why do you have them both listed?" I asked. "Well sir," he explained, "some people likes to order striped bass, and some likes to order rockfish." Chesapeake Bay rockfish have many friends.

Bluefish, similar in size and texture, can be prepared in much the same way as striped bass—or rockfish.

    2 pounds rockfish fillets
    1 teaspoon salt
    2 cups dry bread crumbs
    1 teaspoon dry mustard
    2 tablespoons minced parsley
    2 hard-cooked eggs, chopped
    ½ cup butter, melted
    2 tablespoons lemon juice
    ½ cup ketchup
    few dashes Tabasco sauce

Preheat oven to 375 degrees.
Wipe fillets dry, season with salt, and set aside. Mix all the remaining ingredients into a well-blended paste.
Place half the fillets into a greased baking pan; cover with half of the mixture. Place the other fillets on top and cover with the remaining paste.
Bake for 30 minutes or until flaky. (*4 servings*)

SHAD ROE AND BACON

On the East Coast in the spring the shad begin to run up the rivers to spawn. Starting in the South they move up with the spring and begin to arrive as far north as New York's Hudson River in the middle of March. Long before that they have been shipped north from the Carolinas.

The shad catch had lessened because of river pollution, but has begun to return to its former size as measures to control the pollution have begun to be effective. Shad returned to the Delaware for the first time in the early seventies. The female shad carries the roe, which is a delicacy.

    4 slices bacon
    1 large shad roe, or 2 small
    4 tablespoons flour

Cook bacon until crisp and put onto a hot platter, leaving the fat in the pan.
Wash and dry roe, being careful not to break the skin of the roe. Dip roe in flour until it is lightly coated all over.
Turn heat under bacon fat very low. Place roe carefully in fat and cook, depending on size, 10 to 15 minutes on one side. Turn carefully and cook on the other side as slowly. If the roe is cooked too fast it can burst and will not be attractive to serve.
Some cooks parboil the roe and then fry it. But if the above directions are carefully followed the roe will not burst.
If the roe is large, serve half to each person. If small, one for each person. (*2 servings*)

TERRAPIN À LA MARYLAND

Diamondback terrapin live along the saltwater marshy edges of gulfs, bays, and inlets of the Atlantic Coast and Gulf of Mexico, and are the most prized of the many fresh and saltwater turtles (including "cooters," "sliders," and snappers) traditionally eaten in Delaware and farther south in the Carolinas and Florida. (In North Carolina the slaves at one time protested that they were given too much turtle to eat.) And in Florida a species of cooter was so esteemed as to be known as "the Suwanee Chicken."

Once upon a time terrapin was almost as plentiful on the tables of southern Maryland diners as oysters and crabs. Not so any longer. We had to dig several generations back for the recipe that follows, which, by the way, we have not tested. With complete confidence in its authenticity and workability, however, we offer it to adventuresome cooks who might be able to get their hands on a couple of real live terrapin.

Actually, turtle and terrapin meat are sometimes available frozen. And terrapin are usually available in New York's Chinatown, where they are valued as an aphrodisiac as well as a food. And here's the recipe:

Have two pots of boiling water, one for cleaning and one for cooking the terrapin. Drop the live terrapin in the boiling water for about 3 minutes, remove, and, with a towel, rub off the skin from the legs, clip off the toes and pull out the head and clean skin from same. After this, put in second pot of boiling water and let boil until they feel soft to the touch. A 5-inch terrapin takes about 45 minutes to cook. After cooking, break the shell apart and let terrapin cool off sufficiently to handle. Then break the terrapin in joints, separating the meat from the bones and entrails. Save and wash the eggs. After dicing the meat and liver of the terrapin, add some of the stock in which you have cooked it.

To serve: Put the terrapin meat in a saucepan or chafing dish and cook with plenty of butter, a little pepper and salt. Cook about 10 minutes, then add the eggs and serve. (Add sherry, if desired.)

Note: A 5-inch terrapin should be cooked only 30 minutes and a 7-inch terrapin about 40 minutes, but you can always tell, because when a terrapin is cooked its shell begins to open and it should immediately be taken out of the water. A great deal of care should be taken in cleaning the legs and the neck and head of the terrapin with a rough cloth. When the terrapin is opened, the blood should be carefully saved and poured over the prepared terrapin in the jar when it is to be put away. Some people take out all of the entrails, others very carefully remove only the gall bladder and sand bag. The gall bladder should be completely taken out, even if you have to sacrifice a little of the liver in doing it. The meat of the terrapin itself should be separated from the bones, but only the large bones taken out. All the joint bones should be left in, but separate the meat as neatly as possible into pieces that will be convenient when eating. (If terrapin is not available, substitute 1 calf's brain and 1 chicken .)

MEATS

HOT DOGS

According to legend, the frankfurter sausage, named after the city in Germany, was put into a roll and sold by an enterprising food salesman at the 1903 World's Fair in St. Louis, Missouri. Another legend has been that he introduced them at a baseball game. Whichever it was, I think we can safely say he started something. Frankfurters are sold in rolls throughout the United States; come in several sizes—2-inch cocktail, 6-inch regular, and 12-inch giant; and are served with any number of condiments: mustard, ketchup, chili sauce, relish, sauerkraut, chili con carne. The rolls range from the almost tasteless to homemade parkerhouse, or Vienna bread rolls. There is a frankfurter called a corn dog, dipped in cornmeal batter and fried. They are also added to many family supper dishes, such as macaroni and cheese, baked beans, or spaghetti.

The popularity of frankfurters reached a climax when Eleanor Roosevelt served them to Their Royal Highnesses King George and Queen Elizabeth of England at a picnic at Hyde Park, New York, at the Roosevelt country home. The best frankfurters are kosher frankfurters, to be found in New York City. They are made in the old-fashioned way—pure ground beef and flavored with garlic, stuffed in casings—and served with hot mustard.

Below is a superior recipe for hot dogs.

> 8 kosher frankfurters
> 8 large Vienna rolls
> butter
> Dijon mustard

Simmer frankfurters in water to cover for 15 minutes. Do not cook too fast or the skins will burst.

Heat rolls, and butter them. Keep hot.

Put one frankfurter in each roll and spread a teaspoon of mustard on each. Serve in paper napkins.

The frankfurters can be grilled over charcoal, or in a frying pan, if you belong to the vociferous minority who prefer their hot dogs grilled. (*4 servings*)

ITALIAN SAUSAGE AND PEPPERS

Many Americans of southern Italian ancestry use homemade sausage for this dish, which used to be served on rolls at New Jersey's old Palisades Amusement Park.

        2 pounds or 8 links Italian sweet or hot sausages
        4 green peppers, seed pod removed, quartered
        1 onion, sliced

Put sausages with 1 cup water in frying pan over medium heat; turn sausages when they begin to brown.
Add onion and peppers. Stir, cover, and let cook for 10 minutes.
Uncover and cook until sausages and onions are brown. (*4 servings*)

HERO SANDWICHES

You call them heros because that's what you have to be to finish one. Call them submarines—call them grinders. By any name these multiple-filling sandwiches made with loaves of Italian bread have become in only a single generation a national American dish.
Heros can measure 10 to 36 inches in length, and have been made as long as 14 feet!
Heros come hot or cold.
To make a hot hero fill a 10-inch Italian loaf with hot Italian meatballs, sausages, Italian peppers, eggplant, crushed olives, and/or even veal cutlets. If you wish to go all the way, pour a liberal serving of spicy gravy over all and sprinkle with Parmesan cheese.
To make a cold hero split the bread, spread with olive oil, and fill with your choice of cold sliced Italian meats such as salami, prosciutto, mortadella, bologna, cappicolla, boiled ham. Lay slices of provolone or other cheese on top, add slices of tomato, and pile on shredded lettuce or cabbage. Sprinkle with vinegar and start to work eating.
Totally Americanized heros are sometimes found made with cold sliced roast beef, sliced turkey, liverwurst, or even tuna fish.

AMERICAN SAUERBRATEN

There are many sauerbratens in Germany. Some are made with beef marinated in wine or buttermilk rather than vinegar, and some are made without gingersnap or gingerbread crumbs.

        4 pounds of beef (top or bottom round, or rump)
     1½ cups cider vinegar
        1 cup water
        2 bay leaves
        8 peppercorns
        ½ teaspoon salt
        1 clove
        2 tablespoons fat
        6 carrots, cut in strips
        6 onions, sliced
        2 tablespoons brown sugar
        8 gingersnaps, or ½ cup gingerbread crumbs

Boil vinegar, water, bay leaves, peppercorns, salt, and clove together. Put beef in this mixture in a deep bowl, refrigerate covered for 2 days, turning several times. Drain, save marinade.
Brown meat in fat on all sides in Dutch oven. Add the onions, carrots, and 1 cup of the marinade, cover and simmer for 2 or 3 hours or until tender. If more marinade is needed add ½ cup at a time. (This can be cooked in a 300-degree oven for the same length of time.)
Add crumbled gingersnaps, brown sugar, and more of the marinade, if necessary or if more gravy is desired. Cook 15 minutes. Slice across the grain of the meat.
Serve with potato pancakes or dumplings. (*8 servings*)

SAUSAGES WITH CHOCOLATE

There is a famous dish made in Germany with bear meat, in which chocolate is one of the ingredients. Perhaps this adaptation was a nostalgic reminder of the old country for the early German settlers in Peapack, New Jersey. They had plenty of bear meat there, as well, in those days.

8 pork sausages
8 ounces of unsweetened chocolate,
 melted

Put pork sausages in a frying pan with enough
water to cover the bottom of the pan. Simmer
until water has evaporated, then cook sausages
on all sides until brown.
Pour off excess fat; add a cup of water and the
chocolate. Simmer sausages in chocolate sauce
and serve. (*2 to 4 servings*)

DUTCH PORK PIE

This Pennsylvania Dutch recipe is different
from the every day pork recipes we know, and
is a worthy dish.

Meat:

2 pounds thick sliced loin of pork, diced
1 tablespoon parsley, minced
1 large onion, chopped
1 tablespoon ketchup

Preheat oven to 325 degrees.
Put one-third of the pork into a deep 2-quart
baking dish, cover with parsley. Add another
one-third of the pork, and spread onion over
this. Add remaining pork and spread ketchup
over this.

Sauce:

2 tablespoons butter
2 tablespoons flour
1¾ cups milk
½ teaspoon salt
⅛ teaspoon pepper
3 tablespoons bread crumbs

Melt butter over low heat, stir in flour, and add
milk slowly, stirring all the time until sauce
thickens. Add salt and pepper. Spoon this over
the pork.
Sprinkle all with bread crumbs, put into the
oven and bake 1-½ hours.

Pastry:

 2 cups flour
 ½ teaspoon salt
 ⅓ cup pork fat, chopped fine (or lard)
 ¼ cup water

Mix flour, salt, and pork fat until mealy. Add
water until the pastry leaves the bowl clean.
Roll out ½ inch thick to cover pie. Return pie
to oven. Bake 25 to 30 minutes, until crust is
brown. (*6 servings*)

SCHNITZ UND KNEPP

This is a famous Pennsylvania Dutch recipe.

4 cups dried apples, soaked 8 hours or
 overnight
½ smoked ham (butt end) or smoked
 pork butt
2 tablespoons brown sugar

Soak apples in water overnight or all day.
Cover ham with water and cook for 3 hours. If
tenderized, or a pork butt cook 1½ hours with
apples and the water in which they were
soaked. Add brown sugar.

Dumplings

2 cups flour
4 teaspoons baking powder
¼ teaspoon pepper
1 teaspoon salt
1 egg
1-½ cups milk
3 tablespoons melted butter

Sift dry ingredients into a bowl. Mix egg,
milk, and shortening into the flour mixture to
form a batter.
Drop by spoonfuls into boiling liquid. Cover
pot and cook dumplings 15 minutes. Do not
lift cover of the pot after adding dumplings.
Serve in soup plates with slice of ham, apples,
dumplings. (*8 to 10 servings*)

BEEFSTEAK AND OYSTER PIE

This pie really is made with steak (and really is fit for a king).

First make the pie pastry:

    1¾ cups flour
    1 teaspoon salt
    ⅔ cup shortening
    ⅓ cup ice water

Sift the flour and salt into a mixing bowl, add the shortening and mix with a pastry blender until it is in pea-size bits.
Sprinkle the ice water in by spoonfuls, stirring with a fork, until enough has been added to pat into a ball. Do not knead.
Wrap in wax paper, chill, and roll out on a floured board into 2 pastries, to fit the pan.

Then make the pie:

    2 pounds boneless sirloin steak, cut into
        1½-inch chunks
        flour
    3 tablespoons butter
    3 tablespoons olive oil (or other
        cooking oil)
    1 cup chopped onions
    1 cup beef broth
    1 bay leaf, crumbled
    ½ teaspoon thyme
    2 tablespoons minced parsley
    1 teaspoon salt
    1 teaspoon freshly ground pepper
    12 shucked oysters
    12 mushroom caps

Flour the steak and brown in a mixture of butter and oil, using a heavy skillet. Add the onions and cook for 5 minutes longer.
Pour in the broth, add the mushrooms and seasonings, and cook, stirring, 10 minutes.
Preheat oven to 350 degrees.
Line a casserole or suitable baking dish with one of the pie crusts and pour in the meat mixture.
Place the shucked oysters on top, add the second pie crust, pinch around the edges to seal, and perforate in several places to allow steam to escape.
Bake 30 minutes. If crust browns too quickly cover with foil. (*4 to 6 servings*)

ROAST BEEF WITH YORKSHIRE PUDDING

In early times a roast of beef was threaded on a spit with a drip pan underneath. As the beef roasted fat and juices were caught in the pan and, ½ hour before the beef was done, the pudding was put into the roasting pan to rise and brown, and to absorb the juices. This works just as well in an oven if the beef is removed from the roasting pan first.

    1 three-rib roast (7 to 8 pounds)
    2 cups flour
    1 teaspoon salt
    2 cups milk
    4 eggs

Preheat oven to 325 degrees.
Put roast in oven. Bake 1 hour and 45 minutes or 15 minutes per pound for rare. If medium-rare is desired roast 35 minutes longer, a total of 20 minutes to the pound.
Mix flour and milk and salt. Add eggs and beat 3 minutes. Let sit until ready to put in roasting pan.
Remove roast from pan to heated platter. Turn oven to 400 degrees. Pour off all but ¼ inch fat in roasting pan. Pour batter into roasting pan and bake for 20 to 30 minutes or until it mounds and browns. Serve with the roast. Caution: do not open oven while the pudding is rising. (*8 servings*)

UMBLE PIES

Umbles or humbles were the innards of the deer (kidneys, liver, brains, lesser cuts), which were usually made into pies for the servants after the hunt. They don't seem so humble now.
The following recipe is from *The Accomplished Cook* (1664):

To make Umble Pies:
Lay minced beef suet in the bottom of the pye or flices of interlarded bacon, the umbles cut in the fame form, and seasoned with nutmeg, pepper, salt, fill your pyes with it, and flices of bacon and butter, close it up and bake it, and liquor it with claret butter and ftripped tyme.

(In those days the pies were made up first and a hole made in the top into which the liquor for the pie was poured—in this case a wineglass or two of claret, melted butter, and stripped stalk of thyme.)

HARLEM BARBECUE SAUCE

Migrations of southern blacks to the North in the last twenty years has reinforced the "soul" of northeastern cities. This barbecue sauce has sold untold numbers of spareribs, chickens, and hamburgers over the years, and has made walking along 125th Street a pleasure.

½ cup butter
1 teaspoon dry mustard
⅛ teaspoon cayenne
1 teaspoon Tabasco sauce
2 tablespoons ketchup
2 tablespoons lemon juice
2 tablespoons vinegar
½ teaspoon onion salt
½ teaspoon garlic salt
1 tablespoon tomato sauce
2 tablespoons finely chopped parsley
¼ cup water

Mix all together and cook for 5 minutes. Enough for two chickens, or 8 to 10 pork chops, or 2 sides of spareribs (about 1 cup sauce).
This is best when used for charcoal-broiled meats.

HOG JOWLS AND BLACK-EYED PEAS

Hog jowls are the cheeks and tongue of the hog. Cured like country hams, they have much the same sweet flavor. In New York's Harlem this dish is traditionally served on New Year's Eve for good luck.

1 Virginia country-smoked hog jowl
2 cups dried black-eyed peas, soaked overnight and drained, or 2 pounds fresh peas
½ cup brown sugar
1 teaspoon dry mustard
2 tablespoons vinegar
1 tablespoon whole cloves
1 onion, stuck with 4 cloves

Scrub the jowl well with a brush until all the smoke and black grit is removed. Scrape the hide well and cut the hairs out of the snout, leaving the snout on. Put into a large pot ¾ full of water, bring to a boil, and simmer 2 hours. Remove from the liquid (saving liquid for the peas), and cut off the hide.
Cook the peas in the reserved liquid until tender, about 1 hour.
Preheat oven to 350 degrees.
Mix together the sugar, dry mustard, and vinegar, and spread evenly over the jowl. Dot with cloves, put into a baking dish, bake 20 minutes. Surround with peas, add the onion, and cook in the oven until all are brown and tender. (*6 servings*)

GOULASH

This is *gulyas*, meaning cowboy in Hungarian. Here is an elegant version of a dish brought to the United States by immigrants from Hungary. Do not use Spanish paprika with this—use Hungarian paprika, sweet or hot or both.

2 pounds stewing beef (or lean pork), cut into 1½-inch chunks
1 tablespoon flour
1 teaspoon salt
2 teaspoons paprika (Hungarian hot or sweet as desired)
few grains cayenne
2 tablespoons olive oil or lard
1 onion, chopped
1 clove garlic, chopped
1 green pepper, chopped
1 teaspoon tomato paste
½ cup dry red wine
1 pint sour cream (optional)

Put the meat, flour, salt, paprika, and cayenne into a paper bag and shake until meat is well coated.
Heat the oil in a heavy skillet. Sauté the onions, garlic, peppers, and tomato paste a few minutes, push to one side of pan; then add the meat, brown, add wine. Simmer about 1½ hours or until meat is tender.
Stir in the sour cream, cover, and simmer again about 10 minutes.
Serve on hot noodles. (*4 to 6 servings*)

HUNGARIAN STUFFED CABBAGE

1 medium cabbage, with core removed
2 pounds chopped beef chuck (or a
   mixture of beef and pork)
1 egg
¼ cup partially cooked rice
1 teaspoon salt
½ teaspoon pepper
1 teaspoon paprika
2 onions, chopped
   cooking oil
2 cups sauerkraut, rinsed
1 tablespoon caraway seeds
1 small can tomato juice

Drop the cabbage into boiling water for 2 to 3
minutes to soften the leaves. Drain and set
aside.

Mix together the chopped meat, egg, rice, salt,
pepper, and paprika; form into balls 2½ to 3
inches in diameter. Wrap each ball with a
softened cabbage leaf, tucking the leaves under
to secure. Shred leftover leaves and set aside.
Using a large pot, sauté the onions in oil 2 or 3
minutes or until transparent. Place the stuffed
cabbage leaves onto the onions, toss shredded
leaves on top, and then add the sauerkraut.
Sprinkle with caraway seeds and pour in the
tomato juice.

Cover the pot and simmer over low heat for 2
to 2-½ hours. Shake the pot occasionally and
add a little water if needed.

Serve with boiled potatoes and sour cream on
the side. Stuffed cabbage is better warmed
over, so prepare a day in advance and reheat
just before serving. (*4 to 6 servings*)

HAMBURGERS

There are all kinds of stories about where and
how the hamburger sandwich got started: at
the 1903 World's Fair in St. Louis; at a New
York waterfront restaurant habituated by
sailors from Hamburg, Germany, who wanted
to take their lunch back to the ship in bags; at a
landmark luncheonette in Connecticut . . .
Whenever or however its origins, the hamburger has certainly taken over as America's
number-one food—as a snack to be eaten on
the run, a light lunch, or a main dinner course.
Hamburger is made by grinding certain parts
of the beef, either separately or as a mixture. In
general, the finest grade comes from the round
or from the tail of sirloin or porterhouse cuts.
The neck and chuck meat rank next in quality
and flavor, the cheapest being made by
grinding together the scrap meat from all parts
of the steer.

Flavor and texture are what count most in
good hamburgers; there's nothing wrong with
fat, except that too much is apt to cook up to
nothing, leaving a skillet full of grease.

Since the discovery of high-protein soybeans,
synthetic meat products are being produced to
augment the more-expensive beef. But as yet
the flavor of these soy-meat products does not
compare with that of beef. They look like
hamburger, but they don't taste like it.

Following is a recipe for very special hamburgers, to serve when you feel like putting
forth just a little more effort.

1½ pounds chopped round steak
1 onion, chopped
1 tablespoon chopped shallots
4 tablespoons butter
   dash Worcestershire sauce
   dash Tabasco sauce
1 teaspoon dry mustard
2 teaspoons salt
   freshly ground pepper
1 egg, lightly beaten
2 tablespoons sour cream
4 large hard rolls, buttered

Sauté the onion and shallots in 2 tablespoons
butter, add the seasonings. Mix with the
chopped steak and the beaten egg, using your
hands, not a fork.

Roll loosely into 4 balls the size of tennis balls
and drop onto the kitchen table to flatten.

Pan-broil on both sides in a heavy skillet with
2 tablespoons butter.

Transfer to a heated platter.

Heat buttered rolls. Place a hamburger on
each. To the pan juices add the sour cream,
simmer a minute or two, and pour a spoonful
over each hamburger. (*4 servings*)

PORK LIVER PUDDING

There were few delicatessens around when this country began, and many pigs. This is a liver sausage recipe that should be sliced like liverwurst.

2 pounds pork liver, cut into pieces
1 pound fat pork shoulder, cut into pieces
1 onion
½ teaspoon parsley, chopped
¼ teaspoon thyme
1 teaspoon salt
½ teaspoon pepper
1½ cups beef broth

Preheat oven to 325 degrees.
Put all the ingredients except the broth through a grinder. Mix well and put into baking dish. Pour ½ cup hot broth around it. Bake for 15 minutes. Add ½ cup more of broth, cover, bake another 15 minutes. Add remaining broth. Cook 1 hour, covered; uncover and bake 1 more hour. Let cool, then chill. Slice next day. Serve as cold meat or in sandwiches.

GREEK POT ROAST WITH OLIVES

3 to 4 pounds of beef rump roast
3 tablespoons olive oil
1 clove garlic
½ teaspoon
¼ teaspoon pepper
1 cup red wine
2 tablespoons tomato paste
½ cup green olives

Heat oil in frying pan. Brown meat on all sides.
Put meat, garlic and seasonings into a deep pot with cover.
Pour wine into frying pan, scrape brown bits into sauce and add to pot roast. Simmer over low heat for ½ hour.
Add tomato paste, continue to cook for 3 or 4 hours covered.
Add olives last 30 minutes of cooking. (*6 to 8 servings*)

POULTRY
AND GAME BIRDS

SIXTH AVENUE CHOPPED CHICKEN LIVERS

The Sixth Avenue Delicatessen in New York was famous for years for its Jewish cuisine—most especially for its chicken livers which, we are told, *must* be made with chicken fat (the more chicken fat the better).

1 large onion, chopped
chicken fat
1 pound chicken livers
2 or 3 hard-cooked eggs
salt
pepper

Fry the onions in chicken fat until golden, then add the livers and continue cooking until livers are well done, about 5 minutes.
Season to taste with salt and pepper and run through the meat grinder along with the eggs, or chop fine on chopping board. Do not use blender.
Mix thoroughly and mash with a fork, adding more chicken fat as you proceed.
Check seasoning, spoon into a jar, and spread a dollop of fat on top before sealing.
Serve on crisp crackers as a snack, or on lettuce as an hors d'oeuvre. (*about 2 cups*)

ROAST WILD DUCK, MARYLAND RUDDY DUCK

There is much lore about cooking wild duck. It's a fine art, no doubt, and requires care. The preparation of ducks is important.

Ducks should be dry-plucked, wiped clean, and singed. To quote one cook, "It is insufficient cleaning that gives wild ducks a strong fishy taste. Rinse out the inside and wipe well both inside and out with a wet towel; but do not wash the duck unless you have accidentally broken the gall bladder, as washing destroys the flavor." This cook sprinkles them inside with salt, and stuffs them with celery and raw apple slices, or a peeled onion, halved.

    1 pair of ducks, mallard or canvasback
    salt
    celery and apple or raw onion slices
    pepper
    ½ cup butter
    salt pork, thinly sliced

Preheat oven to 500 degrees.

Rub ducks with pepper, put a lump of butter inside each, and dress according to directions above. Cover breasts with salt pork slices, and place into a baking pan.

Cook 20 minutes if small, 30 minutes if large, basting every 5 minutes. They are done if when pierced with a fork the blood does not run. Serve in a hot dish with their own juice and tart apple or currant jelly on the side. Wild duck is traditionally accompanied by wild rice. (*4 servings*)

RUDDY DUCK

There is a species of duck called ruddy duck, but the "ruddy" in this recipe derives from the method of cooking.

The preparation of the duck for this Maryland specialty is the same as for roast wild duck. Salt pork is replaced with butter and the breasts are removed after 20 to 30 minutes of cooking, and the carcass put in a duck press to extract the juices, to which is added a cup of red wine or sherry. This is all mixed together and served with the duck.

Only canvasback ducks should be used for ruddy duck because they feed on wild celery, which gives them a superior flavor.

CHOPPED CHICKEN HORS D'OEUVRES

    1 chicken breast
    1 tablespoon butter
    1 tablespoon flour
    ½ cup broth
    ¼ teaspoon salt
    ⅛ teaspoon pepper
    ⅛ teaspoon nutmeg
    ½ cup heavy cream

Put chicken breast in water to cover and cook 10 to 15 minutes. Remove bones and chop breast fine. Reserve broth.

Melt butter in small frying pan; add chopped chicken, sprinkle with flour, stir, add broth; stir until thick. Add salt, pepper, nutmeg, cream. Remove from heat. Cool.

Spread on toast or small baking powder biscuits. (*1 cup*)

PUERTO RICAN POLLO EN MOLE

The Caribbean is not far from New York when broiled chicken can be bought in a supermarket and quickly turned into a home-cooked meal.

    2 tablespoons cooking oil
    3 slices stale bread, diced
    1 clove garlic, chopped
    1 onion, chopped
    3 chili peppers, roasted, seeded, and
      ground
    ⅛ teaspoon sesame seed, pounded with
    ⅛ teaspoon anise seed
    ½ teaspoon salt
    2 cloves
    ¼ teaspoon pepper
    1 tomato, peeled and chopped
    1 cup chicken broth
    1 chicken, broiled

Fry bread, chopped onion, and garlic in cooking oil; add peppers, seasonings, tomato, and broth. Simmer until well blended.

Cut a broiled chicken in 8 even pieces and add to the sauce. Simmer 10 minutes and serve with rice. (*4 servings*)

One would think, with all the vast quantities of fried chicken consumed in the state of Maryland, that there could at least be some agreement as to how it should be cooked. Alas, there is great diversity of opinion, and we found ourselves unable to choose. We, therefore, offer you two delicious ways of preparing Maryland fried chicken.

MARYLAND FRIED CHICKEN I

    2 broilers or small frying chickens
    2 cups flour
    3 teaspoons baking powder
    ½ teaspoon salt
    ¼ teaspoon pepper
    2 eggs
    ½ cup milk
      bacon fat or other frying fat

Preheat oven to 225 degrees.
Disjoint the chickens. Halve the breasts.
Separate the leg and second joint.
Make a batter of the flour, baking powder, salt, pepper, eggs, milk.
Heat fat to 375 degrees, or until just smoking.
Dip pieces of chicken into the batter and fry a few pieces at a time until brown. The legs and second joints will take a bit longer to cook than the breasts, so cook these pieces first.
Keep warm in the oven until ready to serve. (*6 to 8 servings*)

MARYLAND FRIED CHICKEN II

    2 tablespoons butter
    4 slices lean salt pork
    2 tablespoons flour
    ½ cup milk
    1 frying chicken
    2 tablespoons parsley, chopped
    2 tablespoons chives, chopped
    2 tablespoons butter
    2 tablespoons flour
    1 cup milk
    ½ cup light cream

Dip salt pork in flour and fry in two tablespoons butter over medium heat.
Disjoint chicken, dip in milk and flour, and cook in butter and pork fat until brown and done, about 20 minutes on each side. Add more butter if necessary.
When chicken is done put on a heat-proof platter with salt pork and keep hot in oven.
Melt rest of butter in pan juices, stir in flour, stir in milk slowly until the sauce is thick and smooth.
Add light cream to gravy and spoon gravy over chicken and salt pork. Sprinkle with chopped chives. Serve with fried tomatoes. (*4 to 6 servings*)

CLUB SANDWICH

The original club sandwich, made with chicken, bacon, tomato, lettuce and mayonnaise, is served in every country club and resort in America, and remains a nostalgic reminder, as well as a present pleasure, to many.

    3 freshly toasted slices white bread
      butter
    3 slices chicken breast
    1 medium lettuce leaf, 1 small
    2 slices bacon, cooked
    1 medium tomato, peeled and sliced
      mayonnaise, preferably homemade
    1 sweet gherkin pickle
      toothpicks

Butter each piece of toast on 1 side.
Lay 3 slices of chicken on one buttered side.
Cover this with buttered side of second slice.
Spread the top of this with mayonnaise and cover with sliced tomato; on top of this put 2 slices of bacon.
Cover this with last piece of toast, buttered side to bacon.
Secure with 2 toothpicks and serve with pickle on a small piece of lettuce. (*1 serving*)

VEGETABLES
AND SIDE DISHES

GLAZED CARROTS

8 to 12 whole young carrots, depending
   on size, scrubbed
5 tablespoons butter
1 tablespoon honey
½ teaspoon salt
½ teaspoon pepper

Place the carrots into a heavy saucepan, cover
with salted water, and cook over low heat
about 15 minutes or until tender. Drain well
and wipe dry.
Melt the butter in a heavy skillet over very low
heat, stir in the honey, season, and add the
carrots. Cook 10 minutes, turning so that
carrots are glazed on all sides. Take great care
not to burn. (*4 servings*)

IRISH COLCANNON

The city of New York becomes Irish (and
unusually open-hearted) on St. Patrick's Day.
Anyone who can imitate an Irish accent does,
particularly when standing at a bar. Corned
beef and cabbage is on every restaurant menu,
not only because it's good business, but for
pure sentiment, because St. Patrick's Day is a
bit like the first crocus.

1 head cabbage, cored and quartered
8 medium potatoes, peeled
½ cup butter
1 teaspoon salt
½ teaspoon pepper

Boil the cabbage and potatoes until soft.
Drain the cabbage and chop.
Mash the potatoes.
Mix together the chopped cabbage, mashed
potatoes, butter, and seasonings. (There
should be twice as much potatoes as cabbage.)
Serve on St. Patrick's Day with corned beef. (*6
to 8 servings*)

POTATO KUGEL

Potato kugel, a favorite dish of Jewish
Americans, was brought here from the old
country. Actually it is a pudding, which,
though better served hot, can be served hot or
cold.

6 medium potatoes, peeled
2 eggs
½ cup flour
1 teaspoon baking powder
1 teaspoon salt
½ teaspoon pepper
2 onions, minced
¼ cup chicken fat (or butter)

Preheat oven to 350 degrees.
Grate the potatoes (or put them through a
meat grinder); drain and place into a blender
with the eggs and blend until smooth.
Sift together the flour, baking powder, and
seasonings; add to the blender.
Sauté the onions in chicken fat until brown,
add to the blender. Mix well and pour into a
greased baking dish.
Bake 1 hour or until crisp and brown. (*4 to 6
servings*)

DUTCH POTATO PANCAKE

4 cups mashed potatoes
2 tablespoons flour
2 eggs, lightly beaten
1 tablespoon baking powder
   pinch salt
1 cup milk

Mix together all the ingredients and beat into a
batter. Place on a hot, greased grill and fry on
both sides until golden brown. (*4 to 6 servings*)

NEW YORK BAKED BEANS

New York baked beans used to be made the same way as New England baked beans, without the molasses. The additions in this recipe only improve on what is a very good dish.

> 1 pound pea beans, washed, soaked overnight
> ½ pound salt pork
> 1 onion
> 2 cloves garlic
> 1 teaspoon salt
> ¼ teaspoon pepper
> 1 teaspoon sage
> 1 teaspoon dry mustard
> ¼ teaspoon allspice

Drain beans and save soaking water. Cover beans with fresh water and bring to a boil slowly over very low heat. Add pork, onion, garlic, salt, pepper, and sage; cook until skins burst, about 1 hour. Take out pork and slice. Preheat oven to 300 degrees.
Put a few slices of pork into the bean pot. Fill pot with beans and water. Put remaining meat on top. Dissolve mustard in a little bean water, add allspice, and pour over beans. Bake in oven for 2 hours. (*8 to 10 servings*)

FRIED TOMATOES

> 4 medium tomatoes, sliced ½ inch thick
> 4 tablespoons flour
> 4 tablespoons bacon fat
> ¼ teaspoon salt
> ⅛ teaspoon pepper

Dip tomato slices in flour.
Heat bacon fat. Fry tomatoes until brown on one side, turn carefully, and brown on other side.
Sprinkle with salt and pepper and serve hot. (*4 servings*)

HOPPING JOHN

Considered by many a dish of the Deep South, this nourishing concoction is made from Philadelphia to Florida and as far west as Ohio.

> 1 cup black-eyed peas (cowpeas)
> 4 cups cold water
> ½ pound bacon strips, cut into squares
> 2 cups boiling water
> 1 cup long-grain rice
> 1 teaspoon salt
> dash pepper

Place the peas and cold water into a heavy pot and simmer, covered, for 1 hour.
Remove cover and continue cooking until peas are almost dry.
Add the remaining ingredients, bring to a boil, cover, and simmer for 30 minutes or until almost dry and rice is tender. (*4 servings*)

BUTTERED BRUSSELS SPROUTS

> 1 pint brussels sprouts
> ½ stalk celery, finely chopped
> ¼ cup butter
> ½ teaspoon salt
> ¼ teaspoon pepper
> 1 tablespoon minced parsley

Boil the sprouts with the celery in water to cover until tender, about 20 minutes. Drain.
Put the butter into a saucepan; add the sprouts, seasonings, and parsley; and cook about 5 minutes, shaking from time to time. (*4 servings*)

RED CABBAGE AND APPLES

> 4 tablespoons bacon drippings
> 1 onion, chopped
> 4 cups shredded red cabbage
> 2 tart apples, peeled and sliced
> 2 tablespoons vinegar
> ½ teaspoon caraway seed
> 1 teaspoon salt
> ½ teaspoon pepper
> ½ cup water
> 2 tablespoons brown sugar

Using a heavy skillet, cook the onion in the bacon drippings until brown.
Add the remaining ingredients, except brown sugar, and cook over low heat until tender, about 45 minutes. Stir frequently to prevent sticking; also, add a little more water if necessary. Add sugar when almost done, watch to prevent burning. (*4 to 6 servings*)

BROILED MUSHROOMS

Southeastern Pennsylvania is a leading producer of mushrooms for the epicurean eastern cities. The delicate flavor of these fungi is a much-sought-after accompaniment to many a fine dish.

> 3 to 4 large mushrooms per person
> 3 tablespoons butter, melted
> 4 slices bacon
> Tabasco sauce

Trim stems from large mushrooms and brush the caps with butter. Place onto a broiler rack and broil about 3 minutes on each side.
Broil bacon until half cooked at the same time. Remove mushrooms from the heat, turn cap side up, dot with butter, and add a small square of half-cooked bacon to each. Season with salt, freshly ground pepper, and a dash of Tabasco. Return to the broiler and cook 3 minutes longer. Serve on buttered toast.

SALADS
AND DRESSINGS

WALDORF SALAD

> 2 cups peeled and cubed apples
> 1½ cups chopped celery
> 1½ cups mayonnaise
> 1 cup chopped walnuts
> salt
> pepper
> nutmeg
> olive oil
> lettuce

Mix together the apples, celery, mayonnaise, ½ cup walnuts, and seasonings to taste.
Toss washed and dried lettuce with oil and arrange on 4 salad plates. Spoon the apple-celery-nut mixture onto each and garnish with remaining walnuts. (*4 servings*)

CHICKEN IN ASPIC

> ½ cup water
> 2 envelopes unflavored gelatin
> 1 can chicken broth
> 2 cups sliced cooked chicken breast
> 1 cup chopped celery

Heat water, add the gelatin, and stir until dissolved.
Stir in the broth, and pour ½ inch into a wet mold and chill until slightly firm.
Add chicken slices and the remaining aspic.
Cover and chill 3 to 4 hours.
Unmold onto a bed of lettuce and serve with mayonnaise. (*4 to 6 servings*)

CRAB SALAD, DELAWARE

> 1 pound lump crab meat
> 1½ cups chopped celery
> 1 teaspoon Worcestershire sauce
> dash Tabasco sauce
> 1 cup mayonnaise
> 1 tomato, sliced
> 2 hard-cooked eggs, quartered
> lettuce

Mix together the crab, celery, Worcestershire, Tabasco, and mayonnaise. Take care not to break the crab lumps.
Serve on lettuce garnished with tomatoes and eggs. (*4 servings*)

TUNA FISH SALAD

Every luncheonette, diner, coffee shop, cafeteria, greasy-spoon, drugstore counter—and not a few elegant restaurants—serves tuna fish salad, has it on hand, makes it up every morning for sandwiches and for lunch. It is one of the mainstays of the home lunch, lunch box, and picnic basket. Canned tuna fish is the base of this nourishing salad, though it can be varied in many ways: a tablespoon of chopped green pepper, bell, poblano, or jalapeño peppers; a tablespoon or two of ripe or green olives—all these can change the flavor, as can different dressings. The latest diner gimmick is to place a slice of American cheese on a tuna-fish-salad sandwich and run it under the broiler to melt cheese.

    1 large can tuna fish
    1 stalk celery, finely chopped
    2 hard-boiled eggs, sliced
    1 tablespoon finely chopped onion
    5 tablespoons mayonnaise or salad
        dressing
    ¼ teaspoon pepper

Put tuna fish in a bowl and break or flake. Add celery, eggs, onion, and mayonnaise. Toss until all are coated with mayonnaise. Refrigerate until ready to serve.
Serve on lettuce leaves that have been lightly dressed with French dressing or oil and lemon juice. (*4 to 6 servings*)

ICEBERG LETTUCE WITH THOUSAND ISLAND DRESSING

Iceberg lettuce is well named. It is a very tight-leaved head lettuce almost the color of an iceberg—and sometimes almost as hard, and must be cut with a knife, which is supposed to be bad manners. Let not Mother Grundy deter you. It ships well and is often served in the following manner as a delicacy in the very best restaurants.

    1 cup mayonnaise
    ⅓ cup chili sauce
    1 tablespoon chopped olives
    1 tablespoon chopped pimento
    1 hard-cooked egg yolk, chopped
    1 head iceberg lettuce

Mix all the ingredients except lettuce together. Cut head of lettuce into 6 wedges. Put each wedge on a salad plate and spoon over each several tablespoons of the dressing. Serve. (*6 servings*)

CHEF'S SALAD

This salad is really the chef's delight because all he has to do is mix together cooked ham, chicken, turkey, tongue, and cheese cut into thin strips, in any combination, and serve on lettuce with any dressing. He can garnish with hard-cooked eggs, olives, anchovies, sardines, or almost anything he has on hand.

BREADS
AND BATTERCAKES

WAFFLES

Waffles were brought to America by the Dutch, who originally settled in New York and New Jersey. They were soon carried to other parts of the country as the pioneers took off in all directions in search of new homes.

Variations on the original recipe gradually appeared: waffles made with heavy cream, sour cream, buttermilk, cornmeal; whole wheat and buckwheat waffles served with maple syrup, molasses, powdered sugar, ice cream, or strawberries or other fruits and topped with whipped cream.

Originally, irons were used that had to be heated on top of the stove and brushed with fat each time batter was poured in. Then the iron had to be turned over to cook the waffle on the other side.

The following recipe is geared to the modern-day electric waffle iron.

    2 cups flour
    2 teaspoons baking powder
    ½ teaspoon salt
    3 eggs, separated
    1¼ cups milk
    ½ cup melted butter

Heat the waffle iron.
Sift together flour, salt, and baking powder. Beat egg yolks, add milk and butter. Beat egg whites until barely stiff. Mix flour mixture and liquids, fold in egg whites. Bake one at a time, ½ cup batter per waffle. (*4 servings of approximately 2 waffles each*)

ITALIAN BREAD

This basic Italian bread is made in round loaves, has no preservatives, and should be eaten within two days of baking.

    1 package dry yeast, or 1 ounce
      brewer's yeast (preferable)
    1 cup lukewarm water
    1 teaspoon salt
    3½ cups flour
    2 tablespoons lard
    2 tablespoons cornmeal

Soften yeast in ¼ cup lukewarm water. Put remaining water in a large bowl, add salt, yeast mixture and 1 cup flour; beat until smooth. Stir in remaining flour. Turn out onto a floured board and knead for ten or more minutes or until smooth and satiny.
Grease a large bowl with lard. Put in the dough and turn over, so that the top is greased. Cover with a cloth and let rise in an unlit oven about an hour or until double in bulk. Punch down and knead, let rest 10 minutes. Form into round loaves and put on greased baking sheet dusted with cornmeal. Let rise until double in bulk.

Preheat oven to 375 degrees. Put a shallow pan of water in bottom of oven—this insures a good crust. Bake bread 40 to 45 minutes or until brown. It is done if it makes a hollow sound when tapped with finger. (*2 loaves*)

CORNMEAL BATTERCAKES

    ¾ cup white water-ground cornmeal
    1 teaspoon salt
    2 eggs
    2 teaspoons baking powder
    1½ cups milk
      bacon fat for cooking

Mix cornmeal, salt, eggs, baking powder, and milk until well blended.
This batter is very thin. The griddle must be very hot (a drop of water will dance on it) and very well greased with bacon fat.
Dip pancakes onto griddle. *Stir batter each time.* Allow four cakes per dipper. They should be no larger than 2-½ inches across. Wait until the cakes are lacy around the edges and covered with bubbles, then turn and brown on the other side.
Serve these thin cakes with bacon and plenty of butter. (*4 servings, 18 to 24 battercakes*)

CINNAMON BUNS

Philadelphia was famous for these buns. When yeast bread was made several times a week, part of the bread dough was rolled and covered with the rich butter and sugar and cinnamon filling. The buns were cut, allowed to rise, and then baked, filling the house with a fragrance so good the cook was hard put to keep them for supper time.

    4 cups flour
    5 teaspoons baking powder
    1½ teaspoons salt
    ¾ cup butter
    ½ cup light cream or milk
    2 eggs
    1 cup brown sugar
    1 teaspoon cinnamon
    ½ cup nuts, chopped fine
    ½ cup raisins (optional)
    2 tablespoons cream

Sift together flour, baking powder, and salt. Rub butter into the mixture. Beat eggs, add cream or milk, add to flour and butter mixture, and mix well. Roll out on a floured board, forming a square ½ inch thick, approximately 12 by 12 inches.

Preheat oven to 400 degrees.

Mix together brown sugar, cinnamon, chopped nuts, and raisins, if desired. Spread over dough evenly. Roll up like a jelly roll, pinch closed and cut the roll into twelve 1-inch slices with a sharp knife. Lay the slices into a buttered baking pan, brush the tops with cream and bake 20 minutes or until brown. (*1 dozen rolls*)

For yeast cinnamon buns, use ½ recipe bread dough, allow dough to triple in bulk, roll out, spread filling, roll up, cut, and bake.

OLE KOOKS

Soft, sweet, fruited Dutch crullers fried in deep fat, ole kooks may have been the forerunner of the doughnut. Ole kooks were a staple of New Amsterdam cooking.

    2 cups milk
    1 cup butter
    3 eggs, separated
    1 cup sugar
    ⅔ package dry yeast
    ¼ cup warm water
 3½ cups sifted flour, to make a soft dough
    3 tablespoons chopped raisins
    3 tablespoons thinly sliced citron
    ¼ teaspoon nutmeg
    ¼ cup milk
      lard for frying

Put the butter into the milk and warm just until butter is soft through. Beat egg yolks and sugar together. Beat egg whites until light. Dissolve yeast in warm water and mix all together. Add the flour, mix, and let rise overnight until double in bulk.

Soak fruits and nutmeg in ¼ cup milk 20 to 30 minutes. Pour off milk and mix fruit into dough.

Pinch off pieces the size of a small egg. Fry in deep hot lard (370 degrees) a few at a time for 10 or 12 minutes, until risen and brown. (*approximately 30 crullers*)

CRACKLIN' BREAD

Cracklings are made from leftover scraps of fresh pork. No longer as available as they once were, cracklings, however, can easily be made at home by cubing fresh fat pork or the rind of ham and frying until crisp and brown. Most of the fat is then squeezed out by wrapping in a cloth while still warm. Bread with cracklings contains enough fat to be eaten without butter.

 1½ cups water-ground white cornmeal
    ½ cup flour
    ½ teaspoon baking soda
    ¼ teaspoon salt
 1½ cups buttermilk
    1 cup cracklings

Preheat oven to 400 degrees.

Mix together all the dry ingredients. Add the buttermilk, stir in the cracklings, put into a greased 1½ quart baking pan, and bake in the oven about 30 minutes.

Serve sliced in squares.

APPLE DUMPLINGS

It was sometimes too time-consuming to start a fire in a brick oven to bake dumplings, so they were often tied in a well-floured pudding cloth and boiled.

    1 recipe Baking Powder Biscuit dough*
    6 apples, peeled and cored
    6 tablespoons sugar (brown or white) or
      maple syrup
    ½ teaspoon cinnamon
    6 pats butter

Preheat oven to 375 degrees.

Make biscuit dough, roll out ¼ inch thick, cut in 6 squares 5 by 5 inches. Place apple on each. Mix cinnamon and sugar, put 1 tablespoon in each apple; put 1 pat of butter in each apple. Fold dough over apples.

Set in shallow baking pan. Bake 30 minutes or until brown. Serve with cream or nutmeg sauce.

Peaches or apricots can replace apples in this recipe. Scrub but do not peel or stone. (*6 servings*)

BEATEN BISCUITS

On the eastern shore of Maryland every family used to have its biscuit block, a little smaller than the butcher's block. The biscuit dough was beaten on this block "100 strokes" or until it crackled. One person wrote, "Every Saturday morning about 8 A.M. you could hear the thump-thump as folks started beating their biscuits. The biscuit dough was placed on a clean towel and beaten out flat with an axe; it was folded up again and again, and beaten until you could hear the dough snap and crackle. The biscuits looked lovely and were delicious to eat and would keep perfectly fresh for a long time."

    4½ cups flour, sifted
    ½ cup lard
    1½ teaspoons salt
    ¾ cup water

Preheat oven to 400 degrees.
Mix all ingredients together using as little water as possible. The dough should be stiff. Place on heavy towel on a block or strong table and beat with a heavy object. Beat flat, fold, and beat again for 30 minutes or until the dough snaps and crackles.

Form into biscuits the size of golf balls, give each a press with the wrist to flatten slightly. Prick each with a fork. Bake 30 minutes. (*2 dozen*)

BRAN MUFFINS

    1 cup bran
    1 cup milk
    1 egg, slightly beaten
    2 tablespoons melted butter
    1 cup all-purpose flour
    3 teaspoons baking powder
    ¼ cup sugar
    ½ teaspoon salt
    raisins or walnuts

Mix the bran, milk, egg, and butter together in a bowl and let stand 10 minutes.
Preheat oven to 400 degrees.
Sift together the flour, baking powder, sugar, and salt. Add this to the moist mixture and stir until flour is dampened. Raisins (½ cup) or chopped walnuts may be added to the moist mixture, if desired.
Spoon into a buttered 12-muffin tin, filling cups ⅔ full, and bake 20 to 25 minutes, or until brown.

DESSERTS

PEARS HÉLÈNE

    4 fresh pears, peeled, halved, and cored
    1 cup sugar
    1½ cups water
    ½ teaspoon vanilla extract
    ice cream
    Chocolate Sauce (recipe below)

Dissolve the sugar in hot water, add the vanilla and the pears. Simmer until pears are tender. Cool in the syrup and serve over vanilla ice cream, topped with chocolate sauce:

    2 squares unsweetened chocolate
    6 tablespoons water
    ½ cup water
    ⅛ teaspoon salt
    3 tablespoons butter
    ½ teaspoon vanilla

Melt chocolate in water over low heat, stir in sugar and salt. Continue stirring until sauce is smooth and begins to thicken.
Add butter and vanilla, Serve hot or cold. (*4 servings*)

CHEESECAKE

Cheesecake used to be the *pièce de résistance* of Reuben's, a famous after-theater supper club on Fifty-Ninth Street in New York City. So good was their cake that visitors to New York used to take it home when they left the city. The best cheesecake is still found in Manhattan.

  1½ cups cottage cheese
  ½ cup sugar
  3 tablespoons heavy cream
     Grated rind of one lemon
  3 eggs, beaten
  1 egg yolk

Crust:

  1 cup butter, softened
  1 cup sugar
  1 egg
  ⅓ cup milk
  3 cups flour
  ½ teaspoon baking soda
  1 teaspoon vanilla

Mix cottage cheese, sugar, cream, lemon rind, and the eggs and egg yolk beaten together. Set aside.
Preheat oven to 350 degrees.
Cream the butter, add sugar gradually. Add egg and beat well. Add milk.
Sift flour with soda and fold into the butter mixture. Add flavoring.
Roll about ¼ inch thick and line deep layer-cake pan. Fill with cottage cheese mixture and bake 30 to 40 minutes.

DUTCH CUSTARD PIE

From the hearty farm cooking of Pennsylvania Dutch country, where a custard pie is made with brown sugar instead of white sugar, cinnamon instead of nutmeg.

  1 cup brown sugar, firmly packed
  1 teaspoon flour
  ½ teaspoon cinnamon
  2 cups milk
  3 eggs, lightly beaten
  ¼ teaspoon salt
  1 unbaked pie shell

Preheat oven to 400 degrees.
Mix sugar, flour, cinnamon, milk, eggs, and salt.
Pour into pie shell and bake 5 minutes; lower heat to 300 degrees and bake 35 to 40 minutes or until a knife comes clean when inserted in the center of the pie. (*6 servings*)

STRAWBERRY SHORTCAKE (CAKE)

The strawberry shortcake controversy resolves itself into a standoff as to whether one uses a light spongecake or biscuit dough. Both schools are adamant that theirs is the one original strawberry shortcake. If your choice is the cake, the recipe below is for you. If you prefer biscuit, see page 29.
This dessert, eaten at strawberry festivals on the Eastern Shore of Maryland in late May and June, is a truly national dessert as well.

  5 eggs, separated
  1 cup sugar
  1 cup cake flour, sifted 4 times
  ¼ teaspoon salt
  1 tablespoon grated lemon rind
     juice of 1 lemon (1½ tablespoons)

Preheat oven to 375 degrees.
Beat egg yolks with rotary beater. Add ½ cup sugar gradually—1 tablespoon at a time. Add lemon juice and rind, and beat all together until thick and lemon-colored. Fold cake flour into mixture.
Beat egg whites with salt until stiff. Add remaining ½ cup sugar a little at a time. Fold into yolk and flour mixture.
Turn into 2 ungreased layer-cake pans and bake 25 to 30 minutes or until cake springs back when touched in center. Invert pans until cake is cold.

  1 quart strawberries, capped and washed
  ¾ cup sugar
  1 pint heavy cream, whipped

Save 8 or 10 good berries for decoration and mash the rest with the sugar.
Put cake together at the last minute: 1 cake layer, strawberries, second cake layer, strawberries, whipped cream on top, extra whipped cream served separately. (*6 to 8 servings*)

SPICE CAKE

Before the days of packaged cake mixes everyone had a favorite plain cake recipe, which could be whipped up without much preparation. Cakes were popular for family Sunday dinners because they could be made the day before, and would keep almost a week—providing they weren't eaten. Sometimes two cakes were made at the same time, one with yolks and one with whites of eggs. These were often called gold cake and white cake. They were filled with different fillings and iced with different icings. There was also a cake called 1,2,3,4 cake—1 cup butter, 2 of sugar, 3 of flour, and 4 eggs. It should have been called mnemonic cake.

Here is the 1,2,3,4 cake, with spices.

1 cup butter, softened
2 cups sugar
4 eggs, separated
3 cups flour, sifted
3 teaspoons baking powder
½ teaspoon salt
1 cup milk
1½ teaspoons vanilla
1 teaspoon nutmeg
1 teaspoon mace
1½ teaspoons cloves

Preheat oven to 375 degrees.
Cream butter and sugar together until lemon-colored; add beaten egg yolks and beat well, until frothy.
Sift the flour, baking powder, and salt together and add alternately to the egg mixture with the milk, beating after each addition. Add vanilla and spices, beat well.
Divide batter evenly in 2 layer-cake pans lined with buttered paper and bake about thirty minutes, until cake springs back when touched. (For loaf or tube pans, set oven at 350 degrees and bake 45 to 50 minutes.)
Ice with Caramel Frosting.

CARAMEL FROSTING

2 cups sugar
1 cup rich milk
1 cup sugar (for caramelizing)
¼ cup butter
1 teaspoon vanilla

Heat 2 cups sugar with milk until dissolved. Brown the 1 cup of sugar in a hot skillet, then add the sugar-milk mixture. Cook this together until a drop forms a soft ball in cold water. Remove from heat.
Add butter and vanilla and beat until thick enough to spread.
Spread over bottom layer of spice cake. Cover with top layer and spread over top layer and around the sides of the cake.

CHRISTMAS FRUITCAKE

Part of the ritual of Christmas in the Tidewater (and in the South as well) was the preparation of the fruitcake or cakes. This had to be done at least four months before Christmas because it was believed that the fruitcakes were at their best when they had at least three pourings on to make them age properly. This custom is still followed. Usually the cake is kept in a tin and opened monthly, when a jigger or so of the best bourbon is trickled over it. In Washington, D.C., cakes are kept from year to year. Next year's fruitcake is made this Christmas, and last year's is eaten this year, so that it is a continuous process. The following is a light fruitcake.

The fruit and nuts:

2 pounds seedless raisins
1 pound currants
1 pound citron
1 cup almonds
1 cup pecans
juice and grated rind of ½ orange
2 tablespoons flour

Chop all the fruits and nuts fine. Mix all together, dredge with flour, and set aside. They will go into the cake last.

Pan:

2 tablespoons butter, softened
1 circle brown or wax paper cut to fit bottom of ring mold
1 strip to line sides
2 tablespoons flour
1 ring-mold cake pan

Put paper in pan, rub paper with butter and sprinkle with flour. Set aside.
Preheat oven to 250 degrees.

The cake:

1 cup butter
1½ cups sugar
6 egg yolks, beaten very light
6 egg whites, beaten stiff
2 tablespoons cane syrup
2 cups flour
1 tablespoon brandy
¼ teaspoon allspice
⅛ teaspoon cinnamon
¼ teaspoon cloves
¼ teaspoon ginger
¼ teaspoon nutmeg

Beat butter until creamy, add sugar, and beat until very light. Add yolks of eggs and beat until fluffy. Fold in egg whites. Add cane syrup. Add the flour little by little to the cake mixture, beating after each addition. Add brandy, beat well. Add spices and fruits, beat well, and pour into ring mold.
Put in pan of water in oven. Cover. Uncover last half hour.
Bake 4 hours or until straw comes out clean. Cool. Wrap and put in a cool place until ready to use.
Every 4 weeks pour on a 2-ounce jigger of the best bourbon whiskey to mellow the cake. Cake will keep for a year.
Serve cut very thin.
It can be served as well for dessert with a bowl of hard sauce.*

RICE PUDDING

Boil the rice tender in milk, then feafon with nutmeg, mace, rofe-water, fugar, yolks of eggs, with half the whites, fome grated bread, and marrow minced with ambergreece, and bake it in a buttered difh.
From *The Accomplifhed Cook* (1664)

We repeat this old recipe only to show how deeply rooted rice pudding is in American cookery. The following more-recent recipe will yield a rice pudding with an old-fashioned flavor. Eastern diners are famous for their rice pudding.

¼ cup uncooked rice
½ cup sugar
½ teaspoon salt
4 cups milk
1 teaspoon vanilla
pinch nutmeg
raisins (optional)

Preheat oven to 300 degrees.
Combine all the ingredients, place into a casserole, and bake uncovered for 3 hours. During the first hour stir occasionally with a fork; then, if desired, add ½ cup raisins. Serve hot or cold. (*4 servings*)

MINCEMEAT FOR PIES

In England, where mince pies originated, mincemeat contained more suet than meat. In the New World, however, meat was plentiful and mincemeat pies were actually made with minced meat. Mincemeat was always made well ahead of time and put aside for the holiday season.
Below we give you a very famous old recipe from the Astor House in New York.

4 pounds lean cooked beef, finely chopped
8 cups unpeeled, finely chopped apple
3 pounds seedless raisins
2 boxes currants
½ pound citron, finely chopped
1 pound brown sugar
4 cups molasses
10 cups sweet cider
1 tablespoon each salt, pepper, mace, allspice, ground cloves
3½ tablespoons cinnamon
3 tablespoons nutmeg

Simmer meat in enough water to cover until tender and almost dry, skimming from time to time. Mix all the other ingredients together, add to the meat, bring to a boil, transfer to 5 hot sterilized quart jars, seal, and put aside until ready for use.
Make pies with crusts. Add 2 tablespoons brandy or bourbon to each jar when making pie (1 quart per pie).

SHOOFLY PIE

In a Lancaster market a Mennonite woman explained to us that this Pennsylvania Dutch pie is made in two different consistencies, wet and dry. The addition of ½ cup more of molasses and ½ cup more of water makes a softer, more moist pie, as in the recipe below. The dry version comes out like a crumb cake.

> ½ cup molasses
> 1 cup water
> 2 cups flour
> ½ cup butter or lard
> ¼ teaspoon salt
> 1 cup brown sugar, firmly packed
> ¾ teaspoon baking powder
> 1 unbaked pie crust
> ½ teaspoon cinnamon

Preheat oven to 325 degrees.
Dissolve the molasses in the water.
Mix together all the other ingredients except the cinnamon to form a crumblike mixture.
Line a 9-inch pie pan with the crust and pour in the molasses. Spread in the crumb mixture and sprinkle with cinnamon. Bake 30 minutes or until brown. (*6 servings*)

CHOCOLATE MOUSSE

This dessert is French, but has been so totally accepted in the United States that we include it here. A richer mousse can be made by folding 2 cups of whipped cream into the mixture below before chilling. In that case follow the same directions, using only 2 eggs.

> 2 squares unsweetened chocolate
> 2 tablespoons hot water
> ½ cup sugar
> 4 egg yolks, beaten until thick
> 1 teaspoon vanilla
> 4 egg whites, beaten until stiff
> whipped cream

Using a double boiler, melt the chocolate in the water over very low heat, stirring constantly.
Beat in the egg yolks and vanilla.
Fold in the egg whites, blending carefully.
Spoon into custard cups or cocktail glasses.
Chill about 10 hours and serve, topped with whipped cream. (*4 to 6 servings*)

BEVERAGES

BLACK VELVET

This was a favorite drink of the U. S. Navy until the advent of national Prohibition. The custom then was to pour the stout and champagne simultaneously into the glass and then to drink without stirring. This was Bismarck's favorite nightcap too, only he believed that neither the champagne nor the stout should be too cold.

> 1 split champagne
> 1 small bottle stout

Pour simultaneously into a chilled glass and serve. (*1 serving*)

SYLLABUB

To make a fine syllabub from the cow—Sweeten a quart of cyder with double refined sugar, grate nutmeg into it, then add milk from the Cow into your liquor, when you have thus added the quantity of milk you think proper, pour half a pint or more in proportion to the quantity of syllabub you make, of the sweetest cream you can get over it.

—*American Cooking*
by Amelia Simmons (1796).

As with cobblers, there are syllabubs to drink and those to serve as a dessert.

2 cups heavy cream
4 tablespoons sugar
2 egg whites, beaten until stiff
¼ cup sauterne, madeira, or sherry wine

Whip the cream until stiff, fold in the sugar and the egg whites. Add the wine slowly while beating. Serve in sherbet glasses.
Spoon onto wine-soaked spongecake and you have tipsy cake. (*4 to 6 servings*)

CHRISTMAS EGGNOG

If you can arrange to do it, make eggnog a day or so before it is to be served. The mellowness achieved by even this slight amount of aging makes a great deal of difference in the flavor.

6 egg yolks, beaten until light
1 cup sugar
pinch salt
6 egg whites, beaten stiff
1 pint heavy cream, whipped
1 pint milk
1 pint bourbon whiskey
½ cup rum

Beat the sugar and salt into the egg yolks and fold in the egg whites. Blend thoroughly.
Add the remaining ingredients, blend well and refrigerate (or keep in a very cool place) in a gallon container or jug, covered, until ready for use.
Shake or stir, pour into a punch bowl, and ladle into small cups. Sprinkle with nutmeg. (*12 servings*)

MEAD

An ancient word for honey, mead is mentioned with great frequency in the Bible and ancient histories. The following recipe, found in Pennsylvania, dates circa 1800.

40 pounds honey (14 quarts)
10 gallons water
7½ ounces dried hops (or 15 yeast cakes)
1 quart brandy or sack

For a smaller amount, use the following:

5 pounds honey
5 gallons water
2 ounces dried hops (or 1 package yeast)
½ cup brandy or sack

Add honey to water and boil 45 minutes. Add hops and boil 30 minutes longer. (Or if yeast is used, cool honey and water to lukewarm and crumble yeast into it.)
Let stand overnight, then add the brandy or sack and pour into a cask. Cover with an oversize lid and let stand until fermentation is complete. Then cover tightly and seal.
Let stand a year and then bottle. (*12 to 14 gallons; 5 gallons*)

IRISH COFFEE

2 teaspoons sugar
1 ounce jigger Irish whiskey
strong black hot coffee
1 tablespoon heavy or whipped cream

Put the sugar and whiskey into mug, fill almost to the top with coffee, stir, and top with cream. (*1 serving*)

BLOODY MARY

Originally a hangover remedy ("the hair of the dog") drunk on the morning after, the Bloody Mary has increased in popularity and become something of a before-lunch favorite, combining aperitif (vodka) with appetizer (tomato juice).

½ ounce fresh lemon juice
dash Worcestershire sauce
dash Tabasco sauce
4 ounces tomato juice
salt and pepper
1½ ounces vodka

Put all the ingredients into a cocktail shaker and shake well. Strain into a 6-ounce glass, or serve on the rocks. (*1 serving*)

SOUTHERN COOKING

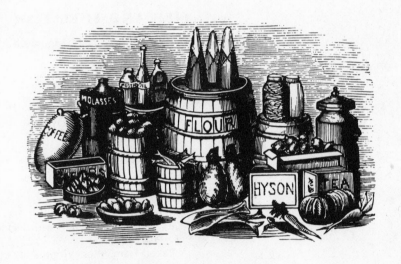

SOUPS AND CHOWDERS

Mulligatawny
She-Crab Soup
Southern Peanut Soup
Old-Fashioned Vegetable Soup
Black Kettle Soup
Oyster Chowder
Florida Velouté Soup
Catfish Soup

PASTA, EGG, AND CHEESE DISHES

Grape-Mint Omelet
Georgia Egg Pie
Cheese Puffs
Virginia Ham Omelet
Egg Pilaf
Cheese and Hominy Casserole

FISH AND SHELLFISH

Fillets of Pompano, Meunière
Soft-shell Crabs
Shrimp Pilaf
Imperial Crab, Mobile
Charleston Shrimp Pie
Cracked Stone Crab
Creamed Crab and Oysters
Catfish Stew
Key West Conch
Baked Shad without Bones

MEATS

Southern Hams
Baked Kentucky Ham with Pickled
   Peaches
Baked Ham, West Virginia Style
Ham Slice and Red-eye Gravy
Raisin Sauce
Kentucky Burgoo
Plantation Pork Chops
Roasted Whole Spareribs
Hog Jowl and Turnip Greens
The Southern Barbecue
Chitterlings
Possum 'n' Sweet 'Taters
Cuban Meat Patties
Maguina

POULTRY AND GAME BIRDS

Brunswick Stew
Southern Chicken Hash
Country Captain
Old Virginia Chicken Pudding
Chicken Pilaf
Chicken Mousse
Southern Chicken Pie

VEGETABLES AND SIDE DISHES

Hominy
Hominy Grits
Fried Grits
Baked Grits
Baked Eggplant
Cymlings
Southern Snap Beans
Charleston Okra Pilaf
Fried Black-eyed Peas
Puréed Broccoli
Dandelion Greens, Southern Style
Old South Succotash
Fried Yams
Appalachian Ramp Feast
Watermelon Pickles

SALADS AND DRESSINGS

Florida Seafood Salad
Chiffonade Salad
Oyster Salad
Sunburst Salad
Golden Apple Salad
Wine Jelly

BREADS AND BATTERCAKES

Homemade Bread and Rolls
Sally Lunn
Spoon Bread
Batter Bread
Buttermilk Corncakes
Hoecake
Corn Pone
Old-fashioned Corn Dodgers
Hush Puppies
Hominy Bread
Peanut Bread
Popovers

DESSERTS

Plain Pastry (and historical recipe)
Sweet Potato Pie
Pecan Pie
Key Lime Pie
Bavarian Cream
Sweet Yam Pudding
Fried Peach Tarts, Georgia Style
Trifle
Charlotte Russe
Lane Cake
Mango Delight
Orange Marmalade
Guava Jelly

BEVERAGES

Old Kentucky Cooler
Southern Eggnog
Cherry Bounce
Planter's Punch
Smuggler's Grog
Plantation Punch
Greenbrier Mint Julep

SOUTHERN COOKING

In 1616 a youth desiring to go from England to the Virginia Company's new colony at Jamestown was advised to take with him, besides other necessary equipment: eight bushels of meal, two bushels of peas, eight bushels of oatmeal, a gallon of wine, a gallon of oil, and two gallons of vinegar.

Household utensils to be used by six persons included an iron pot, a kettle, a large frying pan, a gridiron, two skillets, a spit, platters, dishes, and spoons of wood. There was a charge for sugar, spice, and fruit to be supplied on the voyage. Fifty acres of land had been promised the men after their seven years of servitude.

By 1618, because the young men refused to stay in the Colony without them, one hundred young women, "maids, young and uncorrupt," were sent to the Colony, with the stipulation that they were to marry tenants of the Colony, or be fined the cost of their passage.

At that time the Virginia Company comprised the whole East Coast and included New England (the northern half), and from the Chesapeake Bay down to Florida (the southern half). Later, during the civil wars of the first fifty years of the seventeenth century, Royalists, exiled by their beliefs, came to the Colony—first a few at a time and then in a flood. That was in 1649 when the parliamentary government took over England. They brought with them English court tastes—and their cooks, who knew how to satisfy them.

The Eastern Shore and southern Maryland were parts of the early Jamestown Colony, and in all of these areas the same combinations of foods and drink, as well as many similar old English recipes, are still used.

Governor Tryon of North Carolina wrote to his uncle in 1765:

The Garden has nothing to boaft of except Fruit Trees, Peaches, Nectrs. Figgs and Plumbs are in perfection and of good sorts. I cut a Mufk Melon this week which weighed 17 ½ pounds. Apples grow extremely well here. I have tefted excellent Cyder, the produce of this Province. Moft, if not all kinds of Garden Greens and Pot Herbs grow luxuriant with us. We are in want of nothing but Induftry and Skill, to bring every Vegetable to greater perfection in this Province.

Tidewater cooking—spoon bread, country ham, fried chicken, biscuits, and seafood—extends all the way along the coast from Annapolis down to Norfolk and Williamsburg, and from Jamestown to Charleston in the Carolinas low country, and into Alabama and Georgia to Jacksonville and St. Augustine, and extends up into the foothills of the Appalachian Mountains.

Other early settlers, the Scotch-Irish, emigrated from Northern Ireland to the Colonies, where they moved westward to the foothills of the Appalachian Mountains. There they spread out over the mountains into the fertile fields of the Shenandoah Valley. Grain and corn were hard to transport so they used excess grain for whiskey. Bourbon whiskey, made from corn, is the only native American distilled liquor. Some of these settlers went on down the mountains and across the Cumberland Gap into Kentucky and Tennessee. The valleys between were settled more gradually as people came to claim land.

Southern cooking grew in variety with the plentiful deer in the woods, seafood in the bays and rivers, and wild ducks that fed on the wild marsh celery. Though proud, "the Virginians are not generally rich," said the Duc de Liancourt. "Thus one often finds a well served table, covered with silver, in a room where for ten years half the window panes have been missing and where they will be missed for ten years hence." But in the late eighteenth century, when the steam engine came into use in the processing of cotton cloth in England, the fortunes of the planters were made. The cotton gin had also been invented, and the prosperity of the South was assured for a time. It was a life of ease: games, hunts, parties, hospitality, and the before-breakfast julep for the chosen few. It was a society built on slave labor—a newly rich, ostentatious society. Sumptuous mansions were built and furnished with imported goods. If the soul and spirit of the old South was hospitality, so the very essence and core of that hospitality was the excellence of cuisine, the bounteous—not to say bewildering—repasts that three times a day, each day, made "Welcome!" a concrete and particularly delightful reality. Though they sent to Europe for wines, brandies, and exotic spices, and cooks who taught them to make charlottes and pheasant under glass, nothing could match the luscious pies, fruit-cakes, roast pigs, hams, and turkeys that proliferated in southern kitchens. Within every cook's scope and range there were a dozen variants of fresh fruit pies and puddings in season, potato pies and puddings, molasses pies and puddings, and, all else failing, the perennial custard pie and pudding.

Not all kitchens belonged to the rich. In some poor cabins and farms it took real ingenuity to survive. Game such as possum, squirrel, deer, and salt pork was the backbone of these families' diet. Skill with a rifle meant the difference between meat for dinner and beans, black-eyed peas, and/or salt pork.

During his presidency, Thomas Jefferson's table was noted for fine food and wines served at both the White House and Monticello. So much so that he was eventually impoverished by his hospitality. But at his neighbor George Washington's Mount Vernon and other plantations in Virginia in 1797, the slaves were only allowed small kitchen gardens. They were not allowed to keep either ducks, geese, or pigs, but were permitted chickens. They were given "a peck of cornmeal per week for adults, half as much for children. Twenty herrings a month each, and all the black catfish caught." At harvest time the fieldworkers were given salt meat (corned beef). From their homes, the country cabins and the slave cabins, came what we now call soul food. Such dishes as hog jowl and black-eyed peas, red beans and rice, were and are eaten—and relished—by blacks and whites alike.

Country hams are cured in every state in the South, having been first developed from the lean razorback hogs that roamed the woods. A Tennessee ham might be prepared by a different method than a Kentucky Magnolia, or a Virginia ham, but they are all carefully cured with salt and sugar and are hickory-smoked. When sliced thin and eaten with biscuits or corn bread, the southern country ham compares with the greatest hams of the world.

In the southern tradition are hot breads of every kind and variety: buttermilk corn bread, dabs, bops, dodgers, batter bread, spoon bread, rolls, biscuits, and dumplings. Small pancakes the size of a silver dollar; corncakes with a batter so thin that unless the griddle is well greased with bacon fat they will become small accordions rather than the thin, lacy-edged, flat cakes that are so delicious with hot sausage or ham. Other specialties of the South are hominy, sweet potatoes, rice, shrimp, catfish, pecan pie, tipsy pudding, fruitcake, strong coffee, barbecues, cakes, and pickles. It's mighty good eating, all of it.

SOUPS AND CHOWDERS

BLACK KETTLE SOUP

You don't have to use an old Kentucky black kettle to make this soup, but it helps.

Fill a 1-gallon pot or kettle with water, put in a veal shin, a couple of alligators, and a bit of rattlesnake (substitute 1 dressed fowl and ¼ pound salt pork if alligator and snake not available), cover, and boil for 2 hours, skimming from time to time. Now add whatever you might have on hand—rice, okra, diced potatoes, corn, chopped tomatoes, chopped onion (a cup or so of each), and continue boiling an hour longer.

Thicken as desired with flour and water, season with salt and pepper, add a tablespoon of Worcestershire sauce. (Kentuckians sometimes add 1 cup currant jelly.) Stir and serve.

SHE-CRAB SOUP

Here is a very old recipe from Charleston, South Carolina. We've never made this soup exactly according to recipe, never being able to find enough female crabs with eggs in the market at the time we wanted to make the soup. But we have eaten it in Charleston restaurants and found that the eggs gave the soup a rich flavor and a velvety texture attainable in no other way.

  1 dozen blue-claw she-crabs, or ½-pound crab meat
  1 tablespoon butter
  1 small onion, chopped
  1 teaspoon salt
  ½ teaspoon pepper
  2 cups milk, scalded
  2 teaspoons Worcestershire sauce
  1 tablespoon flour blended with 1 tablespoon butter
  1 tablespoon sherry
  ½ cup heavy cream

Steam or boil the crabs about 20 minutes or until pink-tinted. Remove the eggs and set aside. Pick the meat from the shells.

Put the picked meat and eggs into the top section of a double boiler along with the butter and flour roux, chopped onion, salt, and pepper. Simmer for 5 minutes, then stir in the milk and Worcestershire. Add the sherry and simmer gently for 30 minutes.

Remove from the heat, pour in the cream, stir, and serve. (*4 servings*)

MULLIGATAWNY

This hearty soup showed up in the early days of Charleston's culinary greatness. The recipe, or one very nearly like it, was brought into Charleston Harbor by spice ships plying trade with the Orient.

  1 chicken (3 pounds), disjointed
  2 teaspoons salt
10 peppercorns
  3 tablespoons butter
  1 onion, chopped
  1 apple, peeled, cored, and chopped
  1 small green pepper, seeded and chopped
    Tabasco sauce
  1 tablespoon curry powder, or coriander
  ½ teaspoon nutmeg
  6 tablespoons cooked rice

Put the chicken into a pot or soup kettle with the salt and pepper and 2 quarts water. Cover, bring to a boil, and simmer about 1 hour or until chicken falls from the bone. Remove the bones from the chicken and discard.

Melt the butter in a small skillet, and sauté the onion, apple, and pepper over low heat 10 minutes. Do not brown. Stir in the Tabasco, curry powder and nutmeg. Add to the soup. Cook, stirring, about 15 minutes.

Serve in bowls with a spoon of hot rice in each. (*6 servings*)

SOUTHERN PEANUT SOUP

1 small onion, chopped
2 stalks celery, chopped
5 tablespoons butter
2 tablespoons flour
1 cup freshly ground peanut butter
5 cups chicken broth
1 teaspoon Worcestershire sauce
1 teaspoon salt
½ cup finely chopped peanuts

Sauté the onion and celery in the butter until tender. Stir in the flour, then the peanut butter, broth, and seasonings.
Serve hot in bowls sprinkled with chopped peanuts. (*4 servings*)

FLORIDA VELOUTÉ SOUP

1 celery root, approximately ½ pound
1 green pepper
½ teaspoon salt
1 pint sweet cream
1 tablespoon butter

Peel, chop celery root and pepper into small pieces, put in blender. Set blender at "chop" for 15 seconds, then at "purée."
Melt butter, stir in purée, salt, cream. Heat, but do not boil. Serve in cups. (*4 to 6 servings*)

OLD-FASHIONED VEGETABLE SOUP

2 quarts beef stock
2 small carrots, julienned
4 small onions, sliced
1 turnip, diced
1 cup sliced green beans
1 cup chopped fresh or canned tomatoes
½ cup chopped celery
1 cup peas, fresh or frozen
1 teaspoon salt
1 teaspoon pepper

Combine all the ingredients and cook until vegetables are tender but not soggy. (*6 to 8 servings*)

Note: Almost any seasonal vegetables, and any pasta or noodles, can be used in this soup. Vegetables that cook more quickly should be chopped or diced more coarsely.

CATFISH SOUP

Call this a soup, if you wish, but you can also serve it with boiled rice as a one-dish meal. That's what people do along the Mississippi River.

¼ pound salt pork, diced
2 to 3 pounds catfish, cleaned, skinned, and cut up
1 onion, chopped
1 stalk celery, chopped
1 tablespoon chopped parsley
1 bay leaf
pinch thyme
½ teaspoon pepper
1½ quarts water
1 tablespoon butter
1 tablespoon flour
1 cut hot milk
2 egg yolks, slightly beaten

Put the salt pork into a large saucepan and cook until crisp.
Add the fish, onions, celery, seasonings, and water. Cook slowly until fish is tender, but has not yet begun to fall apart.
Remove the fish to a hot tureen or serving bowl.
In a separate saucepan melt the butter, stir in the flour and then the hot milk. Cook, stirring, until thick and smooth. Add this sauce to the soup, stirring.
Remove from the heat, stir in the egg yolks, pour the soup over the fish, and serve. (*4 servings*)

OYSTER CHOWDER

¼ pound salt pork, diced
2 onions, chopped
2 cups boiling water
2 medium potatoes, peeled and diced
2 cups hot milk
4 tablespoons butter
1½ dozen oysters with their liquor
1 teaspoon salt
½ teaspoon pepper
paprika

Fry the pork slowly in a skillet for 5 minutes. Add the onions and continue frying until pork is crisp and onions are golden. Pour off some of the pork fat.

Add the boiling water and potatoes and simmer about 12 minutes or until potatoes are tender.

Add the remaining ingredients and heat until the edges of the oysters begin to curl. Check seasonings and serve in bowls with a shake of paprika on each. (*4 servings*)

PASTA, EGG, AND CHEESE DISHES

VIRGINIA HAM OMELET

4 eggs, beaten slightly
4 tablespoons water
½ teaspoon salt
¼ teaspoon pepper
2 tablespoons butter
½ cup cooked Virginia ham, finely chopped or ground

Mix together the eggs, water, salt, and pepper. Heat the butter in an omelet pan over low heat. When it begins to sizzle, add the eggs. As the omelet cooks, lift the edges, allowing the uncooked parts to run beneath.

When the omelet is creamy, add the ham, increase the heat slightly, and cook for a few minutes but do not dry out. Fold double and roll onto a heated platter. (*2 servings*)

EGG PILAF

1 cup rice
1 teaspoon salt
2 cups chicken broth
3 eggs
½ cup butter
½ teaspoon pepper

Put the rice, salt, and broth into a pot. Cover securely and cook over low heat about 20 minutes or until rice has absorbed all the broth. Stir in the eggs one at a time. Add the butter and pepper, beat for a minute or two with a whisk, and serve as a luncheon dish. (*4 servings*)

GRAPE-MINT OMELET

This recipe was invented by a cook named Jenna. It's from an old Georgia cookbook.

6 eggs, separated
½ teaspoon salt
⅛ teaspoon rosemary
¼ cup water
4 tablespoons grape or blackberry jelly
1 teaspoon fresh mint, minced

Preheat oven to 400 degrees.

Beat egg yolks with salt and rosemary. Beat whites until stiff but not dry. Fold into yolks. Butter a heavy casserole. Put in a layer of eggs, dot with jelly, another layer, dot with jelly, another layer, dot with jelly. Put casserole in a pan of hot water in the oven and bake for 20 minutes.

Sprinkle with chopped mint leaves and serve. (*6 servings*)

GEORGIA EGG PIE

- 8 eggs
- ½ teaspoon salt
- ¼ teaspoon pepper
- ½ teaspoon dry mustard
- ¼ teaspoon sage
- ¼ teaspoon paprika
- 3 slices cooked bacon, crumbled
- 1 cup milk
- 2 tablespoons butter, melted
- 1 recipe biscuit dough*

Preheat oven to 350 degrees.
Carefully break eggs into buttered pie plate, sprinkle with salt, pepper, mustard, sage, paprika, and crumbled bacon. Add milk and melted butter.
Roll out biscuit dough to fit pie plate, cover pie with it, make slits in dough.
Bake pie 40 minutes. Serve immediately. (*6 to 8 servings*)

CHEESE PUFFS

- 1 cup grated American cheese
- ½ cup lard
- 1 cup flour
- 1 teaspoon baking powder
- 1 egg, lightly beaten
- 1 teaspoon salt
- pinch cayenne

Preheat oven to 350 degrees.
Mix all the ingredients together thoroughly and roll thin on a floured board.
Cut into 1 by 2 inch strips, place onto a greased oven sheet, and bake about 5 minutes.
Serve with salads. (*about 1 dozen puffs*)

CHEESE AND HOMINY CASSEROLE

- 4 cups cooked or canned hominy, washed and drained
- 8 tablespoons butter
- 2 cups grated Cheddar cheese
- freshly ground pepper
- salt
- ½ cup dry bread crumbs
- ½ cup heavy cream

Preheat oven to 350 degrees.
Butter a 2-quart casserole and put in layers of hominy and cheese, dotting each layer with butter and sprinkling each with salt and pepper. (Bottom and top layers should be hominy).
Top off with bread crumbs and dots of butter, and pour the cream over all.
Bake 15 to 20 minutes or until golden brown on top. (*4 servings*)

FISH AND SHELLFISH

SHRIMP PILAF

- 4 slices bacon, cut into pieces
- 1 onion, chopped
- 2½ cups chopped fresh or canned tomatoes
- 1 cup uncooked rice
- 1½ cups peeled cooked shrimp
- 1 teaspoon salt

Fry the bacon pieces until crisp, remove, and set aside.
Brown the onion in the bacon fat, add the tomatoes, and cook for a few minutes.
Add the rice, transfer the mixture to the top part of a double boiler, and cook about 45 minutes or until rice is cooked.
Add the shrimp and bacon bits, transfer to a baking dish, and cook in a preheated 325 degree oven for about 15 minutes. (*6 servings*)

CHARLESTON SHRIMP PIE

3 slices bread
1 cup milk, or sherry
2 cups (about 1 pound) peeled, cooked shrimp
2 tablespoons melted butter
½ teaspoon pepper
1 teaspoon Worcestershire sauce
¼ teaspoon nutmeg, cayenne, or mace
2 tablespoons sherry

Preheat oven to 375 degrees.
Using a casserole soak the bread in the milk or sherry (if wine is used eliminate 2 tablespoons sherry), and mash with a fork.
Add the shrimp, butter, seasonings, and 2 tablespoons sherry. Mix well. Turn into a well-buttered baking dish.
Bake in the oven for 20 minutes, and serve for lunch with a salad. (*4 servings*)

SOFT-SHELL CRABS

The blue-claw crab, like all other crustaceans, must slough its shell in order to grow. While waiting for its new shell to harden, the crab becomes (1) defenseless and (2) delicious. Catching crabs just at the strategic moment of their softness is not easy, so they are caught—at least, commercially—while still in a hard state, and kept in tanks until the sloughing action takes place. They are marketed iced, live or frozen, and are cooked and eaten whole as they come from the market.

8 live soft-shell blue-claw crabs
2 eggs, beaten
¼ cup milk
2 teaspoons salt
½ cup flour
½ cup dry bread crumbs
4 tablespoons butter or bacon fat

Kill the crabs by cutting off the "face." Lift the points of the top shell and remove the gills and digestive organs. Rinse crabs in cold water and drain.
Mix together the eggs, milk, and salt.
Mix together the flour and bread crumbs.
Dip the crabs into the egg mixture and then roll them in the flour-crumb mixture. Pan-fry in butter over moderate heat until brown on both sides.

Or just dust the crabs lightly in flour, sauté in butter, and serve on toast. (*2 to 4 servings, depending upon size of crabs*)

CRACKED STONE CRAB

This little crab, whose body measures only 3 to 4 inches across, was once found in great quantities along the Florida shores. Its disproportionately large claws, tinted cream and brilliant red and tipped with black, are greatly prized by those who are lucky enough to come by them.
Recently stone crabs have been noticeably on the decrease, and conservation measures have been put into effect that prohibit taking the whole crab. The larger claw is cut off and the crab is returned to the sand to develop a new one. In the market, therefore, only the claws of stone crabs are for sale.
To eat these delicious claws simply steam, crack, extract the meat, and dip—hot or cold—into drawn butter, mayonnaise, or the sauce of your choice.

CREAMED CRAB AND OYSTERS

Crab meat and oysters rarely used to come in season together, oysters going out in May and crab still scarce at that time of year. Crab meat is now pasteurized and keeps far better than it used to; but like any shellfish, it should be eaten as soon as possible after purchase.

2 tablespoons butter
1 hard-boiled egg, chopped
¼ cup cream
¼ cup milk
2 tablespoons ketchup
 dash Worcestershire sauce
1 teaspoon salt
½ teaspoon pepper
⅛ teaspoon cayenne pepper
1 cup cooked crab flakes
10 oysters with their liquor

Melt the butter in a saucepan, add egg, cream, milk, ketchup, Worcestershire, and seasonings. Simmer slowly, stirring, for 5 minutes.
Add the crab flakes and oysters with their liquor, and simmer slowly until edges of oysters curl. Serve on toast. (*2 servings*)

IMPERIAL CRAB, MOBILE

4 crabs, or ¾ pound lump or back-fin
    blue-claw crab meat and 4 crab shells
½ onion, chopped
2 tablespoons butter
2 tablespoons flour
½ teaspoon salt
    few grains cayenne pepper
    dash Worcestershire sauce
1 teaspoon dry English mustard
2 tablespoons chopped green pepper
2 cups heavy cream
2 egg yolks
    dry bread crumbs
    butter

Preheat oven to 350 degrees.
Boil the crabs until the shells turn pink, remove the meat. Save the shells.
Sautéé the onion in the butter, add the flour, crabmeat, seasonings, green pepper, and cream. Mix well.
Bind with egg yolks, pile into the shells, sprinkle with bread crumbs, dot with butter, and brown 25 minutes in the oven. (*4 servings*)

FILLETS OF POMPANO, MEUNIÈRE

Many epicures consider the pompano America's finest fish. Caught in the waters off the southern coast, this fish is most delicate in flavor and has a firm but tender texture. Unfortunately it travels poorly, and therefore is not easy to find in northern and western markets.
Elaborate New Orleans methods of preparation notwithstanding, pompano's delicacy is best preserved when cooked in the simplest manner.

8 pompano fillets
    milk
    flour
4 tablespoons butter mixed with
4 tablespoons olive oil
    minced parsley
1 lemon, quartered

Dip the fillets in milk, then in flour. Sauté in the hot butter-oil mixture 3 minutes on each side or until delicately browned.
Remove to a heated platter, add more butter to the pan, swirl around and pour over the fillets. Garnish with parsley and lemon wedges. (*4 servings*)

CATFISH STEW

Catfish are usually associated with the Mississippi, Ohio, and Missouri rivers, and their tributaries. They range in size from less than a pound (the various species of bullheads) to one hundred pounds (the blue catfish and "channel cats"). In the raw, catfish are ugly-looking, smooth-skinned creatures with long barbels resembling cat's whiskers; but the meat is sweet, firm, flaky, and flavorful, and is prized as a delicacy in many parts of the country. The Department of the Interior has recently set up a number of catfish farms in the United States for the express purpose of cultivating this prolific and nutritious fish. Originally concentrated in the state of Arkansas, catfish farms, inexpensive to start and profitable to run, are beginning to show up all over the South and Midwest.

¼ pound bacon, cut into pieces
4 pounds catfish, skinned, dressed, and
    cut into medium chunks
1 cup chopped onion
½ can condensed tomato soup
1 teaspoon salt
½ teaspoon pepper
    pinch sugar

Fry the bacon in a heavy pot. Add all the other ingredients and cook over low heat for 20 to 30 minutes. Serve hot with corn bread. (*6 servings*)

KEY WEST CONCH

The meat of Florida's conch is not unlike that of California's abalone. And the conch shell is collected by souvenir hunters with the same avidity.
To remove the meat from the conch, unfortunately, a hole is usually drilled into the shell, reducing its value to collectors.

4 conchs, fresh or frozen
2 tablespoons butter
1 tablespoon cooking oil mixed with
1 teaspoon dry mustard
1 teaspoon salt
½ teaspoon pepper
1 tablespoon vinegar
½ cup hot water
1 tablespoon flour
1 tablespoon butter
1 cup sliced raw mushrooms

Pound the conch well with a kitchen mallet, and sauté over medium heat in the butter-oil mixture 15 minutes on each side.

Add the seasonings, vinegar, and water; simmer for 30 minutes. Remove conch and chop into small pieces, reserving the gravy.

Brown the flour in the butter, stir in the conch pieces and the mushrooms, cook for 5 minutes, and add to the gravy.

Cook slowly 15 minutes and serve on toast. (*4 servings*)

BAKED SHAD WITHOUT BONES

Shad, a member of the herring family of fishes, is known for the delicate flavor of its flesh, but unfortunately is also known for the multitude of small hairlike bones that appear to permeate the entire fish.

Shad is one of our favorite fishes—bones or not—so we tested this "without bones" recipe and found that the bones really disintegrated. It is not necessary to cook it so long, 2½ hours uncovered is enough to bake out the oily flavor that some people don't like, and all but the larger bones.

    1 shad, 3 to 4 pounds, dressed
    melted butter
    salt
    pepper
    cooking oil
    large brown paper bag

Preheat oven to 250 degrees.

Rub the shad inside and out with melted butter, and sprinkle with salt and pepper.

Oil a paper bag well inside and out, insert the shad, and fold and pin shut to make a tight seal. Place into a covered roaster and bake in the oven for 6 hours. The bones will disintegrate. (*8 servings*)

MEATS

KENTUCKY BURGOO

The burgoo is an outdoor get-together happening, similar in spirit to a New England clambake or a Maryland crab feast. Always prepared on a large scale for lots of celebrants, the burgoo is strictly an outdoor stew containing an ever-changing variety of ingredients, to be consumed, often, from the ever-present tin cups, standing or sitting around on the grass.

Most of the old recipes we've run across call for such quantities of ingredients as 6 squirrels, 6 chickens, 6 pounds beef, lots of tomatoes, corn, onions, and peppers. (A very old recipe lists as ingredients the following: 100 pounds beef, 12 chickens, 1½ bushels potatoes, 1 peck turnips, 1 peck carrots, 1 gallon onions, 30 tomatoes, 12 large ears corn, 3 boxes oatmeal, 4 pounds salt, ¾ pound pepper, 12 heads cabbage. The dish requires 24 hours to cook.) Following is a more reasonable recipe you might be tempted to try:

    1 young squirrel, dressed and jointed
    1 young chicken, dressed and jointed
    1½ pounds beef, cut into 2-inch cubes
    1½ pounds pork, cut into 2-inch cubes
    several tomatoes, skinned and
        quartered
    kernels cut from 6 ears corn
    1 red pepper, cut up
    5 green peppers, cut up
    5 onions, peeled and quartered
    2 teaspoons salt
    1 teaspoon pepper
    ½ teaspoon cayenne

Cover the meat with water, using a suitable heavy pot, and simmer slowly 4 to 5 hours or until meat is well done and most of the water has cooked away.

One hour before meat is done, add the vegetables and seasonings and whatever more water may be necessary.

Check seasonings. Serve with hunks of soda bread, and mint juleps or beer. (*8 to 10 servings*)

SOUTHERN HAMS

The original Smithfields of Virginia learned how to cure hams from the Chinese, who developed their skill over a period of several thousand years. And the hams the Smithfields cured came exclusively from the lean, gamy, half-wild razorback hogs raised in the peanut fields. The hogs are butchered when about a year old, and the hams undergo a dry-salt curing process for several months, after which they are cleaned, coated with black pepper, and smoked very gradually over a smoldering hickory-wood fire for up to six months. After another twelve to eighteen months of aging, the hams emerge flat, shrunken, and blackened—ugly to look at and hard as a rock, but sweet and succulent to the taste.

Not all Virginia hams are razorbacks, and very few are Smithfield, but the general process of peanut-feeding, pepper-coating, and hickory-smoking is applied throughout much of the state to produce superior-flavored and prized hams.

Kentucky hams, rivaling those of neighboring Virginia, are made from the heavier Hampshire hogs, which have been carefully grain-fed. These hams are salt-cured and rubbed with a molasses-pepper mixture before being subjected to several smokings with mixtures of hard woods. They are then hung in specially constructed smokehouses to age.

The people of Tennessee claim that their own particular brand of country ham will stand up to that of Kentucky and Virginia. Wild boars, originally brought to the mountains of North Carolina and Tennessee from Germany, have multiplied and interbred with native razorbacks, they say, to produce a brand of tusked hog with sweet and tangy meat—indigenous only to the Tennessee mountains.

TO CURE HAMS AT HOME

1 gallon of water
8 pounds salt
1 ounce saltpeter
1 ounce baking soda
2½ pounds white sugar
1 fresh ham, 10 to 12 pounds

Bring water, salt, saltpeter, soda, and sugar to a boil, skim, cool. Pour over the ham in a container large enough to allow all the ham to be covered. Turn from time to time in the cure. It should take five weeks. Replace evaporated water. (Small meat, bacon, tongue, or shoulders should remain in the pickle for two to three weeks.) Refrigerate in warm weather, or cure hams only when the weather is cold, below 40 degrees.

Remove from cure, hang up to dry for twenty-four hours by a cord run through the shank. Smoke ham over a good hickory-smoke fire (see below). The pickle can be boiled and skimmed and kept for reuse. It is enough to cure four hams. Add more salt if the pickle won't float an egg. Add an equal amount of sugar to compensate.

TO SMOKE HAMS AT HOME

We found this recipe in an old American cookbook and again verbatim in an old English cookbook.

Take an old hogshead. Stop all the crevices, and fix a place to put a cross-stick at the bottom, to hang the articles to be smoked on.

Next, in the side, cut a hole near the top to introduce an iron pan filled with sawdust and small pieces of green wood. Having turned the tub upside down, hang the articles upon the cross-stick, introduce the iron pan in the opening, place a piece of red hot iron in the pan, this burns the sawdust, cover it with sawdust, and all will be complete. Let a large ham remain for 40 hours, and keep up a good smoke, by adding more sawdust to the fire.

Direct heat should not reach the ham. Hams were smoked in cold weather so they would not spoil. Often the fire was allowed to die down at night and then rekindled in the morning. Count the time smoked, not the length of time the ham has hung in the smokehouse. The outside temperature should be below 40 degrees, the temperature in the smokehouse not above 110 degrees. Wrap smoked ham in a starched, unbleached muslin sack and hang for several months to age.

Note: this same method can be applied with equal success to smoking fish at home.

BAKED HAM, WEST VIRGINIA STYLE

> 1 country ham, soaked overnight in cold water
> 3 lemons, peeled
> 3 oranges, peeled
> 1 cup dried apricots
> 1 cup dried prunes
> 24 whole cloves
> 2 sticks cinnamon

Scrub the ham, transfer to a pot of fresh water and boil for 1 hour. Remove from the pot and trim away the rind.

Return to the pot, cover with water, and add the lemons, oranges, apricots, prunes, about a dozen cloves, and the cinnamon sticks. Cook about 4 hours or until the meat is tender and loosened from the bone.

Preheat oven to 350 degrees.

Remove ham from the pot, drain, and wipe dry with a towel. Cover with brown sugar, stick in a dozen cloves, and place into a shallow baking dish. Bake until browned. The fruit and spices add a new and succulent flavor to the ham.

ROASTED WHOLE SPARERIBS

Roasted spareribs are found throughout the South, and almost always are served with roasted sweet potatoes and/or yams. The succulent meat flavor blends with both the potatoes and the pork-fat and brown-sugar glaze. It's simple, too.

> 1 whole sparerib, both rib sides of pork
> 1 teaspoon salt
> ½ teaspoon pepper
> 3 tablespoons bacon fat
> 3 tablespoons brown sugar
> 8 large sweet potatoes

Preheat oven to 300 degrees.

Rub sparerib with salt, pepper, and bacon fat. Put on a cookie sheet or other large pan with an edge, and bake for 1 hour. Sprinkle with brown sugar. Cook 30 minutes or longer, depending upon the size of the ribs, until tender. Cut into individual rib servings.

Serve with sweet potatoes, baked the last hour of cooking. (*8 servings*)

HOG JOWL AND TURNIP GREENS

Hog jowl is not available everywhere, but if you can find one you'll soon learn why this dish is so popular in the South. The jowl is "country cured," the same as hams.

> 1½ to 2 pounds hog jowl
> 2 quarts turnip tops, well cleaned
> 2 teaspoons salt
> 1 teaspoon pepper

Place the jowl in a large pot, cover with boiling water, and cook for about 40 minutes or until meat is tender and comes easily off the skin and bone. Remove to a heated platter.

Add the turnip tops and seasonings to the pot liquor, cover, and cook slowly for 30 minutes or until greens are tender. Remove from the liquor, drain, cut up, and place around the jowl.

Serve in bowls with the pot liquor. (*about 4 servings*)

HAM SLICE AND RED-EYE GRAVY

Red-eye-gravy experts disagree. Some say that it should be made with water, and some say with coffee. Our preference is for water.

> ¾-inch-thick slice country ham, or other ham steak
> small piece ham fat
> 2 tablespoons brown sugar
> 1 cup water or coffee

Heat frying pan. Slash edge of fat around ham slice to prevent curling.

Add fat to pan, and then ham slice. Cook over low heat until brown on one side. Turn and sprinkle the browned side with 1 tablespoon brown sugar. When brown on second side, turn and sprinkle with remaining tablespoon brown sugar. Turn quickly again to caramelize the sugar on second side.

Put on hot serving dish and keep hot while preparing gravy.

Pour water into pan and swirl around. It will be a rich reddish-brown color. Pour over ham steak, and serve immediately with corn pone. (*2 to 4 servings*)

RAISIN SAUCE

½ cup brown sugar, firmly packed
3 tablespoons cornstarch
⅛ teaspoon salt
½ cup ham liquor
½ cup sherry
½ cup water
⅜ cup vinegar
½ cup raisins

Mix sugar, cornstarch, salt, ham liquor, sherry and water. Cook 10 minutes, stirring constantly. Add vinegar and raisins. Cook until raisins are plump and mixture boils. Serve with ham or ham slice. (*2 cups*)

PLANTATION PORK CHOPS

Here is a fancy pork-chop dish that reputedly was served to Confederate guerilla General Early when he asked the lady of the plantation to feed his men. It has been reduced to household proportions.

6 large rib pork chops
6 slices Bermuda onion, ½ inch thick
6 slices large tomato
3 large green peppers, halved and seeded
1½ cups cooked rice
6 medium sweet potatoes
6 carrots
1 cup brown sugar
1½ teaspoons salt
½ cup chili sauce
½ teaspoon pepper
1½ cups water

Preheat oven to 375 degrees.
Brown chops on both sides in a large frying pan. Place in baking pan. Put a slice of onion on each chop, then a slice of tomato. Sprinkle with salt and pepper.
Fill the pepper halves with the cooked rice and put on top of the tomato. Peel sweet potatoes and carrots and place around the chops. Mix chili sauce and water and pour around the chops and vegetables. Sprinkle brown sugar over potatoes and carrots.
Bake 1½ hours, basting frequently so that the flavor of the sauce is absorbed by the rice and potatoes. Add more liquid if necessary. (*6 servings*)

BAKED KENTUCKY HAM WITH PICKLED PEACHES

1 Kentucky country ham, approximately 12 pounds
1 quart jar sweet pickled peaches (recipe below)
¼ cup whole cloves.

Scrub ham well, remove all curing grit and mold. Put ham in a pan large enough to hold water to cover the ham. Soak 12 hours and drain.
Cover ham with fresh water and bring quickly to a boil. Lower heat and cook the ham, covered, for 4 to 5 hours. Cool in water. Preheat oven to 350 degrees.
Skin the ham, stick the whole cloves in the fat and spread ⅓ of the syrup from the sweet pickled peaches over the ham. Put the ham in the oven for 10 minutes; coat again with ⅓ of the syrup; repeat once again. Remove after 10 minutes. Serve surrounded by sweet pickled peaches:

6 pounds sugar
1 quart vinegar
1 tablespoon stick cinnamon
1 tablespoon whole ginger
1 tablespoon whole cloves
1 tablespoon whole allspice
96 cloves
48 medium-sized peaches, peeled

Boil sugar, vinegar, and spices together 20 minutes. Add peaches and cook 30 minutes, until the peaches are tender. Stick each peach with 2 cloves and fill sterile jars. Continue to boil the syrup until it is thick. Fill jars to cover peaches. Seal.

CHITTERLINGS

Chitlins are an old-time favorite of hog-killing time. The large intestine of the hog is turned inside out, thoroughly cleaned, and cut into pieces 5 or 6 inches in length. The slices are then rolled in cornmeal or cracker crumbs, and slow-cooked by either frying or broiling until crisp. The chitlins are eaten hot, sprinkled with chopped raw onion.

POSSUM 'N' SWEET 'TATERS

Possum has long been a popular food among the country people of Appalachia and the Deep South. Recently the government has been experimenting with possum farms in an attempt to broaden the nation's food supply. Like other game, possum is apt to have a strong flavor unless it is dressed as soon as possible after the kill.

    4 tablespoons butter
    ½ cup chopped onion
    ¾ cup bread crumbs
    1 teaspoon chopped parsley
    1 teaspoon salt
    ½ teaspoon pepper
      beef broth
    1 possum, skinned and cleaned*
    1 tablespoon melted butter
    1 teaspoon Worcestershire sauce
      (optional)
      dash cayenne
    4 slices bacon
    4 sweet potatoes, peeled

Preheat oven to 450 degrees.
Melt 4 tablespoons butter in a skillet and simmer the onions until brown. Add the bread crumbs, parsley, salt, pepper, and a little broth. Mix and stuff into the body of the possum; skewer or sew up the opening.
Place into a greased baking pan with 2 teaspoons water, and roast for 15 minutes. Reduce the heat to 350 degrees. Put slices of bacon across the roast, cook for 30 minutes, and then place sweet potatoes around the meat and continue baking about 1 hour or until possum is tender and brown. Baste frequently with a mixture of melted butter, pan juices, Worcestershire, cayenne, and ½ cup hot water. Remove to a heated platter and serve, surrounded by the sweet 'taters. (*4 servings*)

> *To clean, dip eviscerated possum in a gallon of boiling water containing ½ cup lime. Pull off hair and scrape the body. Cut off tail and feet. Wash in hot water, then cover with cold salted water and let stand at room temperature about 8 hours. Drain, cover with hot water and simmer, covered, about 1 hour or until skin is tender. Let stand in broth until ready to bake.

CUBAN MEAT PATTIES

Here is a recent addition to the great American melting-pot menu, brought to Florida by refugees from Castro's rule.

    1½ pounds chopped meat—beef, veal, or
      meat-loaf mix
    ¼ cup ketchup
    1 teaspoon salt
    ¼ teaspoon pepper
    1 small clove garlic, minced
    ½ teaspoon sage
    ½ teaspoon thyme
    ⅛ teaspoon celery salt, or 1 teaspoon
      chopped celery leaves
    3 bananas
    2 tablespoons butter
    6 slices toast, buttered

Mix meat, ketchup, salt, pepper, garlic, sage, thyme, and celery salt. Form into 6 patties.
Sauté patties slowly in frying pan (they will make their own fat) until browned. Turn and brown on the other side until done. Beef can be rare, but veal or meat-loaf mix should be well done.
Peel and halve bananas, cut each piece lengthwise in half. Melt butter; sauté bananas in butter.
Place each patty on toast with two slices of banana. (*6 servings*)

MAGUINA (BAKED BEEF, JEWISH STYLE)

This recipe came from a well-known hotel in Miami, Florida, to which we were told it had migrated—from New York City.

    1 pound lean beef, thinly sliced
    2 onions, chopped
    1 clove garlic, minced
    3 tablespoons olive oil
    ½ cup tomato paste
    1 cup sliced mushrooms
    2 large potatoes, peeled and thinly
      sliced
    ½ teaspoon salt
      dash paprika
      dash nutmeg
      dash cinnamon
    8 eggs, beaten

Sauté the beef slices, onions, and garlic in hot olive oil for 10 minutes in a heavy skillet. Add the tomato paste, mushrooms, potatoes, and seasonings. Continue cooking, stirring, until potatoes are done. Remove from heat. Preheat oven to 350 degrees.

Grease a baking dish, pour in the skillet contents, and add the beaten eggs. Mix well and bake for 30 minutes. (*4 to 6 servings*)

THE SOUTHERN BARBECUE

The barbecue—a pig roast found throughout the South wherever and whenever people gather together in groups—can serve as an excuse for a political rally or a wedding party; as a fund-raising occasion for the volunteer fire department; a church or Sunday school picnic; as a focal attraction of holiday celebrations; or just as a reason for friends to get together. The barbecue is an outdoor event regulated by strict traditional procedures peculiar to locality or region. A hardwood (oak or hickory) fire is built in a shallow trench and reduced to hot embers. The pig—very young six or seven weeks old, which has been well fattened on cornmeal—is killed and split down the backbone from "barbe" (beard) to "cue" (tail). It is then laid skin side up on a grill placed over the coals, and slowly roasted. The skin is well greased and the pig turned over and basted with a special barbecue sauce or "soption" (usually hot vinegar, salt, red pepper, and butter), some of which, mixed with the pig juices, becomes the sauce to serve with the meat. When the meat is done and the skin is crisp, the feast begins. Slices of the pig, doused liberally with sauce, are dealt out with corn bread or beaten biscuits, corn on the cob, green beans, cymlings, tomatoes, coleslaw, or whatever the area and season produce. And, of course, the dessert is watermelon.

POULTRY
AND GAME BIRDS

BRUNSWICK STEW

This historic dish is said to have originated in Brunswick County, Virginia, although there is a Brunswick County, North Carolina, that also lays claim to it. But there is a difference: The Virginia stew is often made with rabbit or chicken, the North Carolina stew with squirrel meat. A popular picnic and barbecue dish throughout the South, the recipe varies from location to location. There is a Brunswick stew made in Georgia that uses a combination of beef, lamb, and pig's liver instead of either chicken or squirrel.

We believe the following recipe to be the most widely accepted and perhaps the oldest. We give it with chicken, but many cooks prefer squirrel. Use your own judgment.

1 large chicken, disjointed (or 6 cleaned and dressed squirrels, if available)
½ pound bacon, chopped
6 quarts water
1½ cups lima beans
1½ cups corn
2 tomatoes, cut up
1 teaspoon salt
½ teaspoon pepper
¼ teaspoon cayenne
2 tablespoons butter
4 cups mashed potatoes
½ loaf sliced bread

Put the chicken, bacon, and water into a large pot. Cover and bring to a boil. Cook for 30 minutes or more, until chicken is ready to fall from the bones.

Remove chicken, remove meat from bones, and return meat to the pot. Add lima beans, corn, tomatoes, and seasonings, and cook for 25 minutes longer.

Add the butter, potatoes, and bread slices and cook, stirring, a few minutes longer or until ingredients can scarcely be distinguished. Add a little boiling water if too thick to stir.
Serve very hot in bowls, with corn pone on the side. (*6 to 8 servings*)

CHICKEN MOUSSE

A good dish for a summer lunch or buffet.

1 whole breast of chicken (both halves)
2 egg whites
1 pint heavy cream
½ teaspoon salt
¼ teaspoon pepper
2 tablespoons sherry

Cook chicken breast 15 minutes in water to cover. Cool. Chop chicken. Put into blender, turn to "chop" 15 seconds, then to "purée" 15 seconds. Put into saucepan. Add egg whites, beat, and put saucepan into a bowl of ice. Stir until mixture begins to get cold.
Add cream very gradually to the chicken mixture, beating it all the time until it is well worked in. Add the salt, pepper, and sherry. Beat in.
Put into serving dish and refrigerate until ready to use. (*6 servings*)

SOUTHERN CHICKEN PIE

Chicken was a treat in the old days, to be enjoyed only on special occasions, or on Sunday. At the start of World War II, poultry growers were given incentives by the U. S. Government to increase their production. Their success in so doing now makes chicken and turkey among the least costly of protein foods. A chicken pie was designed to stretch the flavor of the Sunday bird to feed a hungry family. Often two different kinds of pastry were made, one for the dumplings and one for the crust. Here is a simplified version of some of those elaborate pies.

1 chicken (3 to 4 pounds), disjointed, breast halved
1 teaspoon salt
2 tablespoons butter
1 cup milk or cream
1 tablespoon flour
1 cup broth in which chicken was cooked

Pastry:

3 cups flour
1 teaspoon baking powder
1 teaspoon salt
¾ cup lard or shortening
½ cup sour cream

Put the chicken parts into a large pot or saucepan, cover with water, add salt, and bring to a boil. Lower heat and simmer 1½ to 3 hours, or until tender. Cool in the broth. Remove meat from bones.
Preheat oven to 375 degrees.
Mix and sift together flour, baking powder, and salt, cut in shortening, and add the sour cream and enough water to hold the pastry together. Roll out on a floured board, cut a wide strip, and line the sides of a 3-quart baking dish. (There is no bottom crust.) Cut the remaining pastry into 1-inch strips.
Place a layer of chicken into the dish and dot with butter. Cover with strips of pastry. Add another layer of chicken and cover with the remaining pastry strips in a lattice fashion. Bake about 30 minutes or until pastry is light brown.
Mix 1 tablespoon flour with a small amount of milk, then add to the remaining milk and a cup of the broth. Spoon this mixture into the pie and bake another 20 minutes. The inside pastry will be cooked without becoming soggy. (*4 to 6 servings*)

SOUTHERN CHICKEN HASH

4 tablespoons butter
3½ teaspoons flour
5 tablespoons chopped celery
2 cups chicken broth
1 onion, peeled and cut in half
4 cups cooked chicken (or turkey), diced
1 teaspoon Worcestershire sauce
1 cup heavy cream
1 teaspoon salt
½ teaspoon pepper
⅛ teaspoon mace

Melt butter, stir in flour and celery. Stir-fry a few moments, then slowly add the broth, then the onion. Simmer 10 minutes.
Add the chicken and the remaining ingredients, heat, remove the onion, and serve—preferably with corn bread. (*6 to 8 servings*)

COUNTRY CAPTAIN

Why this delicious concoction has been hidden in Alabama and Georgia all these years we don't understand. It should be a national dish . . . an international dish. It is worthy of worldwide recognition. We made it with walnuts instead of almonds, and it is just as good. Some recipes serve the currants and other condiments after the chicken has been passed, as one would with curry.

    2 cups lard, for deep-frying
    2 chickens, disjointed
    ¾ cup flour
    ½ teaspoon salt
    ¼ teaspoon pepper
    1 medium onion, sliced
    1 bell pepper, sliced
    2 cloves garlic, sliced
    2 stalks celery, chopped
    6 large tomatoes, sliced
    1 teaspoon salt
    1 teaspoon ground black pepper
    1 teaspoon whole thyme
    1 teaspoon curry powder
    1 teaspoon parsley, chopped
    ½ cup currants
    ½ cup chopped almonds
    2 cups raw rice
    4 cups hot chicken broth, or water

Heat lard slowly in a deep frying pan with a lid.
Roll the chicken in flour mixed with salt and pepper. Place chicken pieces into lard when it just begins to smoke. Cook until golden on one side, then turn, large pieces first. When all are golden brown, remove to a hot platter.
Pour off all but 4 tablespoons lard, and reserve for future use.
Cook the onion, pepper, garlic, and celery in the 4 tablespoons lard left in the pan, until the onion is light brown, then add the tomatoes and seasonings. Cook 5 minutes. Add the chicken. Sprinkle the currants, almonds, and parsley over all. Cover, allowing a vent for steam, and cook over very low heat another 45 minutes.
Preheat oven to 325 degrees.
Meanwhile, melt butter in a frying pan, stir in raw rice, and cook until rice is light yellow. Add hot water or broth. Bake in saucepan or 2-quart covered casserole 45 minutes.
Dish the chicken onto a large platter, surround with rice mixed with the sauce. (*6 servings*)

OLD VIRGINIA CHICKEN PUDDING

It's not always easy to understand the names Virginians give to their favorite dishes. Spoon bread and batter bread are fairly explicit, but chicken pudding . . . Let's just say that chicken pudding has no relationship whatsoever to bread pudding, rice pudding, or tapioca pudding. In short, chicken pudding is *not* a dessert.

    1 chicken, disjointed (or the meat of a
        boiled fowl)
    2 sprigs parsley
    1 bay leaf
      pinch thyme
    ½ teaspoon pepper
    3 eggs, lightly beaten
    2 cups milk
    3 tablespoons melted butter
    1½ cups flour
    1 teaspoon salt

Place chicken in heavy pot with the seasonings, cover with water, cover pot, and bring to a boil. Cook for 20 minutes or until chicken is almost done. (Cook fowl 1 to 1½ hours.)
Preheat oven to 350 degrees.
Remove chicken to a buttered baking dish, reserving the cooking liquid for gravy.
Mix eggs and milk together and sift in 1 cup of flour mixed with ½ teaspoon salt, stirring until smooth. Pour this mixture over the chicken and bake about 45 minutes.
Meanwhile boil down the chicken liquid to about half. Mix the remaining flour and ½ teaspoon salt with 1 cup of water until smooth, and stir bit by bit into the liquid until the desired thickness is reached.
Serve the chicken from the baking dish and pass the gravy separately. (*4 servings*)

CHICKEN PILAF

In the days when Charleston was a great seaport, before there was even a South Carolina, early traders brought in the standard Oriental dish of rice mixed with meat and spices. Southern cooks quickly adopted the dish, shuffled the ingredients about, and in one form or another *pilaf* resulted, and has remained in Charleston ever since. The following recipe is very old. It is sometimes found with ¼ teaspoon curry powder added.

6 tablespoons butter
1 onion, chopped
6 stalks celery, cut up
2 tomatoes, sliced
2 cups raw rice
1 chicken (2½ pounds), disjointed
4 cups chicken broth
1 teaspoon salt
½ teaspoon pepper

Brown the onion in the butter, add the celery and tomatoes, and cook over low heat 10 minutes.

Put the rice into a saucepan; add the onion, celery, and tomato mixture, the chicken parts, broth, and seasonings.

Cover tightly and cook slowly for 30 minutes or more, until chicken is tender. (*6 servings*)

VEGETABLES
AND SIDE DISHES

HOMINY

The name is said to be derived from the Algonquian word *tuckahummin*, to grind corn. The many Indian tribes for whom corn was a staple of the diet not only ground corn, but also parched it and treated it with lye or lime. In Colonial times this lye-treated hominy was called samp. The whole dry kernels of corn were soaked a day and a half in a lye bath made of five ounces of lye to six quarts of water, and five quarts of shelled whole corn kernels. They were then washed in six or seven waters to remove the lye. During this washing process the hulls were rubbed off the corn, which had swollen to two or three times its original size. This "hominy" was then boiled for several hours or until soft.

Hominy grits or grist are made of polished dry-corn kernels that are milled or ground and used to come in several gradations. Grits are a staple of southern diet and are served in many ways and at any meal. Plain boiled hominy grits are served for breakfast along with bacon and eggs or with butter or sugar and cream. Baked grits can be served for lunch; fried grits are served as an accompaniment to other dishes. Boiled hominy grits are incorporated into fritter batter and fried and served as a starch at dinner. There is no end to the ingenuity with which southern cooks have used this mild-flavored corn product as a complement to other foods.

HOMINY

2 cups whole hominy
3 cups water
2 teaspoons salt
½ cup light cream
½ cup butter

Soak the hominy in warm water overnight. Drain, put into a double boiler with 3 cups water and salt. Simmer all day, adding more water if necessary.

When water has been taken up, add cream and butter, and simmer 2 hours longer. Stir and serve with meat. (*4 servings*)

HOMINY GRITS

Hominy grits are ground hominy. When cooking grits, it is a good idea to make more than you need; reserve the rest for another meal.

5 cups water, boiling
1 teaspoon salt
1 cup hominy grits

Stir the grits slowly into the boiling, salted water. Lower heat and cook 45 minutes, covered, stirring from time to time to prevent the cereal from sticking to the bottom of the pan.

Serve as a side dish with butter or gravy, or as a hot cereal with sugar and cream. (*6 servings*)

FRIED GRITS

Pour the cooked grits into a loaf pan, cool, refrigerate overnight or until firm. Unmold and cut into 12 slices.

  2 eggs, beaten
  1 cup bread crumbs
  4 tablespoons bacon fat

Dip the sliced grits into the beaten egg, then into bread crumbs. Fry in hot bacon fat until brown and crisp around the edges. Serve with bacon for breakfast. (*6 servings*)

BAKED GRITS

  4 cups water
  1 teaspoon salt
  1 cup hominy grits
  3 tablespoons butter
  2 eggs, beaten
  1 tablespoon butter

Preheat oven to 375 degrees.
Bring water to a boil. Add salt, stir in grits slowly, and cook until thick, about 45 minutes. Remove from heat, stir in butter and beaten eggs.
Butter 1½ quart baking dish. Pour in grits. Bake in oven until brown, 20 to 30 minutes. Serve for lunch or as an accompaniment to a main dish. (*6 servings*)

SOUTHERN SNAP BEANS

Southern beans are cooked to death, according to northern cooks, but they taste good, which sometimes is all that matters.

  ½ cup diced salt pork
  2 pounds fresh green beans

Fry diced pork over low heat in a pot until crisp.
Snap off the stem ends of green beans, cut up, and wash.
Put them into the pot undried, season to taste with salt and pepper, cover and cook over very low heat for about 1 hour. Note: If you keep the heat down, no water is needed. (*8 servings*)

APPALACHIAN RAMP FEAST

Ramps are a species of wild garlic indigenous to, but by no means exclusive to, the mountains of West Virginia, Tennessee, and North Carolina. In the spring, when wild garlic is in bloom, there are sections of these states in which ramp feasts are rampant.
As soon as the ground is soft enough, the ramps are uprooted and prepared for eating. The roots that clustered about the base are torn away, and the bulbs are cleaned and readied for cooking over hastily built fires.
First they are cut into 1-inch pieces, then they are salted, put into a skillet with bacon grease and vinegar, covered, and cooked over hot coals for about 20 minutes.
Ramps have a sweet mouth-watering garlicky flavor and a pungent odor mountain folk boast about ("something on the order of wild onion but magnified and intensified a thousand-fold"). Although consumed raw by a hard-bitten minority, ramps are most often eaten fried, accompanied by meats, potatoes, beans, and plenty of corn bread, all topped off with sassafras tea. Beer and mountain whiskey also help to make the occasion festive—to say the least.
When April comes to Appalachia, you can tell by the hootin' an' ahollerin' an' square-dancing, if not by the smell alone, that the mountain folk are on their annual ramp rampage.

WATERMELON PICKLES

Slice rind of 1 large watermelon into 6-inch pieces, cover with water, and boil 6 minutes. Drain, cool, and slice off the tough skin and some of the soft pulp. Cut with a knife or cookie cutter into fancy shapes.
Cover with lime water (2 tablespoons calcium oxide—from the drugstore—per quart of water), and allow to stand 3 hours.
Drain, rinse, and cover with fresh water. Simmer until tender, drain again.
Prepare a pickling syrup by simmering in a separate saucepan together 1 quart vinegar, 2 cups water, 2 pounds sugar, 1 tablespoon whole cloves, 1 stick cinnamon, and 1 tablespoon allspice.
Add the watermelon rind to the pickling syrup and simmer until syrup is clear and rind is clear. Transfer to sterilized jars and seal.

BAKED EGGPLANT

2 medium eggplants, peeled and cut
  into ¾-inch strips
  salt
2 tablespoons butter
1 onion, chopped
2 tomatoes, peeled and cut up
1 teaspoon chopped parsley
1 pinch basil
½ teaspoon pepper
4 tablespoons cooking oil
1 tablespoon butter

Preheat oven to 350 degrees.
Sprinkle the eggplant liberally with salt and allow to sit for an hour.
Sauté the onion in butter until golden, add the tomatoes, herbs, and seasoning. Simmer until tomatoes are soft. Strain through a coarse sieve.
Drain eggplant, dry with a towel, dust with flour, and brown in oil. Drain.
Place eggplant into a buttered baking dish with alternate layers of the tomato sauce, dot with butter, and bake in the oven 20 to 30 minutes.
(*4 to 6 servings*)

CYMLINGS

In the South they're called cymlings—in the rest of the country they're scalloped white (or "patty pan") squash. Whatever they're called, they're best when small and tender, before the skins are so tough that they have to be peeled. To cook cymlings southern style, pack them close together in a saucepan and pour over them about 1 cup hot water, cover, and cook over low heat 30 to 40 minutes, depending upon size. The idea is to steam them rather than boil them.
Drain and mash. Place over very low heat for 15 or 20 minutes to dry out, stirring occasionally to prevent burning.
Add plenty of butter, and season to taste with salt and pepper.

PURÉED BROCCOLI

When broccoli was brought to this country from Italy in the 1920s it was served as a new and exotic vegetable, but old Charleston cookbooks had recipes for broccoli more than one hundred years ago.

2 pounds broccoli, washed
6 tablespoons butter
1 teaspoon salt
1 teaspoon freshly ground pepper
  pinch grated nutmeg
2 tablespoons heavy cream
¼ cup grated American cheese

Separate the stems and flowers of the broccoli and chop both into small pieces.
Put the stems into a saucepan of boiling salted water and cook 10 minutes. Add the flowers and continue cooking until tender about 5 minutes. Drain and put through a food mill or blender.
Preheat oven to 350 degrees.
Place puréed broccoli into a baking dish, add the seasonings and cream, sprinkle with cheese, and bake 10 minutes. (*4 servings*)

DANDELION GREENS, SOUTHERN STYLE

young dandelion greens (picked
  before they blossom)
2 cups water
1 tablespoon butter
1 tablespoon lard
1 cup fine, dry bread crumbs
2 tablespoons lemon juice
2 tablespoons onion juice
½ teaspoon salt
½ teaspoon pepper
4 tablespoons crisp, crumbled bacon
2 hard-cooked eggs, chopped

Pick over, wash, and cook the greens in slightly salted water until tender. Drain, chop fine, and set aside (you'll need 2½ cups).
Melt the butter and lard in a saucepan, add the bread crumbs and cook until browned.
Add 2½ cups greens, the lemon juice, onion juice, and seasonings. Mix together well and heat thoroughly.
Garnish with bacon and egg, and serve at once.
(*4 servings*)

OLD SOUTH SUCCOTASH

2 pounds fresh green beans
¼ pound of salt pork
4 or 5 ears of corn, scored and scraped, (green corn if possible), or 1 can (16 ounces) cream-style corn

Trim beans, cover, and cook in boiling water just to cover until tender.
Cut pork in small slices, brown well on each side, and add to beans. Add the corn. Cook all together for 1 hour over low heat—2 hours is better. Stir frequently to prevent sticking or burning. (*6 to 8 servings*)

CHARLESTON OKRA PILAF

4 slices bacon, cut up
1 cup okra, cut into small pieces
1 cup rice
2 cups water

Brown the bacon, remove it from the fat, and set aside.
Fry the okra in the bacon fat over very low heat for 10 minutes. Add the rice and water. Cover and simmer about 40 minutes.
Add the bacon and serve. (*4 servings*)

FRIED BLACK-EYED PEAS

½ pound shelled black-eyed peas
1 teaspoon salt
8 slices bacon
1 onion, sliced

Soak the peas in cold water for 30 minutes. Drain and cook in salted water for 1 hour or more, until tender. Drain again.
Fry the bacon until well done but not crisp. Remove and set aside.
Add the sliced onion to the bacon fat and fry until lightly browned. Add the peas and cook, mashing them a little so they will be dry and crusty when done.
Serve with the bacon slices on top. (*4 servings*)

FRIED YAMS

Fried yams have long been a favorite dish throughout most of the Deep South. Accompanied with ham or sausage and grits, hot biscuits, or corn bread, fried yams make a country breakfast fit for a king.
The yams are peeled, cut into thick slices, soaked in salted water for half an hour or so, drained, and dried. They are then fried on both sides, a few slices at a time, in smoking-hot fat until brown.

SALADS
AND DRESSINGS

FLORIDA SEAFOOD SALAD

2½ cups several varieties fish and shellfish washed and dried salad greens
1 grapefruit, sectioned
½ cup olives, ripe and/or green
½ cup olive oil
1½ tablespoons vinegar
½ teaspoon Dijon mustard
¼ teaspoon salt
⅛ teaspoon pepper

Place cold cooked shrimp, lobster, crab meat, scallops, and flaked white fish in any combination you wish into a bowl lined with salad greens. Add grapefruit sections, ripe olives, and green olives.
Pour in a vinaigrette sauce made by mixing together oil and vinegar, a little Dijon or dry English mustard, salt and freshly ground pepper to taste.
Toss all together well and serve. (*4 servings*)

OYSTER SALAD

½ pint shucked raw oysters
½ cup chopped celery
2 hard-cooked eggs, chopped
3 tablespoons mayonnaise
  fresh salad greens
½ teaspoon salt
⅛ teaspoon pepper

Place well-drained oysters into a bowl lined with salad greens, add celery, eggs, and mayonnaise. Season with salt and pepper, toss, and serve. (*2 to 4 servings*)

SUNBURST SALAD

1½ cups grapefruit sections
1½ cups orange sections
  lettuce
1 package (3 ounces) cream cheese
  mixed with 2 tablespoons cream until
  fluffy
¼ cup French dressing
4 maraschino cherries

Arrange grapefruit and orange sections in a petallike manner on lettuce leaves, spoon cream cheese mixture in center, and dot with cherries. Pour dressing over all. (*4 servings*)

GOLDEN APPLE SALAD

Once on a high hillside in West Virginia, a man saw that one tree produced a flavorful yellow apple. He put a fence around it and carefully began to propagate the tree. He called it the Golden Grimes, and here is a salad made for these apples.

2 cups cubed yellow apples
  juice of 1 lemon
½ cup dates, halved and pitted
¼ cup hickory-nut meats
½ cup heavy cream
½ cup mayonnaise
¼ cup orange marmalade
1 teaspoon salt

Cube apples, mix with lemon juice.
Put first three ingredients in a bowl.
Whip cream, mix with mayonnaise, add the remaining ingredients, and chill until ready to serve. (*6 servings*)

CHIFFONADE SALAD

1 grapefruit, sectioned
4 tomatoes, quartered
1 green pepper, cut in thin strips
  romaine lettuce, washed and dried
5 tablespoons olive oil
1 tablespoon vinegar
¼ teaspoon Dijon mustard
  salt
  pepper
⅛ teaspoon rosemary

Place grapefruit sections, quartered tomatoes, and julienned green peppers into a bowl lined with shredded romaine.
Make a vinaigrette sauce by mixing together oil and vinegar, a little Dijon or dry English mustard, salt and freshly ground pepper to taste. Shake in a bottle or jar with a pinch or two of rosemary.
Pour the sauce over the salad, toss well, and serve. (*4 servings*)

BREADS
AND BATTERCAKES

HOMEMADE BREAD AND ROLLS

When I was a little girl we had a very good cook whose name was Diana Montague. Whenever she made hot rolls the aroma of baking bread spread over the neighborhood and I would come running from wherever I was and beg Diana for rolls until she refused to give me any more. Those rolls were so light they melted in my mouth like ice cream.

Watching her work the dough was like watching an artist at work. The following is not her recipe, because it is impossible to put the skill that was in her brain and hands into a recipe. There are too many variables in yeasts, flours, and doughs; knowledge of them can only come from experience.

In making bread it is important to remember that the dough should be kept warm (about 80 degrees Fahrenheit) during fermentation. Extremes of heat and cold destroy the action of the yeast. Once kneaded, it is also important to cover the dough with soft butter or lard and a damp cloth. This prevents the formation of a crust which, when the dough is kneaded again, would form hard lumps.

Homemade yeast is slower to rise than commercial yeast. It will have a better aroma if "started" with baker's or brewer's yeast.

To make a sponge to raise overnight:

　3 cups warm water
　2 tablespoons lard
　2 tablespoons sugar
　1 teaspoon baking soda
　1 cup homemade yeast or 1 cake yeast or 1 package dry yeast dissolved in 1 cup warm water
　3 cups flour

Put the lard and sugar into 3 cups water, just hot enough to dissolve them. Add the yeast and soda (dissolved in 1 cup water), then gradually add the flour. Stir well, cover, and let rise in unlit oven with door open until morning (the pilot light will keep it dry and warm), or at room temperature.

In the morning, add to this sponge:

　8 cups sifted flour
　1 teaspoon salt
　¼ cup water rinsed in the mixing bowl

Put flour in wide bowl or tray, make a well in the center and put in the sponge. Knead flour in toward the center of the bowl, make a ¼ turn and knead again. (If too soft, add more flour; if too stiff, add more water). Always flour hands lightly when kneading.

After 20 minutes (30 minutes if using homemade yeast) of kneading, when dough is smooth and silky, cover and set aside 4 to 5 hours (in unlit oven 2½ hours), until it doubles in bulk.

Knead lightly again for 8 minutes.

1. To make loaves:
Divide dough into 4 loaves, mold and put into 4 well-greased loaf pans. Let rise in unlit oven or at room temperature until double in bulk. Bake 40 to 60 minutes in a preheated 400-degree oven, until brown. (When done, bread has a hollow sound when tapped.)

2. To make cloverleaf rolls:
Refrigerate dough for 2 hours or overnight. Butter hands and make small balls, 1 inch in diameter. Put 3 of these into each section of a well-buttered muffin tin. Let rise until double in bulk.
Bake 12 to 15 minutes in a preheated 400-degree oven. For a soft crust, brush with melted butter on removing from oven.

3. To make parkerhouse rolls:
Refrigerate dough for 2 hours or overnight.
Roll dough into a ½-inch-thick sheet. Cut with
biscuit cutter and fold over each biscuit,
leaving ¼ inch on bottom half. Press lightly
and place in a well-buttered pan, allowing
room for the rolls to rise. Let rise until double
in bulk.
Bake in a preheated 400-degree oven 12 to 15
minutes. For a soft crust, brush with melted
butter on removing from oven. (*about 4 dozen
rolls*)

SPOON BREAD

Spoon bread is found throughout the South, in
Virginia where it may have originated, the
Carolinas and Mississippi. It is also found on
Nantucket Island, in Massachusetts, where it is
called Bannock. All southern recipes call for
white water-ground cornmeal, milk, eggs,
butter or bacon fat. The essential difference
between the spoon bread of one area and that
of another lies in the proportions of the
ingredients. More important is the method of
mixing and baking. It should be cooked, but
soft when served, soft enough to be served
with a spoon.

   3 cups milk
   1 cup white water-ground cornmeal
1½ tablespoons melted butter
   3 eggs, beaten
   1 teaspoon salt
   3 teaspoons baking powder
   2 tablespoon bacon fat or melted butter

Preheat oven to 400 degrees.
Put two cups milk in saucepan, stir in meal and
salt and bring to a boil. Cook until thickened.
Put bacon fat in 1-quart baking dish and put in
oven.
Mix third cup of milk with eggs, baking
powder, and 1½ tablespoons melted butter.
Mix mush and egg mixture, pour into hot dish
and bake 30 to 35 minutes. It should have a
jiggle in center when done. Serve immediately.
(*6 servings*)

SALLY LUNN

When the bread cupboard was bare, it wasn't a
matter of running to the store for a loaf—
something had to be done. Sally Lunn was a
good, quick standby for cooks over the
centuries.

   1 package or 1 cake yeast dissolved in ¼
     cup warm water
   2 tablespoons butter
   1 cup warm milk
   2 eggs, well beaten
  ¼ teaspoon salt
   3 cups sifted flour

Melt the butter in the milk, but do not boil. Stir
in the yeast, eggs, and salt.
Blend this mixture into the flour until smooth,
pour into a buttered 2 quart baking pan, and
cover with a towel.
When the dough has risen to double (1 to 1½
hours), place into a preheated 375-degree
oven, and bake for 30 minutes or until golden.
Cut into squares and serve hot. (*8 servings*)

BATTER BREAD

This bread is used at family meals because it is
not as rich as spoon bread. The essential
difference is that the meal is scalded with
boiling water, then mixed with the other
ingredients and baked.

   2 tablespoons bacon fat or lard
1½ cups boiling water
1½ cups white water-ground corn meal
   1 tablespoon melted butter
  ¾ teaspoon salt
   2 eggs, beaten
   2 teaspoons baking powder
1½ cups milk

Preheat oven to 400 degrees
Put bacon fat in 1 quart baking dish and put in
oven.
Pour boiling water over cornmeal, stirring out
lumps. Stir in butter, salt, eggs, milk, baking
powder.
Pour into hot baking dish and bake 30 to 40
minutes. Remove from oven while there is still
a jiggle in the center.
Serve immediately. (*6 servings*)

CORN PONE

Richer than hoecake, which is said to have sustained the Confederate Army for three years, corn pone is softer and not as chewy.

    2 cups water-ground cornmeal
    1 cup boiling water
    1 tablespoon shortening or bacon
        drippings (or 2 tablespoons cracklings)
    1 cup buttermilk mixed with ½ cup cold
        water
    2 eggs, well beaten
    ½ teaspoon baking soda
    1 teaspoon salt

Preheat oven to 425 degrees.
Put the cornmeal into a bowl, stir in the boiling water and shortening or bacon drippings.
Stir in the buttermilk, eggs, soda, and salt. Beat thoroughly and turn into a well-greased, hot baking pan (batter should be about ¾ inch deep).
Put into the oven and bake for 30 minutes.
Cut into squares and serve as you would hot bread. (*4 servings*)

OLD-FASHIONED CORN DODGERS

Cousin to hoecake and hush puppies, these can be served either as bread or as a side dish with eggs or meat.

    2 cups water-ground cornmeal
    ½ teaspoon salt
    ½ teaspoon baking soda
    1 tablespoon cooking oil
        buttermilk or water
        bacon fat

Mix together the cornmeal, salt, and soda. Add the cooking oil and enough buttermilk or water to make a stiff dough.
Form the dough into 8 oblong shapes, and cook on a griddle in hot bacon fat until golden brown.
Southern cooks today often add 1 teaspoon baking powder to the batter, making it somewhat lighter. (*4 servings*)

HOMINY BREAD

    ½ cup hominy grits
    3 cups water
    ½ teaspoon salt
    2 tablespoons butter
    2 eggs, beaten
    2 cups milk
    1 cup white water-ground cornmeal

Put the grits into the water with the salt and bring to a boil, stirring. Reduce heat to a slow simmer, cover, and cook for 45 minutes.
Preheat oven to 425 degrees.
Remove hominy from the stove, stir in the butter, eggs, and 1 cup milk.
Stir in the cornmeal and the remaining milk.
Pour into a greased baking dish, place into the oven, and bake 45 minutes or until golden.
Serve with a spoon as batter bread. (*8 servings*)

PEANUT BREAD

We sometimes forget that peanuts are not just a snack or something to mash into a spreadable "butter." In many Oriental countries, notably Thailand, peanuts are used in sauces, gravies, and stuffings. Even in America sauces and soups are made from peanuts. So it is scarcely surprising to find this rich and delicious bread made from the lowly goober.

    ½ cup sugar
    3 teaspoons baking powder
    4 cups flour
    ½ teaspoon salt
    1 teaspoon baking soda
    1½ cups milk
    ½ cup corn syrup
    1 cup ground raw peanuts.

Preheat oven to 350 degrees.
Mix together the sugar, baking powder, flour, salt, and soda.
Mix together the milk and corn syrup.
Combine the dry ingredients with the liquids, add the peanuts, form into a loaf, and place onto a greased baking pan.
Bake about 45 to 60 minutes or until straw tests clean.

HUSH PUPPIES

These crisp little cornmeal fritters seem to have originated in Florida as an accompaniment to fried fish and were often, it is said, tossed to the dogs to quiet them. They can still be found in almost any part of the South, served in the home and in restaurants.

2 cups water-ground cornmeal
1 tablespoon flour
3 teaspoons baking powder
1 teaspoon salt
1 egg, well beaten
2 cups milk
5 tablespoons chopped onion
½ teaspoon red pepper (cayenne)

Mix all the dry ingredients together.
Mix together the egg, milk, pepper, and onion.
Combine the two mixtures and beat into a stiff batter.
Drop by the tablespoonful into the deep fat in which fish are being fried. Cook until brown and with a good crust. They float when done. Drain on paper towel. Serve with the fried fish. (*8 servings*)

HOECAKE

2 cups white or yellow water-ground cornmeal
1 teaspoon salt
water or milk

Sift together cornmeal and salt. Stir in enough water or milk to make a soft, but not runny, dough.
Pour into a heavy, hot, well-greased skillet or griddle and form into a round cake about ½ inch thick.
Cook slowly about 15 minutes or until well browned. Turn and brown 15 minutes longer on the other side, or until the cake is well done through and through. Serve as you would hot bread. (*2 to 4 servings*)

BUTTERMILK CORNCAKES

Southerners never use sugar in corn bread or in pancakes.

2 eggs, lightly beaten
1 cup buttermilk (or sour milk)
1 cup water
1 cup white water-ground cornmeal
1 cup flour
½ teaspoon baking soda
½ teaspoon salt
bacon fat or vegetable oil

Mix together the eggs, buttermilk, and water.
Mix together the cornmeal, flour, soda, and salt.
Combine the two mixtures and blend well.
Drop by the tablespoonful onto a well-greased, hot griddle.
Cook and turn. Serve as any pancake. (*4 servings*)

POPOVERS

These totally American muffins are known in the Deep South, where they are nearly as common as biscuits, as puff popps. Actually, they are made from a thin batterlike dough similar to that of Yorkshire pudding. Properly prepared, popovers should be crisp on the outside and moist inside.

1½ cups flour
¼ teaspoon salt
2 eggs lightly beaten
1½ cups milk
2 tablespoons melted butter

Preheat oven to 425 degrees.
Sift together the flour and salt, and blend in the eggs, milk, and butter to make a smooth batter.
Beat with rotary beater 3 minutes.
Fill hot buttered muffin cups two-thirds full with this batter and bake about 30 minutes. Do not open oven until the muffins pop and brown. (*12 popovers*)

DESSERTS

"TO MAKE A PASTE FOR A PYE"

Take a gallon of flour a pound of butter, boil it in fair water and make the paste up quick.

The foregoing recipe appeared in *The Accomplished Cook*, printed in 1664. Someone must have been in a great hurry when it was written, since anyone attempting to follow this recipe would end up with a sticky mess.

Pies were a staple of Colonial cooking all along the Eastern Seaboard. It would be a long list if we tried to enumerate the variety of southern pies. A few of the best known are pecan pie, sweet potato pie, key lime pie, peach tarts, all included here.

A basic pie crust usable for most pies is easy to make, and can be refrigerated until ready to be rolled out.

PLAIN PASTRY

Double crust:

    2 cups sifted flour
    ⅔ cup lard
    ½ teaspoon baking powder
    ¾ teaspoon salt
    4 tablespoons water

Single crust:

    sifted flour
    ⅓ cup lard
    ¼ teaspoon baking powder
    ¼ teaspoon salt
    2 tablespoons water

Sift flour, baking powder, and salt together. Mix with lard until it is the texture of coarse crumbs. Mix lightly so that the heat of the hands will not melt the fat. Add the water in several places and mix lightly again. Form the dough into a ball. If double crust, form into two balls.

Flour board and roll the dough with light strokes outward to form a circle ¼ inch thick (or thinner). Put pie pan upside down on the dough and cut around 1-¼ inches beyond the lip of the pan. Turn the pan over, fold dough in half, and place it in the pan; unfold and fit. If a hole develops, put a piece of pastry over it and work it into the surrounding dough.

For a two-crust pie, roll the other ball the exact size of the pie pan, put on over filling, slit for steam vents and crimp the edges of both crusts together. For a single prebaked crust, prick the pastry on the bottom with a fork (to prevent rising into bubbles) and bake for approximately 12 minutes (until light brown) in a 375 degree oven.

PECAN PIE

This dessert is, and always has been, a favorite throughout the South. The ingredients have varied down through the years. Sorghum was probably used originally, but recent recipes call for dark corn syrup or light molasses. Maple syrup, brown sugar, even white sugar have been and are used to make these sugar pies throughout the country.

    3 eggs, slightly beaten
    ½ cup brown sugar, firmly packed
    1 cup dark corn syrup
    ¼ teaspoon salt
    ½ teaspoon vanilla
    1 cup coarsely chopped pecans
    1 unbaked 9-inch pie crust
      whipped cream

Preheat oven to 450 degrees.

Mix together the eggs, sugar, syrup, salt, vanilla, and pecans and spoon into a 9-inch pie pan lined with pie crust.

Bake 12 minutes, reduce the heat to 350 degrees, and cook 30 minutes longer.

Chill and serve in very small slices topped with unsweetened whipped cream. (*8 servings*)

KEY LIME PIE

Key limes are a special variety found on the Florida Keys. Part of the rich flavor of key lime pie is that the limes are picked just before the pie is made. Ordinary limes can be substituted and should be ripe. The pie is sometimes prepared with a meringue on top and then baked, to brown. It can also be served with whipped cream.

- ½ cup key lime juice, room temperature
- 1 package unflavored gelatin
- 2 eggs, separated
- 1½ tablespoons sugar
- 1 can sweetened condensed milk
- 1 pastry shell, baked (see Plain Pastry*)
- 1 tablespoon grated lime rind

Mix lime juice and gelatin, set aside for half an hour. Add 1 tablespoon sugar to the egg yolks, beat until lemon-colored. Add the gelatin mixture to this, stir, add the condensed milk.

Beat egg whites and gradually add remaining sugar. When stiff fold into the lime mixture. Pour into baked pastry shell and refrigerate until ready to use.

Sprinkle with grated rind before serving. (6 servings)

SWEET POTATO PIE

Sweet potato or yam pies are famous throughout the southland. Sometimes the potatoes are mashed and at other times sliced, as in the pie below. A superior pie.

This pie is also sometimes called a cobbler, and is made with less brandy, or sometimes water mixed with rum or bourbon.

- 3 medium yams
- 3 crusts pie pastry (1½ recipes plain pastry* for two-crust pie)
- ½ cup butter
- 1 cup brown sugar, firmly packed
- 1 teaspoon allspice
- ¾ cup brandy

Preheat oven to 375 degrees.

Wash, peel, and slice yams ¼ inch thick. Boil until tender and drain 10 minutes.

Cut one crust pie pastry in strips, lay on a cookie sheet, and put in oven. Line one deep pie pan with pastry and put to bake in oven. Bake both 12 to 15 minutes.

Line cooked pie pastry with half the sliced sweet potatoes, sprinkle over half the sugar, half the spice, and dot with half the butter. Cover this with strips of cooked pastry in a latticework. Add another layer of potatoes, sprinkle with remaining sugar and spice and dot with remaining butter.

Cover with uncooked crust. Crimp edges well. Make a slit in the top of this and with a funnel pour in the brandy.

Bake 5 minutes, reduce oven to 325 degrees, and bake pie 25 to 30 minutes longer.

Serve hot with whipped cream. (6 to 8 servings)

BAVARIAN CREAM

- 1 package unflavored gelatin
- ¼ cup water
- ⅛ teaspoon salt
- 2 eggs, separated
- ¼ cup granulated sugar
- 1 cup milk
- ¾ teaspoon vanilla
- 1-½ cups heavy cream
- ¼ cup confectioners' sugar

Soak gelatin in water. Put gelatin and salt in saucepan.

Beat egg yolks, add granulated sugar and milk. Add to gelatin. Cook over low heat about 5 minutes, stirring until all gelatin is dissolved. Add vanilla.

Set over bowl of ice cubes and stir until mixture begins to stiffen. Fold in stiffly beaten egg whites.

Whip cream with confectioners' sugar until stiff. Reserve 1 cup whipped cream, add remaining cream to mixture. Rinse a 1-½-quart glass serving bowl with cold water. Spoon mixture into bowl.

Chill at least two hours. Decorate with reserved cream before serving. (6 servings)

MANGO DELIGHT

- 8 ripe mangoes, unpeeled, washed and cut into small pieces
- 2 cups sweetened whipped cream
- ½ cup shaved sweet chocolate

Simmer the mangoes in a little water about half an hour or until tender. Put through a sieve and spoon into glass dessert dishes.

Top with whipped cream and chocolate, chill, and serve. (4 servings)

LANE CAKE

This famous cake, a favorite at Christmas time, is claimed by the Carolinians (who call it Rocky Mountain cake), by the the Alabamans, and by almost everybody south of the Mason-Dixon Line. It varies somewhat—sometimes drastically—from locality to locality, but the recipe herewith was recommended to us as the most generally accepted one.

    3 cups flour
    2 teaspoons baking powder
    ½ teaspoon salt
    2 cups sugar
    1 cup butter
    1 cup milk
    1 teaspoon vanilla
    8 egg whites, beaten until stiff (yolks
        reserved)

Preheat oven to 375 degrees.
Sift together the flour, baking powder, and salt several times. (The more you sift the lighter the cake.)
Sift the sugar; cream in the butter. Add the flour mixture and milk alternately, a little at a time, beginning and ending with flour.
Add the vanilla, then fold in the egg whites. Line four 8-inch layer cake pans with greased paper, spoon in the cake mixture, and bake 30 to 35 minutes.
Cool slightly, turn out, and fill.

Filling:

    8 reserved egg yolks, beaten
    1 cup sugar
    ½ teaspoon salt
    ½ cup butter
    1 teaspoon vanilla
    1 cup chopped seedless raisins
    1 cup grated coconut
    1 cup chopped pecans
    ½ cup brandy

Beat together the egg yolks, sugar, and salt. Melt the butter in a double boiler and stir in the egg mixture and vanilla until thickened.
Remove from the heat and stir in the remaining ingredients, cool, and spread between the cake layers. Then ice the cake with vanilla icing:

    1¼ cups sugar
    ½ cup water
    2 egg whites
    ½ teaspoon cream of tartar
    ½ teaspoon vanilla

Boil sugar and water together until syrup spins a thread.
Whip egg whites with cream of tartar until stiff. Add syrup gradually to egg whites in a thin stream, beating all the while. Add vanilla. Spread icing over cake.

TRIFLE

There are many ways of preparing trifle, the dessert George Washington is said to have preferred over all others. Modern cooks use store-bought ladyfingers and/or macaroons topped with custard, whipped cream, blanched almonds, strawberry jam, and seasoned with sherry wine, cinnamon, cherries, and so forth. This is sometimes called tipsey parson.
But there is something charming about the simple old recipe passed down from who-knows-where.

First make custard:

    2 cups milk
    1½ teaspoons cornstarch
    ¼ teaspoon salt
    2 egg yolks, lightly beaten
    ¼ cup powdered sugar
    ½ teaspoon vanilla extract

Mix 2 tablespoons of milk with the cornstarch and salt. Scald the rest of the milk and pour over the cornstarch mixture. Season and cook in the top section of a double boiler until thickened.
Mix the egg yolks with the sugar and add to the double boiler, stirring. Add the vanilla, stir, heat through, remove from the stove, and chill.

Then make trifle:

    1 recipe spongecake or other plain cake
        (fresh or stale), cut into ½-inch slices
    1 cup sherry
    1 jar strawberry jam
    1 cup heavy cream, whipped

Place slices of cake into a cut glass dish, soak with sherry, and cover with a layer of strawberry jam. Spoon a layer of cold custard over all, and add a second layer of cake and jam. Chill and serve topped with whipped cream. (*8 servings*)

GUAVA JELLY

    1 pound guavas, washed, with blossom
       end removed, sliced
    2 pints water
      sugar
      lime juice

Cook the guavas in the water about an hour. Cool, pour into a gauze bag and strain, pressing to extract all the juices. Strain juices again.

Add 1⅛ cups sugar and 1 tablespoon lime juice for each cup guava juice, boil rapidly 5 minutes, and test for "sheeting." (Cool a spoonful of juice and pour back into the pan from the side of the spoon. When juice is ready to jell, it will come together and sheet off the spoon). Jelly thermometer should read 223 degrees.

Skim, pour into jelly glasses, and seal. (*about 2 pints*)

FRIED PEACH TARTS, GEORGIA STYLE

      stewed peaches, drained and
      chopped
      sugar
      powdered ginger
      biscuit dough
      fat for deep frying
      confectioners' sugar

Sweeten and season stewed peaches with sugar and ginger.

Roll out biscuit dough thin and cut into saucer-sized rounds.

Spoon the chopped peaches onto one half of each round, fold over the other half and pinch edges together firmly.

Drop, a few at a time, into hot deep fat (370 degrees) and cook until golden. Drain and sprinkle with confectioners' sugar. Serve hot or cold.

SWEET YAM PUDDING

    3 cups yams, peeled and coarsely grated
    2 eggs
 1½ cups molasses
    ½ cup brown sugar, firmly packed
    1 cup milk
    2 tablespoons flour
    ½ cup butter, softened
    ½ teaspoon ginger
    ½ teaspoon cinnamon
    ½ teaspoon nutmeg
    1 teaspoon allspice
    1 teaspoon grated orange peel
    1 cup heavy cream

Preheat oven to 350 degrees.

Mix all ingredients, except cream, together until they are thoroughly blended.

Cook in heavy skillet on the top of the stove over medium, then low, heat until it thickens. Then put skillet in oven 20 to 30 minutes to brown.

Serve with heavy cream. (*4 servings*)

CHARLOTTE RUSSE

This dessert is found in almost every cookbook from Charleston to Louisville. Less elaborate than a trifle, it makes a lovely party dessert. Some recipes call for stale cake.

    4 cups heavy cream
    6 tablespoons confectioners' sugar
    1 package unflavored gelatin, dissolved
       in ¼ cup water
    ½ teaspoon vanilla
    1 tablespoon sherry
    ½ pound ladyfingers or cake

Dissolve gelatin in water.

Line cut-glass dish with lady fingers or thinly sliced cake.

Add sherry to gelatin, stir.

Whip the cream, add sugar gradually.

Add vanilla to gelatin and mix carefully into cream mixture. Be sure the gelatin has dissolved. Stir.

Pour cream into bowl with ladyfingers, and refrigerate 3 to 4 hours. (*8 servings*)

WINE JELLY

This is a very old recipe that has withstood the test of time in southern kitchens. It can be served with custard and pound cake.

    2 envelopes unflavored gelatin
    ½ cup cold water
    1 cup boiling water
    ¾ cups sugar
    2 cups sweet sherry
    ¼ cup lemon juice
    ½ cup rum
    1 tablespoon peanut oil
      whipped cream

Put gelatin in a bowl with cold water. Soak for 10 minutes. Boil water and add to gelatin. Stir well and add sugar, sherry, lemon juice, rum. Rub mold with peanut oil and pour in gelatin mixture.
Mold 3 to 4 hours. Unmold and serve with whipped cream. (*6 servings*)

ORANGE MARMALADE

Orange marmalade is not as awesome an undertaking as one would think. Here is a recipe that should keep a good supply on hand.

    1 quart thinly sliced oranges, with peel
      and pulp (seeds removed)
    1½ quarts water
    1½ quarts sugar

Put the oranges and water into a large pot and allow to stand overnight.
Cover and cook 40 minutes to 1 hour or until peel is tender. Add 1-½ quarts sugar.
Cook, uncovered, at a fast boil to the jelly stage (jelly thermometer should read 220 degrees).
Pour into sterilized jelly glasses. (*5 pints*)

BEVERAGES

CHERRY BOUNCE

This delectable drink was made traditionally throughout the South during the cherry season and southerners take great credit for it. However, there can be little doubt that the very same drink, or one quite similar, was made in the English countryside before the Colonies were established.

    12 pounds sour red cherries, washed,
       stones removed
       sugar
       ground mace
       ground allspice
    1 quart brandy
    1 quart rum

Place the cherries into a heat-resistant container and set it into a pot containing boiling water. Cook gently until the juice is extracted from the cherries. Strain through a jelly bag and measure the juice obtained.

To each gallon juice add 4 pounds sugar and ½ teaspoon each of mace and allspice. Simmer gently until scum ceases to rise.
Skim, cool, add the brandy and rum and bottle for use.

OLD KENTUCKY COOLER

    4 ounces brandy
    2 ounces Jamaica rum
    2 ounces bourbon whiskey
    2 ounces water
    1 tablespoon sugar
    2 slices lemon peel

Mix all the ingredients together thoroughly and pour into prechilled Old Fashioned glasses full of shaved ice.
Garnish with twists of lemon peel. (*4 servings*)

PLANTER'S PUNCH

            juice of ½ lemon
            juice of ½ orange
    4 or 5 dashes curaçao
    1½ ounces Jamaica rum
            slice orange
            slice lemon
            maraschino cherry
            slice fresh pineapple

Combine all the ingredients in a cocktail shaker, shake, and pour into a tall glass filled with cracked ice. Decorate with the fruit and serve with straws. (*1 serving*)

SOUTHERN EGGNOG

In the South it is very bad form to buy eggnog. It should always be homemade, usually by the host.

    12 egg yolks
     1 cup fine sugar
     1 quart bourbon whiskey
     1 quart whole milk
     1 quart light cream
     1 teaspoon nutmeg
     ½ teaspoon cinnamon
     ½ pint heavy cream, whipped

Beat egg yolks until light and fluffy. Strain. Add the sugar gradually and continue beating, then add all whiskey to this mixture and stir well. Add the milk and light cream.
Whip cream; add nutmeg and cinnamon. Mix whipped cream into eggnog last. (*32 servings, half-cup portions*)

SMUGGLER'S GROG

    1½ ounces Jamaica rum
     1 lump sugar
     1 teaspoon butter
        twist lemon peel

Combine all ingredients in a mug. Fill with boiling water, and serve with a stick of cinnamon for stirring. (*1 serving*)

PLANTATION PUNCH

     1 bottle Jamaica rum
     ½ bottle grenadine
     1 cup orange juice
     1 cup lime juice
     ½ cup pineapple juice
     1 orange, sliced
     2 cups pineapple chunks
        maraschino cherries

Combine all the ingredients in a punch bowl with a large block of ice. Stir to chill thoroughly. (*about 20 servings*)

GREENBRIER MINT JULEP

Crush 5 mint leaves with a dash of sugar syrup in the bottom of a tall glass and allow to steep for 15 minutes. Add 3 or 4 ounces of good bourbon whiskey, and pack the glass tightly with shaved ice.
Stir gently in a circular motion until glass is well frosted, decorate with a sprig of mint, wrap bottom of glass with paper napkin to absorb condensation, and serve. (*1 serving*)

GULF COAST
COOKING

SOUPS AND CHOWDERS

Crayfish Bisque
Shrimp Bisque
French Watercress Soup
Oyster Gumbo Filé
Cream of Crab Soup
Onion Soup New Orleans
Creole Soup
Parsley Soup

PASTA, EGG, AND CHEESE DISHES

Eggs au Beurre Noir
Eggs Benedictine
Omelet Fines Herbes
Eggs Mornay
Puffy Omelet

FISH AND SHELLFISH

Louisiana Court Bouillon
Bouillabaisse Louisianne
Pompano en Papillote
Red Snapper Creole
Oysters Rockefeller
Oysters en Brochette
Shrimp Rémoulade
Shrimp Marinière
Shrimp Gumbo
Shrimp Creole with Rice
Shrimp Patties
Fried Frogs' Legs

MEATS

Jambalaya
Gumbo Suprême
Tripe Piquante
Sweetbreads à la Reine
Kidneys à la Française
Blanquette of Lamb
Creole Pilaf
Flank Steak de Luxe
Steak a l'Oignon Belle Alliance
Burgundian Beef

POULTRY AND GAME BIRDS

New Orleans Gumbo Filé
Poulet au Diable
Canvasback Duck with Delta Dressing
Creole Chicken Pie
Chicken Fritters
Quail in Wine
Roast Squab Pilaf

VEGETABLES AND SIDE DISHES

Potatoes Soufflées
Mushrooms Under Glass
Cauliflower au Gratin
Baked Carrots
Corn Fritters Beauregard
Creole Corn Pudding
Baked Candied Yams
Baked Bananas

SALADS AND DRESSINGS

Papaya-Shrimp Salad
Salad Macédoine
Avocado Henri
Shrimp Mousse
Creole Mustard Dressing

BREADS AND BATTERCAKES

Calas
Kush-Kush
Rice Muffins
Pain Perdu
Louisiana Honey Bread
Hop Yeast

DESSERTS

Blackberry Roll
Apricot Sherbet
Chess Pie
Jeff Davis Pudding
Raspberry Meringues
Fig Pudding
Strawberry Mousse Frappé
Creole Pecan Pralines
Bar-le-Duc
Red Pepper Jam
Wedding Cake
Creole Fritters

BEVERAGES

Old-fashioned Creole Cocktail
Sazarac Cocktail
Ramos Fizz
Mississippi Punch
Port Sangaree
Creole Coffee
Café Orleans Flambé
Café Brûlot

GULF COAST COOKING

The peace treaty that officially ended the Revolutionary War was signed in Paris in 1783. A boundary line was drawn below the thirteen original states above Florida, which then belonged to Spain, as did the "Island of New Orleans," having been ceded to Spain in 1763 by the French, who had retained all the territory west of the Mississippi.

This uneasy balance continued for twenty years until New Orleans was ceded to Napoleon by the Spanish, alarming the newly elected American President Thomas Jefferson. He bought Louisiana from France in 1803. The Louisiana Purchase included part of West Florida, and the western boundary of that territory was not defined until the treaty with Spain in 1819.

From the mixture of French and Spanish with a touch of African (African slaves had been imported as early as 1717) and American Indian came a hybrid society with its own very special brand of cooking not found anywhere else in the world. A native seasoning called filé, made from dried and powdered sassafras leaves, was added to okra (brought from Africa) and used to concoct dishes with native shrimp, crayfish, rice, and corn such as no one anywhere had eaten before. Crayfish à la creole, jambalaya, and gumbo filé became as common as baked beans and chowder in New England. Famous *calas*, light rice cakes, were cooked in deep fat right on the street by freed black women, a custom that began after the War Between the States when former slaves had no other means of support.

About the Natchez Indians, who lived on the Mississippi and in Louisiana north of New Orleans, Maturin Le Petit (1693-1739) a Jesuit, said,

This nation of savages inhabits one of the most beautiful and fertile countries in the World. . . . Their religion at certain points is very similar to that of the ancient Romans. [In death] the rewards to which they look forward consist principally in feasting. . . . They will be conducted to a region of pleasures where exquisite viands will be furnished them in abundance.
Violators of their laws will be cast upon lands unfruitful and entirely covered with water, where they will not have any kind of corn . . . and they will never eat meat, and have no nourishment but the flesh of crocodiles [alligators] and spoiled fish and shell fish.

The Choctaw tribe's territory was once the whole state of Mississippi, and eventually dwindled to a reservation on Bayou Lacombe, near Mandeville. The women of the tribe gathered young sassafras leaves; dried, pounded, and sieved them; and took them to sell in the old French market in New Orleans. The Creoles learned to use the filé, as it was called. The skill of the black cooks put it into *gombo*, an African word. All the tribes cultivated pumpkins, squash, corn, and sunflowers. They hunted wild turkey, duck, partridge, quail, and fished for red snapper, redfish, flounder, striped bass, grouper, and many others. They also used wild berries, nuts, and persimmons in their cooking. Most of the Indians were later pushed across the Mississippi after the Cherokee and Creeks lost their last war with the whites.

In 1755 the Acadians came down the Mississippi, or sailed to the Gulf Coast from Grand Pré, Nova Scotia, exiled by the English for their assistance to the French Canadians. They reinforced the French element of Gulf Coast cooking, and being mostly fishermen they took to the gulf with energy. Their name was slurred to "Cajun." In the late eighteenth and early nineteenth centuries English, Scots-Irish, and other settlers drifted westward from the Carolinas and settled in Alabama, Tennessee, and Arkansas, Louisiana, and Mississippi.

The French *beignets* had become fritters that were served either with the meat without sugar, or as a light dessert dusted with powdered sugar. Finely chopped fish added to them turned them into a delightful lunch; and fruits, marinated in brandy, dipped in fritter batter and fried, were served with ham.

By the time Andrew Jackson took New Orleans, stately houses were being built on the profits of sugar cane, sorghum, rice, and many other crops. The American stereotypical picture of "the South" was based on those things, and slaves and cotton. The slave economy fostered good food. There were many hands and plenty of time to watch a pot or to make meticulous preparations. Riverboats carried people to New Orleans in luxury, and carried city delicacies to them. One such delicate custom was the serving of a middle-course drink or punch. It was often a champagne brandy or fruit punch, frozen until almost a sherbet, and served between courses at dinner parties to refresh the appetites of the guests. They could well use refreshment, because the "business" of these plantations was food. Everything they needed was produced there: hogs for hams, bacon, fat, and soap; cattle for beef; milk for butter and cheese; chickens for eggs (and for eating); fruit trees and grapes for wine.

When potatoes are spoken of in the Deep South, sweet potatoes or yams are meant (white potatoes are "Irish potatoes.") Fields of corn yielded food for everyone, including the horses; corn was also made into meal and hominy—big hominy, little hominy, lye hominy (samp). The corn fields also yielded bourbon whiskey. Vegetables, herbs, and flowers were produced for the table, for medicines, and for perfumes.

In those days a poor relative would "board around," which meant that a cousin—or even a friend—would come to visit and stay for months, sometimes a lifetime. One more person was not a great strain on a household economy that grew its own sustenance and commonly sustained sixty to one hundred people, including the slaves. An ordinary plantation breakfast then would feed a whole family for a day now. There were often three main dishes, as well as batter cakes, biscuits, eggs, and bacon. At holiday times and big meetin' times, having a dozen weekend guests was not unusual. The dark side was that this way of life was only possible with slave labor.

The storehouse contained barrels of molasses, flour, brown sugar, white sugar; firkins of green coffee; whole cheeses; kits of mackerel; brown sedge for brooms; homemade mops of corn shucks; and stacks of dried onions, pumpkins, and gourds.

The smokehouse rafters were hung with hams, sausages, and bacon. Barrels of lard and homemade lye soap stood on the floor. The milk house, usually situated over a spring, was filled with crocks of butter and pans of cream and milk. They liked their coffee strong—two tablespoons for each cup plus two for the drip pot—and on cold mornings and after dinner they would fortify it with a jigger or so of rum.

Four weeks of cold weather were required for hog-killing time, a maximum of forty-two degrees per morning, usually in November. The entire population of the plantation was called into service to scald and scrape the white-skinned hogs, and to cut them up, to render the lard, to make the sausage and head cheese, and to clean the chitterlings. A warm spell before the four weeks were up was a disaster which brought everyone to cutting again to preserve the meat from spoilage.

Their stomachs were stronger than ours. They were used to skinning and cutting up game, and to whole calves' heads in a pot to make head cheese, beheaded chickens and turkeys—sights we never see. The process was straight from animal to pot, but they ate wonderful food.

In 1840 Antoine Alciatore opened his restaurant, adding to the already lustrous fame of New Orleans cooking. Even when garlic as a seasoning was eschewed by a good number of American cooks—an odd phenomenon, because colonial cookbooks mention it often— the art of its use was never lost in the great kitchens of New Orleans. Shallots, leeks, peppers and other seasonings and spices unheard of by most of America then, were always in a Creole kitchen.

Antoine became famous for his pompano en papillote, pommes soufflées, fresh mushrooms sous cloche, oysters à la Rockefeller (still a secret recipe), chicken creole, bisque d'écrevisse cardinale, café brûlot diabolique, and other dishes not surpassed then or now, even in the restaurants of New York or Paris.

There were other restaurants as famous.

Gallatoire's, Arnaud's, and other great hotels and bars. The St. Charles was well known for its Sazarac Bar, also its cocktail, which in the old days was made with Sazarac de Forge et Fils brandy at the Sazarac Coffee House, but is now made with bourbon. The Ramos fizz, another drink which originated in New Orleans, which most people know as the gin fizz, was invented by Henry C. Ramos.

The Gulf Coast has a generous supply of wild game, from doves, quail, and wild turkey to wild ducks that come in from Arkansas, along with pigs fattened on the nuts and berries in the woods. From the Texas Gulf come game fish, redfish, speckled trout, grouper, red snapper, pompano, mackerel, and an infinite number of other fish.

A new shellfish was added to the cornucopia of the Gulf Coast in 1951. A Cajun fisherman, caught out in the gulf one night, threw his nets over the side, expecting to catch a few while he slept. The nets filled quickly—and in them were the largest shrimp he had ever seen. The giant shrimp, running three to four to a pound, had missed discovery before because of the Cajun custom of fishing only in daylight, and the shrimps' habit of rising to feed on the surface only at night.

With such supplies at hand, inventiveness is encouraged, and so is appreciation. A Creole cook expects to be complimented. Where one hears about food, good food, and eats fine flavorful meals all the time, it is difficult to cook anything really bad. The great care taken with even simple dishes that are eaten every day adds a sheen to just living. On top of all this there are the gardens and the flowers: azaleas, roses, magnolias, calla lilies, and cape jasmine spilling over fences and walls, and on the streets in cities and towns, sending their fragrance into the air, delighting the other senses as well as the palate.

SOUPS AND CHOWDERS

FRENCH WATERCRESS SOUP

This delightful soup is easy to make, and its delicacy makes it especially suitable as a first course for a light luncheon.

    3 large potatoes, peeled and cubed
    2 cups milk, scalded
    1 teaspoon salt
    1 large bunch watercress, stems
      removed
    4 tablespoons butter
    4 tablespoons chopped parsley

Boil the potatoes in 1 quart water until soft. Mash while still in the pot with a potato masher.
Add the milk, salt, and watercress. Cook 10 minutes.
Add the butter and parsley, stir well, and serve hot in cups. (*4 servings*)

CREOLE SOUP

    3 tablespoons chopped green pepper
    3 tablespoons chopped onion
    2 tablespoons butter
    ⅓ cup flour
    1 quart beef stock
    2 cups chopped tomatoes
    1 teaspoon salt
    1 teaspoon pepper
    ¼ teaspoon cayenne
    ½ cup cooked macaroni, cut into rings
    2 tablespoons grated horseradish

Cook the pepper and onion in butter 5 minutes, then add the flour, stock, and tomatoes.
Cover and simmer 15 minutes.
Strain; add seasonings, macaroni, and horseradish. Cook 5 minutes and serve. (*4 servings*)

CREAM OF CRAB SOUP

2 tablespoons butter
1 tablespoon flour
2 quarts milk
1 medium onion, chopped
2 teaspoons chopped parsley
1 stalk celery, chopped
1 teaspoon salt
½ teaspoon pepper
3 cups cooked crab-meat flakes
   unsweetened whipped cream

Cream the butter and flour together, and put into the top portion of a double boiler with the milk. Add the vegetables and seasonings and cook slowly for 30 minutes, stirring every few minutes, until soup is well blended and thickened.

Add the crab flakes, cook 10 minutes longer, and serve hot with dabs of unsweetened whipped cream. (*4 servings*)

CRAYFISH BISQUE

This is a way-out dish from old New Orleans, popular in the days when servants were plentiful and cheap and had nothing to do but sit around all day singing and stuffing crayfish heads. If you have time on your hands—and patience—and if you can get hold of four dozen fresh crayfish, this could be fun. By the way, the lake crayfish are the largest, and therefore have the largest heads.

4 dozen fresh crayfish, soaked in salt
   water and well scrubbed
2 quarts hot water
4 slices of bread, crusts removed, wet
   and squeezed dry to make 1 cup
1 tablespoon butter
1 tablespoon flour
1 onion, finely chopped
1 teaspoon chopped parsley
   pepper
   salt
1 egg
   flour
   butter

Sauce:

3 tablespoons flour
2 tablespoons butter
1 carrot, chopped
½ cup chopped celery
1 teaspoon chopped parsley
   salt
   pepper

Boil the crayfish in 2 quarts water for 30 minutes, until bright red; cool in own water. Pour off the broth and set aside for the sauce. Pick the crayfish, clean the heads, and save them and the meat from the bodies.

Soak the bread in water and squeeze it dry. Chop the crayfish meat fine and add it to the bread.

Melt the butter, blend in the flour, add the onion, parsley, salt, and pepper. Cook gently a minute or two, then add the crayfish and bread. Cook a minute or two longer and transfer to a bowl.

Add egg, mix well, and stuff into the crayfish heads.

Sprinkle the heads lightly with flour, fry a few minutes in butter, and serve with sauce made by adding a browned roux of butter and flour to the crayfish broth seasoned with carrot, celery, parsley, salt, and pepper. (*6 servings*)

OYSTER GUMBO FILÉ

This is a very old recipe for a favorite New Orleans soup. Rich and savory, if served with rice it suffices well as a one-dish meal. Shrimp are often used in this dish in place of oysters, and are equally delicious.

1 tablespoon lard
2 tablespoons flour
1 onion, chopped
1 spring onion top, chopped
½ teaspoon thyme
1 bay leaf
1 teaspoon salt
½ teaspoon pepper
   few dashes Tabasco
2 quarts hot water
3 dozen oysters with their liquor
2 teaspoons chopped parsley
1 tablespoon filé

Using a large pot or saucepan, heat the lard and brown the flour.

Add the vegetables and seasonings and simmer 5 minutes. Pour in the hot water and oyster liquor and simmer over moderate heat for 20 minutes.

Add the oysters and parsley. Cook 10 minutes longer or until oysters crinkle.

Remove from heat, drop in the filé, and stir vigorously.

Serve with rice. (*6 servings*)

ONION SOUP NEW ORLEANS

Though onion soup comes from France, the onion soup of Louisiana is sufficiently different to show how changes are wrought by a change of venue and the passage of time.

  6 large onions, peeled
  2 tablespoons butter
  5 tablespoons olive oil
  7 cups boiling water
1½ teaspoons salt
  ¼ teaspoon pepper
  ¼ teaspoon cayenne
  6 slices thin French bread, toasted
  1 cup Parmesan cheese, grated
  6 thin slices Swiss cheese

Brown the whole onions in butter. Remove, hold with a two-pronged fork, and slice thin. Heat olive oil in a 4-quart pot. Add the sliced onions and brown slowly. Cook, stirring constantly, until they are as dark as possible without being burned.

Add the boiling water, salt, pepper, and cayenne. Boil 20 minutes.

Put the toast in soup plates, and put a heaping tablespoon of Parmesan cheese on to each; top with Swiss cheese. Spoon the soup evenly into the soup plates. (*6 servings*)

PARSLEY SOUP

Soup made from parsley and hard-cooked eggs? An unusual idea—an unusual dish, one to talk about and to enjoy.

  5 hard-cooked eggs
  2 cups cold water
  1 tablespoon lard
  8 tablespoons chopped parsley
  6 cups hot water
  1 teaspoon salt
  ½ teaspoon pepper
  1 clove garlic, crushed
  1 cup croutons (bread cubes fried in butter)

Remove the yolks from the eggs, break them up, mash into the cold water, and pass through a colander sieve.

Heat the lard and cook the parsley in it for a few minutes, then add the egg-yolk-and-water mixture and remaining ingredients except for the croutons. Cook for 10 minutes.

Chop the egg whites, add them to the soup, and serve with croutons. (*4 to 6 servings*)

SHRIMP BISQUE

  4 tablespoons butter
  1 stalk celery, chopped
  2 large mushrooms, chopped
  ½ onion, chopped
  ½ carrot, chopped
    pinch marjoram
    few grains mace
  ½ teaspoon freshly ground pepper
  ½ teaspoon salt
  1 cup chicken broth
  1 cup cooked shrimp, finely chopped
  1 cup heavy cream
  2 teaspoons dry sherry

Put the butter, celery, mushrooms, onion, carrot, and seasonings into a large pot and sauté slowly for 10 minutes.

Add the chicken broth and cook 5 minutes longer. Put through a sieve.

Add the chopped shrimp, simmer 1 minute or so, check the seasoning, and stir in the cream and sherry.

Heat through and serve at once. (*4 servings*)

PASTA, EGG,
AND CHEESE DISHES

EGGS MORNAY

Here is a really elegant luncheon dish, served at fine restaurants and good enough to serve at parties.

        3 tablespoons butter
        3 tablespoons flour
    1½ cups half-and-half
        salt
        pepper
        nutmeg
     ½ cup grated Swiss cheese
     ½ cup grated Parmesan cheese
        8 hard-cooked eggs, halved

Preheat oven to 450 degrees.
Melt the butter over low heat, blend in the flour and then the half-and-half, season to taste, and cook until thickened. Add the cheese. Stir-cook until cheese has melted and the mixture is well blended.
Meanwhile place the eggs cut side down in a buttered shallow baking dish. Pour the sauce over the eggs, and bake about 10 minutes or until browned. (*4 servings*)

EGGS AU BEURRE NOIR

From France via New Orleans, a different way to serve your breakfast eggs. The rich piquancy of the dish also makes it an ideal one to serve as a light lunch.

        4 eggs
     ½ cup dry white wine mixed with ½ cup water
        2 tablespoons vinegar
        2 tablespoons butter
        2 teaspoons minced parsley
     ½ teaspoon salt

Poach the eggs one at a time in the water to which the wine has been added.
Remove eggs, place into 2 heated shirring dishes, and keep warm in a 200-degree oven. Boil the vinegar down to ½ quantity and pour over eggs.
Simmer butter a few minutes in same pan, add parsley and salt. Continue cooking until browned. Pour over eggs and serve at once. (*2 servings*)

OMELET FINES HERBES

This is the classic omelet, Louisiana style, with herbs of your choice added. Do not make with more than 4 eggs; make several 4-egg omelets instead.

        4 eggs, beaten very slightly
        4 tablespoons water
     ½ teaspoon salt
     ⅛ teaspoon pepper
        mixture of ½ teaspoon each of minced parsley and/or minced chives and/or minced watercress and/or ½ teaspoon thyme and/or 1 teaspoon minced fresh tarragon or chervil. Herbs can be used in combination, and increased or decreased
        2 tablespoons butter

Mix together the eggs, water, salt, pepper, and herbs.
Melt the butter in an omelet pan over high heat. When it begins to sizzle, reduce the heat slightly and add the egg mixture.
As the omelet cooks, lift edges, allowing uncooked parts to run under until the entire omelet is creamy.
Fold double and turn onto a heated platter. (*2 servings*)

EGGS BENEDICTINE

Not to be confused with the popular eggs Benedick, this relatively little-known dish had its roots in France.

    4 eggs
    4 tablespoons cream
    4 thin slices cooked ham
    4 slices tomato

Preheat oven to 350 degrees.
Place a tablespoon of cream, a slice of ham, and a slice of tomato into each of 4 shirring dishes. Break an egg into each, and bake in the oven 15 minutes or until set.

Meanwhile make the sauce:

    1 tablespoon butter
    1 tablespoon flour
    ½ teaspoon salt
    ⅛ teaspoon pepper
    1 cup milk
    ½ cup grated American cheese
    2 egg yolks, well beaten
    ½ cup sherry

Melt the butter and stir in the flour and seasonings. Stir in the milk gradually, and cook until the sauce thickens. Then add the cheese and cook a few minutes longer, until cheese melts.

Remove from the heat, stir in the egg yolks and sherry. Pour the sauce over the baked eggs and serve at once. (*4 servings*)

PUFFY OMELET

    4 egg yolks, beaten until thick and
        lemon-colored
    4 tablespoons hot water
    ½ teaspoon salt
    ¼ teaspoon pepper
    4 egg whites, beaten until stiff
    2 tablespoons butter

Preheat oven to 375 degrees.
Mix together the beaten egg yolks, hot water, and seasonings.
Fold in the stiff egg whites until well blended. Heat an omelet pan and butter the sides and bottom thoroughly. Pour in the egg mixture and cook very slowly, until light brown on the bottom and puffy on top.
Place the pan in the oven to finish cooking the top. Test by touching the top lightly with a finger. If the egg does not stick it is done. Do not overcook or dry out.
Fold double, turn onto a heated platter, and serve hot. (*2 servings*)

FISH AND SHELLFISH

SHRIMP PATTIES

    2 cups cooked, shelled shrimp,
        deveined
    4 slices not-too-fresh bread, crusts
        removed
    ¼ cup melted butter containing:
        ½ teaspoon mace
        ½ teaspoon pepper
        ½ teaspoon salt
    2 cups cream sauce

Preheat oven to 275 degrees.
Pound the shrimp in a mortar, run them through a meat grinder, or put them into a blender.
Soak the bread slices in water, squeeze dry, and crumble into the shrimp. Mix in the savory butter and shape into small cakes.
Place in a buttered pan, and bake for 15 minutes or until brown.
Serve with cream sauce. (*4 servings*)

SHRIMP CREOLE WITH RICE

1 medium onion, thinly sliced
1 green pepper, chopped
1 cup boiling water
5 large mushrooms, sliced
2 tablespoons butter
2 cups chopped tomatoes
3 tablespoons chopped ham
1 cup tomato juice
1 teaspoon Tabasco sauce
½ teaspoon salt
⅛ teaspoon pepper
1 pound fresh gulf shrimp, cooked, peeled, and deveined
4 cups cooked rice

Cook onion and green pepper in 1 cup boiling water until tender.
Sauté mushrooms in butter. Add tomatoes.
Combine the onion, green pepper, and water with the mushrooms and tomatoes. Add the ham, tomato juice, and seasonings. Add shrimp.
Cook together for a few minutes and serve over hot rice. (*6 servings*)

SHRIMP MARINIÈRE

The Gulf of Mexico might possibly be the shrimp capital of the world. Certainly the giant shrimp that inhabit the depths of the gulf and rise to the surface only at night must be the largest.
Here is an elegant way to serve this popular shellfish.

1½ pounds raw shrimp, shelled and deveined
2 shallots, minced (or ½ cup minced spring onion)
2 cups dry white wine
1 cup oyster liquor, fish stock, or clam broth, strained through cheese cloth
2 tablespoons butter
2 tablespoons flour
1 teaspoon salt
1 tablespoon lemon juice
2 egg yolks, beaten with ½ cup heavy cream
1 tablespoon minced parsley
toast

Simmer the shrimp and shallots in the wine and oyster liquor 15 minutes, using a medium skillet.
Melt butter in a small skillet, stir in flour, salt, and a cup of the shrimp liquid. (If clam broth is used, omit salt.) Cook-stir until mixture thickens.
Add the sauce to the shrimp, and cook over low heat 10 minutes. Add the lemon juice, then the egg-cream mixture, stirring constantly. Do not boil after eggs and cream have been added. Serve on toast, garnished with parsley. (*4 to 6 servings*)

SHRIMP RÉMOULADE

1 teaspoon mace
1 teaspoon thyme
1 bay leaf
1 red pepper pod, seeds removed
6 cloves
1 tablespoon chopped celery leaves
3 quarts boiling water
2 pounds fresh shrimp

Put all spices in boiling water. Cook 10 minutes. Add shrimp, cook 10 minutes more, cool in the water.
When cool, peel and devein shrimp. (If frozen shrimp are used, drop them into boiling water, turn off heat, let cool in water.)

Sauce:

1 bunch watercress, chopped
3 tablespoons parsley, chopped
1 clove garlic, finely chopped
1 medium onion, finely chopped
1 teaspoon dry mustard
½ teaspoon salt
¼ teaspoon pepper
⅓ cup olive oil
2 tablespoons vinegar

Put chopped watercress, parsley, garlic, and onion into a salad bowl. Add mustard, salt, pepper, olive oil, and viengar. Stir well. Add shrimp, toss shrimp in dressing, cover, and refrigerate until ready to serve. (*4 to 6 servings*)

SHRIMP GUMBO

1 slice salt pork, cubed (about 1 ounce)
1 clove garlic, minced
½ cup chopped scallions
4 tablespoons flour
4 cups water
1 bay leaf
  pinch thyme
1 teaspoon salt
½ teaspoon freshly ground pepper
2 cups chopped and drained, fresh or
  canned tomatoes
1 cup cubed cooked ham
½ pound fresh okra or ½ package (10
  ounces) frozen okra
2 pounds medium raw shrimp, peeled
  and split lengthwise
1 cup cooked rice.

Sauté the pork in a large heavy skillet until crisp. Remove and set aside.

To the pork drippings add the garlic and scallions. Sauté until tender. Sprinkle in the flour, stirring. Then gradually pour in water, stirring until smooth.

Add the bay leaf, thyme, salt, pepper, tomatoes, and ham. Cover the skillet, and simmer 15 minutes over low heat.

Add the okra, cook 20 minutes longer, add the shrimp, and cook 10 minutes more or until shrimp are tender.

Serve in soup bowls with a bit of rice in each. Top with crisp salt-pork bits. (*6 servings*)

RED SNAPPER CREOLE

The Gulf of Mexico and other southern waters abound with red snapper, a delectable fish running two pounds or more. It is the favorite New Orleans fish, served simply oven-broiled. But the Creoles can't seem to resist dressing it up with their own special piquant sauce.

1 red snapper, about 2 or 3 pounds,
  dressed
5 tablespoons olive oil
1 teaspoon salt
½ teaspoon pepper
2 cups chopped fresh or canned
  tomatoes
1 clove garlic, crushed
3 sprigs parsley, chopped
  pinch cayenne
2 teaspoons lemon juice

Preheat oven to 325 degrees.

Rub the fish well with 1 tablespoon olive oil, salt, and pepper, and gash across the side in 2 or 3 places.

Place fish into a baking pan and bake for 30 minutes or until done.

Meanwhile place the remaining ingredients into a heavy skillet with 4 tablespoons olive oil and cook, stirring, for 10 minutes.

Transfer the fish to a heated platter and serve topped with the creole sauce. (*4 servings*)

BOUILLABAISSE LOUISIANNE

Bouillabaisse originated in Marseilles and, according to the Marseillaises, cannot be duplicated anywhere else in the world due to the presence in it of certain fish indigenous only to local waters. This, however, does not prevent other cities from producing their own *memorable* brand of "bouillabaisse"—and New Orleans is no exception. Following is a very old recipe for a dish justly famous.

3 tablespoons finely chopped parsley
3 cloves garlic, finely chopped
  pinch thyme
1 teaspoon salt
½ teaspoon pepper
  pinch cayenne
3 pounds red snapper or redfish or
  both, split, boned, dressed, and sliced
2 onions, chopped
1 cup olive oil
6 fresh tomatoes, peeled and sliced
2 cups hot water
1 bay leaf
½ lemon, sliced
  pinch Spanish saffron

Mix together the parsley, garlic, thyme, salt, pepper, and cayenne. Rub into the fish and set aside for 15 minutes in a covered dish.

Meanwhile heat the oil in a large heavy skillet, and sauté the onion for 5 minutes or until golden. Now add the fish slices and cook for 10 minutes, turning from time to time.

Remove the fish slices and set aside, adding the tomatoes to the skillet. Add also the water, bay leaf, and lemon slices.

Bring to a boil, cover, and cook for 10 minutes, then return the fish slices.

Remove a little of the sauce, mix in the saffron, and stir into the skillet.

Serve on toast. (*4 to 6 servings*)

POMPANO EN PAPILLOTE

Here is a famous dish attributed to Antoine's in New Orleans. It is said to have been created in honor of a now-forgotten but then-famous Brazilian balloonist who was visiting New Orleans. Because of the inflated appearance of the cooked papillote, it was originally named Pompano Montgolfier, after the inventor of the balloon. The dish was a favorite of Franklin D. Roosevelt.

We watched the late Michael Field demonstrate the preparation of pompano fillets en papillote a few years before his death. His dexterity made the dish seem simple to prepare.

> 4 pompano fillets, about 7 inches long
> ½ cup chicken stock, with fat removed
> ¼ cup dry white wine
> 1 teaspoon salt
> 2 tablespoons butter
> 2 tablespoons finely chopped shallots (or scallions)
> 3 tablespoons flour
> 2 tablespoons cream
> ½ teaspoon lemon juice
> ½ teaspoon salt
> ⅛ teaspoon cayenne
> 1 cup coarsely chopped cooked shrimp
> 1 cup coarsely diced crab meat (fresh or canned)
> parchment cooking paper

Fold the fillets end to end, to prevent breaking, and poach them for about 6 minutes in the chicken stock and wine. Remove, carefully unfold, and season with salt. Reserve.

Strain the poaching liquid into a saucepan and reduce over high heat to 1 cup. Reserve.

In another saucepan, cook the shallots in butter for 2 or 3 minutes, stir in the flour, cook for a moment or two, add the reduced poaching liquid, and continue cooking until smooth and thick. Add the cream, lemon juice, salt, and cayenne. Taste for seasonings.

Preheat oven to 450 degrees.

Cut 4 sheets of parchment cooking paper into 12-by-14-inch heart shapes, fold lengthwise, then open again.

Lay a fillet on the right half of each papillote, spoon on equal amounts of shrimp and crab meat on the lower half of each, moisten with a tablespoon of the sauce, and fold the top half of the fillet over it, enclosing the stuffing. Spoon the remaining sauce over each fillet.

Fold the left half of the parchment over, and seal by crimping and rolling the edges together.

Place the papillotes on a lightly greased cookie sheet and bake for about 8 minutes.

Serve in the puffed, browned parchment hearts. (*4 servings*)

LOUISIANA COURT BOUILLON

This elegant Creole dish is not to be confused with the fish broth so heavily depended on in French cooking. It is a rich seafood stew, often made in New Orleans of red snapper. Make it using whatever fish you might have in your area, and you will find it delicious.

> ½ cup flour
> ¼ cup olive oil
> ½ cup butter
> 4 medium onions, chopped
> 2 cloves garlic, chopped
> 2 tablespoons tomato paste
> 3 pimentos, seeded and chopped
> 2 cups boiling water
> 2 cups dry white wine (or dry red wine)
> 2 teaspoons salt
> ½ teaspoon pepper
> pinch cayenne
> pinch thyme
> 1½ pounds red snapper or redfish fillets
> 4 sprigs parsley, chopped

Make a thick roux of the flour and oil in a large, heavy skillet. Add the butter, onions, garlic, tomato paste, and pimentos. Blend well. Slowly add the boiling water, stirring to make a smooth mixture.

Stir in the wine, and add the seasonings.

Simmer gently for 30 minutes, then add the fish fillets, and cook 15 minutes longer or until fish flakes when fork-tested. Do not overcook.

Serve in bowls, garnished with chopped parsley. (*4 servings*)

FRIED FROGS' LEGS

When the French came to Louisiana they found a bonanza of frogs in the bayou country; frogs' legs were a favorite food back home in France. These days, frogs are cultivated on frog farms to satisfy the demand for the delicate, succulent meat of the legs.

    12 pairs large frogs' legs, skinned and
        well washed
        salt
        flour
     2 eggs, lightly beaten
        dry bread crumbs
     2 cups olive oil
     3 cloves garlic, crushed
    ½ cup minced parsley

Salt the frogs' legs, dredge them with flour, dip them into beaten eggs and then into bread crumbs.
Heat the oil to the smoking point in a heavy skillet, add the garlic, and fry the frogs' legs a few at a time until golden. Drain on paper napkins, keep warm.
Serve garnished with parsley. (*4 servings*)

OYSTERS EN BROCHETTE

An indescribably succulent dish made famous by Antoine Alciatore at the time of the War Between the States.

     6 slices bacon, cut into quarters,
        partially cooked
    24 large raw oysters
        flour
        salt
        pepper
    ½ cup butter
    ¼ cup olive oil
     1 teaspoon minced parsley
     1 lemon, quartered

On each of 4 skewers, string 6 pieces bacon alternately with 6 oysters (skewering through the eye of the oyster).
Roll in flour seasoned with salt and pepper.
Heat the butter and oil and sauté the skewered oysters, turning to cook on all sides.
Serve garnished with parsley, with a wedge of lemon. (*4 servings*)

OYSTERS ROCKEFELLER

This dish, "rich as Rockefeller," was developed in a New Orleans restaurant—most likely at Antoine's. The recipe, we have found, differs sometimes significantly, sometimes subtly, from restaurant to restaurant and from region to region.

     1 cup melted butter
    ¼ cup minced shallots (or scallions)
    ¼ cup minced parsley
    ½ cup minced fresh watercress or
        spinach
    ½ clove garlic, minced
    ½ teaspoon dried tarragon
    ¼ cup bread crumbs
        few drops Worcestershire sauce
        few drops Tabasco sauce
    ½ teaspoon salt
        few drops Pernod
     2 dozen oysters on the half shell
    ½ cup crumbled cooked bacon

Preheat oven to 450 degrees.
Mix all the ingredients, except the oysters and bacon, together in a blender, or grind them in a mortar.
Line 4 shallow pie pans with damp rock salt (to hold the heat) and arrange the half-shell oysters on them. Place a dab of the mixture just made on each oyster and sprinkle with bacon bits.
Bake in the oven about 5 minutes, or until sauce bubbles. (*4 servings as a main dish, 8 as an appetizer*)

MEATS

JAMBALAYA

This Creole dish can be found in one form or another throughout the Mississippi delta area. Essentially it is a rice-tomato-base stew with almost anything added—whatever the country yields.

Most often a heavy iron pot is used to make jambalaya. Chopped onions are browned lightly in lard, and the mixture is thickened with flour. Chopped tomatoes are added, and from then on anything goes—chopped ham, salt pork, chicken, shrimp, oysters, quartered crabs, and so forth; and seasonings—salt, pepper, garlic, chili powder, cayenne. The preparation ends with the addition of boiling water or oyster liquor and rice. The pot is tightly covered and the jambalaya is slow-cooked without stirring until done (the rice absorbs the water).

Jambalaya is an ideal dish for church socials, picnics, or other large gatherings.

GUMBO SUPRÊME

Filé is a powder made from the tender young leaves of sassafras used as a flavoring and thickener. Choctaw Indian squaws used to bring filé into the French market in New Orleans to sell. Today it can be found in gourmet spice shops. The recipe below is a delicate mixture of shrimp, oysters, crab meat, chicken, and filé—hence it is surely the ultimate gumbo.

    1 tablespoon butter
    1 tablespoon flour
    1 medium onion, chopped
    1 teaspoon minced parsley
    1 quart oyster liquor
    1 pint boiling water
      salt
      pepper
    1 bay leaf
    1 cup cooked shelled shrimp
    1 cup crab meat
    1 dozen shucked oysters
    1 cooked chicken breast, diced
    1 tablespoon filé powder
      freshly boiled rice

Simmer flour in butter until golden; add onion and simmer until lightly browned. Add parsley, oyster liquor gradually, boiling water, seasonings, and the bay leaf. Stir constantly until smooth and boiling.

Add seafood and chicken, and stir gently. Cook only until oysters begin to crinkle. Remove from heat.

Carefully sift or sprinkle in filé, stirring gently to prevent filé from lumping. Do not reheat once filé is added.

Put in tureen. Serve at once in soup bowls, passing boiled rice at the table. (*6 to 8 servings*)

SWEETBREADS À LA REINE

The Creoles call these milk glands of the calf *ris de veau*, the same word as "laugh" in French. It is an apt name for this light delicacy. Scarce and expensive they are, because calves have to be still nursing to have them; and when properly cooked a delectable dish. Real sweetbreads should be a delicate cream color when cooked.

    2 pairs veal sweetbreads
    2 tablespoons butter
    2 tablespoons flour
    1 cup light cream
    1 teaspoon salt
      pinch cayenne
    1 cup cracker crumbs
    1 egg, lightly beaten
      minced parsley

Simmer the sweetbreads 20 minutes in hot water with a little salt and vinegar added. Drain. Cover with cold water and let stand until chilled. Drain again, slip off the thin membrane, and cut out the dark tubes.

Over low heat melt the butter, stir in flour, then add the cream slowly. Stir until thickened. Season, and set sauce aside.

Dip the sweetbreads into cracker crumbs, then egg, and again in cracker crumbs. Fry in hot fat.

Serve with the sauce, garnish with parsley. (*4 servings*)

TRIPE PIQUANTE

Tripe is rarely cooked in America except in soups. In the Gulf Coast cities there are many ways to cook it, and it can be bought already cooked in special markets.

1 pound honeycomb tripe, cut into 4-inch pieces
2 tablespoons butter
2 tablespoons chopped onion
1 clove garlic, minced
1 tablespoon chopped parsley
  pinch thyme
1 bay leaf
1 tablespoon flour
1 cup hot water
1 teaspoon lemon juice or vinegar

Simmer the tripe in water to cover over low heat about 4 hours. Remove from heat and set aside.
Sauté the onion and garlic in the butter for a minute or so; stir in the parsley, thyme, and bay leaf.
Stir in the flour and cook 1 minute, then add 1 cup water. Stir.
Add the tripe and lemon juice. Stir, cover, and simmer 1 hour.
Serve with French bread. (*4 servings*)

CREOLE PILAF

1½ cups diced cooked lamb or veal
1 cup rice
1½ cups cooked tomatoes
1 cup chicken broth
1 large onion, chopped
½ green pepper, chopped
2 stalks celery, chopped
1 teaspoon salt
  pinch cayenne
  buttered bread crumbs

Preheat oven to 350 degrees.
Mix together the meat, rice, tomatoes, and broth. Cook 10 minutes.
Add the chopped vegetables and seasonings, turn into a casserole, and cover with bread crumbs.
Bake 1 hour or until golden brown, and serve from the casserole. (*4 servings*)

FLANK STEAK DELUXE

1 medium onion, chopped
2 tablespoons butter
1 medium flank steak, sliced on the bias into ½-inch strips
  flour
1 teaspoon dry mustard
1 tablespoon vinegar
1 teaspoon salt
1 teaspoon paprika
  few grains cayenne
2 cups water

Sauté the onion in the butter, using a heavy skillet.
Dredge the steak slices with flour, fry them quickly in the same skillet, remove, and set aside.
Add to the same skillet 1 tablespoon flour, the mustard, vinegar, salt, paprika, and cayenne. Stir, add the water, stir again.
Add the meat slices to the sauce, cover, and simmer about 15 minutes. (*4 to 6 servings*)

STEAK À L'OIGNON BELLE ALLIANCE

An unusual steak recipe—very different, and very good.

2½ pounds steak, 1½ inches thick (porterhouse, club, or Delmonico)
3 tablespoons butter
4 tablespoons flour
2 cups water
6 onions, sliced
2 shallots, chopped
1 teaspoon salt
1½ teaspoons freshly ground pepper
  chopped parsley

Trim excess fat from steak, score edges, and pan-broil on both sides in a heavy skillet to desired doneness. Remove to a heated platter and keep hot.
In the same skillet melt the butter, stir in the flour to make a thick roux, and gradually add water, continuing to stir.
Add the onions, shallots, and seasonings. Stir and simmer until onions are soft.
Pour the sauce over the steak, garnish with parsley, and serve. (*4 servings*)

KIDNEY À LA FRANÇAISE

    2 beef kidneys
    4 tablespoons flour plus flour for
      dredging
    4 tablespoons fat
    2 cups boiling water
    1 bay leaf
    1 teaspoon salt
    ½ teaspoon pepper
    1 slice lemon

Soak the kidneys in water for 1 hour, changing water 2 or 3 times.

Cover with fresh water, heat slowly to boiling. Drain. Repeat this procedure twice, remove from heat, cool, then cut out the cords and center fat.

Cut into thin slices, dredge with flour, and sauté in hot fat until brown, using a heavy skillet. Remove and reserve.

Add 4 tablespoons flour to fat, stir well, and cook until brown. Add the boiling water, stirring until sauce is smooth. Add the bay leaf, seasonings, and lemon. Return the kidneys and simmer over low heat 1 hour, adding water if necessary. Remove bay leaf and serve on rice. (*4 servings*)

BLANQUETTE OF LAMB

Most lamb stews and fricassees develop from browned meat. This recipe—like that of blanquette de veau—breaks the rule, and the dish emerges a rich cream color.

    4 pounds stewing lamb, excess fat
      removed
    2 stalks celery, chopped
    1 clove garlic, chopped
    8 shallots, chopped
    1 large bay leaf
    4 sprigs parsley, chopped
      pinch thyme
   12 peppercorns
    2 teaspoons salt
    3 tablespoons butter
    3 tablespoons flour
    4 carrots, julienned

Put the first nine ingredients into a large pot, add enough water to cover, bring to a boil, cover, and simmer 2 ½ hours.

Remove from heat, take out meat and set aside, strain the broth, cool, and skim off all fat.

In a small pan melt the butter, stir in the flour, cook for 2 minutes, and add to the broth.

Parboil the carrots 10 minutes and add to the broth.

Add the meat to the broth, and heat 10 minutes.

Serve with new potatoes. (*4 servings*)

BURGUNDIAN BEEF

    ¼ pound salt pork, diced
    2 pounds lean top or bottom round of
      beef, cut into cubes
    1 large onion, chopped
    1 clove garlic, minced
    2 shallots, minced
    ½ carrot, sliced
    1 tablespoon minced parsley
    6 peppercorns
    1 bay leaf
    1 tablespoon fresh minced tarragon
      pinch thyme
    1 teaspoon salt
    1 cup dry red wine

Sauté the salt pork in a heavy skillet until crisp. Remove from skillet and reserve.

Put the beef cubes into the skillet and brown on all sides in the pork fat. Remove from skillet and reserve.

Put the onion, garlic, shallots, and carrot into the skillet and cook until onion is light yellow. Return the beef cubes to the skillet, and add the seasonings and wine. Cover; cook over very low heat 3 hours or in 300 degree oven, adding more wine if necessary.

Add the crisp pork bits, and serve with creole corn pudding, or on rice or hominy. (*4 to 6 servings*)

POULTRY
AND GAME BIRDS

CANVASBACK DUCK WITH DELTA DRESSING

Here is a delightful way to prepare the delicious canvasback ducks that settle in the delta country to feed upon the wild celery. Traditionally these most-prized ducks are served rare, but there are those who prefer them cooked through.

    2 tablespoons butter
    1 onion, chopped
    ½ cup chopped celery
    1 teaspoon salt
    ½ teaspoon paprika
      few grains cayenne
   12 slices toast, crumbled
    1 dozen shucked oysters
    1 cup chopped pecan meats, lightly
      toasted
    2 canvasback ducks, dressed, cleaned
      inside and out with a wet cloth (see
      p. 60)

Preheat oven to 450 degrees.
Melt the butter and sauté the onions, celery, and seasonings 5 minutes, stirring. Add the toast, oysters, and pecans, and cook-stir for 5 minutes longer.
Stuff the ducks with this dressing, skewer, and tie legs together.
Place on a greased oven rack and cook about 20 to 30 minutes for rare duck, longer if desired. It is done when the blood does not run when the duck is pierced with a fork. Duck is traditionally served rare; if, however, you want it well done, lower oven heat to 300 degrees and cook 2 hours longer.
Serve with wild rice. (*4 servings*)

POULET AU DIABLE (DEVILED CHICKEN)

This old New Orleans dish was originally made by parboiling a fowl and pouring the sauce over it. This can still be done, but with today's tender chickens the recipe can be made more easily as follows.

    1 broiler or fryer, cut into serving
      portions
    1 teaspoon salt
    1 teaspoon pepper
    ½ cup lard or cooking oil
    2 tablespoons flour
    1 cup chicken broth
  1½ teaspoons dry mustard
    2 teaspoons Worcestershire sauce
    2 teaspoons ketchup
    1 teaspoon paprika
    1 cup dry white wine
    2 cups mashed potatoes

Preheat oven to 400 degrees.
Season the chicken parts with salt and pepper, and brown on all sides in melted lard, using a heavy skillet. Remove and set aside.
Stir the flour into the fat, add the broth, and cook until thickened. Stir in the mustard, Worcestershire, ketchup, and paprika.
Return the chicken to the skillet, cover, and simmer about 30 minutes or until tender.
Transfer to a casserole, add the wine, pipe mashed potatoes around edges and across the top, and brown in the oven 10 minutes longer.
(*4 servings*)

NEW ORLEANS GUMBO FILÉ

This is a typical New Orleans gumbo. You can make it with shrimp as well as with chicken.

>   2 tablespoons lard
>   2 medium onions, chopped
>   2 chickens, cut into serving pieces
>   2 pounds fresh or frozen okra, cut into
>   thin slices (or canned okra)
>   2 cloves garlic, crushed
>   1 cup tomatoes, canned or fresh
>   1 sprig fresh thyme
>   2 quarts water
>   2 teaspoons salt
>   2 tablespoons filé
>   cooked rice

Melt the lard in a large heavy skillet, add the onions, and cook until golden. Push aside onions and brown chicken.

Add the okra, garlic, tomatoes, and thyme, and cook over low heat for 10 minutes, stirring from time to time.

Add the water very gradually and sprinkle with salt. Cover and simmer 1 hour longer. Remove from heat.

Sprinkle with filé, stir well. Do not heat after adding filé or it will curdle.

Serve in soup plates with a spoonful of cooked rice in each. (*6 servings*)

CHICKEN FRITTERS

>   2 eggs, separated
>   1 cup flour
>   1 tablespoon melted butter
>   ½ teaspoon salt
>   1 cup water
>   2 whole chicken breasts (4 halves),
>   boned
>   lard for frying

Beat the yolks of eggs until lemon-colored. Add the flour, and beat together. Add the melted butter and salt. Add the water and beat well.

Beat whites of eggs until stiff, and add to the batter.

Cut each half chicken breast into 2 or 3 pieces depending on size.

Heat lard to 370 degrees.

Dip each piece of chicken in fritter batter and then drop in boiling lard. Cook until golden brown. Drain on brown paper or paper towels. Keep hot until all are done.

Serve on napkin-covered dish, garnished with lemon slices and parsley. Fish fillets can be cooked the same way. (*4 servings*)

QUAIL IN WINE

>   ½ cup fat
>   2 small onions, chopped
>   2 whole cloves
>   8 peppercorns
>   1 clove garlic, minced
>   ½ bay leaf
>   4 quail, cleaned and trussed
>   1½ cups dry white wine
>   ½ teaspoon salt
>   ¼ teaspoon pepper
>   few grains cayenne
>   1 teaspoon minced chives
>   2 cups heavy cream

Using a heavy skillet, melt the fat; stir in the onions, cloves, peppercorns, garlic, and bay leaf.

Add the quail and brown on all sides.

Add the wine, seasonings and chives, cover, and simmer slowly about 30 minutes or until birds are tender.

Remove quail to a heated platter. Strain the sauce, stir in the cream, heat almost to the boiling point, and pour over the quail. Serve with rice (wild rice if available). (*4 servings*)

ROAST SQUAB PILAF

>   6 slices bacon, diced
>   1 cup chopped celery
>   1 onion, chopped
>   2 cups raw rice
>   4 cups chicken broth
>   4 eggs, beaten
>   1 teaspoon salt
>   pinch cayenne
>   4 squabs, dressed
>   mustard-pickle juice

Fry the bacon until crisp, remove, and set aside.

Brown celery and onion in the bacon drippings.

Boil the rice in the broth until tender. Add the bacon, celery, onion, and beaten eggs. Season and mix well.

Preheat oven to 400 degrees.

Stuff the squabs with the rice mixture, and place on mounds of remaining rice. Bake in the oven for 25 minutes, basting with pickle juice. A side dish of candied yams will complement the squabs perfectly. (*4 servings*)

CREOLE CHICKEN PIE

- 6 tablespoons flour
- 1 young chicken (3 to 4 pounds) disjointed, breast halved
- 6 tablespoons bacon fat
- 1½ cups water or broth
- 2 tablespoons flour

Pastry:

- 3 cups flour
- 1 teaspoon baking powder
- 1 teaspoon salt
- ¾ cup lard or shortening
- ½ cup sour cream

Flour the chicken parts, and sauté in bacon fat 20 minutes or until brown. Add water or broth, cover the pan, and simmer over low heat about 30 minutes or until tender.

Make sour cream pastry dough (see recipe for Southern Chicken Pie*). Cut 2 round crusts, and line bottom of a 3-quart baking dish with one. Cut remaining pastry into 1-inch strips. Lay chicken parts onto the crust and put strips of the dough on top of the chicken.

Preheat oven to 375 degrees.

Mix 2 tablespoons flour into the pan gravy, add broth or water, and stir over low heat until thickened. Pour over the chicken, cover with second round crust, crimp around the edges, slit top twice, and bake about 30 minutes or until brown. (*6 servings*)

VEGETABLES
AND SIDE DISHES

POTATOES SOUFFLÉES

The famous puffed potatoes, *pommes soufflées*, originated in Paris. The secret was passed on to Antoine Alciatore, who brought it to this country in 1840 when he opened his famous restaurant in New Orleans. The authentic recipe from Antoine's restaurant follows.

Peel the potatoes and cut into ⅛-inch-lengthwise slices, place in a wire basket, and run cold water over to remove extra starch. Dry thoroughly.

Have 2 frying kettles of fat ready—one at moderate (370 degrees) temperature, the other very hot (390 degrees). Place several slices into frying basket in moderately hot fat and cook until they rise to the surface and the edges show faint signs of puffing. (If the puff does not develop, check temperatures and start over with another slice). If the faint puffing appears, then immediately transfer potatoes in basket to the very hot kettle of fat; cook until fully puffed and browned. Drain on absorbent paper, sprinkle with salt, serve immediately. If desired, the potatoes may be set aside after the second cooking and given a final dip in the very hot fat, then rushed to the table. If this is to be done, do not fully brown the potatoes in the second fat pot. Finish them in the third cooking.

MUSHROOMS UNDER GLASS

This was a very glamorous dish at Antoine's during the late 1800s. The mushrooms were baked under glass to preserve their delicate flavor and aroma until the moment they were served.

The dish is rarely encountered today, but glass bells are still available in hotel-supply or gourmet shops.

    ½ cup butter
    1 tablespoon minced parsley
    1 tablespoon minced shallots
    1 teaspoon dried tarragon
    1 tablespoon butter
    4 slices dry toast, cut into rounds
  16 large mushroom caps
     salt
     freshly ground black pepper
    ½ cup heavy cream

Cream the butter and seasonings with the back of a spoon until well blended, and butter the toast on both sides.

Preheat oven to 350 degrees.

Place the buttered toast rounds onto 4 round baking dishes; place 4 mushroom caps onto each. Put the remaining herbed butter onto the mushrooms, season with salt and pepper, and top each with 2 tablespoons heavy cream.

Cover the 4 dishes with 4 glass bells and bake in the oven for 20 minutes.

Do not remove bells until mushrooms are served. (*4 servings*)

BAKED BANANAS

    4 large ripe bananas, unpeeled
    4 teaspoons butter
    4 teaspoons brown sugar
    1 teaspoon lime juice
     sour cream (optional)

Preheat oven to 350 degrees.

Arrange unpeeled bananas on a baking sheet, slice open the skins and insert slivers of butter, brown sugar, and lime juice in each.

Bake about 25 minutes, or until skins are quite black. Serve warm, with or without sour cream. (*4 servings*)

CAULIFLOWER AU GRATIN

    1 medium head cauliflower
    1 small onion, chopped
    1 cup milk
    ¼ pound American cheese, grated
    1 egg yolk
    ½ teaspoon butter
    ½ teaspoon white pepper
    ½ teaspoon paprika
     bread crumbs

Preheat oven to 375 degrees.

Boil the cauliflower until just tender. Drain, and set aside.

Put the onion and milk into a saucepan and simmer over low heat 5 minutes.

Add the cheese (reserving a little for garnishing), allow to boil up again, remove from the heat, and cool. Stir in the egg yolk, butter, and seasonings. Pour half of this into a baking dish, put in the cauliflower, then add the remaining sauce.

Dot with grated cheese and bread crumbs and bake until brown, about 25 minutes. (*4 servings*)

BAKED CANDIED YAMS

The yam (or sweet potato) is to the southland what the white potato is to the rest of the country, and more. It's a side dish to be served with meat, an important "specialty" dish, and is made into desserts (pies and puddings). Here's an easy way to fix yams, which brings out their best qualities.

    6 medium yams
    ½ cup butter
    1 cup brown sugar, firmly packed
    ¼ cup water

Boil yams 30 minutes in water to cover. Cool. Melt butter. In a separate pan melt sugar in the water over low heat.

Preheat oven to 350 degrees.

Butter an 11 by 13-inch baking pan. Peel potatoes and cut lengthwise. Lay the potatoes in the pan in one layer. Spoon melted butter over all. Spoon melted sugar over all. Bake until candied, 35 to 40 minutes. (*6 servings*)

CORN FRITTERS BEAUREGARD

- 2 cups raw corn kernels
- 1 teaspoon salt
- 2 eggs, yolks and whites beaten separately
- 1 tablespoon milk
- 1 cup flour
- 1 teaspoon baking powder
  cooking oil or fat

Add the salt to the corn. Stir the egg yolks into the milk, and add to the corn.
Sift the baking powder with the flour; stir into the corn mixture.
Fold in the egg whites, and drop by tablespoons into deep fat heated to 370 degrees. Fry until brown. (*4 servings*)
This is only one aspect of the famous Creole fritter, for others, see p. 135.

BAKED CARROTS

- 8 medium carrots, peeled, sliced lengthwise
- 2 tablespoons butter
- 1 tablespoon flour
- 1 teaspoon salt
- ½ teaspoon white pepper
- 1 cup milk
  bread crumbs
  butter

Preheat oven to 375 degrees.
Boil the carrots until tender, and drain.
Melt the butter (do not brown), stir in the flour and seasonings, and then the milk. Continue stirring until thickened.
Put the carrots into a buttered baking dish, pour in the sauce, sprinkle with bread crumbs, dot with butter, and brown in the oven, about 25 minutes. (*4 servings*)

CREOLE CORN PUDDING

Corn pudding is by no means an exclusive Louisiana dish, since it enjoys great popularity throughout the South. This recipe with fresh corn, struck us as extra good eating.

- 4 ears fresh sweet corn
- 1 pint milk, warmed
- 3 eggs, beaten to a froth
- 2 teaspoons melted butter
- 1 teaspoon salt
- ½ teaspoon pepper
- 1 teaspoon baking powder

Preheat oven to 325 degrees.
Grate the corn from the cobs and mix with the tepid milk. Stir in the eggs, butter, and seasonings, and then the baking powder.
Place all in a buttered baking dish, and cook in the oven for 30 or 40 minutes. Serve with ham or other main dishes. (*4 servings*)

SALADS
AND DRESSINGS

CREOLE MUSTARD DRESSING

Make a paste of dry mustard and warm water. Beat olive oil into it very, very slowly with a wire whisk. When the mixture has taken up all the oil possible, add a little vinegar, sugar, and salt to your taste.
This mustard is especially good on cold fish and shellfish.

SALAD MACÉDOINE

Chop cold leftover cauliflower, beans, carrots, peas, beets—any vegetables on hand—and mix together with mayonnaise. Serve on lettuce that has been coated with olive oil.

SHRIMP MOUSSE

    2 large tomatoes, seeded and chopped
    1 medium onion, chopped
    1 tablespoon vinegar
    1 tablespoon sugar
    1 teaspoon salt
      few grains cayenne
    1 envelope unflavored gelatin, soaked
      in ½ cup cold water
    2 pounds cooked shrimp, chopped
    2 stalks celery, chopped
    4 hard-cooked eggs, chopped
      chopped parsley

Cook the tomatoes, onion, vinegar, sugar, salt, and cayenne in 1-½ cups water for 10 minutes, using a medium saucepan. Remove from heat and stir in the gelatin.

Mix together the shrimp, celery, eggs, and parsley and spoon into a mold, or 4 individual molds.

Pour the gelatin liquid over the mixture, and chill. Serve cold. (*4 servings*)

AVOCADO HENRI

    1 cup finely minced cooked shrimp
    ½ cup finely minced stuffed olives
    ½ cup finely chopped green pepper
    2 tablespoons mayonnaise
      few grains cayenne
    2 ripe avocados, sliced in half, pits
      removed, and brushed with lemon
      juice
    8 anchovies

Mix together the shrimp, olives, pepper, mayonnaise, and cayenne, and spoon into the avocados.

Garnish each with crossed anchovies, chill slightly, and serve. (*4 servings*)

PAPAYA-SHRIMP SALAD

Papayas—"melons that grow on trees"—are an important food in the Carribbean and are popular in the warmer parts of the United States. Rich in vitamins and low in calories, this versatile fruit can be eaten in a large variety of ways: peeled, sliced, and served with other fruits as a breakfast food; in salads, simply halved and sprinkled with lime juice; halved and filled with shrimp, crab meat, flaked fish, chopped chicken, etc.

Papaya juice is used in facial creams; the seeds are used in salad dressings; green papaya is used as a meat tenderizer.

This exotic, nutritious fruit can nowadays be found at any time of the year in many big-city markets.

    2 fresh ripe papayas, chilled
    1½ cups chopped cooked shrimp
    1 cup chopped celery
    ½ cup toasted slivered almonds
    ½ teaspoon curry powder
    ½ cup mayonnaise
      juice of ½ lime
    1 lime, quartered

Halve the papayas and remove the seeds.

Mix together the shrimp, celery, almonds, curry, and mayonnaise, and pile into the papaya halves. Sprinkle with lime juice and serve with lime wedges. (*4 servings*)

BREADS
AND BATTERCAKES

HOP YEAST

As bread was the staff of life, so was yeast the staff of bread. Such was the necessity in every household, that yeast sometimes had to be made from scratch. This recipe was not resorted to very often because of the custom of reserving a part of the last batch of dough or batter to use with the next batch.

- ¼ cup hops
- 2 cups boiling water
- 1 cup flour

Mix hops into boiling water. When lukewarm, stir in sifted flour to make a thin batter, and let rise in sun or by the fire overnight. Peach leaves and fodder with a little vinegar will also make good yeast. Cover crock with cheesecloth and store the yeast not to be used at 60 to 70 degrees, or refrigerate.
1 cup of yeast makes 4 loaves of bread. (*5 to 6 cups*)

CALAS

Calas were sold in the streets of New Orleans in post-Civil War days by black woman vendors freed from slavery by the war. "*Toute calas chaude!*" was their familiar early-morning cry.

- 2 eggs, separated
- 1 cup sugar
- 1 cup cooked rice
- 2 cups flour
- 2 teaspoons baking powder
  cooking oil or fat
  confectioners' sugar

Mix together the egg yolks, sugar, rice, flour, and baking powder.
Beat the egg whites and fold them into the rice mixture.
Drop by the spoonful into hot cooking oil (370 degrees), and cook until golden.
Drain on paper, dust with confectioners' sugar, and serve hot. (*4 to 6 servings*)

KUSH-KUSH

A breakfast dish, sometimes called couche-couche, but no relation to the African dish couscous.

- 2 cups cornmeal
- ½ cup hot water
- 2 cups milk
- 1 egg, beaten
- 1 teaspoon sugar
- ¾ teaspoon baking powder
- 1 teaspoon salt

In a heavy skillet scald the cornmeal in the water, and stir in the remaining ingredients. Cook over moderate heat about 15 minutes or until well browned, stirring often.
Serve with cream or pure cane syrup. (*4 servings*)

LOUISIANA HONEY BREAD

This is a very old Creole recipe, and one that produces a delicious and unusual bread. We recommend that you try it.

- 2 cups flour
- 1 teaspoon baking soda
- 1 teaspoon baking powder
- 1 teaspoon salt
- 1 teaspoon powdered ginger
- ½ teaspoon cinnamon
- 1 cup milk
- 1 cup honey
- 1 egg, slightly beaten

Sift together all the dry ingredients. Add the milk, honey, and egg, and put into the bowl of an electric mixer. Mix for at least 30 minutes, until thoroughly blended, and spoon into a buttered loaf pan.
Preheat oven to 375 degrees.
Bake for about 45 minutes, and serve thinly sliced and well buttered.

PAIN PERDU

This is a sweet Creole version of "French toast." On the Gulf Coast the liquid, instead of milk, is orange-flower water and 3 tablespoons brandy.

    ½ cup milk
    ¼ cup sugar
    ½ teaspoon grated lemon rind
    ½ teaspoon salt
    6 slices bread, crusts trimmed off, cut
      into strips
    5 eggs, well beaten
      bread crumbs
      cooking lard
      confectioners' sugar, if desired

Put eggs into a bowl and beat well. Add the milk, sugar, lemon rind, and salt.
Dip the bread strips into the egg mixture. Squeeze gently by pressing with a pancake turner to keep them from being too moist, dip into the bread crumbs, and fry in hot fat until golden.
Serve with the meat course or sprinkle with confectioners' sugar and serve as a dessert. (*4 servings*)

RICE MUFFINS

A major crop in gulf states and therefore plentiful, rice was served at least once a day and many recipes were changed to incorporate it. The rice gives a nice chewy quality to muffins.

    1 cup flour
    1 tablespoon sugar
    1 teaspoon baking powder
    ½ teaspoon salt
    2 eggs
    ½ cup milk
    4 tablespoons melted butter
    1 cup boiled rice

Preheat oven to 375 degrees.
Sift flour, sugar, baking powder, salt, into a bowl. Make a hole and put in the eggs, milk, and melted butter.
Beat all together until just mixed. Add rice. Stir well.
Fill buttered muffin tins ⅔ full and bake 12 to 15 minutes. (*12 muffins*)

DESSERTS

FIG PUDDING

Mississippi has a plentiful crop of figs and other semitropical fruits, so it is not at all surprising that fig pudding has become a favorite native dessert.

    ½ pound fresh figs, finely chopped
    ½ pound suet, minced
    1 cup milk
    2½ cups bread crumbs
    2 eggs, beaten
    ¼ teaspoon cinnamon
    ¼ teaspoon nutmeg
    ¼ teaspoon cloves
    ½ teaspoon salt
      unsweetened whipped cream

Mix all the ingredients together, spoon into a buttered mold, cover tightly, and place onto a rack in a deep pot. Add boiling water until it reaches halfway up around the mold. Cover the pot and simmer 3½ to 4 hours. Add more boiling water as necessary.
Serve topped with whipped cream. (*4 servings*)

CREOLE PECAN PRALINES

This is a candy well known to Louisianians and all who have visited the gulf area. What you probably did not know is how easy it is to make.

    2 cups brown sugar, firmly packed
    1 cup boiling water
    ¼ cup molasses
    4 cups shelled pecans

Put the sugar into a saucepan, add the boiling water, stir well, and place over low heat.

Add the molasses. Stir until syrup forms balls when dropped into cold water.

Remove from heat, add nuts, stir, and drop 2 tablespoons at a time onto a buttered marble or plastic slab to form pralines. Let cool and wrap in wax paper. Store in tins or glass jars until needed. (*35 to 40 candies*)

RASPBERRY MERINGUES

Light and airy, containing few calories, meringues can be baked in layers and filled with ice cream; with chocolate filling they serve as "cake." Used singly they serve as a base for a rich ice cream, or whipped cream, or stewed fruit. As versatile as they are, they are easy to make.

    6 egg whites
    ¾ cup sugar
    ½ teaspoon cream of tartar

Preheat oven to 275 degrees.

Beat egg whites with cream of tartar until stiff. Add sugar by tablespoons; beat until shiny points can be made. Drop 12 spoonfuls on brown-paper-covered pastry sheet.

Bake 30 minutes for chewy meringues, 1 hour for crisp meringues. Allow them to cool in closed oven.

This meringue can also be baked in two layers. When done spread ice cream on one layer and top with second layer, or fill with raspberries and top with whipped cream (see below).

Filling:

    1 pint heavy cream
    1 pint fresh raspberries
    4 tablespoons confectioners' sugar

Wash and stem fruit, and cover with sugar. Whip cream.

Cover one half the meringues with a spoonful of whipped cream and a spoonful of berries. Put one of each of the remaining meringues on top, and heap whipped cream on each. Decorate with one or two berries. Serve immediately. (*6 servings*)

JEFF DAVIS PUDDING

In the later years of the Confederacy food was scarce and the rich ingredients for plum pudding were not available. This "patriotic" version is good even without the costly brandy and many fruits of prewar years.

    1 cup molasses
    1 cup sour milk
    1 cup finely chopped suet
    3 cups flour
    1 teaspoon baking soda
    ½ teaspoon salt
    ½ teaspoon cloves
    1 teaspoon cinnamon
    1 teaspoon allspice
    1 cup raisins, seeded and chopped
    1 cup currants
    ½ cup citron, chopped fine

Mix together the molasses, milk, and suet.

Mix together 2½ cups of flour, the soda, salt, and spices.

Add the dry mixture to the liquid mixture, and blend well with a whisk.

Mix the fruit with the remaining ½ cup of flour and stir into the mixture.

Spoon into a buttered mold, cover, and place onto a rack in a deep pot. Add boiling water until it reaches halfway up around the mold. Cover the pot and simmer 4 hours adding more water as necessary. Serve wtih Hard Sauce*. (*8 servings*)

RED PEPPER JAM

    20 sweet red peppers or pimentos,
        washed, seeds removed, finely
        chopped
    2 teaspoons salt
    6 cups sugar
    2 pints cider vinegar

Sprinkle the peppers with salt and let stand about 6 hours. Drain, place in kettle with the sugar and vinegar, and simmer until it reaches the consistency of jam.

Pour into jelly glasses and seal. (*2 pints*)

BAR-LE-DUC

Originating in Lorraine, where red currants are plentiful, this much-prized jam made its way to the United States through New Orleans. Although still not as plentiful as other jams, bar-le-duc is obtainable commercially in many specialty food stores. It is served as a jam and with meats and game.

    4 cups sugar
    1 quart water
    2 quarts currants, washed

Boil the sugar in the water for 8 minutes. Add currants and cook 15 minutes longer. Let cool.
Pour into jelly glasses and seal. (*3 pints*)

APRICOT SHERBET

Sherbets are different from ice creams in that no milk or cream is used in the basic mixture. They are most refreshing—so refreshing that in the long dinners of the midnineteenth century they were served in the middle of dinner to refresh jaded appetites. In Louisiana these inter-dinner ices were called middle-course drinks, and were not true sherbets in that they were made with wines and brandies and barely frozen. Elegant restaurants took up the custom and began to serve between-courses sherbet. Once in a while one still encounters this in old-fashioned restaurants.

    1 can (1 pound) or 6 fresh cooked
        apricots put through a sieve
    2 cups sugar
    4 cups water
    2 tablespoons lemon juice

Boil sugar, water, and apricot pulp together for 5 or 10 minutes. Add lemon juice. Cool.
Put in freezer as directed in Vanilla Ice Cream*.
When frozen, pack to mellow for 2 to 3 hours and serve.
If done in freezing compartment of refrigerator, half-freeze mixture. Take out and beat well. Return to mold and freeze until ready to serve. Serve in glasses or sherbet cups. (*12 servings*)

CHESS PIE

In South Carolina this pie is called a transparent pie. The only difference is that the meringue is folded into the butter-yolk mixture, otherwise it is the same. Pecan meats are often added to this pie, too, and everyone believes the pie passed down in his or her family to be the best.
"The secret of the pies not becoming heavy is in cutting them and distributing them on the plates as soon as they are cooked and still hot. If they are allowed to cool without cutting them, they will fall." (from *Practical Cooking and Dinner Giving*, by Mary Henderson, 1876)
All ingredients should be at room temperature.

    3 eggs, separated
    6 tablespoons butter, softened
    ½ cup sugar
    1 teaspoon vanilla or ground nutmeg
    1 tablespoon sugar
    1 pie crust*, in 8-inch pie plate

Preheat oven to 425 degrees.
Beat yolks and sugar together until lemon-colored.
Beat butter until creamy.
Mix the butter and egg-sugar mixture together quickly with ½ teaspoon vanilla. Put in unbaked pie crust and bake 5 minutes at 425 degrees. Lower heat to 300 degrees and continue baking for 30 minutes or until a knife will come clean when inserted in custard.
Have ready the whites of eggs beaten stiff, with 1 tablespoon sugar, added gradually with remaining vanilla.
When pie is done spread meringue over it and return to oven for 15 minutes, to brown. (The meringue can be folded into the above mixture before it is baked, if desired)
Cut and put on serving plates immediately. (*4 servings*)

STRAWBERRY MOUSSE FRAPPÉ

    1 quart strawberries, decapped,
        washed, and halved
        confectioners' sugar
    1 pint heavy cream, whipped
    1 jigger brandy

Cover the berries with sugar, let stand an hour or so, drain, and reserve juice.

Mix the berries with the whipped cream, add a little of the juice, and chill or freeze. Add brandy to remaining juice and pour over mousse before serving. (*4 to 6 servings*)

CREOLE FRITTERS

Fritters are light, batter-covered fried shellfish, fruits, or plain puffy fried cakes, often flavored with vanilla, brandy, rum, or whatever the cook may feel will benefit the batter treatment. A favorite in Creole country, when they are well made, they are a delight. This batter is for fruits.

- 2 eggs, separated
- 1 cup flour
- 1 tablespoon melted butter
- ¼ teaspoon salt
- 2 tablespoons brandy
- 6 tablespoons water
  confectioners' sugar
- 3 bananas, peeled, sliced lengthwise twice and crosswise in thirds
  peeled and sliced apples
  peach or apricot halves
  orange sections
  large strawberries
  pineapple slices
  Lard heated to 370 or 390 degrees.

Beat the egg yolks until lemon-colored. Beat in the flour. Add butter, salt, brandy, and water. The batter should be thick enough to cover and coat whatever is immersed in it, but not so thick that it is heavy. Creole cooks say it should be about the consistency of thick starch, or thick cream.

Beat egg whites until stiff and fold into batter. If food to be immersed is uncooked, the deep fat should be at 370 degrees; if cooked, 390 degrees.

Dip a slice of fruit in batter and then place into boiling lard with a slotted spoon. (Be sure the fruit is covered with batter.) Fry to a golden brown, lift out, drain on paper. Continue until all are done. Put on serving plate on clean napkin, sift confectioners' sugar over all, and serve hot.

Serve as light dessert or with meats. (*12 servings*)

WEDDING CAKE

Once upon a time, no matter how elaborately decorated, wedding cakes were made at home for the most part. Loving hands chopped fruits and nuts and beat and iced these cakes—spongecake, buttercake, poundcake, any kind of cake was used.

The fruitcakes were mostly in the South and were often elaborate, with candied orange blossoms and rosebuds that can only be found in professional bakeries now. The most glorious of all, a Creole wedding cake: a fruitcake covered with orgeat (almond) paste, then iced, piped with blossoms and rosebuds, and finished with a wreath of blush roses.

The old cookbook where this simpler recipe was found said: "This, as you may infer, is ample to serve both his kinfolks and her kinfolks and give away samples for all the yearning spinsters to dream on."

- 1¾ pounds butter
- 2 pounds sugar
- 2 pounds sifted flour
- 19 eggs, whites and yolks beaten separately
- 4 ounces best bourbon whiskey
- 2 tablespoons cloves
- 6 nutmegs, grated
- 6 pounds seedless currants
- 5 pounds seedless raisins
- 2 pounds citron, chopped finely

Preheat oven to 275 degrees.

All ingredients should be at room temperature. Cream butter well. Add sugar, beat until very light.

Beat yolks of eggs until lemon-colored. Add to sugar and butter, and beat until very light.

Beat egg whites very stiff and fold into batter. Sift flour, and add gradually to butter-and-egg mixture. Beat after each addition.

Add whiskey and then spices.

Mix all the fruits together and dust with flour. Add to cake, mix well. Beat again.

Line deep graduated baking pans, 8 quart, 4 quart, 3 quart, with 2 layers of well-buttered brown paper. Fill ⅔ full. Bake in oven 1½ to 3 hours, until a washed broom straw comes out clean. (Time depends on baking pans used.)

Frost with white icing in which chopped maraschino cherries and citron have been mixed. Four ordinary recipes of icing will be needed.

BLACKBERRY ROLL

This is from an old New Orleans cookbook, and is like a pie without spice or sugar. It makes a delicious combination with the hard sauce.

>6 cups ripe blackberries, washed
>1 recipe biscuit dough (see p. 164)

Hard sauce:

>½ cup butter, softened
>1 cup granulated sugar
>½ teaspoon vanilla
>1½ tablespoons brandy

Preheat oven to 400 degrees.
Divide dough into two parts and roll each part thin. Lay one on a cookie sheet. Put in berries, level, and cover with other crust, roll the two crusts up around edges to seal in the juices. Bake 30 minutes.
To make hard sauce, beat sugar into softened butter until thick and creamy. Add vanilla and brandy. Beat again.
Serve blackberry roll hot with hard sauce in a separate bowl to be passed at the table. (*6 to 8 servings*)

BEVERAGES

OLD-FASHIONED CREOLE COCKTAIL

The original Old Fashioned was made with cognac, gin, sherry, or vermouth, as well as the very good old bourbon with which it is made today. The old recipe called for 1 tablespoon of liquor in this drink.

>1 lump sugar
>3 tablespoons seltzer or soda water
>1-inch strip lemon peel
>2 ounces orange juice
>1 tablespoon lemon juice
>1½ ounces of bourbon, cognac, sherry, gin, or vermouth
>1 maraschino cherry
>1 sprig mint

Put sugar lump in a large Old Fashioned glass. Add 3 tablespoons soda water and muddle to melt sugar.
Add lemon peel, orange and lemon juices. Add liquor, cherry and a large piece of ice.
Stir well, and decorate with sprig of mint. (*1 serving*)

PORT SANGAREE

A sangaree is a tropical drink made with wine, spiced and sweetened. In Mexico and other Spanish-speaking countries it's *sangría*.

>½ teaspoon confectioners' sugar
>1 teaspoon water
>2 ounces port
>soda water
>1 ounce brandy
>nutmeg

Using an 8-ounce glass, dissolve confectioners' sugar in water. Add port, 2 ice cubes, and nearly fill with carbonated water. Float brandy on top, and serve sprinkled with nutmeg. (*1 serving*)

MISSISSIPPI PUNCH

Mississippi punch was traditionally made up in quantity for festive occasions, and was served from large cut-glass bowls. It is a powerful drink, guaranteed to have a powerful effect on the life of a party. The recipe below, for a single drink, can be expanded as needed.

>1 ounce brandy
>½ ounce Jamaica rum
>½ ounce bourbon
>1 ounce water
>1 teaspoon confectioners' sugar
>shaved ice
>sprig mint

Put the brandy, rum, bourbon, water, and sugar into a shaker, mix thoroughly, and pour into a 12-ounce glass filled with shaved ice. Garnish with a sprig of mint and serve with a straw. (*1 serving*)

SAZARAC COCKTAIL

Many cocktails were invented during Prohibition to mask the flavor of bathtub gin and bootleg whiskey. This cocktail was known in New Orleans long before that noble experiment. It was named Sazarac after a well-known hotel whose bartender invented the drink.

½ cube sugar
cracked ice
1 jigger (1-½ ounces) rye whiskey
2 dashes Peychaud bitters
1 twist lemon peel
few drops absinthe (or Pernod)

Muddle the sugar with a little water in mixing glass. Add ice, whiskey, bitters, and lemon peel.
Stir until well chilled. Remove ice, add several drops of absinthe, stir a little, and strain into a chilled glass. Serve with water on the side. (*1 serving*)

RAMOS FIZZ

This drink, invented by Henry Ramos, was made famous by Louisiana's flamboyant senator, Huey Long, who is said to have introduced it to Washington (and the nation) when he was in office.

2 teaspoons confectioners' sugar
4 teaspoons lemon juice
½ teaspoon orange-flower water
2 egg whites
2 jiggers (3 ounces) dry gin
½ cup cream
cracked ice
soda water

Put all the ingredients into a shaker, and shake thoroughly. Strain into 8-ounce glasses and add a squirt of soda water. (*2 servings*)

CREOLE COFFEE

The very best coffee is made in a drip pot. In gulf and delta country the making of coffee is a rite to be approached reverently, with the best coffee beans "parched" to a dark brown and shaken at the last moment of roasting with a teaspoon of sugar and brushed with the white of an egg. They are then ground as needed in a hand grinder—not pulverized or coarse, but medium. A Brazilian or Colombian coffee is used.

Before the advent of the drip pot, water was poured onto the grounds in a pot and brought to just boiling, then a small glass of cold water was poured in, as in Camp Coffee*. The spout of the pot is covered or stuffed with a cloth, and the grounds too are kept covered when the water is not being spooned into them. It is really essence of coffee, dark and flavorful.

1 cup very finely ground coffee
4 cups boiling water

Using a drip coffeepot, pour 2 tablespoons boiling water over coffee grounds. Wait 5 minutes and repeat, never adding more water until grounds have ceased to bubble. Pour back over the grounds repeatedly until desired strength is obtained. Serve very hot, but never allow to boil.
Add hot milk, if you wish. (*4 cups*)

CAFÉ ORLÉANS FLAMBÉ

4 tablespoons brown sugar
2 whole allspice
1 cinnamon stick
1 teaspoon grated lemon peel
2 cups extra-strong coffee, very hot
½ cup cognac

In a chafing dish or other suitable container combine the sugar, spices, lemon peel, and coffee. Heat, stirring, to just below boiling. Place the cognac into a ladle, warm, ignite, and pour over the coffee mixture. Ladle while still flaming into demitasse cups. (*4 servings*)

CAFÉ BRÛLOT

8 lumps sugar
4 whole cloves
1 cinnamon stick
1 lemon peel cut into a spiral
1 orange peel cut into a spiral
½ cup cognac
2 cups extra-strong coffee, very hot

Place sugar, cloves, and cinnamon into a chafing dish or other suitable container.
Add lemon and orange peels.
Add cognac, set over flame, and heat, stirring. Ignite cognac, continuing to stir.
Ladle into demitasse cups ¾ full of hot coffee while still flaming (do not serve the spices or peels). (*4 servings*)

MIDWESTERN
COOKING

SOUPS AND CHOWDERS

Green Corn Soup
Pea Soup with Pigs' Hocks
Salsify Soup
Milwaukee Beer Soup
Madzoon Soup with Oatmeal
Michigan Black Bean Soup
U.S. Senate Bean Soup

PASTA, EGG, AND CHEESE DISHES

American Fondue
Macaroni Pie
Indiana Spaghetti
Cheese Dumplings
Wisconsin Welsh Rabbit

FISH AND SHELLFISH

Boiled Crayfish
Planked Michigan Whitefish
Lake Trout, Horseradish Sauce
Stuffed Baked Bass
Wisconsin Fish Stew

MEATS

Pan-Broiled Steak
Braised Short Ribs of Beef
Stuffed Lamb Shanks
Veal Kidney Stew
Veal Cutlets, Romanian Style
Country Sausage
Roast Beef Hash
Roast Rabbit with Sage Dressing
Kielbasa and Kraut
Stovepipe Hash
Stuffed Cabbage
Creamed Chipped Beef

POULTRY AND GAME BIRDS

Old-fashioned Roast Turkey
Chicken Pot Pie
Smothered Fried Chicken
Baked Chicken in Cream
Pickled Chicken
Roast Goose with Apple Stuffing

VEGETABLES AND SIDE DISHES

Potato Pancakes
Carrot Croquettes
Spinach Ring
Rutabagas and Mushrooms
Baked Cabbage
Buttered Radishes
Sauer Beans
Zucchini with Sour Cream Sauce

SALADS AND DRESSINGS

Indiana Potato Salad
Hot Dutch Salad
Celery Vinaigrette
Stuffed Endive
Molded Asparagus Salad
Tossed Salad, Blue Cheese Dressing

BREADS AND BATTERCAKES

Hominy Fritters
Wisconsin Beer Bread
Baking Powder Biscuits
Bohemian Houska
Huckleberry Muffins
Indiana Corncake
Swedish Rye Bread
Gaelic Oatcakes
Soy Biscuits

DESSERTS

Vanilla Ice Cream
Old-fashioned Chocolate Cake
Orange Cake
Butternut Squash Pie
Pumpkin Chiffon Pie
Brown-Sugar Pie
Sour Cherry Pie
Old-fashioned Apple Crisp
Buttermilk Raisin Cake
Coffeecake
Strawberry Jam
Special Picnic Watermelon

BEVERAGES

Iced Tea
Mulled Cider
Elderberry Wine
Rice Wine
Sherry Cobbler

MIDWESTERN COOKING

Even before the War for American Independence, bands of settlers had made their way westward beyond the Allegheny Mountains. Afterward many more crossed these mountains on a new turnpike built to the Ohio country. The migration became a flood when the Erie Canal opened in 1825. "A cent and a half a mile, a mile and a half an hour," was the slogan. Whole families moved westward with all their possessions, pushed by poverty and hope.

The alliance of the League of Six Nations of the Iroquois had been broken by separate allegiances of the tribes during the American Revolution, and the tribes had either been pushed west or onto reservations. A traveler in 1797 said, "To the American farmer the Geneze [Genesee] near Lake Ontario, Kentucky, Tenasee [Tennessee], in a word the whole Western Territory is the promised land. . . ."

The migrants ate the simplest food because the land had to be cleared before crops could be raised. A clearing was made by cutting down a number of trees. The logs were cut and notched to make a lean-to shelter. The tree stumps were set afire to burn away. Meals were prepared outdoors over an open fire above which a frame had been rigged to suspend the cooking pots. And bread was baked in Dutch ovens, in the hot coals. The first year buckwheat was planted among the stumps and, if there was a cleared area, corn. The farm animals rooted for their own food in the woods and fields.

Corn was the most important food and was served three times a day in one dish or another, usually with salt pork. An Englishman named Ashe reported, "The dinner consisted of a large piece of salt bacon, a dish of hominy, and a tureen of squirrel broth. I dined entirely on the last dish, which I found incomparably good, and the meat equal to the most delicate chicken." His host ate nothing but bacon and drank nothing but whiskey. If time permitted, the corn was carried to the nearest mill to be ground. Otherwise it was pounded in a mortar, or was ground in a hand mill consisting of a flat stone placed on a stump with another stone hung over it. Rubbed around and around, it ground the corn.

As work progressed, an *out oven* was built by piling chips and twigs in an oblong about 2 feet high and covering the pile with a thick layer of clay. The chips were then set afire. The fire hardened the clay into brick, the ashes were cleaned out, and the oven was ready to use. Out ovens were heated by setting a fire within the cavity. When the coals were raked out, the oven remained very hot, 500 degrees perhaps, and bread or pies were put in to absorb the heat and to bake.

Pigs were easy to raise and were valuable because they could eat scraps from the family table and root for their own food. Pork that could not be eaten fresh was salted down and some parts hung to smoke in the family chimney. Salt pork, ham, and game were the only meats available in those early days.

Fowl, both domestic and wild, gave variety to their diet, and they set about to gain the best qualities of each in their domestic fowl, as they had in New England, from whence they came. A traveler's diary of the time observed:

I saw a flock of geese, wild and domestic mixed. Their necks are completely black and slender. Their meat has much better taste than that of common geese. Citizens introduce this species by slightly wounding the wild birds in flight or by gathering their eggs and setting them under the domestic geese. It is in this same fashion that in Virginia they mix the wild with the domestic turkeys and crossbreed them, with infinite improvement.

All this led to inventiveness to use and combine available foods, and rich farms, villages, and towns grew and expanded. In them, many nationalities merged and became Americans. St. Louis became the gateway to the Far West; and Chicago, which had been a trading post at the juncture of the Mississippi River and Lake Michigan, became a city. With the growth of the cattle business and the railroads, Chicago developed into the packing center of the country. Steak, once a cattle-trail delicacy, grew in popularity to become an American ritual feast. Not that steak hadn't been eaten before, but now, with better distribution, uniform butchering, and ice refrigeration beginning to build the packing industry, steak was available to more people. The sirloin or porterhouse steak is still the great American dinner and the terms "Chicago cut" and "New York cut" are now a part of the language.

When Scandinavians settled in Wisconsin and Minnesota, it became a dairy region, one of the most important in the U.S., and many fine dishes were added to the wealth of Midwestern cooking. "Danish" became an American term for coffeecake, and Wisconsin cheeses are nationally distributed.

In the flood of immigration of the late 1800s many ethnic groups of Europe and the Middle East—Ukrainians, Poles, Czechoslovakians, Armenians—settled in Chicago, Detroit, Pittsburgh, St. Louis, Gary, and other cities, as well as on farms. Neighborhood restaurants served kielbasa and sauerkraut, houska at Christmas time, madzoon soup, or Gaelic oatcakes—any number of "foreign" dishes. If they weren't served in restaurants, they were cooked at home. Recently soul foods—basically southern, like hominy fritters—have been added to the ethnic mix of the Midwest, with the migration of blacks from the South. The Midwest was one of the first areas to welcome escaped slaves before the Civil War.

Next to the state fair, the annual fish fry was *the* event in the small towns of the Middle West. It compared in mood to the clambakes, oyster roasts, and barbecues of other regions. The hosts were often the mayor and council of the town, or other local figures like the mill owner. A grove was selected and barrels of fish in ice were sent from the Great Lakes. A stove with a large cast-iron sheet was washed and oiled, and a fire was built. When the sheet was hot the cooking began.

In the meantime the fish had been cleaned and washed and rolled in salted cornmeal. People had been arriving all morning with large picnic baskets filled with potato salad, every kind of cake and pie imaginable, and iced tea (which was new, having been served for the first time at the St. Louis Fair). The smell of frying fish spread for miles around. After all had eaten, the band would strike up, and songs from leading operettas and the rousing marches of that day were played.

There were other big events in the year, such as strawberry festivals, Fourth of July celebrations, and harvest-home suppers given by the ladies of the churches, the firemen, or the Grange. They were all excuses to show off the fine home cooking on which most of them feasted all their lives.

Edna Ferber captured the earthy beauty of this region when she described the prairie land just outside Chicago in the early part of this century. Selina, a character in Ferber's novel *So Big*, had taken a job as a schoolteacher in a Dutch community.

The last week in October found her on the way to High Prairie, seated beside Klaas Pool in the two-horse wagon with which he brought his garden stuff to the Chicago market. She sat perched next to him on the high seat like a saucy wren beside a ruminate Holstein. So they jolted up Halstead road through a late October sunset. . . . Today it was stretched away and away in the last rays of the late autumn sunlight over which the lake mist was beginning to creep like chiffon covering gold. Mile after mile of cabbage fields, jade green against the earth. Mile after mile of red cabbage, a rich plummy burgundy veined with black. Between these heaps of corn were piled up sunshine. Against the horizon an occasional patch of woods showed the last russet and bronze of oak and maple. These things Selina saw with her beauty-loving eye, and she clasped her hands in their black cotton gloves.
"Oh, Mr. Pool," she cried, "Mr. Pool! How beautiful it is here!"

SOUPS AND CHOWDERS

GREEN CORN SOUP

6 ears fresh corn
2 cups water
1 quart milk
2 tablespoons butter
2 tablespoons flour
2 teaspoons Worcestershire sauce
1 teaspoon salt
½ teaspoon pepper
1 egg yolk, beaten

Cut the kernels from the ears of corn and set aside.
Boil the cobs 15 minutes in 2 cups water, remove them, and discard, reserving liquid.
Add the kernels to the liquid and cook 10 minutes, then pour in the milk.
Make a roux by blending the flour and butter. Add to the soup along with the Worcestershire, salt and pepper. Cook 5 minutes longer. Slowly stir in the egg yolk, and serve. (*4 servings*)

PEA SOUP WITH PIGS' HOCKS

Back in old Holland this delicious and hearty soup was known as *snert*.

1 pound pigs' hocks
2 quarts water
1 pound split green peas
2 leeks, white part only, chopped
2 stalks celery, chopped
2 teaspoons salt
1 teaspoon pepper

Boil the hocks in the water about 1 hour or until tender, skimming the scum as it rises to the surface. Remove hocks and set aside.
Add the peas to the liquid and simmer for 30 minutes, then add the remaining ingredients, and continue simmering for 30 minutes longer. Remove the meat from the hocks, dice, and add to the soup. (*6 to 8 servings*)

SALSIFY SOUP

1 bunch salsify (oyster plant)
1 tablespoon vinegar
2 cups milk
1 tablespoon butter
1 tablespoon flour
salt
pepper
½ cup unsweetened whipped cream

Scrape the salsify and cook with the vinegar, in enough water to cover, until soft.
Press through a sieve, add the milk, and simmer. Thicken with a roux made by creaming together the butter and flour.
Season to taste, and continue cooking until smooth and thickened. Remove from the heat, stir in the whipped cream, and serve. (*2 to 4 servings*)

MILWAUKEE BEER SOUP

This is a light, nourishing soup with the dry taste of beer and the thickness of very light custard. The egg white gives it a texture like Chinese egg drop soup and it takes but 5 minutes to make.

2 cups beer
1 cup water
1 teaspoon salt
½ teaspoon freshly ground pepper
2 eggs, separated
1 tablespoon flour
1 cup milk
toast

Put the beer, water, and seasonings into a pot; bring to a boil.
Beat the egg yolks with the flour, add milk, and stir until smooth.
Stir the egg mixture into the hot beer, and bring back to a boil.
Beat the egg whites, fold into the soup, and serve hot with toast. (*4 servings*)

MADZOON SOUP WITH OATMEAL

Yogurt is called *madzoon* by the Armenians, many of whom migrated to the United States when their country was conquered by Turkey in 1896. Yogurt is milk treated with bacteria, which curdles it into a semisolid mixture more digestible than milk.

This and other Armenian foods can be found in most big cities.

    2 cups water
    ½ cup regular oatmeal
    1 teaspoon salt
    2 cups yogurt
    2 tablespoons butter
    1 small onion, chopped
    1 teaspoon chopped fresh mint leaves

Boil water, add oatmeal and salt, and cook 5 minutes.

Put yogurt into a large bowl or tureen and gradually pour in the oatmeal, stirring so the yogurt won't curdle. Return to pan and put over very low heat.

Melt the butter, fry the onion until golden, and add the chopped mint. Pour over the soup and serve. (*4 servings*)

MICHIGAN BLACK BEAN SOUP

Michigan claims to produce more beans of all sorts than any of the other forty-nine states. And, as you can imagine, the state abounds with all varieties of bean soup. This black bean soup is a justly famous Michigan treat, although by now it appears all over the country.

    2 cups black beans, soaked overnight
    3 quarts hot water
    1 ham bone, with meat
    2 onions, chopped
    1 tablespoon Worcestershire sauce
      few grains cayenne
    ½ cup sherry
    1 lemon, thinly sliced
    2 hard-cooked eggs, chopped

Drain the beans, put them into a kettle with 3 quarts hot water, the ham bone, onions, Worcestershire sauce, and cayenne.

Cover and cook slowly 3 to 4 hours or until beans are soft. Remove ham bone, chop the meat, and return meat to soup. Stir in sherry. Serve in bowls, garnished with lemon slices and sprinkled with chopped egg. (*6 to 8 servings*)

U. S. SENATE BEAN SOUP

This famous soup, long served in the U. S. Senate restaurant, is composed, as it should be, of ingredients from several regions of the country. Michigan lays claim to the white beans; Virginia, Tennessee, and Kentucky argue about the origin of the ham bone; the potatoes come from Maine; and the remaining ingredients are grown in Maryland. Truly a soup worthy of the United States Senate—here is the "official" recipe:

    2 cups dried white beans, soaked
      overnight
    1 "country" ham bone, with meat
    3 quarts water
    ½ cup mashed potatoes
    3 onions, finely chopped
    1 bunch celery with leaves, finely
      chopped
    1 clove garlic, minced
    2 tablespoons minced parsley
      salt and pepper to taste

Drain the beans, put them into a kettle with the ham bone and 3 quarts water. Cover, bring to a boil, lower the heat, and simmer 2 hours.

Stir in the potatoes and add the remaining ingredients. Continue slow-cooking until beans are done.

Remove the ham bone, and discard after trimming away the meat bits, which are added to the soup. Check seasoning, and serve piping hot. (*8 servings*)

PASTA, EGG,
AND CHEESE DISHES

AMERICAN FONDUE

This is not really a fondue in the Swiss sense of the dish, but is nonetheless very popular in the cheese region of America. It is more like a cheese soufflé, or a quiche without the crust.

    1 cup scalded milk
    ¼ cup soft bread crumbs
    1 cup grated mild cheese
    1½ tablespoons butter
    ½ teaspoon salt
    2 egg yolks, beaten
    2 egg whites, beaten until stiff

Mix together the milk, bread crumbs, cheese, butter, and salt. Cook, stirring, over low heat until smooth. Remove from heat.
Preheat oven to 350 degrees.
Stir in the egg yolks, then fold in the egg whites. Pour into a buttered 1-quart casserole, and bake about 20 minutes or until firm. Cut as you would a pie and serve with drinks, or for 2 at lunch. (*4 servings as side dish, 2 servings as main dish*)

MACARONI PIE

We found this recipe in Michigan. Seems to us it's the old recipe for baked macaroni and cheese found in the East and South. The mystery is why it is referred to as *pie*.

    ½ pound macaroni, straight or elbow
    1 teaspoon salt
    1 tablespoon butter
    1 egg, well beaten
    1 teaspoon dry mustard
    1 teaspoon pepper
    ½ teaspoon cayenne
    2 cups grated cheese
    ½ cup milk

Preheat oven to 350 degrees.
Boil the macaroni in salted water until tender, drain, and stir in the butter and egg.
Mix the mustard, pepper, and cayenne with a tablespoon of hot water and add to the macaroni, together with the cheese and milk. Mix thoroughly and spoon into a buttered baking dish. Bake in the oven about 30 minutes or until cheese is melted and macaroni is golden on top. (*4 servings*)

INDIANA SPAGHETTI

Here is a spaghetti dish we discovered in, of all places, Indiana. We seriously doubt that this recipe or its creator ever saw Italy, but we tested the dish and heartily approve.

    4 slices bacon
    5 onions, sliced
    1 pound chopped chuck
    ½ pound fresh mushrooms, chopped
    2 cups chopped tomatoes
    1 package, (1 pound), spaghetti
    1 cup grated Parmesan cheese

Fry the bacon until crisp. Remove from pan, break into pieces and set aside.
Fry the onions in the bacon fat until brown. Remove and set aside.
Cook the meat in the same skillet until well done.
Combine the onions, meat, mushrooms, and tomato, and simmer 10 minutes.
Cook the spaghetti in boiling water not more than 15 minutes. Drain.
Preheat oven to 250 degrees.
Put the spaghetti, sauce, and bacon bits into a casserole, cover with grated cheese, and bake until golden brown. (*4 to 6 servings*)

CHEESE DUMPLINGS

Though we found it in Chicago, this recipe has its roots in Hungary, where it is served for light lunch, or at dinner with meat. It is also served with sugar, cinnamon, and sour cream as a dessert.

    1 pound creamed cottage cheese, or
      ricotta
    ¾ cup flour
    4 eggs, lightly beaten
    ½ teaspoon salt
    4 tablespoons butter, melted
    ½ cup bread crumbs
      sour cream

Mix cheese, flour, eggs, and salt, until smooth. Wet hands and form into balls. Drop them into a pot of salted boiling water and cook for 20 minutes. Drain.
Brown bread crumbs lightly in melted butter.

Put dumplings in melted butter and shake pan to cover.
Serve with sour cream. (*4 servings*)

WISCONSIN WELSH RABBIT

    1¾ cups milk
    ½ pound American cheese, grated
    2 eggs, beaten slightly
    ½ teaspoon paprika
    1½ teaspoons salt
    ½ teaspoon pepper

Preheat oven to 300 degrees.
Heat the milk in a double boiler and stir in the cheese.
Mix the seasonings into the eggs, and stir into the milk and cheese mixture.
Pour into a buttered baking dish, place into a pan of hot (not boiling) water, and bake about 30 minutes or until set. (*2 to 4 servings*)

FISH AND SHELLFISH

STUFFED BAKED BASS

    5 slices white bread crumbled
    3 tablespoons butter
    1 small onion, chopped
    1 tablespoon chopped parsley
    ½ teaspoon salt
    ⅛ teaspoon pepper
    ⅛ teaspoon thyme

Crumble bread, set aside.
Melt butter and sauté onion and parsley until onion is transparent. Stir in bread and seasonings.

    1 bass (2 pounds), or other whole fish of
      similar size, dressed and cleaned
    2 tablespoons melted butter
    2 tablespoons lemon juice
    1 teaspoon salt
    1 teaspoon paprika
    ½ teaspoon pepper

Preheat oven to 350 degrees.
Wash and dry the fish, place into a greased shallow baking dish and pack the stuffing loosely into the cavity. Close and fasten with toothpicks.
Mix together the butter, lemon juice, and seasonings, and brush the fish well with this sauce. Put into the oven and bake about 30 minutes or until fish flakes when fork-tested. (*4 servings*)

PLANKED MICHIGAN WHITEFISH

The Great Lakes, especially Lake Superior and Lake Michigan, have long been famous for whitefish, a firm-fleshed, rich, and flavorful fish weighing from two pounds up. At the turn of the century it was discovered that this delicate fish took on additional flavor when charcoal broiled or cooked on a well-seasoned oak or maple plank.

In 1880 seventy percent of the fish caught in the Great Lakes were whitefish and lake trout; they had declined to five percent in 1964 from overfishing, pollution, and the depredations of the sea lamprey. But now these fine fish are beginning to come back, as control measures have begun to be successful.

Even if whitefish is not available to you, almost any not-too-fatty fish is delicious cooked this way.

> 1 whitefish (3 pounds) cleaned and
> dressed
> salt
> pepper
> paprika
> melted butter
> lemon juice
> minced parsley
> lemon wedges

Heat a suitable-sized thick oak or maple plank under the hot-water tap.

Split the fish, remove the backbone, and lay onto the plank skin side down.

Season with salt and pepper, dust with paprika, brush with melted butter, and cook under a hot broiler for 30 minutes or until fork-tender (or bake in a preheated 400-degree oven). Brush occasionally with a mixture of lemon juice and melted butter.

Serve on the plank, sprinkled with minced parsley and garnished with lemon wedges.

Or, if you wish, surround the fish with cooked mushrooms, tomatoes, and peas, and squeeze (from a pastry bag) hot mashed potatoes around the edges of the plank. (*4 servings*)

WISCONSIN FISH STEW

> 2 pounds fresh pickerel or pike,
> cleaned, cut into serving pieces
> 3 cups water, or to cover
> ¼ cup vinegar
> ½ teaspoon salt
> 2 bay leaves
> 3 whole allspice
> 1½ cups milk
> 1½ cups light cream
> 1 tablespoon butter
> 1 tablespoon flour
> 4 to 6 boiled potatoes
> 1 teaspoon chopped fresh dill

Place vinegar and seasonings in water in a large pot, bring to a boil, and add fish. Lower heat and simmer about 10 minutes or until a fork will pierce fish easily. Set aside.

Heat milk and cream to same temperature as fish stew (to prevent curdling), and add to stew. Mix butter and flour together, and add to stew. Stir gently. Add boiled potatoes. Heat through.

Serve in soup bowls. (*4 to 6 servings*)

BOILED CRAYFISH

Many midwestern streams abound with small crayfish, which make delicious eating. The head, body, and legs are discarded, the tail being the only part that is eaten.

Boiled in a little water, then peeled, the little crayfish tails are eaten as is, with a little salt and a squeeze of lemon, with cocktail sauce, or in a salad. Or they may be sautéed in butter.

> 2 pounds fresh crayfish
> 2 quarts boiling water
> 2 tablespoons salt
> 1 tablespoon caraway seeds
> 1 teaspoon chopped fresh dill

Place the live crayfish into the boiling water, to which the salt, caraway seeds, and dill have been added. Cook 5 minutes, no longer.

Drain, chill, and serve whole. (*6 servings*)

LAKE TROUT, HORSERADISH SAUCE

The deep northern lakes are noted for fine big trout. Poaching retains the delicate flavor of this fish, and horseradish adds just the right piquancy to make this a memorable dish.

    4 pounds lake trout, cleaned and
      dressed
    1 teaspoon salt
    ¼ cup grated fresh horseradish
    1 tablespoon vinegar
    ¼ teaspoon salt
      few grains cayenne
    ½ cup heavy cream, whipped
    ¼ cup melted butter
    1 tablespoon minced parsley
    1 lemon, sliced

Wrap the trout in cheesecloth, and simmer gently in salted water about 10 minutes or until fork pierces easily to the backbone. Remove the cheesecloth and carefully transfer the fish to a heated platter. Keep warm.

Mix together the horseradish, vinegar, salt, and cayenne, and fold into the whipped cream. Spoon into a sauce boat.

Sprinkle the trout with melted butter, dust with minced parsley, garnish with lemon slices, and serve with the horseradish sauce on the side. (*6 servings*)

MEATS

CREAMED CHIPPED BEEF

Dried beef was carried across country; often the cow went along too on whatever transportation was available. Many families, including their animals, made their way to the Ohio River and the Middle West on barges after the Erie Canal was opened. Creamed chipped beef has gone on to become an all-American quick-meal dish, and is often served on baking powder biscuits.

    ½ pound dried chipped beef
    3 tablespoons butter
    1 onion, chopped fine
    2 tablespoons flour
    2½ cups milk
    ¼ teaspoon pepper

Pull chipped beef apart, place in bowl, run water into bowl, rinse beef, and pour out water.

Melt butter in a heavy skillet. When hot, spread beef in pan, add chopped onion, stir, and let brown slightly. Sprinkle flour over all, stir-fry for 2 minutes. Add milk, stir until thickened. Add pepper.

Serve on toast, noodles, rice, or waffles. (*2 servings*)

STOVEPIPE HASH

    2½ cups coarsely chopped cooked meat
        (lamb, beef, and/or corned beef)
    2 slices bread
    2 medium onions, chopped
    3 teaspoons chopped parsley
    1 cup mashed or diced cooked potatoes
    1 tablespoon ketchup
    1 teaspoon Worcestershire sauce
    2 tablespoons melted butter
    ½ cup milk
    1 teaspoon salt
    ½ teaspoon pepper
      few grains cayenne
    ½ cup ketchup

Preheat oven to 375 degrees.

Put the chopped meat, bread, onion, and parsley through the meat grinder, using the finest blade. Mix in the potatoes, 1 tablespoon ketchup, Worcestershire, butter, milk, and seasonings.

Pile high into a buttered baking dish, pour ½ cup ketchup over all, and bake 30 minutes or until brown. (*4 to 6 servings*)

COUNTRY SAUSAGE

When winter comes to American farms and cold covers the countryside, it is time to slaughter the hogs, salt down the hams and bacon, and make the sausage for the coming year. Sausage has been a part of the American gastronomic scene since the very earliest days. Incoming settlers brought traditional sausages from home which were slowly modified by time, necessity, and preferences. The highly flavored sausages of France grew peppery on the Gulf Coast, and even more so as it moved to the Southwest and into real pepper country—the territory of Spanish sausages in New Mexico. Mild English sausage was ground even finer and highly seasoned with sage and black pepper in Virginia. Inevitably, a wide range of sausage forms and flavors resulted. Further west, beef and pork were made into bologna and summer sausage—one originating in Italy, and the other in Pennsylvania. The most common is pork sausage made everywhere.

In addition to the almost infinite variety of native country sausages, you can still find throughout America the specialized sausages of ethnic groups—chorizos from Spain; kielbasa from Poland; bratwurst and liverwurst from Switzerland; knockwurst, blutwurst, liverwurst, and all the other wursts from Germany; salami and hot and sweet pork sausages from Italy.

American pork sausage may be found loose, as meat, rolled, packed in casings, or sewn into bags. It may be fresh or smoked. It may be lightly or heavily seasoned with sage, thyme, cayenne, black pepper, savory, chili powder, bay leaf, anise, or almost any herbs and spices imaginable.

Below is a simple recipe for country sausage that can be made easily in your own kitchen. Vary the seasonings to meet your own taste preferences.

3 pounds fresh lean pork
3 pounds chine fat (fat from the spine)
3 tablespoons salt
2 tablespoons black pepper
   pinch or more cayenne (optional)
4 tablespoons powdered sage
2 tablespoons summer savory

Put the meat with the fat through a meat grinder, using the coarse blade. Mix in the seasonings, knead well, and put through the grinder again, using the fine blade.

Pack mixture into clean, tightly woven muslin bags, and dip in hot lard. Freeze or hang in a cool place, or pack into jars, seal with melted lard, and refrigerate. When ready to cook, form into flat cakes, and fry until brown on both sides. (*6 servings*)

ROAST BEEF HASH

2 tablespoons butter or cooking oil
3 cups roast beef, finely chopped
2 cups cold boiled potatoes, finely chopped
1 medium onion, finely chopped
1 teaspoon salt
2 tablespoons water
4 eggs, poached

Melt butter in a heavy skillet, stir in beef, potatoes, onion, and salt. Stir a few minutes, add water, and form into a flat cake 1½ inches thick, allowing space around the edge.

Cook over low heat without stirring, about 30 minutes, or until a crust has formed on the bottom.

Fold over like an omelet. Divide into quarters. Top each serving with a poached egg. (*4 servings*)

ROAST RABBIT WITH SAGE DRESSING

2 cups bread crumbs
½ teaspoon salt
¼ teaspoon pepper
1 teaspoon crushed fresh sage leaves, or ½ teaspoon dried sage
1 tablespoon minced onion
½ cup melted butter
1 rabbit, dressed, washed, and seasoned with salt and pepper
2 tablespoons cooking fat

Preheat oven to 350 degrees.

Combine the first 6 ingredients, mix well, and stuff into the rabbit. Skewer, spread with fat, and roast, uncovered, in the oven 1½ hours, or until tender. (*4 to 6 servings*)

PAN-BROILED STEAK

    4 pounds of porterhouse or sirloin
      steak, 1½ inches thick
    3 tablespoons butter, melted
    1 teaspoon salt
    ½ teaspoon pepper
    1 lemon, sliced
      parsley

Heat a large frying pan or griddle over high heat. Cook steak until a brown crust forms on one side, then turn and cook on the other side (17 minutes total for rare steak, 20 minutes for medium-rare).
Put the butter onto a heated platter with the salt and pepper. Lay the steak in the butter; turn. Carve in ¾-inch slices, surround with lemon and parsley, and serve. (*6 servings*)

BRAISED SHORT RIBS OF BEEF

    3 pounds short ribs of beef
    1 teaspoon salt
    ½ teaspoon freshly ground pepper
      flour
      cooking oil
    1 carrot, peeled and sliced
    1 turnip, peeled and sliced
    1 onion, sliced
    1 green pepper, sliced
    1 stalk celery, sliced
    3 sprigs parsley, chopped
    2 cups boiling water
    4 medium potatoes, peeled and halved
    2 tablespoons flour

Preheat oven to 400 degrees.
Season the ribs, dredge lightly with flour, and brown on all sides in cooking oil.
Place ribs in a roasting pan, surround with the vegetables, add water, cover, and bake in the oven 2 hours.
Place potatoes around meat and continue cooking, uncovered, about 40 minutes or until meat and potatoes are done and well browned.
Remove meat and potatoes to a hot platter.
Thicken the liquid in the pan with flour mixed to a smooth paste with a little water, and bring to a boil. Add water if needed.
Pour the gravy over the ribs and serve. (*4 servings*)

STUFFED CABBAGE

    2 cups finely ground cold cooked pork
    ½ cup leftover cooked rice (or ⅓ cup
      raw quick-cooking rice)
    1 teaspoon salt
    ½ teaspoon pepper
      few grains cayenne
    1 can condensed tomato soup
    8 large cabbage leaves

Mix together the meat, rice, and seasonings. Add enough of the soup (1 tablespoon or so) to hold the mixture together.
Soften the cabbage leaves by immersing in boiling water for 2 or 3 minutes. Drain, and spoon an equal amount of the meat mixture onto each leaf. Fold over filling, and fasten with toothpicks.
Place the cabbage rolls into a deep pan, pour in the soup mixed with half a can of water, cover, and simmer over low heat for 20 minutes. (*4 servings*)

STUFFED LAMB SHANKS

    4 lamb shanks
    2 tablespoons butter
    3 cups water
    1 teaspoon salt
    ¼ teaspoon pepper
    1 cup barley
    1 tablespoon flour mixed with ½ cup
      water

Brown the lamb shanks on all sides in the butter, using a heavy skillet.
Add the water, seasonings, and barley. Cover and simmer 1½ hours or until tender, adding water as needed.
Remove the meat, cool, and take out the bones.
Cook the barley in the lamb broth about 30 minutes longer, then stuff into boned shanks.
Thicken the lamb broth with the flour-water mixture, stir-cook until thick, and pour over the shanks.
Cover, heat 15 minutes, and serve with Swedish rye bread or biscuits. (*4 servings*)

VEAL KIDNEY STEW

If you shudder at the thought of "innards," we defy you to try this recipe and then say you don't like kidneys, but you *must* remove the fat and skin, and you *must* soak them.

2 veal kidneys
½ small onion
1 thin slice lemon
2 tablespoons butter
1 teaspoon salt
½ teaspoon pepper
2 tablespoons flour
½ pound mushrooms, diced
1½ cups chicken broth
⅓ cup cream
1 teaspoon chopped chives
  butter bread crumbs

Wash the kidneys, remove the fat and skin and hard membrane. Soak in cold water 3 hours, changing the water several times. Put into a saucepan with the onion and lemon, cover with cold water, and simmer for 30 minutes. Drain and cool. Cut away all veins, and dice.

Melt the butter. Season the flour and stir it into the melted butter until smooth. Add the mushrooms, kidneys, and broth. Simmer 15 or 20 minutes. Add the cream and chives.

Transfer to a hot casserole, sprinkle with bread crumbs, brown slightly under the broiler, and serve.(*4 servings*)

KIELBASA AND KRAUT

Spell it any way you like—kielbasa or kielbasy—this spicy sausage is a great favorite among Americans of Slavic extraction. It also plays a prominent role in the religious ritual of Poles, Ukrainians, and Russians, especially during the Christmas and Easter seasons.

Kielbasa can be eaten cold in thin slices, but is best boiled, sautéed, or baked. The recipe that follows is a fairly standard one among kielbasa aficionados.

1 kielbasa (about 2 pounds), cut into thick slices
1 pound sauerkraut, rinsed
1 onion, chopped
1 teaspoon peppercorns
1½ cups beer

Put all the ingredients into a pot. Simmer, covered, about 1 hour or until sauerkraut is tender. (*4 to 6 servings*)

VEAL CUTLETS, ROMANIAN STYLE

4 veal cutlets (about 3 pounds)
1 teaspoon salt
½ teaspoon pepper
3 tablespoons melted butter
1 pound of fresh tomatoes or 1 can (number 2) tomatoes, cut up
1 can condensed tomato soup
1 clove garlic, slivered
1 pound fresh string beans, cut diagonally in thin slices, or 1 can (number 2) french-cut string beans
1 medium onion, peeled and chopped
2 tablespoons butter
2 tablespoons flour

Preheat oven to 375 degrees.

Sprinkle the cutlets with salt and pepper, and place into a casserole with the butter. Cover with the tomatoes, ½ can of soup, ½ can of water, and sprinkle the garlic on top. Bake sbout 1 hour.

Sauté the string beans and onion in 2 tablespoons butter, using a small skillet. Push vegetables to one side of pan, stir in the flour and continue cooking until flour is thoroughly browned. Add the remaining ½ can soup and ½ can water, stir, bring to a boil, and pour into the casserole.

Bake 20 minutes longer, and serve from the casserole. (*4 servings*)

POULTRY
AND GAME BIRDS

OLD-FASHIONED ROAST TURKEY

Wild turkey, like other game, was often parboiled before it was roasted. Domestic turkeys don't need the extra cooking because they're more tender due to special feeding, but the custom has stayed on in some parts of the country.

    1 turkey, 12 to 14 pounds (defrosted if frozen)
    1 stalk celery
    1 small onion
    2 teaspoons salt
    3 cups water

Put turkey in roasting pan with a cover, with celery, onion, salt, and water. Cover, bring to a boil, and simmer over very low heat for 1 hour. Baste the top of the turkey with pan juices once or twice. Reserve pan juices in a bowl.

Stuffing:

    3 eggs, beaten
    8 to 12 cups crumbled day-old bread
    2 teaspoons poultry seasoning
    ⅔ cup celery, chopped
    1 medium onion, chopped

Mix all ingredients together. Sprinkle pan juices over stuffing, mix quickly and stuff lightly into turkey.
Preheat oven to 325 degrees.
Rub turkey with butter or bacon fat. Roast turkey, uncovered, for 1½ to 2 hours (until juices near the second joint run clear when pierced with a fork).
Make gravy from pan juices. Some turkeys give off more juice than others. Use 1 tablespoon of flour and 1 cup water stirred into pan per cup of pan juices. (*8 servings*)

CHICKEN POT PIE

Chicken pot pie moved westward into the valley of Virginia and the Ohio Valley and from there throughout the Middle West. The farms were rich with fat chickens, good fresh vegetables, milk, butter, and flour to make good fricassees and pies. Pot pie was sometimes made the next day with what was left of a large fowl and the vegetables that had been served with it (there were often as many as six vegetables on farm tables). But it was more likely to be started by stewing a fresh chicken, and adding fresh vegetables to the broth (see Southern Chicken Pie*). Chicken shortcakes made with biscuit or corn bread are variations of this basic recipe.

First, make standard pie crust:

    1½ cups flour
    1 teaspoon salt
    ⅔ cup vegetable shortening, or ⅓ cup lard
    ¼ cup ice water

Sift the flour and salt into a mixing bowl, add the shortening, and work with a pastry blender or rub between fingers until the mixture is in pea-size pieces. Add the ice water bit by bit, stirring with a fork until pastry is wet enough to hold together in a ball.
Divide into two balls, one larger than the other, and roll each out on a floured board to fit the casserole.
Preheat oven to 425 degrees.
Line a 1½-quart casserole with the larger pastry, and fill with the following ingredients:

2 cups diced cooked chicken
½ cup cooked chopped celery
½ cup cooked peas
½ cup diced cooked potatoes
¼ cup chopped pimentos
¼ cup pearl onions
2 cups chicken gravy, or cream sauce
 made with half chicken broth and half
 milk
1 teaspoon salt
½ teaspoon pepper

Cover with the second pastry, crimp the edges, cut steam vents, and bake 20 to 25 minutes. (*4 servings*)

SMOTHERED FRIED CHICKEN

1 fryer (2½ to 3 pounds), disjointed
1 teaspoon salt
½ cup butter
½ cup lard
½ cup flour

Gravy:

2 tablespoons flour
1½ cups milk
1 teaspoon salt
¼ teaspoon pepper

If fresh-killed, sprinkle chicken with 1 teaspoon salt, and refrigerate overnight.
Put lard and butter in an iron skillet or Dutch oven with a cover. Heat.
Flour chicken and place in the hot fat. Cover tightly and lower heat. Cook 20 minutes on one side, then turn, cover again, and cook 20 minutes on the other side. Remove chicken to a hot platter.
To make gravy, stir flour into pan drippings. Add milk gradually. When gravy forms, add salt and pepper. Serve with chicken. (*4 servings*)

BAKED CHICKEN IN CREAM

1 chicken (3 pounds), disjointed
½ cup flour
1 teaspoon salt
¼ teaspoon pepper
 bacon fat
2 tablespoons finely chopped onion
2 tablespoons finely chopped celery
1 tablespoon finely chopped parsley
2 cups heavy cream

Preheat oven to 325 degrees.
Put flour, salt, and pepper into a paper bag, and shake the chicken pieces in the mixture to coat.
Brown chicken pieces in hot bacon fat in a heavy skillet.
Transfer to a greased casserole, cover with the remaining ingredients.
Cover the casserole, and cook slowly in the oven for 1½ hours or until chicken is tender. (*4 servings*)

PICKLED CHICKEN

In very hot countries chickens are put into brine as soon as killed to keep them from spoiling in the heat.
This recipe is unusual, but even more unusual is finding this "hot-country" dish in midwestern America. Actually it serves as an interesting variation on chicken aspic.

1 fowl (5 to 6 pounds)
1 teaspoon salt
1 cup vinegar
⅛ teaspoon allspice
⅛ teaspoon cinnamon

Boil fowl in enough salted water to cover until meat falls from the bones. Remove and discard the bones, reserving the broth.
Put the meat into a bowl that has a cover.
Mix 1 cup vinegar with 1 cup of the broth, add a little allspice and cinnamon.
Pour this mixture over the chicken, cover, and set aside in the refrigerator for at least 2 days. Serve cold. (*4 servings*)

ROAST GOOSE WITH APPLE STUFFING

Wisconsin geese are force-fed, Strasbourg style, to produce enormous livers for making paté and liverwurst. The geese themselves are fat and succulent, and are delicious roasted with tart apples and raisins.

    1 goose (8 pounds)
    salt
    pepper
    powdered ginger
    3 large tart apples, peeled, cored, and chopped
    1 cup raisins
    1 tablespoon finely chopped onion
    grated rind of 1 lemon

Preheat oven to 350 degrees.
Rub the goose inside and out with a mixture of salt, pepper, and a little ginger.
Mix together the apples and raisins, and stuff loosely into the goose.
Place the goose on the rack of an oven pan and roast in oven for 2 to 2½ hours or until juice runs clear when breast is pierced with a fork. Remove the goose to a heated platter, and keep hot.
Skim off the fat from the pan juices, stir in the onion and lemon rind, and bring to a boil on top of the stove, adding a little hot water if needed. Pour the sauce into a gravy boat and serve with the goose. (*6 to 8 servings*)

VEGETABLES
AND SIDE DISHES

RUTABAGAS AND MUSHROOMS

Rutabagas are the Swedish, or yellow, turnips. A great favorite of the English who brought them to this country, they are known throughout the British Isles as "Swedes." In this country they are most often peeled, sliced, or diced, and cooked in boiling water with a little salt. Sometimes they are mashed, buttered, and combined with an equal amount of mashed potatoes. The following recipe is a midwestern favorite.

    1 medium rutabaga, peeled and sliced
    salt
    6 tablespoons butter
    1 cup coarsely chopped mushrooms
    ½ teaspoon freshly ground pepper

Cook the rutabaga in salted water until soft. Drain, mash, and stir in 3 tablespoons butter. Sauté the mushrooms in the remaining butter until brown, and add to the rutabagas. Season and serve. (*4 servings*)

SAUER BEANS

Some ingenious gardener must have come up with this recipe. If it worked for sauerkraut, why wouldn't it work for green beans? We have lost the art of preserving foods in salt. Freezers are convenient and easy to use, so old methods that require time and tending are falling into disuse.

    15 pounds fresh green beans
    ¾ cup salt
    1 gallon crock, sterilized with boiling water

Remove tips of beans and slice once lengthwise. Mix well with salt and pack in gallon crock. Cover the crock with a clean white cloth and a plate, and weigh it down with a stone. Let work 3 weeks. After the working is finished (the liquid will be still) the beans can be packed in jars.
Use with pork, ham, spareribs, hocks, or knuckles as one would use sauerkraut.

ZUCCHINI WITH SOUR CREAM SAUCE

8 small zucchini, peeled or scraped
  dash vinegar
1 teaspoon salt
½ teaspoon pepper
  dash sugar
1 slice of onion
2 tablespoons vinegar
1 tablespoon water
1 teaspoon minced fresh dill
1 teaspoon minced parsley
1 cup sour cream
1 tablespoon butter
1 tablespoon flour

Halve the zucchini lengthwise, and discard the center pulp and seeds. Slice lengthwise into strips, and boil 8 minutes in a little water with vinegar, salt, pepper, sugar, and onion. Drain and keep warm.
In a saucepan mix together 2 tablespoons vinegar, 1 tablespoon of water, the dill, parsley, and sour cream.
Make a roux of the butter and flour and add to the saucepan. Blend well and heat (do not boil).
Serve the zucchini with the sour cream sauce spooned over it. (*4 servings*)

BUTTERED RADISHES

With so many radishes grown in home gardens this is a very simple way to cook them (cooking reduces the "bite"). Radishes are very good creamed, too.

4 cups small red radishes, washed and
  stemmed
  water to cover
2 tablespoons butter
¼ teaspoon salt

Cook radishes in water to cover, over low heat, for 30 minutes.
Drain, add butter and salt.
Serve hot. (*6 servings*)

POTATO PANCAKES

This recipe comes from Wisconsin and is unusual because it doesn't use flour. We tried to make potato pancakes with grated potatoes when we first started to cook. When they turned purple we threw them away.

2 large potatoes, peeled and grated
2 eggs, well beaten
½ teaspoon salt
2 tablespoons bacon fat or cooking oil

Grate potatoes into a bowl and add just enough cold water to cover them. Let stand 5 minutes, then pour into a colander with a bowl under it to catch the water. Let the starch settle in the bowl of water a few minutes and carefully pour off the purple liquid on top.
Mix the starch with the grated potatoes and the well-beaten eggs. Add salt.
Cook on a very hot griddle until brown. Turn and brown on the other side. (*4 servings*)

BAKED CABBAGE

Cabbage was the mainstay of the winter months in the years before canning and freezing. Without cabbage and a few other green vegetables, many people would have died of scurvy, a disease caused by a lack of vitamin C. Cabbage was cooked in every possible way, and by spring people were heartily sick of it—but not sick enough to pass up the tender, green, new cabbage leaves that sprouted from the stalks left in the garden for that very purpose.

1 medium-size cabbage, cut in eighths
2 eggs, well beaten
2 tablespoons melted butter
4 tablespoons cream
1 teaspoon salt
½ teaspoon paprika

Cover the cabbage with boiling water, and cook about 15 minutes or until tender. Drain and cool.
Preheat oven to 325 degrees.
Chop the cabbage finely and add eggs, butter, cream, and seasonings. Cook in a buttered baking dish about 30 minutes. (*4 servings*)

SPINACH RING

3 cups chopped cooked spinach (fresh or frozen), drained and pressed dry
1 cup heavy cream
2 eggs, beaten
1 teaspoon salt
½ teaspoon pepper
pinch nutmeg
juice of ½ lemon

Preheat oven to 350 degrees.
Mix together all the ingredients and place into a buttered ring mold.
Set the mold into a pan of hot water and bake about 40 minutes or until firm.
Unmold onto a heated platter. Fill the center with small braised onions, buttered cooked peas, mushrooms, or a mixture of all of them. (*4 to 6 servings*)

CARROT CROQUETTES

This recipe came from Zion, Illinois. Perhaps it is a reminder that the first Mormons camped there—they often used dishes like this one to take the place of meat. Swiss chard, spinach, or squash, cooked and drained, can be used in this recipe instead of carrots.

2 medium carrots, ground
⅔ cup cracker crumbs
1 small onion, finely chopped
⅓ cup milk
4 eggs, beaten
bacon fat

Mix all ingredients together.
Fry by tablespoons in bacon fat on hot griddle, like pancakes. Turn and cook on the other side. (*4 servings*)

SALADS
AND DRESSINGS

HOT DUTCH SALAD

¼ pound bacon, chopped
1 egg, beaten
½ cup sour cream
2 tablespoons vinegar
salt
3 or 4 spring onions, sliced and chopped
lettuce leaves

Brown the bacon in a heavy skillet over low heat. Stir in the beaten egg, then the cream, then the vinegar. Season to taste and remove from heat.
Stir in the onions but do not cook. Pour over the lettuce leaves while still hot, and toss. (*2 servings*)

CELERY VINAIGRETTE

2 celery hearts
2 tablespoons vinegar
6 tablespoons olive oil
¼ teaspoon paprika
1 teaspoon salt
¼ teaspoon pepper
1 tablespoon chopped green pepper
1 tablespoon chopped pimento

Cut celery hearts in half and simmer in boiling water until tender, about 20 minutes. Remove to serving dish.
Mix remaining ingredients, and spoon over celery. Refrigerate until ready to serve. (*4 servings*)

STUFFED ENDIVE

cottage cheese
salt
pepper
chopped chives
endive
French dressing
paprika
stuffed olives

Season the cottage cheese to taste and mix with chopped chives.

Dip the endive into French dressing, sprinkle with paprika, and fill with the cottage cheese mixture.

Arrange on a plate like flower petals and fill the center with stuffed olives.

MOLDED ASPARAGUS SALAD

When it comes to making salad, canned asparagus seems to be universally preferred to the fresh or frozen variety.

1 can (16 ounces) asparagus tips, drained (liquid reserved)
2 tablespoons melted butter
2 tablespoons flour
4 egg yolks, beaten
1 package unflavored gelatin, soaked in 2 tablespoons cold water
juice of 1 lemon
1 cup unsweetened whipped cream
salt
pepper
lettuce
julienned pimento
mayonnaise

Mix together the butter, flour, and the liquid drained from the asparagus, and cook for 2 minutes. Remove from the heat and stir into the beaten egg yolks.

Return to the heat and cook 1 minute, stirring constantly. Add the gelatin and stir until it dissolves. Cool.

Add the lemon juice and whipped cream. Season to taste.

Line a mold with a layer of asparagus, pour over half the sauce, add the remaining asparagus and the rest of the sauce. Chill.

Serve on lettuce garnished with pimento and mayonnaise. (*6 to 8 servings*)

INDIANA POTATO SALAD

Potato salad is a truly national dish and is made differently in every section of the country. In the East it is made with hard-boiled eggs, celery, minced onion and mayonnaise or sour cream; and in the South and Midwest, with a boiled dressing made with whipped cream, or mayonnaise, pimentos, olives, and chopped red or green peppers. Wisconsin potato salad is dressed with chopped cucumbers, chopped hard-boiled eggs, celery seed, minced onion, sour cream, and salt and pepper. The beef broth in this recipe is unusual and may be of French or German origin.

3 cups diced cooked potatoes, cold
6 tablespoons olive oil
4 tablespoons vinegar
½ cup beef broth
1 teaspoon salt
few grains cayenne
1 tablespoon minced onion

Mix together all the ingredients, chill, and serve on lettuce. (*4 to 6 servings*)

TOSSED GREEN SALAD, BLUE CHEESE DRESSING

Among the many uses of Wisconsin's blue cheese is this dressing, very much like a Roquefort cheese dressing. The French cannot believe that Americans eat cheese in salads.

6 tablespoons olive oil
1 tablespoon vinegar
2 tablespoons blue cheese
½ teaspoon salt
⅛ teaspoon pepper
½ head romaine and ½ head chicory, washed, dried, and torn into small pieces.

Put oil, vinegar, blue cheese, salt, and pepper in salad bowl and mix well, mashing the cheese into the dressing.

When ready to serve, add the romaine and chicory and toss all together. (*6 to 8 servings*)

BREADS
AND BATTERCAKES

BOHEMIAN HOUSKA

Come Christmas, in the midwestern cities, this bread-cake was baked and sold in bakeries, or was lovingly homemade to keep alive the memory of Bohemia. Bohemia has long since become a memory; formerly a province of Czechoslovakia, it was abolished in 1949.

    1 package dry yeast, or 1 cake
    ½ cup sugar
    2 cups milk, scalded
    8 cups flour
    1 teaspoon salt
    ¼ teaspoon mace
    1 cup lard, or butter and lard mixed
    3 eggs, well beaten
    1 cup seedless raisins
    ½ cup chopped almonds

Make a sponge with yeast, 2 tablespoons sugar, 1-½ cups milk and 2 tablespoons flour. Beat and allow to rise until double in bulk.
Sift remaining flour with salt and mace, three times.
Add the lard or butter and the rest of the sugar to the remaining ½ cup hot milk. When melted and slightly cooled, mix with the beaten eggs, and add this to the yeast sponge.
Dust raisins and chopped almonds with flour. Add yeast mixture to flour, beat well, add raisins and almonds. Allow to rise until double in bulk.
Divide dough into 3 sections, then divide each section into 3. Roll into strips. Make one braid out of each 3 strips and place into greased loaf pans. Let double in bulk.
Preheat oven to 400 degrees.
Bake houska 15 minutes, reduce heat to 350, and bake 20 to 25 minutes longer or until brown. (*3 loaf-sized cakes*)

BAKING POWDER BISCUITS

    3 cups flour
    1 teaspoon salt
    3 teaspoons baking powder
    6 tablespoons shortening
    1 cup milk

Preheat oven to 425 degrees.
Sift the dry ingredients together. Work in the shortening with fingers or a pastry blender until it is the consistency of coarse cornmeal. Add the milk and stir until mixture lumps together. Place on a floured board, and roll out until ½ to 1 inch thick.
Cut biscuits with floured cutter, place into a baking pan, and allow to stand at room temperature 15 to 30 minutes.
Bake 12 to 15 minutes.(*about 20 biscuits*)

HUCKLEBERRY MUFFINS

    3 cups flour
    3 teaspoons baking powder
    4 tablespoons sugar
    ½ teaspoon salt
    1 cup milk
    1 egg
    5 tablespoons melted butter
    1 cup huckleberries or blueberries,
        mixed with 2 tablespoons sugar

Preheat oven to 400 degrees.
Mix and sift the flour, baking powder, sugar, and salt.
Beat together the milk and egg, and mix with the dry ingredients.
Stir in the butter and huckleberries, and pour into buttered muffin tins to ⅔ full, and bake 15 to 20 minutes. (*12 muffins*)

INDIANA CORNCAKE

This is an unusual recipe, coming as it does from Indiana, because it calls for the use of white water-ground cornmeal, a product of Maryland, Virginia, and other southern states. The answer has to be that it was brought there by settlers, as so many other recipes indigenous to one region have been spread about the country.

2 cups white water-ground cornmeal
2 teaspoons baking powder
1 egg yolk, lightly beaten
2 cups milk
1 tablespoon melted fat
1 egg white, beaten stiff

Preheat oven to 375 degrees.
Mix together cornmeal and baking powder. Mix together egg yolk with milk and fat, and stir into the cornmeal. Fold in the egg white; pour into a greased shallow pan and bake 30 minutes. (*4 servings*)

WISCONSIN BEER BREAD

In Bavaria and other beer-consuming parts of the world, beer is used extensively in cooking. It is not surprising, therefore, to find in America's beer belt a bread made with beer.

1½ cups beer
1 package dry yeast
4 cups flour, sifted
½ teaspoon sugar
1 teaspoon salt

Heat beer to lukewarm and stir in yeast until dissolved.
Stir in flour until the consistency is that of thick pancake batter. Cover with cloth and let rise until double in bulk. Add remaining flour, sugar, and salt.
Knead dough until it comes away from the sides of the bowl easily.
Grease bowl and set dough in it. Grease top of dough, cover again, set in a warm place, and let rise again until double in bulk.
Form into one loaf. Let rise again 1 hour.
Preheat oven to 375 degrees.
Bake 40 to 60 minutes or until golden brown on top. (*1 loaf*)

GAELIC OATCAKES

These cakes were brought to the Midwest from Wales and Ireland, where they are made without sugar or flour and with oats fresh from the mill.

2 tablespoons butter
4 cups long-cooking oatmeal, put through meat grinder
1 cup white flour
1 tablespoon sugar
½ teaspoon salt
1 cup milk, warmed

Rub butter into oatmeal, flour, salt, and sugar until very fine. Add enough milk to make it malleable enough to roll out. Take a piece as big as a baseball and roll until very thin, using plenty of oats to "flour" board. Cut in quarters and put on a buttered cookie sheet. Repeat until all is used.
Preheat oven to 375 degrees.
Bake cakes 12 minutes or until brown. Serve with butter. (*4 to 6 servings*)

SOY BISCUITS

Soy flour, made from toasted soybeans, is a relative newcomer to the American kitchen. Soy flour has an abundance of protein and has become a popular protein "health food." Until this rich resource was discovered, there were few vegetable proteins that could take the place of meat in vegetarian and health diets. Soy flour has a richness of flavor that, to many palates, shows up better in combination with whole wheat or other flours.

¼ cup soy flour
¼ cup white flour
1 cup whole wheat flour
½ teaspoon salt
¾ cup milk
3 tablespoons vegetable oil

Preheat oven to 425 degrees.
Mix together all the ingredients, using enough milk to make a soft dough.
Roll out on a floured board to a thickness of ½-inch, and cut into biscuits.
Place onto an oiled cookie sheet and bake 10 or 15 minutes or until golden. (*about 24 biscuits*)

SWEDISH RYE BREAD

    3 cups milk, scalded
    1 cake yeast (or 1 package dry yeast)
    ½ cup white sugar
    3 tablespoons brown sugar
    ¾ cup dark corn syrup
    2 cups rye flour
    3½ cups white flour, or enough to make a
        stiff dough

Dissolve yeast in ¼ cup milk. Add yeast, brown and white sugars, corn syrup, and rye flour to the scalded milk and beat well.
Add white flour, mix well, cover, and let rise overnight.
Shape into 2 loaves and place on buttered cookie sheet. Cover with towel, let rise until double in bulk.
Preheat oven to 350 degrees.
Bake bread 1 hour, or until loaf sounds hollow when tapped with finger. (*2 loaves*)

HOMINY FRITTERS

    2 cups cold cooked hominy
    2 eggs, beaten
    ½ cup milk
    ½ teaspoon salt
    1 teaspoon baking powder
    1½ cups flour
       fat for frying

Mix hominy, eggs, milk, and salt.
Sift flour with baking powder, and add to hominy mixture. Beat well.
Heat fat until just smoking, and drop batter into it by tablespoonfuls. Fry until brown.
Drain on paper towels and serve hot. (*6 to 8 servings*)

DESSERTS

VANILLA ICE CREAM

Few people now remember taking turns at the hand-cranked ice cream freezer at picnics or Fourth of July celebrations, but it was part of the ritual of Sunday evenings in summer. The stronger boys had a chance to show off as the "cream," as it was called, hardened, and everyone watched and waited for the feast to come. The last turn was the hardest, and then the person in charge would say, "That's enough." Then the paddle was removed, (all the children begged to lick it), and the freezer was packed with salted ice to ripen until time to serve. Almost always someone made chocolate or fudge sauce to go with the ice cream. The beauty of the recipe below is that Vanilla Ice Cream can be converted into strawberry, peach, or other fruit ice creams by simply adding chopped fruit.

    1 quart milk or cream
    1½ cups confectioners' sugar
    6 eggs if all cream, 8 if milk, separated
    2 teaspoons vanilla

Scald the milk or cream.
Beat the egg yolks until lemon-colored. Add the sugar and beat until light. Beat the egg whites until stiff.
Pour the scalded milk or cream into the egg-and-sugar mixture slowly, stirring all the time. Fold in the egg whites and vanilla. Let cool.
Prepare freezer. Have plenty of ice cubes or crushed ice on hand, and rock salt. Put a 3-inch layer of ice on the bottom, and 1½ inches of salt.
Turn the above mixture into the can and cover carefully. Be sure the lid is tight so salt will not get into the ice cream.
Adjust the can to fit in the freezer and fill the space around it with alternate layers of ice and salt. When full, turn the crank until it is difficult to turn. Pour off water, refill with ice, and cover with canvas or heavy cloth. Let stand to ripen 1 hour or more.

OLD FASHIONED CHOCOLATE CAKE

What could be better than a good chocolate cake? Compared to many European desserts and cakes this is a simple one, yet it needs no embellishment and is as American as apple pie. Chocolate cake was usually made with white or yellow cake and chocolate icing. The present trend is to all-chocolate cake.

    1 cup butter, softened
    2 cups sugar
    5 eggs, separated
    4 squares unsweetened chocolate, melted, or ⅔ cup cocoa (can be omitted to make a white cake)
    3½ cups flour
    2 teaspoons baking powder
    1 cup milk
    2 teaspoons vanilla

Frosting:

    1¼ cups sugar
    1 cup heavy cream
    5 squares unsweetened chocolate
    ½ cup butter
    1 teaspoon vanilla

Preheat oven to 375 degrees.
In bowl large enough to hold all cake ingredients cream butter, add sugar, and beat until lemon-colored. Add egg yolks and beat again. Add chocolate.
Sift flour before measuring, and sift again with baking powder. Add alternately to butter mixture with milk, beating all the time. Beat egg whites until stiff and fold in. Add vanilla. Line 3 layer-cake pans with buttered paper. Spoon one-third the batter into each one. Bake 30 to 40 minutes, until cake springs back when touched.
Remove from oven, cool on rack ten minutes, then turn pans to remove layers. Peel off buttered paper.
To make frosting, put sugar and cream in a heavy saucepan, bring to a boil, stirring constantly. Quickly lower heat under pan, add chocolate, butter, and vanilla. Stir until all are melted. Cool and chill until mixture begins to thicken.

Beat until thick enough to spread.
Put one layer on cake plate. Spread with half the filling, covering top and sides. Repeat with each layer. Save a little icing for patching.(*8 servings*)

ORANGE CAKE

This cake fed many generations of a middle western family for birthdays, picnics, and other celebrations. For all we know it may still be doing so. The base is sponge cake.

    7 egg whites
    1¼ cups sugar
    5 egg yolks
    1 tablespoon lemon juice
    1 teaspoon grated lemon rind
    1 cup flour, sifted 4 times
    ¼ teaspoon salt

Preheat oven to 350 degrees.
Beat egg whites until stiff. Gradually beat half the sugar into the whites.
Beat egg yolks, lemon juice, and rind until lemon-colored. Add remainder of sugar, continue beating.
Combine the two mixtures. Stir in the flour and salt. Pour into unbuttered layer-cake pans. Bake 25 or 30 minutes.

Filling:

    juice and grated rind of 4 oranges
    juice of 2 lemons
    1 teaspoon cornstarch
    1 cup sugar
    3 eggs, beaten

Mix all together and stir over low heat until thick. Cool.

Frosting:

    ½ cup confectioners' sugar
    1 orange, sliced thin (discard seeds)

When cake is done, cool. Spread filling between layers. Sprinkle top with confectioners' sugar, and decorate with orange slices.

BUTTERNUT SQUASH PIE

Squash pie, like pumpkin pie, is usually considered a winter dessert. But squash pie, which is equally as good eating, has an advantage. It can be served in August and September, before pumpkins are ripe.

    1 cup mashed butternut squash
    1 cup heavy cream
    1 cup sugar
    3 eggs, slightly beaten
    ¼ cup brandy or bourbon
    1 teaspoon nutmeg
    1 teaspoon cinnamon
    ¾ teaspoon ginger
    ½ teaspoon salt
    ¼ teaspoon mace
    1 unbaked pie crust (see Plain Pastry*)

Peel and cook half a butternut squash, cut into pieces, in one cup of boiling water, about 10 minutes. Drain and mash.
Preheat oven to 400 degrees.
Brush pie pastry with white of egg.
Mix squash, cream, sugar, eggs, brandy, and seasonings together.
Pour into crust and bake 5 minutes. Reduce heat to 300 degrees, and bake 40 to 50 minutes or until a knife blade comes clean when inserted in the center of the pie. (*6 to 8 servings*)

PUMPKIN CHIFFON PIE

Here is an old favorite in a new guise. This recipe can be used with butternut squash as well.

Crust:

    3 cups graham cracker crumbs
    ½ cup brown sugar, firmly packed
    ½ cup butter, at room temperature
    2 tablespoons finely chopped nutmeats

Preheat oven to 300 degrees.
Mix all the ingredients together and form a layer in the bottom and sides of a greased 10-inch pie pan. Toast in the oven for 10 to 15 minutes. Remove and set aside for the filling.

Filling:

    2½ cups cooked (or canned) pumpkin
    1 cup brown sugar, firmly packed
    1 cup milk
    1 cup heavy cream
    ½ cup orange juice
    ½ teaspoon cinnamon
    ½ teaspoon ground cloves
    ½ teaspoon allspice
    2 tablespoons unflavored gelatin,
      soaked in 4 tablespoons cold water
    2 egg whites, beaten until stiff
      whipped cream

Put the pumpkin, sugar, milk, cream, orange juice, and seasonings into blender, and mix until thoroughly blended.
Add the gelatin and blend again.
Remove to a mixing bowl, fold in the egg whites, and fill the prepared crust. Top with whipped cream and chill. (*8 to 10 servings*)

BROWN-SUGAR PIE

The unending number of luscious pies that were and are baked in Ohio and other states of the Midwest is a marvel to foreigners. I once knew an Italian who, on his first visit to the United States, went into a diner and ordered apple pie. After having eaten the whole pie, he then proceeded to eat a lemon pie, and then a custard pie. He couldn't stop eating them! Despite what should have been a monumental state of indigestion, he said, "American pies, I love them, they are marvelous!" Then he kissed his fingers in a gesture of appreciation.

    3 cups brown sugar, firmly packed
    ½ cup melted butter
    ½ cup light cream or evaporated milk
    3 eggs, beaten
    1 unbaked 9-inch pie crust

Preheat oven to 400 degrees.
Mix all ingredients together and pour into pie shell.
Bake 5 minutes at 400 degrees, reduce heat to 350, and continue baking 25 minutes. (*6 servings*)

SOUR CHERRY PIE

"As American as apple pie"—or cherry pie, in this case. Cherry pie has become the symbol of Washington's Birthday in bakeries around the country, though cherries don't ripen until June. There are few desserts as good—or as honest—as fresh cherry pie. A teaspoon of almond flavoring can be added to the filling, if desired.

    4 cups sour red cherries
    ½ cup sugar
    2 tablespoons flour
    2 unbaked 9-inch pie crusts

Preheat oven to 400 degrees.
Stone cherries, reserve juice.
Line pie plate with pastry. Put cherries in pie plate on top of bottom crust. Sprinkle flour and sugar over cherries. Cover with top crust. Cut slits in top crust and crimp edges.
Bake 5 minutes, lower heat to 350 degrees, and cook 40 minutes more, until crust is light brown and juice bubbles up through vents. (*6 servings*)

BUTTERMILK RAISIN CAKE

This old midwestern country recipe has existed for a long time—probably because of its simplicity.

    ½ cup butter
    1 cup sugar
    3 eggs, separated
    ½ cup buttermilk
    2 tablespoons prune juice
    2 cups flour
    ½ teaspoon baking soda
    ½ pound seeded raisins, chopped
      butter

Preheat oven to 350 degrees.
Cream the butter and sugar. Beat the egg yolks, and stir in. Stir in the buttermilk and prune juice.
Blend the flour and soda, and add.
Beat the egg whites until stiff, and fold in.
Stir in the raisins, pour batter into a buttered 9-inch square cake pan, and bake in the oven until done when tested with a skewer, about 35 minutes. (*8 servings*)

COFFEECAKE

This is the original coffee cake, made with coffee.

    5 cups flour
    1 teaspoon cinnamon
    1 teaspoon allspice
    1 teaspoon baking soda
    ¾ cup butter
    2 cups brown sugar, firmly packed
    3 eggs, beaten
    1 cup molasses
    1 cup cold coffee
    1 cup raisins
    1 cup dried currants

Preheat oven to 275 degrees.
Sift flour, cinnamon, allspice, and soda together twice.
Cream the butter, and mix with sugar and beaten eggs.
Mix the coffee and molasses.
Beat these two mixtures alternately into the flour mixture. Add the raisins and currants last.
Butter an 11- by 14-inch baking pan and bake 45 to 50 minutes. (*12 servings*)

STRAWBERRY JAM

    4 cups strawberries (ripe but not
      overripe), washed and capped
    4 cups sugar

Place a layer of strawberries into a pot, then a layer of sugar. Repeat until all ingredients are used.
Let stand overnight or until sugar has dissolved.
Bring to a boil and cook for 10 minutes. Set aside overnight, then fill sterile jelly glasses, and seal. (*16 six-ounce glasses*)

SPECIAL PICNIC WATERMELON

Cut a 2-inch square plug in a ripe watermelon, and slowly pour in rum, applejack, bourbon, or even champagne. Replace the plug and refrigerate for a day, turning from time to time to allow liquor to permeate evenly. Serve sparingly.

OLD-FASHIONED APPLE CRISP

 2 cups dry bread crumbs
 ¼ teaspoon grated nutmeg
 ¼ teaspoon cinnamon
 1 cup brown sugar, firmly packed
 4 cups thinly sliced peeled and cored
   apples
 1 cup grated sharp cheese
   butter

Preheat oven to 350 degrees.

Mix together the bread crumbs, nutmeg, cinnamon, and sugar.

Place alternate layers of this mixture, apples, and cheese into a buttered baking dish.

Cover with bread crumbs, dot with butter, and bake about 40 minutes or until tender and crisp. Serve with cream or your favorite dessert sauce. (*4 to 6 servings*)

BEVERAGES

ICED TEA

Once a foreign visitor told me that the one drink he couldn't abide was iced tea. I was astonished at my own surprise, then I realized that iced tea is almost unknown outside of America.

 4 cups boiling water
 8 teaspoons orange pekoe tea
 1 lemon, sliced
   sugar

Pour boiling water over tea in a china teapot. Let steep 5 minutes. (If making for later use, do not refrigerate, or it will become cloudy.) Pour the tea into 4 glasses filled with ice cubes. Put a lemon slice on the rim of each glass, and serve with sugar on the side. (*6 to 8 servings*)

MULLED CIDER

 1 quart cider
 2 whole allspice berries
 2 whole cloves
 1 stick cinnamon (3 inches long)
 ½ cup brown sugar, firmly packed

Mix together cider, allspice berries, cloves, cinnamon, and brown sugar.

Bring to a boil in a saucepan and cook 5 minutes. Remove spices, and serve hot in mugs. (*6 servings*)

ELDERBERRY WINE

The elderberry is especially suited for wine making, its juices containing a considerable portion of what is necessary for vigorous fermentation, and its beautiful color imparting a rich tint to the wine made from it. It is, however, deficient in sweetness and requires a great deal of sugar. Elderberry wine is one of the best and more popular of the homemade wines.

 6 pounds ripe elderberries, washed
 3 gallons boiling water
   sugar
 1 pound seedless raisins
 6 whole cloves
 1 cake yeast, crumbled
 1 cup brandy or whiskey

Pour the boiling water over the berries, and let stand 24 hours. Crush well and strain through a jelly bag, measuring the juice obtained.

For each gallon of juice add 3 pounds sugar. Add the raisins and cloves. Boil 1 hour, then cool to room temperature, and add the yeast. Transfer to a small keg, cover the bunghole with a cloth, and let stand 14 days. Stir in the brandy, and let stand 6 months.

Strain into bottles and cork tightly. (*about 12 quarts*)

RICE WINE

It doesn't take much skill to make a rice wine of sorts. Just put the ingredients together at the right temperature and nature will do the rest. (The trick is to know just when to bottle it.) Recipes for rice wine can be found all over the country. This very simple one turned up in—of all places—Champaign, Illinois.

    3 pounds raw rice (any kind)
    6 pounds white sugar
    1 pound seeded raisins
    2 oranges, sliced
    2 gallons boiling water
    2 yeast cakes, crumbled

Place the rice, sugar, raisins, oranges, and water into a stone crock. When cool, stir in the yeast cake.

Keep at room temperature (65 to 70 degrees), and stir every day for 3 weeks with a wooden spoon.
Strain and let settle for 24 hours.
When fermentation has stopped, siphon into bottles, and cork. (*8 to 10 quarts*)

SHERRY COBBLER

    1 teaspoon confectioners' sugar
    2 ounces carbonated water
      shaved ice
    3 ounces sherry
      maraschino cherry

Dissolve confectioners' sugar in carbonated water, using a goblet. Fill goblet with shaved ice, add sherry, stir, and serve with straw. Garnish with a cherry or other fruit. (*1 servings*)

PRAIRIE
COOKING

SOUPS AND CHOWDERS

Cream of Turnip Soup
Vegetable Beef Soup
Corn Chowder
Cream of Tomato Soup
Swedish Fruit Soup
Winnebago Cheese Soup
Black-Walnut Bisque

PASTA, EGG, AND CHEESE DISHES

Squaw Dish
Scalloped Cheese
Egg Croquettes
Cheese Squares
Potato Omelet
Deviled Eggs

FISH AND SHELLFISH

Campfire Smelt
Broiled Salt Herring
Baked Pike with Dill Sauce
Baked Muskellunge Steak

MEATS

Crisp-Roasted Fresh Ham
Fruit-Stuffed Spareribs
Baked Dakota Pork Pancake
Campfire Steak
Missouri Kitchen-Barbecued Steak
Kitchen-Barbecued Lamb
Iowa Goulash
Rolled Pot Roast of Beef
Steak and Kidney Pie
Hunters' Hamburger Stew
Danish Kodfars
Swedish Meatballs
Cornish Pasty
Oxtail Stew

POULTRY AND GAME BIRDS

Goose with Hominy
Fried Prairie Chicken with Cream Gravy
Chicken Fricassee with Dumplings
Roast Duck, Sage Dressing
Pheasant Mulligan

VEGETABLES AND SIDE DISHES

Wild Rice
Indian Corn on the Cob
Kansas Potatoes Fried Whole
Norwegian Potato Pancakes
Squash Pudding with Bacon
Creamed Spinach with Bacon
Spiced Pumpkin

SALADS AND DRESSINGS

Wilted Lettuce Salad
Nebraska Herring Salad
Stuffed Tomato Salad
Scandinavian Macaroni Salad
Jellied Orange-Carrot Salad
Gooseberry Mold

BREADS AND BATTERCAKES

Skillet Corn Bread
Salt-Rising Bread
Kansas Cracked-Corn Griddlecakes
Missouri Hoecake
Buttermilk Biscuits
Swedish Coffee Bread

DESSERTS

Cream Pudding
Old-fashioned Lemon Pie
Hickory Nut Pie
Danish Skillet Cake
Bread Cake
Tomato Soup Cake
Black-Walnut Ice Cream
Black-bread Torte
Plum Coffeecake
Bread Pudding
North Dakota Honey Custard

BEVERAGES

Glögg
Cider Punch
Dandelion Flower Wine
Prairie Mary

PRAIRIE COOKING

The first persons to ride across the wild lands beyond the Mississippi were the Indians who had lived there for generations. The French fur trappers, called *coureurs du bois*, named it "the praerie," meaning in their language an extensive tract of grassland. It is doubtful that they had any conception of the true vastness of the region, for it constitutes one of the largest areas of fertile soil in the world.

In the spring when the trappers rode across the prairie, their horses' hooves were stained red by the wild strawberry juice, and in early summer they were purple from the huckleberries that grew in the thick grass. Deer fed there, and buffalo roamed. Beaver dams blocked the rivers and streams where trout leaped. In the lakes there were whitefish and black bass, the flesh of the first snow-white and tender when cooked. Prairie chickens, a kind of grouse, flew up from the grass, and prairie dogs popped into their holes as the men passed.

At first there were trails, known as "traces," across this vast land. Treaties with the Indians permitted the white men to use them, and wagon trains followed them to the rich lands beyond. The Oregon Trail split into two in what is now Idaho, one fork going to Oregon, the other to California. The Mormon Trail paralleled closely until it, too, diverged for Salt Lake. An early stagecoach traveler complained of the food at the stops: "Doughnuts green and poisonous with saleratus [baking soda], suspicious eggs in a massive greasy fritter, and rusty bacon intolerably fat." Another complained of the coffee. They all blamed the high cost of food on the depredations of the Indians.

But a later traveler said,

Our meals at the stage stations continued good throughout the trip. The staples were bacon, eggs, hot biscuits, green tea and coffee, dried peaches, and the apple pies were uniform. Each meal was the same: breakfast, dinner, supper were indistinguishable save by the hours, and the price was $1.00 to $1.50 each.

Lacking wood, the first settlers built huts out of the thick heavy sod, which they cut into large bricks three feet long. These huts provided adequate shelter until a frame house could be built. Some sod huts are still in existence. Fuel consisted of dried buffalo chips. Wild pigeons were a major food source—they could be caught by hand as they settled for the night, their tameness proving their undoing since the last passenger pigeon was seen in 1914. The tender little birds were eaten in pies, stuffed with corn bread, spitted, or stewed. The Canadian goose, a warier bird, still lives to fly south across the prairie every fall.

Eventually the railroads came, and with them came the Irish. The Swedes and Danes found that the profusion of bright blue lakes and the crystal-clear air reminded them of home. The Amish, a part of the same sect that settled Pennsylvania, came too.

New foods were adapted to old recipes, and new ones were invented. Pike was baked with dill. Spareribs were filled with fruit stuffing and baked like goose. Prairie chickens were fried and served with cream gravy, like chickens. Hickory nuts were used in pies that had called for walnuts or chestnuts. When the settlers couldn't get to the mill, they ground corn in a meat grinder and called it cracked corn. When the butter was done in the churn, they used the buttermilk to make biscuits with a rich flavor not to be forgotten. At Christmas they drank glögg, as had been their custom.

Often back East the lure of new land was too much to resist. The farm would be sold and the family would move west with horses, wagon, buggies loaded with bedding, and a food box filled with hams, butter-roasted chickens, eggs, bacon, bread, cakes and pies, fruit jams and preserves. One family moved west in May of the year 1869, right after the Civil War, from Illinois to Kansas. They crossed the Mississippi at St. Louis, Missouri, went westward to St. Charles where they followed the Missouri River's southern shore and then, when the river turned northward, followed their westward course to the eastern border of Kansas,

through woods and fields of millions of wild flowers. Along the river, cliffs on one side were filled with the gold glory of wild columbines in full bloom. Across streams to the valley, prairie hills, past farms with fields of oats and barley. Our way sometimes took us through miles and miles of rolling prairie whose virgin soil was green as a sea of emerald, and starred by millions of wild flowers—wild phlox in full bloom, white, pink, crimson; sensitive plants of pink and yellow; red masses of verbenas; the blue of spiderwort and scores of others.

When the wagon stopped at eventide, fires were built and the Dutch oven and coffeepot were set on the coals for supper. Florence Kelly, who later became a well-known journalist, went on to say,

The Dutch oven was large and round, a rather shallow, flat-bottomed iron pot standing on legs two or more inches high. It was set on a bed of red hot coals, and coals were heaped on its iron cover until it was

heated all through to the right degree. Then the food was put in, the cover was replaced and piled with fresh coals and the oven left to do its work. . . . My mother was expert in its use, and produced for our camp table hot biscuits, corn bread, roast meats done to a turn and tasty with special flavor. . . .

And the breakfasts:

soon the air was fragrant with inviting smells of frying ham, bacon, eggs and potatoes, corncakes cooking on a griddle set on a bed of red hot coals, and a steaming pot of coffee.

It must have been on such trips that the love of outdoor cooking developed into an American custom; it has remained one of the joys of the summer months throughout the country. All that is needed is an iron kettle, a griddle, a skillet, a Dutch oven, a coffeepot, and food to cook.

Though there were many hardships— tornadoes and droughts—the settlers and their families survived them to pass down through the years the good foods of many origins, as well as the sense of independence that such a simple way of life permitted. Part of this heritage has become a boon to the whole world. It was a colony of Ukrainians who first planted the special strain of wheat that was to survive in the prairie climate. This wheat has proved valuable not only to the United States, but to other nations as well, who benefited by its bounty to feed their peoples.

SOUPS AND CHOWDERS

BLACK-WALNUT BISQUE

  3 tablespoons butter
  3 tablespoons flour
  4 cups beef stock
  ½ teaspoon dried marjoram
  ½ bay leaf
  1 teaspoon salt
     few grains cayenne
  1 cup crushed black-walnut meats
  ½ cup sour cream
  ½ cup heavy cream

In a large saucepan melt the butter, stir in the flour until smooth, then gradually stir in the stock. Add the seasonings.
Mix together the walnuts and sour cream, and stir into the stock. Cook for a minute or so, remove from the heat, and stir in the cream. Serve hot. (*4 servings*)

CREAM OF TURNIP SOUP

In the old days turnips were stored all winter in the root cellar. It is not surprising, therefore, that the following recipe shows up repeatedly in one form or another in early cookbooks.
You'll need some stock from the pot on the back of the stove. You can make your own by stewing a veal knuckle in water and reducing to a concentrate—or use canned beef broth.

  1½ cups stock or beef broth
  10 small white turnips, peeled and grated
   1 teaspoon salt
   ½ teaspoon pepper
   1 tablespoon flour
   1 tablespoon butter
   1 cup light cream

Place the broth, turnips, and seasonings into a large pot. Cover and simmer 15 minutes.
Make a roux of the flour and butter and stir into the soup until smooth. Cook 2 minutes.
Add the cream, stir, and serve. (*6 servings*)

VEGETABLE BEEF SOUP

Vegetable soup, of one kind or another, can be found in all parts of the country—and of the world, in fact. It varies subtly or greatly from region to region according to the availability of ingredients. The recipe below is a good one, and fairly typical of the prairie states.

  1 beef shin (4 to 5 pounds)
  1 veal knuckle
     marrow bones
  4 quarts water
  1 tablespoon salt
  1 teaspoon pepper
  2 onions, sliced
  2 carrots, sliced
  2 stalks celery (including leaves),
     chopped
  2 potatoes, peeled and sliced
  2 cups chopped tomatoes, fresh or
     canned
  1 cup shelled peas

Place the meat and bones with salt and pepper into a large kettle or pot with 4 quarts water. Cover and boil 3 to 4 hours. Skim.
Remove the meat from the bones, chop, and return to the stock. Discard the bones.
Add the vegetables, bring to a simmer, and cook until vegetables are soft. Check seasonings and serve hot. (*4 to 6 servings*)

SWEDISH FRUIT SOUP

Scandinavians settling in the prairie country brought with them many of their traditional dishes. Prominent among these is fruit soup, a dish for which Scandinavians have long been famous.

    4 cups dried apricots, prunes, and
      raisins
    1 stick cinnamon
    2 quarts water
    1 tablespoon cornstarch mixed with ½
      cup water
    ¼ cup quick-cooking tapioca
    ¼ cup sugar
      juice of ½ lemon

Put the fruit, cinnamon, and water into a large saucepan, bring to a boil, and cook 15 minutes. Combine the cornstarch and water mixture with the tapioca, add to the fruit, and cook 20 minutes longer.
Stir in the sugar, and then add the lemon juice. Remove the cinnamon stick and serve hot. (*8 servings*)

WINNEBAGO CHEESE SOUP

    3 tablespoons butter
    4 tablespoons flour
    4 cups chicken bouillon
    2 cups milk
    ½ cup minced onion
    ¾ pound Cheddar cheese, grated
    1 cup light cream
    1 teaspoon salt
      few grains cayenne

In a large saucepan melt the butter, stir in the flour, then gradually stir in the bouillon until smooth.
Stir in the milk and add the onion. Cook over low heat 5 minutes, then add the cheese and continue cooking until cheese is melted.
Remove from the heat and stir in the cream, salt, and cayenne. Check for seasoning and serve hot. (*6 to 8 servings*)

CORN CHOWDER

    ¼ pound salt pork, cubed
    1 onion, chopped
    3 cups water
    3 large potatoes, peeled and diced
    2 cups raw corn kernels
    2 cups milk, scalded
    2 tablespoons butter
      dash Tabasco sauce
    1 teaspoon salt
    ½ teaspoon pepper
      chopped parsley

Sauté the salt pork in a heavy skillet until almost crisp. Add the onion and cook over low heat until soft.
Boil 3 cups of water in a saucepan, add the potatoes and corn, and cook until tender. Add the salt pork, onions, and fat drippings to the saucepan, and then the milk, butter, and seasonings.
Cook the chowder about 15 minutes and serve garnished with parsley. (*4 servings*)

CREAM OF TOMATO SOUP

    4 cups chopped tomatoes, fresh or
      canned
    2 tablespoons butter
    2 tablespoons flour
      pinch baking soda
 1½ cups light cream or warm evaporated
      milk
    1 teaspoon salt
    ½ teaspoon cayenne

Cook the tomatoes in a medium saucepan for 15 minutes. Strain.
Make a roux by blending the butter and flour, and add to the strained tomatoes. Add the soda, and cook until mixture thickens.
Spoon some of the mixture into the cream or warmed evaporated milk, and slowly stir into the soup. Season, stir, and serve. (*4 to 6 servings*)

PASTA, EGG,
AND CHEESE DISHES

SCALLOPED CHEESE

This is a soufflé with bread crumbs—an interesting variation, and one of the many dishes that make much of a small amount of cheese. Up until about twenty-five years ago the only cheeses available in ordinary American food stores were American Cheddar, sometimes called "rat cheese"; Philadelphia cream cheese; and Liederkranz, a New York cheese.

    1 quart milk
    3 cups dry bread crumbs
    ¼ pound American Cheddar cheese,
      grated
    ½ teaspoon salt
    ¼ teaspoon paprika
    4 eggs, separated, yolks and whites well
      beaten
    1 tablespoon melted butter

Preheat oven to 225 degrees.
Heat the milk, add the bread crumbs, then add the cheese. Cook 5 minutes, stirring. Cool. Stir in the seasonings, egg yolks and butter. Beat egg whites until stiff, and fold into mixture. Pour into a buttered baking dish, and cook slowly 40 to 45 minutes or until done. (*4 servings*)

EGG CROQUETTES

    3 tablespoons butter
    3 tablespoons flour
    ¾ cup milk
    ½ teaspoon salt
      few grains cayenne
    4 hard-cooked eggs, chopped
      dry bread crumbs
    1 egg, slightly beaten

Melt the butter in a medium saucepan over low heat. Stir in the flour and then gradually add the milk and seasonings. Cook-stir until thickened.
Remove sauce from heat, add chopped eggs, and cool.
Shape into croquettes, roll in crumbs, dip in beaten egg, and fry in deep fat at 365 degrees about 3 minutes or until golden. (*4 servings*)

DEVILED EGGS

A perennial garnish for buffets, summer suppers, and picnics; a luncheon dish; an elegant dish often served with sauces such as Mornay or hollandaise—the deviled egg (sometimes called stuffed eggs) has held its place in American cooking for as long as anyone can remember.

    4 hard-cooked eggs
    2 tablespoons mayonnaise
    1 tablespoon lemon juice
    1 teaspoon dry mustard
    ¼ teaspoon salt
    ⅛ teaspoon pepper
      dash cayenne
      paprika

Remove shells of eggs under cold water. Cut eggs in half carefully, and remove yolks.
Mash the yolks with the mayonnaise, lemon juice, mustard, salt, pepper, and cayenne. Mix well and fill each half white with a spoonful of the mixture. Shape each to mound the yolk mixture, leaving clean white edges.
Sprinkle with paprika, and place on lettuce or decorate a dish of cold meat with them and serve. (*4 servings*)

SQUAW DISH

This authentic American Indian dish has survived for generations as a breakfast dish in the Dakotas, attesting to its general acceptance and excellence.

    ½ pound bacon or salt pork, cubed
      kernels from 4 ears corn, or 1 16-
      ounce can whole kernel corn
    3 eggs, beaten
    1 teaspoon salt
    ½ teaspoon pepper

Fry the bacon cubes in a heavy skillet until brown and crisp, and pour off most of the fat. Mix together the corn and eggs, season with salt and pepper, and pour over the bacon. Cook until eggs are done. (*4 servings*)

CHEESE SQUARES

    1 loaf day-old bread, crusts trimmed
    ¼ pound butter, melted
    ¼ pound hard cheese, grated

Preheat oven to 300 degrees.
Cut bread in 2-inch strips and then cut each strip into 4 cubes.
Dip the cubes in melted butter, roll in grated cheese, and bake 10 to 15 minutes or until golden brown.
Serve at cocktail time, or with soups or salads.

POTATO OMELET

    2 tablespoons butter
    4 eggs, beaten slightly
    4 tablespoons water
    ½ teaspoon salt
      pinch pepper
    1 cup finely cubed cooked potatoes,
      warmed

Melt the butter in an omelet pan and heat to a sizzle.
Mix together the eggs, water, and seasonings, and pour into the omelet pan. As the omelet cooks, lift edges so that uncooked parts come into contact with the hot pan.
Add the warmed potatoes, fold double, brown, and turn onto a hot platter. (*2 to 3 servings*)

FISH AND SHELLFISH

BAKED PIKE WITH DILL SAUCE

    1 pike, 3 or 4 pounds, dressed
    1 tablespoon salt
    1 egg, lightly beaten with 1 tablespoon
      water
      bread crumbs
    4 thin, 2-inch-wide strips salt pork, 5
      inches long
    2 cups light cream or half-and-half
    2 cups pearl onions, cooked 10 minutes
      in salted water
    2 tablespoons butter
    1 teaspoon sugar
      Dill Sauce (recipe follows)

Preheat oven to 425 degrees.
Wash the fish, rub the inside with salt, and brush the outside with egg mixture.
Roll in crumbs, and place on its side in a buttered baking dish. Cut 4 shallow slashes across the fish; lay salt pork strips in the slashes.
Bake in the oven 40 minutes, basting with cream several times until the fish has begun to brown.
Brown the onions in butter and sugar until golden.
Serve the fish on a heated platter, garnished with the onions. (*4 to 6 servings*)
Serve the Dill Sauce separately—recipe follows:

DILL SAUCE

yolk of 1 hard-cooked egg
½ cup salad oil
1½ teaspoons vinegar
dash Worcestershire sauce
½ teaspoon dry mustard
½ teaspoon sugar
¼ teaspoon salt
dash pepper
¼ teaspoon dried dill, or 1 teaspoon fresh dill
¼ cup unsweetened whipped cream

Rub the egg yolk through a sieve and beat in the salad oil, then the vinegar, Worcestershire, mustard, sugar, and seasonings.
Fold in the whipped cream, and refrigerate until ready for use. (*about 1 cup*)

BROILED SALT HERRING

Herrings are not indigenous to the prairie states—they cannot even be found in the waters thereabouts—but the Scandinavians who settled there like them and import them, dried and salted, by the bucketful.

4 salt herrings
4 large potatoes, peeled, halved, and boiled

Soak herrings overnight in cold water. Wash well, drain, and cut off heads.
Place fish onto a greased broiler rack and brown slightly under the broiler.
Serve with boiled potatoes. (*4 servings*)

BAKED MUSKELLUNGE STEAK

If you are lucky enough to catch a muskellunge, or are given a piece by another fisherman who has made the great catch of this big and wily fish of the Great Lakes region, here is the way it should be prepared. Otherwise any fish of the pike family will have to do.

3-pound muskellunge steak or slice
2 teaspoons salt
2 cups sour cream
½ cup dry bread crumbs

Preheat oven to 425 degrees.
Wipe steak dry, rub fish with salt, and place into a well-greased baking dish. Place in oven, and bake 10 minutes.
Reduce heat to 350 degrees. Pour the sour cream over the fish, sprinkle with bread crumbs, and bake 20 minutes longer or until golden brown. (*4 servings*)

CAMPFIRE SMELT

The smelt, originally a saltwater fish, was introduced into the Great Lakes around the turn of the century to serve as food for larger lake fish. It thrived and has become an important food fish for people.
Each spring, like their marine cousins the shad and the salmon, these little fish, averaging seven or eight inches in length, swarm up the small rivers and streams to spawn where they are scooped up literally by the basketful by enthusiastic campers and picnickers.
In the market, they are available fresh in season, and frozen almost year-round. The meat is sweet, lean, and firm.
The following recipe (no doubt borrowed from the American Indian) is the classic camper's method of pan-frying small, fresh-caught fish. It goes for all kinds of small fish—butterfish, croakers, spots, brook trout, pickerel, perch, and the small freshwater bass family.

16 smelts, cleaned, but with heads intact
1 teaspoon salt
½ teaspoon pepper
½ cup cornmeal
½ cup flour
½ cup butter
3 tablespoons bacon fat or cooking oil
parsley

Wipe the fish dry with a paper towel, season with salt and pepper, and roll in a mixture of cornmeal and flour.
Heat the butter and bacon fat in a heavy skillet until it almost smokes, and fry the smelts two or three at a time for about 3 minutes on each side or until golden.
Serve garnished with parsley. (*4 servings*)

MEATS

ROLLED POT ROAST OF BEEF

This simple rolled roast can be found in many parts of the country, but we found it most often in the prairie, which is famous for good substantial meals that stick to the ribs.

- 5 pounds chuck, bottom round, or rump, boned, rolled, and tied
- 4 tablespoons flour
- 2 teaspoons salt
- 1 teaspoon pepper
- ½ teaspoon sugar
  suet, cooking fat, or cooking oil
- 2 medium onions, sliced
- 1½ cups water, tomato juice, beef stock, or a combination
- 1 bay leaf
- 1 teaspoon thyme
- 1½ cups water or beef stock
  minced parsley

Mix together 2 tablespoons flour, the salt, pepper, and sugar (for browning), and rub into the surface of the beef.

Melt a little suet, fat, or oil in a deep heavy pan, and brown the beef on all sides over high heat. Lower the heat, add the onions, brown a little, then add the liquid, bay leaf, and thyme. Cover and cook very slowly for 3 to 4 hours or until meat is fork-tender. Add more liquid from time to time as needed.

Transfer the meat to a heated platter and keep warm.

Stir into the gravy 2 tablespoons flour, then add 1½ cups water or beef stock. Heat, check seasonings, and pour into a gravy boat.

Serve the pot roast, garnished with parsley, with boiled potatoes and carrots. The gravy is served on the side. (*10 to 12 servings*)

STEAK AND KIDNEY PIE

Filling:

- 3 cups of round steak, cut in 1½ inch cubes
- 1 beef kidney, fat removed, cut in 1½ inch cubes, soaked in cold water 30 minutes
- 3 tablespoons flour
- 3 tablespoons chopped beef fat
- 1 large onion, chopped
- 1 teaspoon salt
- ¼ teaspoon pepper
- ⅛ teaspoon cayenne
- 1 teaspoon Worcestershire sauce (optional)
- 2 cups water or stock

Roll beef cubes in flour. Drain kidney pieces and roll in flour.

Melt beef fat in large skillet. Brown the beef, then the kidney and onion. Add seasonings and water or stock. Stir, cover, and simmer 2 hours or until the meat is tender. Add a little more water if needed.

Preheat oven to 400 degrees.

Biscuit Crust:

- 2 tablespoons fat
- 2 cups flour
- 1 teaspoon salt
- ½ to ¾ cup milk, water, or buttermilk (enough to make a stiff dough)

Mix fat into flour and salt. Stir in liquid, form into dough. Roll out on floured board or cloth to size of 1½-quart casserole.

Put beef and kidney stew into casserole. Put biscuit crust on top and crimp around the edges. Cut 2 slits in crust. Bake 30 minutes or until brown. (*4 to 6 servings*)

CAMPFIRE STEAK

Here is a way to cook steak, either over a campfire or under a broiler, which preserves the juices and keeps the meat from becoming too charred. Some believe a wood fire gives a better flavor than charcoal, but wood fires are easier to prepare in the open than at home. One way to get around this is to sprinkle wood shavings over a charcoal fire when it has burned down to coals.

> 1 sirloin steak, 1½ inches thick
> 1 cup rock salt
> ¼ cup butter
> ½ teaspoon pepper

If cooking over a wood fire or charcoal coals, have grate 10 inches from coals. Cover steak with a thick layer of salt, press into meat on each side. Broil on one side 10 minutes. Brush salt off cooked side. Turn and broil on the other side 10 minutes for rare steak. Brush salt off second side when cooked. Juice runs red for rare, pink for medium, and clear for well done. Put steak on platter, butter it, and sprinkle with pepper.
Under broiler, salt well the side under fire. Cook 10 minutes. Scrape off salt and turn. Salt raw side, broil 10 minutes. Butter and pepper the steak on platter, and serve. (*4 to 6 servings*)

MISSOURI KITCHEN-BARBECUED STEAK

This excellent recipe was found in a church cookbook published in a small Missouri town. The cut of meat used in all probability, was taken from grass-fed stock, in which case the condiments used would add needed piquancy.

> 3 pounds porterhouse or sirloin steak, about 2 inches thick
> 4 tablespoons butter
> 2 tablespoons dry mustard
> 2 tablespoons paprika
> 1 teaspoon salt
> 1 teaspoon freshly ground pepper
> 2 tablespoons olive oil
> 1 tablespoon Worcestershire sauce minced parsley

Trim excess fat from steak, and wipe dry.
Make a paste of the butter, mustard, paprika, salt, and pepper, and rub both sides of the steak with it.
Place steak on a rack in a broiling pan and broil close to the heat for 5 minutes. Brush this cooked surface with a mixture of oil and Worcestershire sauce.
Turn, broil 5 minutes on the other side, and brush this surface with the same mixture.
Repeat this operation until steak reaches desired doneness.
Remove to a heated platter, rub in a little more dry mustard, spoon on the pan juices, and garnish with minced parsley. (*4 servings*)

CRISP-ROASTED FRESH HAM

James Beard calls this a truly outstanding dish, eminently suitable to serve at a holiday meal. Buy either a whole or half fresh ham, according to your needs, and have the butcher leave the skin on.

> 8 pounds fresh ham, whole or half
> 2 bay leaves, crumbled
> 1 teaspoon dried sage or thyme
> 1 clove garlic, crushed (optional)
> 2 teaspoons salt
> 2 teaspoons freshly ground pepper or crushed peppercorns
> 2 tablespoons flour
> 1 cup chicken broth

Preheat oven to 300 degrees.
Score the pork by cutting cross-hatched gashes through the rind and fat.
Mix together the bay leaves, sage, garlic, salt, and pepper, and rub into the gashes. Place ham on a rack in roasting pan, fat side up, and place in oven. Roast slowly about 2½ hours (25 minutes per pound).
During the last 20 minutes of roasting, increase the temperature to 375 degrees, and baste frequently with the drippings. This will produce a crisp, brown skin. When done, set aside on a heated platter.
Skim most of the fat from the drippings, and stir in the flour. Gradually add the broth and cook briskly, stirring continually, until thickened. Check seasonings and serve in a gravy boat. (*about 10 servings*)

FRUITED-STUFFED SPARERIBS

2 spareribs (2 pounds each)
1 teaspoon salt
1 teaspoon pepper
3 large apples, peeled, cored, and chopped
2 cups chopped uncooked prunes
2 tablespoons chopped onion
½ teaspoon sage

Preheat oven to 350 degrees.
Rub the spareribs on both sides with salt and pepper.
Mix together the apples, prunes, onion, and sage.
Stuff the hollow side of one of the spareribs with the fruit, cover with the other, and skewer together.
Bake in the oven about 2 hours or until crisp and brown. (*4 servings*)

BAKED DAKOTA PORK PANCAKE

This interesting dish, found in North Dakota, has a distinct Swedish look to it.

½ pound lean fresh pork, cut into thin strips
2 cups flour
1 tablespoon sugar
½ teaspoon salt
1 teaspoon baking powder
1 quart milk
1 egg, beaten

Preheat oven to 375 degrees.
Fry the pork lightly in a large baking pan on top of the stove. Remove pork from pan and set aside.
Sift together the flour, sugar, salt, and baking powder.
Mix together the milk and egg, and stir into the dry ingredients until well blended.
Pour the batter into the baking pan with the pork fat. Place the pork strips on top and bake about ½ hour or until pancake is done and pork is crisp. (*6 servings*)

CORNISH PASTY

This is an old English recipe which came to us by way of Wisconsin and the Minnesota iron country. The following will make a portable dinner for four men.

Pasty:

4 cups flour
2 teaspoons salt
4 tablespoons lard
½ cup cold water

Mix flour and salt. Cut lard into it until the flour becomes mealy. Add water slowly, adding just enough for the dough to hold its shape. Roll out in 4 rounds a little thicker than pie crust (5 to 6 inches in diameter).

Filling:

4 onions, sliced
8 large potatoes, peeled
½ teaspoon pepper
1 teaspoon salt
1 stick butter (½ cup), cut in 4 pieces
1½ pounds round steak, cut in thin strips
1 cup heavy cream

Preheat oven to 400 degrees.
Put 1 sliced onion on each pasty, leaving room at the edge to seal it later. Chip 2 potatoes for each pasty over the onion in small pieces. Sprinkle with pepper and salt. Cut butter pieces in half and put 1 on each side of potatoes on each pasty. Over this, lay ¼ of the steak strips. Sprinkle meat with pepper and salt.
Bring both sides of dough up over the top of the meat and potatoes; pinch these together.
Repeat on all four pasties. Put on cookie sheet.
Bake in oven 25 minutes.
Take out and make a slit in the top of each and pour ¼ cup of cream into each pasty. Return to oven until cream bubbles out of the hole. (*4 servings*)

OXTAIL STEW

    3 oxtails, cut into serving-size pieces
      flour
    3 cups beef stock
    1 stalk celery, chopped
    1 carrot, chopped
    1 leek (white part only), chopped
    2 sprigs parsley, chopped
    ½ teaspoon pepper
    ½ teaspoon cayenne
   10 whole allspice
    1 teaspoon Worcestershire sauce

Dredge the oxtails with flour and put into a heavy pot with the stock, vegetables, and seasonings.

Cover and stew over low heat about 3 hours or until meat is tender. (*6 servings*)

HUNTERS' HAMBURGER STEW

    3 slices bacon, diced
    1 onion, finely chopped
    1 large clove garlic, finely chopped
    2 pounds chopped beef
    1 can (1 pound) tomatoes
    1 teaspoon salt
    ¼ teaspoon pepper
    1 can (1 pound) sauerkraut
    1½ cups beer

In heavy skillet fry bacon, add onion and garlic, and cook until brown. Crumble hamburger into this mixture and stir until browned.

Add the tomatoes and seasonings. Stir, and let cook over low heat until tomato juice is almost absorbed and the stew has a thick texture, not dry.

Rinse sauerkraut and put in separate saucepan. Cover with beer. Bring to a boil, lower heat, and cook until most of the beer is absorbed but sauerkraut is not dry.

Serve meat mixture with sauerkraut. (*6 servings*)

DANISH KODFARS

    1½ pounds finely ground pork loin
    ⅓ cup flour
    ½ cup milk
    1 teaspoon salt
    ½ teaspoon pepper
    1 tablespoon minced onion
      white grapes (optional)

Preheat oven to 325 degrees.

Blend together the meat and flour, and then the milk, mixing until creamy.

Add the seasonings and onion, mix well, shape into small cakes, and bake for almost 1 hour. Remove to a warm platter and serve with brown skillet gravy made by stirring a tablespoon of flour and a cup or so of water into the pan drippings. Remove all but 2 tablespoons of fat before adding the flour. White grapes can be added to the gravy for variety. (*4 servings*)

KITCHEN-BARBECUED LAMB

    1 8 pound leg of lamb
    1 tablespoon salt
      flour
    1 cup chopped onion
    1 cup hot water
    ½ cup chili sauce
    ¼ cup Worcestershire sauce
    ½ teaspoon cayenne

Preheat oven to 450 degrees.

Wipe lamb dry, rub with salt, and dredge well with flour.

Place on rack in oven pan, slide into the oven, and cook about 30 minutes or until well browned all over.

Reduce the oven heat to 350 degrees, mix all the other ingredients together and pour over the lamb.

Cook about 20 minutes per pound, basting thoroughly every 15 minutes. (*6 to 8 servings*)

SWEDISH MEATBALLS

Now a national favorite of the buffet table, Swedish meatballs used to be made by laboriously grinding the meat at home. One ingenious housewife discovered that she could use ground pork-sausage meat and chopped beef instead. We have given the exact recipe below without short cuts.

        2 cups bread crumbs
        2 cups milk
        ¼ pound finely ground lean pork
      1½ pounds finely ground lean beef
        2 eggs, lightly beaten
        1 small onion, minced
        1 teaspoon salt
        ½ teaspoon pepper
        ¼ teaspoon nutmeg
        ¼ cup each of cornmeal and flour,
          mixed
          butter

Mix together all the ingredients except the cornmeal and flour mixture and the butter, and form into small 1-inch balls, dusting the hands with flour-meal mixture while shaping the balls.

Fry slowly in butter over low heat until brown. Cover the pan and steam 30 minutes. Serve with noodles or mashed potatoes. (*6 servings*)

IOWA GOULASH

        1 pound stewing beef, cut into 1½-inch
          cubes
        ½ pound lean pork, cut into 1½-inch
          cubes
        ½ pound veal, cut into 1½ inch cubes
        1 veal kidney, cut into 1½ inch pieces
        3 tablespoons cooking oil
        1 cup chopped onion
        ½ cup flour
        2 cups chopped tomatoes, fresh or
          canned
        1 tablespoon salt
        ¼ teaspoon cayenne
        2 tablespoons paprika
          pinch thyme
          pinch sweet marjoram
        1 quart hot water
        1 cup sherry

Sauté the meat in a little oil until brown on all sides. Add the onion, sprinkle in the flour, and cook until flour is browned.

Add the tomatoes, seasonings, and hot water. Cover and simmer slowly for about 2 hours or until meat is tender.

Stir in the sherry and serve with noodles. (*4 to 6 servings*)

POULTRY
AND GAME BIRDS

ROAST DUCK, SAGE DRESSING

        1 duck, 4 to 5 pounds, cleaned and
          dressed
        ½ cup butter
        1 cup chopped onions
        4 cups dry bread crumbs
        1 teaspoon fresh or ½ teaspoon dried
          sage, or ¼ teaspoon thyme
        ½ teaspoon salt
        ½ teaspoon pepper
        2 tablespoons chopped fresh parsley

Preheat oven to 325 degrees.

Sauté the onions in all but 2 tablespoons butter until soft, add the bread crumbs and seasonings.

Stuff the duck loosely with the above dressing, sew up, tie the legs together, and tuck in the wings.

Rub the duck with remaining butter, and sprinkle with salt and pepper. Place on a rack in a roasting pan and roast 1½ to 2 hours or until skin is crisp and brown. Do not baste.

Pour off fat, leaving only the meat drippings. Season to taste, and stir in about a cup of water—1½ cups for thin gravy. Do not add flour to gravy. (*4 servings*)

FRIED PRAIRIE CHICKEN WITH CREAM GRAVY

Prairie chickens are today an endangered species, attesting to the thoroughness with which they were hunted and the relish with which they were eaten by prairie settlers. Mongolian pheasants have been introduced in many areas to replace the prairie chickens, which do not replenish themselves as quickly and are not as hardy. The following historic recipe can be used today for pheasant or chicken.

    1 young prairie chicken, dressed, cut
      into serving portions
    salt
    pepper
    flour
    4 tablespoons bacon fat
    1 cup heavy cream (or cream gravy, see
      below)

Dip the chicken pieces into cold water, sprinkle with salt and pepper, and dredge with flour. Using a heavy skillet, cook slowly in hot oil about 40 minutes or until tender.

Remove to a hot platter. Pour off all but 2 tablespoons fat from skillet. Mix cream with pan juices and pour over chicken. Or make cream gravy:

    2 tablespoons flour
    ½ teaspoon salt
    ⅛ teaspoon pepper
    1 cup milk

Stir flour into the skillet, season, gradually stir in the milk. Cook until thickened, pour over the prairie chicken, and serve. (*2 to 4 servings*)

CHICKEN FRICASSEE WITH DUMPLINGS

    1 fowl, 4 to 6 pounds
    1 teaspoon salt
      water to cover
    2 tablespoons chopped celery leaves
    ½ cup flour mixed with 2 tablespoons
      soft butter
    ¼ teaspoon pepper

Put fowl with giblets, salt, celery leaves, and water in large pot with a tight cover. Cook 2½ to 3 hours, until tender. Take fowl from broth and remove bones, gristle, and skin; separate meat so that there are an even number of pieces per serving.

Mix the flour and butter into a roux and drop in broth. Stir and bring to a boil until the gravy thickens. Add pepper.

Dumplings:

    2 tablespoons butter, lard, or cooking
      oil
    1½ cups flour
    1½ teaspoons baking powder
    1 teaspoon salt
    ¾ cup milk or light cream

Mix lard into sifted baking powder, flour, and salt until grainy, and add the milk. Stir. Drop by spoonfuls onto the simmering fricassee. Cover tightly and do not lift cover for 15 to 20 minutes, to allow the dumplings to rise. (*4 to 6 servings*)

PHEASANT MULLIGAN

The dictionary defines mulligan as "a kind of stew containing meat, vegetables, etc." Both mulligans and slumgullions are popular western camp concoctions. You might say that almost anything goes: meat or fowl, vegetables, potatoes. Often, at the last minute, dumplings are added. These days, stewing pheasant seems rather a crude way to treat such a delicacy, but pheasant mulligan is an old recipe for an old pheasant. (See Pheasant Western Style*)

    2 pheasants, dressed and jointed
    2 cups (more or less) diced carrots
    1 cup (more or less) chopped onion
    1 or more cups shredded cabbage
    2 or 3 cups diced potatoes
    3 to 4 tablespoons butter
    salt
    pepper

Put the pheasants, carrots, onion, and cabbage into a pot or kettle, cover with water, bring to a simmer, and cook slowly about 1 hour or until tender.

After 45 minutes of cooking, put in the potatoes and butter, and season to taste. (*4 to 6 servings*)

GOOSE WITH HOMINY

1 goose, 8 to 10 pounds, dressed, washed and dried
4 tablespoons butter, softened
   salt
   pepper
1 onion, chopped
1 cup hickory-nut meats
8 cups bread, cut in small cubes
2 apples, diced
4 stalks celery, diced
1 tablespoon minced parsley
5 cups water
2 cans (1 pound) hominy or 1 cup hominy grits
1½ teaspoons salt
⅛ teaspoon pepper
1 cup cider or water
2 tablespoons butter

Preheat oven to 325 degrees.
Rub goose with 2 tablespoons softened butter, sprinkle with salt and pepper.

Put giblets on to cook in water to cover.
Melt remaining butter, add onion, and cook only until transparent. Add nuts, bread, apple, celery, and parsley, toss, and set aside.
Chop goose liver and heart. Mix with bread mixture, and stuff into goose, leaving space for stuffing to expand. Put goose in open baking pan and put in oven.
Bake until the drumstick moves easily, 2½ to 3 hours. Do not baste.
Put 5 cups water on to boil, with 1 teaspoon salt, in heavy saucepan. Stir grits slowly into boiling water. Reduce heat under pan and cook grits slowly, stirring occasionally, 25 to 30 minutes.
Keep hot until ready to serve.
Remove goose from oven. Put on platter and keep warm. Pour all fat from pan juices. Add ½ teaspoon salt, ⅛ teaspoon pepper, and 1 cup cider or water to pan juices. Stir, let boil up, and serve in gravy boat, with the goose, with buttered hominy on the side. (*6 to 8 servings*)

VEGETABLES
AND SIDE DISHES

SPICED PUMPKIN

1 quart vinegar
4 pounds sugar
1 teaspoon whole cloves
2 sticks cinnamon, broken up
5 pounds pumpkin, peeled and cut into 1-inch cubes

Boil the vinegar, sugar, and spices together 5 minutes.
Put the pumpkin into a pot, pour the liquid over, and cook 15 minutes or until pumpkin can be pierced with a fork.
Pour into sterilized jars and seal. Serve on special occasions with the meat course. (*3 quarts*)

WILD RICE

Wild rice is not true rice, but an aquatic seed, *Zizania aquatica*, growing from four to eight feet high in shallow lakes, inlets, and rivers. Early settlers and frontiersmen learned to like this pleasant, smoky, nutty-flavored grain from Indians who gathered it in canoes paddled into the shallow lakes of northern Minnesota and Wisconsin. Wild ducks and geese are attracted to it.
Until 1928 the Indians of the Ojibwa tribe traditionally had the exclusive right to harvest wild rice in Minnesota. Because it grows in quantity only in the northern lake regions, and because it is greatly prized as an accompaniment to wild duck and other game, it has

always commanded a high price. Wild rice grows in Texas, Louisiana, Arkansas, and other parts of the South as well.

Preparing the wild seed is tedious and troublesome because it requires hulling and careful picking over before it can be cooked. The Indians and early settlers fixed it by pouring boiling water over it several times, allowing it to sit 15 or 20 minutes after each washing.

Today wild rice is packaged and sold commercially with directions for preparing spelled out on the box or bag. It is also sold mixed with regular rice. If directions for cooking have not been included on your package, follow this recipe:

    1 cup wild rice, washed in 4 waters
2½ cups cold water
    1 teaspoon salt
    2 tablespoons butter

Put the rice into the water with the salt, and bring to a boil. Stir, lower the heat, and cook, covered, 25 to 40 minutes—or less—until water is absorbed. Overcooking darkens wild rice and decreases its flavor.
Serve with butter. (*2 to 4 servings*)

CREAMED SPINACH WITH BACON

    1 pound fresh spinach, well washed and chopped
½ teaspoon salt
    3 slices bacon
    2 tablespoons chopped onion
    1 tablespoon flour
½ teaspoon pepper
½ cup sour cream

Simmer the spinach in a quart of salted water 10 to 12 minutes. Drain.
Sauté the bacon until crisp in a skillet, drain, crumble, and set aside.
Sauté the onion in the bacon fat, stir in the flour and pepper and then the spinach. Heat thoroughly, stirring well. Add the sour cream and heat a few minutes longer, but do not boil. Serve topped with the crumbled bacon. (*4 servings*)

SQUASH PUDDING WITH BACON

    1 small yellow (crookneck) squash
    1 teaspoon salt
½ teaspoon pepper
    3 tablespoons butter
    2 eggs, well beaten
½ cup milk
    8 slices bacon

Preheat oven to 350 degrees.
Peel the squash, cut in pieces, and boil until soft. Mash thoroughly or put through a ricer, season with salt and pepper, and stir in the butter until melted.
Mix in the eggs and milk, spoon into 4 individual oven-proof dishes. Cover each dish with 2 slices bacon, and bake about 15 minutes or until bacon is crisp. (*4 servings*)

INDIAN CORN ON THE COB

The Indians heated water by tossing hot stones into it until it boiled.

    8 ears fresh corn
    water
½ cup butter, melted

Remove coarse and blemished outer husks of corn. Pull remaining husks back and remove silk, then replace husks and twist tops. Wash unblemished outer leaves and put a layer in a large pot with cover. Lay the ears on this bed and cover the corn with more husks. Cover with cold water and bring to a boil. Boil 3 minutes.
Serve (with or without husks) with melted butter.
Here's another Indian way to cook corn, passed down to Nebraskans where a lot of corn is grown—and eaten. The full flavor and freshness of the corn is preserved by this method.
Peel back the husks, remove the silk, replace husks, twist tops, and roast in coals covered with wood ashes, turning to cook on all sides, about 20 to 25 minutes.

KANSAS POTATOES FRIED WHOLE

The following entrancing recipe was included in *The Kansas Home Cook Book*, 1879.

Peel and lay in cold water potatoes of a uniform size—those about the size of a hen's egg are the best. Have hot in a kettle enough lard or beef drippings to cover them, wipe the potatoes, and drop them in. They will cook in 20 minutes, should be a fine yellow-brown when done, and are much better than the thin, greasy, fried potatoes which grace so many breakfast tables.

Use a kettle, because it is the neatest; the hot fat cannot fly out on the stove. Use one that you can spare, and it can be used again and again without changing the fat.

NORWEGIAN POTATO PANCAKES

4 medium baking potatoes, peeled
2 tablespoons chopped fresh chives
2 teaspoons salt
   freshly ground black pepper
2 tablespoons butter
2 tablespoons oil

Slice the potatoes into thin slivers. Place into a large mixing bowl with the chives and seasonings.

In a heavy skillet heat the butter and oil over high heat to just under the smoking point. Spread potato slices to form pancakes, two tablespoons each, and flatten with a spatula. Fry on both sides over medium heat until crisp and golden. Serve immediately. (*4 servings*)

SALADS
AND DRESSINGS

GOOSEBERRY MOLD

1 package (3 ounces) lemon gelatin
1 cup hot water
1 cup canned or fresh gooseberries
1 cup chopped celery
½ cup grated Cheddar cheese
   lettuce leaves, washed and dried

Put the gelatin into a mold and stir in the hot water until gelatin is dissolved. Add a little cold water and the juice from the gooseberries, and let cool until almost set.
Stir in the gooseberries, celery, and cheese, and chill until set. Unmold onto the lettuce and serve. (*4 to 6 servings*)

NEBRASKA HERRING SALAD

2 salt herring
2 small apples, peeled and finely diced
2 cups finely diced cooked beets
½ cup minced onion
¼ cup minced dill pickle
¼ cup French dressing
2 hard-cooked eggs, chopped

Soak herring 2 hours in cold water. Flake meat. Toss the herring meat well with the apples, beets, onion, pickle, and French dressing. Chill for 2 hours.
Serve on a chilled platter, sprinkled with chopped egg on top. (*4 to 6 servings*)

SCANDINAVIAN MACARONI SALAD

> 4 ounces elbow macaroni
> ¼ cup French dressing
> 1 apple, peeled and diced
> 1 tablespoon lemon juice
> 1 small onion, minced
> ½ cup mayonnaise
> paprika

Cook the macaroni in salted water about 15 minutes or until tender. Drain, rinse, and cool. Add the French dressing and chill for 2 hours. Mix in the apple, lemon juice, onion, and mayonnaise.
Serve dusted with paprika. (*4 servings*)

JELLIED ORANGE-CARROT SALAD

Molded salads of infinite variety can be found in the west. It must be those long hot summers on the prairies that give a cool salad such an inviting taste after sundown.

> 2 envelopes unflavored gelatin
> ½ cup cold water
> 1 cup boiling water
> 1 cup sugar
> 2 cups orange juice
> juice of 1 lemon
> 4 carrots, shredded
> 1 tablespoon peanut oil
> 1 head Boston lettuce, washed
> 3 tablespoons olive oil
> 1 tablespoon lemon juice, or vinegar
> ½ teaspoon salt
> ¼ teaspoon pepper
> mayonnaise

Soak gelatin in cold water 10 minutes. Pour on boiling water. Stir. Add sugar, stir to dissolve. Add orange and lemon juice.
Add shredded carrots.
Oil mold with peanut oil. Pour in gelatin mixture. Refrigerate 3 to 4 hours. Unmold on bed of lettuce.
Mix oil, lemon juice, salt and pepper. Spoon over salad. Serve with a bowl of mayonnaise. (*6 to 8 servings*)

WILTED LETTUCE SALAD

This is a very old salad stemming from covered-wagon days. Made from whatever greens were found along the way, it seldom tasted the same twice.

> 2 heads any kind salad greens, washed, dried, and broken into bite-size pieces
> 4 thin slices bacon or salt pork, cut into small pieces
> ¼ cup vinegar
> ¼ cup sugar
> 1 teaspoon dry mustard
> ½ cup chopped onions

Put the greens into a salad bowl.
Fry the bacon or pork in a heavy skillet until crisp. Remove and add to the salad bowl.
Add the vinegar, sugar, and mustard to the skillet, stir into drippings, and pour all over the greens.
Add the chopped onion, toss, and serve. (*4 servings*)

STUFFED TOMATO SALAD

> 4 medium tomatoes
> ½ banana, diced
> 1 sour apple, peeled and finely chopped
> 1 stalk celery, diced
> ¼ cup peeled and chopped cucumbers
> 2 tablespoons French dressing

Peel the tomatoes by dipping into hot water. Then remove the pulpy centers.
Mix together the remaining ingredients and stuff into the tomatoes. Chill. (*4 servings*)

BREADS
AND BATTERCAKES

BUTTERMILK BISCUITS

4 cups flour
2 teaspoons salt
1 teaspoon baking soda
6 tablespoons lard
2 cups buttermilk

Preheat oven to 425 degrees.
Sift flour, salt, and soda together, cut in the lard, and add the milk, making a relatively stiff dough.
Knead slightly, roll out on a floured board to ½-inch thickness, and cut into biscuits.
Place on greased cookie sheet and bake 10 to 12 minutes. (*4 servings*)

SWEDISH COFFEE BREAD

2 cups milk, scalded
1 cake yeast, softened in ¼ cup lukewarm water
2 tablespoons sugar
6½ cups flour
½ cup shortening
¾ cup sugar
15 cardamom seeds, finely ground
½ teaspoon salt

Beat together the scalded milk, yeast, sugar, and 3 cups flour. Set aside in a warm place to rise until double in bulk.
Cream the shortening and sugar, mix with cardamom seed, and add to the risen milk-flour mixture.
Mix the remaining flour and salt, add to the above mixture, and knead into a soft dough.
Cover with a cloth and allow to rise in a warm place until double in bulk.
Shape into 2 loaves, let rise in a warm place to double again, and bake in a preheated 375-degree oven about 35 minutes or until a straw inserted comes out clean. (*2 loaves*)

SALT-RISING BREAD

The following is an old Scotch-English recipe "discovered" in Nebraska by Crosby Gaige, a well-known American cooking authority and gourmet during the thirties. We give it to you verbatim.

At night scald three tablespoons white cornmeal with new milk, wrap and set in warm place (not hot). In the morning make a stiff batter of one quart of warm water (hot enough to bare hand) and flour, adding tablespoon salt and the fermented cornmeal yeast. Cover your bowl and set in kettle of warm water and keep at even temperature for five and one-half hours. The rising should at this time be near the top of bowl. Make into a stiff dough, adding warm water and flour and one tablespoon sugar and one half cup of butter. Form into loaves and keep warm for one hour. Bake in hot oven, as a hotter oven is required than for yeast bread.

KANSAS CRACKED-CORN GRIDDLECAKES

1 cup cracked corn, cooked 3 hours in salted water
2 cups milk
2 eggs
1 tablespoon lard, melted
2 cups flour
4 teaspoons baking powder
1 teaspoon salt

Mix together the corn, milk, eggs, and oil.
Add the flour, baking powder, and salt, and stir until well blended.
Brown on both sides on a greased hot griddle.
Serve with butter. (*6 to 8 servings*)

SKILLET CORN BREAD

Early prairie pioneers, always on the move, had no ovens for baking bread. Corn bread was often cooked in a heavy skillet placed directly onto hot coals. To produce ovenlike heat, the skillet was covered with a lid onto which some of the hot coals were heaped.

    1 cup cornmeal
    1 teaspoon baking soda
    1 teaspoon salt
    2 cups buttermilk (or use sweet milk
       and omit the baking soda)
    2 eggs, lightly beaten
    2 tablespoons cooking oil

Preheat oven to 425 degrees.
Mix together the dry ingredients, and then blend in all the rest. Pour into a greased heavy skillet, and bake 20 minutes or until done. (*4 servings*)

MISSOURI HOECAKE

    2 cups yellow cornmeal
    ½ teaspoon baking powder
    ½ teaspoon salt
    1 tablespoon lard
       hot water

Sift together the dry ingredients, then add the cooking fat and enough water to make a soft dough.
Form into small, thin cakes. Fry on a hot, greased griddle until brown on both sides. (*4 servings*)

DESSERTS

BREAD PUDDING

The following recipe showed up in Missouri. How it got there would probably make a nice story if the facts could be learned, because the recipe was taken from Amelia Simmons's *American Cookery*, published in Hartford, Connecticut, around 1796.

One pound soft bread or bifcuit foaked in one quart milk, run thro' a fieve or cullender, add 7 eggs, three quarters of a pound fuger, one quarter of a pound butter, nutmeg or cinnamon, one gill rofewater, one pound ftoned raisins, half pint cream, bake three quarters of an hour, middling oven.

This more modern recipe might be easier to follow:

    1 tablespoon butter
    ½ cup sugar
    ¼ teaspoon salt
    2 cups milk, scalded
    2 cups diced bread or biscuit
    ½ teaspoon nutmeg or cinnamon
    4 tablespoons rose water
    1 cup seedless raisins
    ½ cup heavy cream
    2 eggs, separated, whites beaten until
       stiff

Preheat oven to 350 degrees.
Stir the butter, sugar, and salt into the scalded milk, and put in the bread. Soak for 1 hour or more.
Stir in the nutmeg or cinnamon, rose water, raisins, cream, and yolks of eggs, then fold in the beaten egg whites.
Put into a greased baking dish, set into a pan of hot water, and bake 30 minutes. Serve hot with cream. (*4 servings*)

OLD-FASHIONED LEMON PIE

Old recipes say to use one lemon—grated rind and juice. We added more to suit modern tastes. It was also customary then to fold the egg whites into the pie mixture to bake, rather than to put the meringue on top of the pie as we do now. This pie can be made either way.

    4 eggs, separated
    1 cup sugar
    ½ cup lemon juice
    2 tablespoons hot water
    ⅛ teaspoon salt
    1 prebaked pie shell

Beat egg yolks into ½ cup sugar until thick and lemon-colored. Add lemon juice and hot water, and put all into the top part of a double boiler. Set over simmering hot water and stir until thick. Cool.
Beat the egg whites with salt and remaining sugar, added a little at a time until the mixture is thick and quite stiff. Fold this into the lemon mixture and fill the baked pie shell.
Preheat oven to 400 degrees.
Bake the pie until light brown, 15 to 20 minutes. (*6 servings*)

HICKORY NUT PIE

When most of the red and yellow leaves have fallen from the trees in the woods, it is time to collect hickory nuts, black walnuts, walnuts, and once upon a time, before the blight, chestnuts. These were taken home to be roasted, or cracked and shelled for pies and cakes, or just eaten plain.

    4 eggs
    1 cup sugar
    1 cup hickory-nut meats
    12 round soda crackers
    1 pie crust

Preheat oven to 400 degrees.
Beat eggs until light. Gradually add the sugar.
Grind nutmeats and crackers together, and add to egg-and-sugar mixture.
Pour into pie crust.
Bake 5 minutes at 400 degrees, reduce heat to 300 degrees, and bake 20 minutes more. (*6 servings*)

BLACK-WALNUT ICE CREAM

This recipe came from Iowa. The ice cream can be frozen in a hand or electric freezer or molded in the freezing compartment of an ordinary refrigerator. There is nothing quite like the flavor of ice cream that comes from an old-fashioned hand-crank freezer. All the work seems to make it taste better.

    3 egg yolks
    1 cup sugar
    1/16 teaspoon salt
    2 cups scalded milk
    ⅔ cup chopped black-walnut meats
    1 cup heavy cream
    ¾ teaspoon vanilla

Beat egg yolks and sugar together. Add salt and gradually add scalded milk.
Cook in double boiler over hot water until the custard thickens, stirring constantly. Add walnuts. Cool.
Whip cream until stiff, add vanilla. Fold into custard, and freeze or mold until ready to serve. (*6 to 8 servings*)

DANISH SKILLET CAKE

This is probably how pineapple upside-down cake became a national dish. Whether or not it was brought to this country from Denmark, it was found in Minneapolis.

    ½ cup butter
    1 cup sugar
    5 slices pineapple
    2 eggs
    ½ cup flour
    ¼ teaspoon baking powder
      whipped cream

Preheat oven to 350 degrees.
Melt the butter in a heavy skillet over medium heat until lightly brown. Sprinkle ½ cup sugar over browned butter. Lay the pineapple slices in butter-sugar mixture to cover the pan.
Mix the remaining sugar, eggs, flour, and baking powder into a batter, and spoon evenly into the pan. Bake 35 to 40 minutes.
Serve in small slices with whipped cream. This cake is very rich. (*6 servings*)

BLACK-BREAD TORTE

This recipe comes from Minnesota, where there are both German and Scandinavian influences in the kitchen. This sounds very German, but may be a combination of both nationalities.

    4 slices dry rye bread, broken into
      pieces
    ¼ cup red wine
    1 cup sugar
   12 eggs, separated
      grated rind of 1 lemon
    2 tablespoons chopped citron
    1 teaspoon cloves
    1 teaspoon cinnamon
    1 tablespoon flour
    1 cup finely chopped almonds

Preheat oven to 250 degrees.
Put rye bread slices, into a blender. Process for 15 seconds, until fine crumbs.
Mix wine with crumbs. Add sugar and the egg yolks, and beat all together for 15 minutes.
Stir in the rind, citron, cloves, cinnamon, flour, and nuts. Beat egg whites until stiff and fold into crumb mixture. Pour into spring-mold pan and bake for 1 hour. Allow to cool 10 minutes before serving.
Serve with whipped cream or ice cream. (*6 to 8 servings*)

NORTH DAKOTA
HONEY CUSTARD

    4 cups milk
    8 tablespoons strained fireweed honey
    5 eggs, beaten
    ¼ teaspoon salt
      nutmeg

Preheat oven to 300 degrees.
Scald the milk in a double boiler, add the honey, then the beaten eggs, stirring rapidly.
Stir in the salt, pour into 6 buttered custard cups, sprinkle with nutmeg, and set cups into a pan of warm water.
Bake in the oven until a knife inserted into the custard comes out clean.
Serve hot or cold. (*6 servings*)

TOMATO SOUP CAKE

Contrary to expectations, this unusual, tangy cake shows up in many parts of the country. This one was found in a small town in Missouri. It is usually made without an icing.

    ½ cup lard
    ½ cup sugar
    ½ teaspoon baking soda
    1 can condensed tomato soup
    2 cups flour
    2 teaspoons baking powder
  1½ teaspoons powdered cinnamon
    1 teaspoon allspice
    ½ teaspoon powdered cloves
    1 cup chopped raisins
    1 cup chopped nutmeats
      butter

Preheat oven to 350 degrees.
Cream the lard and sugar. Stir the soda into the soup, and blend with the lard-sugar mixture.
Mix together the flour, baking powder, and seasonings, and blend with the soup mixture.
Stir in the raisins and nuts, pour into a buttered 9-inch square cake pan, and bake in the oven until done when skewer-tested, about 35 to 40 minutes. (*10 to 12 servings*)

PLUM COFFEECAKE

    2 eggs, beaten
    1 cup sugar
    2 cups flour
    2 teaspoons baking powder
    ½ cup milk
    ⅓ cup shortening, melted
    1 teaspoon vanilla
      chopped walnuts
      fresh purple plums, pitted and split

Preheat oven to 375 degrees.
Combine the eggs and sugar. Sift the flour and baking powder together. Mix together the egg mixture, dry ingredients, and milk. Beat until smooth.
Add the melted shortening and vanilla, and pour into a greased 9-inch square baking pan.
Sprinkle with nuts, cover with plum halves, and bake about 30 minutes.
Cut into squares, and serve hot or cold. (*6 to 8 servings*)

BREAD CAKE

The receipt for this cake dates back to 1834 that I know about and has been used continuously by all branches of our family for 104 years. . . .

This is a partial quote from Mrs. Frank Enthrup of Ohio, about 1939. The virtue of the bread cake was that it did not dry out, and carried well as the covered wagon made its slow way across the country.

Following is a verbatim copy of the original recipe (courtesy the Browns in their book, *America Cooks*):

After the bread has been mixed and raised just before making into loaves, take out 3 cups of the bread dough. Place in a large crock (or bowl). Add 2 cups brown sugar, 1 cup shortening, ½ teaspoon cloves, 1 teaspoon cinnamon and a dab of allspice, 3 eggs, ½ cup raisins, and a handful of currants.

Mix all of the above together thoroughly 15 or 20 minutes with the hands and then add 1 teaspoon soda dissolved in a tablespoon or more of hot water. Do not add more flour. Pour into 2 loaf pans and bake immediately in a moderate oven, 350 degrees. Use a broom splint to test for doneness, or when the cake leaves the sides of the pan it is done. When inserting a broom splint (or cake tester) if it comes out clean, with no dough on it, the cake is done.

CREAM PUDDING

This dessert was not uncommon in earlier days in dairy country, where thick cream was in such abundance that it often soured before being used up. With today's refrigeration facilities and at today's prices, thick cream has become so valuable commercially that this delightful and simple dessert has tended to disappear from the gastronomic scene.

    2 cups thick cream, slightly soured
    ½ cup water
    ½ cup sifted flour
    ½ teaspoon salt
    2 cups hot milk
      sugar
      cinnamon

Simmer cream and water over very low heat for 45 minutes.

Mix together the flour and salt, and sift into the hot cream. Beat until smooth.

Simmer slowly again until thick and butterfat rises to top of pudding. Remove fat and reserve.

Stir in hot milk and beat again until smooth and creamy. Pour into a bowl, make depressions on top and spoon in the reserved butterfat.

Sprinkle with sugar and cinnamon and serve hot. (*6 to 8 servings*)

BEVERAGES

GLÖGG

This Scandinavian drink is popular from Nebraska to Minnesota during the cold winter months. It is easy to make because there is so much room for improvisation, but since it is somewhat troublesome you might like to mix up enough to last through the winter. Spice foundation:

    4 or 5 whole cloves
    8 or 10 cardamom seeds
    2 sticks cinnamon
    2 cups seedless raisins
    ½ cup candied orange peel
      wine

Put all the ingredients into a small saucepan, cover with some kind of wine, and bring to a boil. Let this spice foundation cool and put aside in a jar until ready for use.

Glögg:

    1 bottle sweet wine (port or muscatel)
    1 bottle dry wine (sherry, claret, burgundy, etc.)
    ½ bottle whiskey, brandy, or rum
    ½ cup sugar
      spice foundation (above)
      almond slivers
      raisins

Heat, but do not boil, the above ingredients in a suitable pot. Ignite the fumes by tossing in a jigger of flaming brandy or whiskey. Put out the flames by covering the pot and serve hot in glasses containing almond slivers and raisins. (*30 3-ounce servings*)

PRAIRIE MARY

    1½ ounces gin
    2 ounces tomato juice
    2 ounces chili sauce
      squeeze of lemon juice
      dash Tabasco sauce
      dash Worcestershire sauce
      dash curry powder
      dash black pepper
      dash salt
      slice celery

Shake all the ingredients together with cracked ice and strain into a 6-ounce glass. Insert a slice of celery and serve. (*1 serving*)

CIDER PUNCH

    2 quarts cider, sweet or hard
    2 cups orange juice
    1 cup lemon juice
    1 stick cinnamon
    1 teaspoon cloves
      sugar or honey to sweeten as desired

Mix together all the ingredients. Heat, but do not boil. Serve hot. (*15 cups*)

DANDELION FLOWER WINE

No one knows when dandelions were first used to make wine, but since almost everything that grows will ferment if given the right conditions, dandelion wine must have a long history.

The recipe below may be varied in a number of ways, as long as it contains yeast and as long as the mixture is kept warm enough to ferment.

    4 quarts washed dandelion flowers
    4 quarts boiling water
    3 lemons, sliced
    3 oranges, sliced
    3 pounds sugar
    1 yeast cake, crumbled

Pour the boiling water over the flowers and allow to stand 3 days, stirring frequently.
Strain, add the fruit and sugar, and boil 30 minutes.
Cool to room temperature and add the yeast. Allow to stand 2 days at room temperature. Transfer to a small keg and keep bunged (with an escape valve for the gas) for 8 or 9 weeks. When fermentation has stopped, strain into bottles and cork. (*1 gallon*)

NORTHWESTERN
COOKING

SOUPS AND CHOWDERS

Venison Broth
Leek and Potato Soup
Rocky Mountain Borsch
Oxtail Soup
Canadian Cabbage Soup
Bean Chowder

PASTA, EGG, AND CHEESE DISHES

Hood River Omelet
Noodles and Sausages
Cheese Blintzes
Denver Omelet
Tomato Rabbit

FISH AND SHELLFISH

Baked Columbia River Salmon
Rocky Mountain Rainbow Trout, Camp
  Style
Poached Trout with Scallions
Washington Salmon Loaf
Dried Ling (Lutefisk)
Kala Lootaa
Alaskan King Crab Rémoulade

MEATS

Roast Venison
Montana Buck Stew
Charcoal-broiled Antelope Steak
Pemmican
Nevada Baked Steak
Rocky Mountain Oysters
Idaho Lumber-Camp Hash
Salt Pork with Mormon Gravy
Oregon Beef-Fruit Stew
Shashlik
Roast Lamb, Utah Style with Hot Minted
  Applesauce
Ranch Barbecued Beef with Cowboy
  Sauce
Seal Alaskan
Chicken-fried Steak

POULTRY AND GAME BIRDS

Braised Chicken with Tomatoes
Sage Hen or Ruffed Grouse, Hunter Style
Creamed Smoked Turkey
Pheasant, Western Style

VEGETABLES AND SIDE DISHES

Bacon Peas
Baked Idaho Potatoes
Fried Apples
Scalloped Asparagus
Idaho Potato Loaf
Montana Baked Corn

SALADS AND DRESSINGS

Wyoming Bean Salad
Tongue and Spinach Salad
Sour Cream Lettuce Salad
Hot Potato Salad
Chicken Salad with Cream Dressinng

BREADS AND BATTERCAKES

Buttermilk Buckwheat Cakes
Sourdough Hotcakes with Berry Syrup
Alaskan Sourdough Waffles
Spider Corn Bread
Hunters' Hotcakes
Eskimo Sourdough Doughnuts

DESSERTS

Rhubarb Pie
Wild Blackberry Pie
Washington Applesauce Cake
Buttermilk Raisin Pie
Washington State Peach Pie
Shortbread
Idaho Potato Doughnuts
Gooseberry Chiffon Pie
Peach Ice Cream
Oregon Apple Pie
Eskimo Ice Cream
Wild Chokecherry Jam
Venison Mince Pie

BEVERAGES

Elderberry Cordial
Blue Blazer
Rocky Mountain Flip
Old-fashioned Boiled Camp Coffee

NORTHWESTERN COOKING

In 1790 the ship *Columbia* left Boston to sail around Cape Horn to the Pacific Northwest on a trading expedition. A sailor aboard named John Boit wrote on May 18, 1792,

> We directed our course up this noble river. . . . Capt. Grey named this river Columbia. This river in my opinion would be a fine place to set up a factory; the river abounds with excellent salmon.

Reports of this voyage inspired Thomas Jefferson some years later to send Merriwether Lewis and William Clark to explore the Northwest in hopes that a link by water might exist between the Columbia River and the Missouri. The expedition left St. Louis on May 14, 1804. Among the instructions given Lewis by President Thomas Jefferson was to take note, along the way, of the customs of the Indians.

By winter the expedition had traveled as far as the five Mandan villages in what is now South Dakota. There they met and hired a French trapper named Toussaint Charbonneaux, and his wife, Sacajawea, who two years before had been stolen from her Shoshone tribe by the Minnetarees and sold by them to Charbonneaux. Sacajawea proved invaluable as an interpreter, as well as an advisor on Indian customs, and provider of food lore.

One day Lewis noted in his diary that Charbonneaux prepared a *poudinque blanc* which he said was "six feet of the lower end of the big buffalo gut, stripped of its fecal matter by squeezing through the fingers and stuffed with meat, kidney, suet, flour, and seasoning. It was boiled a while, then fried in bear oil until brown." George Bird Grinnell, in *Blackfoot Lodge Tales*, mentioned that . . .

> during the stuffing process the entrail was turned inside out, thus combining with the meat the sweet white fat that covers the intestine. The next step was to roast it a little, after which the ends were tied to prevent the escape of juices, and it was thoroughly boiled in water. This is a very great delicacy and when properly prepared is equally appreciated by whites and Indians.

The Eskimo eats the small intestine of the seal, washed in several waters, in soups and stews with seal meat. It is also possible that the "coureurs du bois" introduced the Indians to this recipe. There is a sausage called *andouilles* in France made of the large pig's intestine and filled with strips of chitterling and stomach of the same animal.

Susan Magoffin, who traveled across the Plains in 1846, wrote in her diary,

> It is a rich sight, indeed, to look at the fine fat buffalo meat stretched out on ropes to dry for our sustenance, when we are no longer in the regions of the living animal. Such soup as we have, made of the hump ribs, one of the most choice parts of the buffalo. I never eat its equal in the hotels of N.Y. or Philada. And the sweetest butter and most delicate oil I ever tasted, 'tis not surpassed by the marrow taken from the thigh bone.

Several of Lewis's men returned up the Missouri River to establish an American fur-trading company. Later, trappers' rendezvous were established on the Yellowstone River, Wind River, Snake River, and on other waterways. At Jackson's Hole, Brown's Hole, Pierre's Hole, and Ogden's Hole, trappers, accompanied by their Indian families, would meet to trade the year's catch, and to feast. Whole buffalo were roasted over coals day and night as it was the easiest way to feed so many people. The hump and tongue were great delicacies.

North and south of the Yellowstone, and on what is now the broad wheat lands of Montana, were vast herds of buffalo and elk. It was also Indian territory, so forts were built to protect the trappers—Forts Bonneville, Piegan, Boise, Hall, and Robidou. They were connected by trails that later became the overland routes for the miners who streamed into the Black Hills and into Montana when gold was discovered.

In the spring the Indians had great feasts of duck eggs and those of other waterfowls. Dogs were a delicacy to some tribes, mainly the Gros Ventres, Sioux, and Assiniboines. Other tribes such as the Piegans did not eat dog. A Piegan was quoted as saying, "Men say they are our friends and then turn against us, but our dogs are always true."

The camass root was dug and cooked, or roasted in pits. A starchy root called bitterroot was gathered, dried, and boiled. And a root called *mats* was eaten in great quantity in the spring. This plant was known to the trappers of the Hudson's Bay and American Fur companies as *pomme blanche*.

The Indians ate all parts of the deer, elk, and buffalo except the gall bladder and lungs. The paunch was eaten raw, and sometimes liver too was eaten raw. Meat was boiled or roasted. When boiled, it was eaten rare; and when roasted, well done.

Indians often ate as much as three to four pounds of meat for breakfast. For trips and times of scarcity the tribes made pemmican from dried buffalo meat and buffalo tallow. There were even different grades of pemmican—the best was seasoned with buffalo berries and made with marrow fat. Crushed chokecherries, stones and all, provided the seasoning for another kind of pemmican. It sustained the tribes on trips and when buffalo were scarce. When the buffalo began to disappear, killed indiscriminately for its hide, it was a disaster the Plains tribes were never able to overcome. Their diet was supplemented by seasonal foods such as duck eggs in the spring, other game in the fall, berries and roots at other times. Buffalo meat was the staple they were unable to do without.

In 1840 a man named Henderson Lewelling, a nurseryman, transported a wagonload of fruit-tree seedlings over the Oregon Trail. All went well until he reached the Wyoming Territory, when, on the North Platte, the oxen began to tire. He was urged to jettison his precious cargo. Instead, he and his family and wagons slowed to rest the oxen, then started alone over the Rockies from Fort Bridger to Soda Springs, and across Idaho into Oregon. It was from his seedlings that the first great orchards of Oregon and Washington were developed. There cultivated strawberries grew so big that a single one would serve one person. Cabbages, carrots, beets, cauliflower, and beets, grew to giant size in the virgin soil. Over a part of the same trail, the Mormons, expelled from Iowa, traveled the following year to found Salt Lake City.

By 1860 English and American capital was invested in vast cattle ranches in Montana, Wyoming, and the Dakotas. Cattle were driven to the main trails, and thence to the railheads in Independence, Missouri, and later in Dodge City, Kansas. The drives were serviced by chuck wagons, many with Mexican or Chinese cooks. Tortillas, chili con carne, frijoles, barbecued spareribs, and many southwestern dishes came north with the always-good hunter's stew, steak, roast beef, and the barbecue. The best roast beef in the world can still be eaten in the Northwest. The cowboys found that the juice from a can of tomatoes was a safe drink, and tasted even better mixed with beer. In the towns, the cattle barons feasted on some of the best foods, imported for their pleasure. One French cattle baron brought his own chef with him. As early as the war of the copper kings there wasn't a delicacy to be found in New York and San Francisco that was not served at some political or social dinner in Butte.

The settlers in Idaho had in the meantime discovered that the soil there produced a very light, fluffy potato. Baked and served with butter, salt, and pepper, it was a dish good enough for anyone. It was much later that it became the custom to pass a tray of condiments with baked potato: crisp bacon crumbled, chopped chives, sour cream, grated cheese, and chopped parsley could be sprinkled on the potato for additional flavor. Lamb is grown and prepared for market on the Snake River plain. The long cool nights of those high northwestern valleys are also right for peas, beets, celery, and many other vegetables.

Yeast and sourdough starters were as

valuable as fire to the early pioneers, and were tended as carefully as fire, as they bounced across the country in wagons and on saddlehorns. A cup or so of the yeast was always left to start the next batch of bread or pancakes. When gold was discovered in Alaska in the eighties, sourdough was such standard equipment that the men who crowded into the small cities of Anchorage and Nome were themselves nicknamed "Sourdoughs." Food was scarce; prices were high. Eggs sold for one hundred dollars a dozen, and beef was unavailable. Sourdoughs learned to eat the native fish, seal, walrus, whale, duck, ptarmigan, and other game. And they passed their sourdough on to the Eskimos in exchange.

Alaskans have had to rely heavily on canned and packaged staples. One compensation is the fresh fish which is abundant and in great variety. There is also exotic fare like seagull eggs, and braised bear chops, and moose and caribou steaks and stews. Russia contributes to Alaskan cooking with breads and desserts.

Game is still plentiful in the mountain states. It is said that, "In an average year . . . a quarter of a million game animals and two dozen hunters are killed in this region." It is possible to eat, in season, fresh tender venison steak, domesticated buffalo steak, and Canadian goose. Elk can be had if the hunter is lucky, but it is scarce and inhabits only the highest valleys. Mountain sheep and goats and antelope are available but wary, and as with moose, states are careful to give out only a certain number of hunting licenses each year.

In the spring the rivers are filled with melting snow. Trout stir out of their winter lethargy, and up the rivers from the Pacific come the salmon to spawn—the chinook, largest and most prized; the sockeye and the blue back, which are red. Then there are the coho; the pink, light in color and delicate in flavor; and the chum or keta. Salmon roe is called red caviar.

The Finns who migrated to the Northwest in the eighties and nineties especially appreciated the delicacy of salmon. *Kala lootaa* is salted salmon with onions and potatoes; *lipija kalaa*, rich with milk and butter, is a kind of salmon chowder. Creamed *lutefisk* (salt salmon soaked in mild lye water) is served with a shaker of mustard and a shaker of allspice.

Newcomers to the Northwest are the Basques who came to the ranches of Wyoming and Idaho during World War II to help with the sheep. Famous for such foods as béarnaise sauce, stuffed steak, Basque rice, they add a certain old-world spice to the plain ranch food, and in some parts of the Rockies the scent of garlic can be sniffed in the clear, fresh air of the Big Sky Country, as the flavors of western Europe and western United States mingle.

SOUPS AND CHOWDERS

LEEK AND POTATO SOUP

5 leeks (white part only), thinly sliced
3 tablespoons butter
4 cups peeled, diced potatoes
4 cups chicken broth
1½ teaspoons salt
½ teaspoon celery salt
pinch cayenne
nutmeg

Sauté the leeks in the butter, using a medium saucepan, for 5 minutes or until soft but not brown.

Add the potatoes, broth, and seasonings, except nutmeg. Cook for 15 minutes or until potatoes are soft.

Remove from heat, mash with a potato masher, and strain off the remaining solids.

Reheat a minute or so, and serve with dash of nutmeg on top. (*4 servings*)

OXTAIL SOUP

1 pound oxtail, cut into 2-inch pieces
flour
salt
pepper
3 tablespoons fat or cooking oil
3 cups beef consommé or stock
3 cups water
2 teaspoons Worcestershire sauce
½ cup chopped onion
½ cup diced carrot
½ cup diced celery
½ cup diced turnip
Madeira wine

Flour and season the oxtail pieces. Brown on all sides in hot fat or oil, using a heavy skillet. Transfer to a large pot; add the consommé, water, and Worcestershire sauce. Simmer, covered, for 2 or 3 hours or until meat falls from the bones.
Remove and discard the bones, add the vegetables, and simmer until vegetables are tender. Add hot water if necessary. Serve in bowls with ½ teaspoon Madeira added to each. (*6 servings*)

ROCKY MOUNTAIN BORSCH

1 quart meat stock (or beef or chicken bouillon)
2 cups raw, peeled, minced beets
1 cup minced celery
1 cup minced cabbage
1 tablespoon vinegar
1 teaspoon salt
1 teaspoon pepper
1 cup chopped tomatoes
½ cup sour cream

Put the meat stock, beets, celery, cabbage, vinegar, salt, and pepper into a large pot. Bring to a boil, turn down heat, and simmer for 1 hour.
Add the tomatoes and cook 10 minutes longer. Serve in soup bowls with a dab of sour cream in the middle of each. (*4 to 6 servings*)

VENISON BROTH

A hearty soup and an effective restorative served in the Rocky Mountain country to ward off the cold.

4 pounds venison bones with meat attached
4 stalks celery, with leaves
3 onions, finely chopped
1 clove garlic, chopped
2 carrots, finely chopped
5 sprigs parsley, chopped
2 tomatoes, peeled and chopped
1 teaspoon salt
½ teaspoon pepper

Combine all the ingredients in a large pot or kettle with 3 quarts water.
Bring to a boil, turn down heat, cover, and simmer about 2 hours.
Strain, chill, and skim the fat. Check for seasoning, heat, and serve. (*4 to 6 servings*)

BEAN CHOWDER

1 cup navy beans, soaked overnight in cold water, drained
1½ quarts water
1 cup diced carrots
1 cup chopped tomatoes
1 cup chopped green pepper
1 cup chopped onion
2 teaspoons salt
1 teaspoon pepper
2 tablespoons raw cracked wheat
2½ cups milk

Put the beans and water into a large saucepan, bring to a boil, and cook about 20 minutes (they should be about half done).
Add the vegetables, and cook 20 minutes longer or until beans and vegetables are soft. Put through a sieve, return to the saucepan with the liquid, add the seasonings and cracked wheat, bring to a boil, and cook 10 minutes. Add the milk, heat, and serve. (*8 servings*)

CANADIAN CABBAGE SOUP

¼ cup water
½ medium head cabbage, shredded
1 large, potato, peeled and thinly sliced
1 large onion, peeled and thinly sliced
3 cups milk
¼ cup butter
1 teaspoon salt
¼ teaspoon pepper
  grated mild cheese

Put ¼ cup water in a heavy saucepan; add cabbage, potato, and onion. Stir, cover tightly, and cook over very low heat until very tender. Mash into a pulp with a potato masher. Add the milk, butter, salt, and pepper. Stir. Keep hot, but do not boil. Serve in bowls with grated cheese on top. (*4 servings*)

PASTA, EGG,
AND CHEESE DISHES

NOODLES AND SAUSAGES

4 ounces broad noodles
2 tablespoons butter
¼ cup hot milk
2 eggs, beaten
½ teaspoon salt
½ teaspoon pepper
1 pound small sausages, parboiled for 10
  minutes
  bread crumbs

Drop the noodles into a pot of boiling salted water, and cook about 5 minutes or until just tender. Drain.
Preheat oven to 325 degrees.
Mix together the noodles, butter, milk, eggs, and seasonings. Place into a buttered baking dish.
Stick the half-cooked sausages vertically into the noodles, around the sides and into the center.
Sprinkle with bread crumbs and bake 30 minutes. (*4 to 6 servings*)

DENVER OMELET

The original western omelet probably came from the Southwest via the cattle trails. Denver was the first place easterners encountered this dish.

1 tablespoon butter
½ cup chopped onion
½ cup chopped green pepper
½ cup chopped ham or cooked bacon
2 eggs, lightly beaten
1 teaspoon salt
½ teaspoon pepper
  few dashes Tabasco sauce
2 slices toast

Melt the butter in a heavy skillet; sauté the onion, pepper, and ham for 3 minutes.
Stir in the eggs and seasonings, and let brown on one side. Turn and brown on the other, and serve on hot buttered toast. (*2 servings*)

TOMATO RABBIT

½ pound Cheddar or American cheese, shredded
1 tablespoon butter
1 can condensed tomato soup
1½ tablespoons Worcestershire sauce
½ teaspoon dry mustard
dash Tabasco sauce

Cook the cheese in the butter until melted. Add the remaining ingredients and cook, stirring, until well mixed and thickened. Serve on toast. (*4 servings*)

HOOD RIVER OMELET

3 large Oregon apples, pared, cored, and sliced
1 teaspoon sugar
½ teaspoon cinnamon
½ teaspoon lemon juice
3 eggs
butter

Cook the apples in a little water until soft. Drain, mash, and beat with the sugar, cinnamon, and lemon until light. Set aside to cool. Separate the three eggs, and beat yolks and whites separately. Stir the yolks into the applesauce, and then fold in the whites. Butter an omelet pan, heat, and pour in the egg-apple mixture. Cook on top of stove 2 to 3 minutes, then put under the broiler a few minutes longer to brown on top. (*2 to 4 servings*)

CHEESE BLINTZES

"When the United States purchased Alaska from the Russians, they acquired as a bonus this popular Russian dish," so said our Alaskan friend who gave us this recipe. Somehow we doubt his story of the origin of this dish. But it tested well and tastes good, so we decided to include it.

3 eggs, beaten until light
½ teaspoon salt
1 cup water
1 cup flour
2 pats butter
8 ounces cottage cheese
2 tablespoons butter

Beat 2 of the eggs, salt, water, and flour into a smooth batter.
Melt ½ pat butter in a skillet, and put in 2 tablespoons of the batter. Fry on one side over low heat until firm. Slide out of the pan onto a cloth, uncooked side up. Make 4 pancakes in this manner.
Make a filling of the remaining egg, cottage cheese, and butter, and spread onto each pancake.
Roll, tuck in the edges, and sauté in hot oil. Serve hot or cold, topped with sour cream. (*4 servings*)

FISH AND SHELLFISH

KALA LOOTAA

The Finns of the Northwest serve this on Friday night with cole slaw, buttered peas, and dill pickles.

8 medium potatoes, peeled and sliced
1 small onion, sliced thin
3 tablespoons flour
¼ teaspoon pepper
4 tablespoons butter, diced
½ pound salt salmon, diced
3 cups milk

Preheat oven to 350 degrees.

Butter a 2-quart baking dish, and fill half full with sliced potatoes. Spread the onion over this, and sprinkle the flour over the potatoes and onions.

Distribute evenly half the diced butter, and half the diced salmon. Add the remaining potatoes, then the remaining salmon, butter, and pepper. Add the milk to cover the potatoes.

Bake 1¼ hours or until brown. Serve with coleslaw and dill pickles. (*6 to 8 servings*)

WASHINGTON SALMON LOAF

2 cups flaked, cooked fresh salmon (or canned salmon)
1 cup fine bread crumbs
½ teaspoon dry mustard
1 teaspoon Worcestershire sauce
1 teaspoon salt
2 eggs, slightly beaten
½ cup fish stock or chicken broth
butter
flour

Preheat oven to 350 degrees.

Mix all the ingredients except butter and flour together, moistening if necessary with chicken broth or fish stock.

Form into a loaf and place into a buttered baking dish, dot with butter, sprinkle with flour or bread crumbs, and bake 30 minutes. Serve in slices, with or without a cream sauce. (*4 servings*)

BAKED COLUMBIA RIVER SALMON

1 salmon, 4 to 6 pounds, dressed
¼ cup flour
8 slices bread, wet and crumbled
¼ cup butter, melted
1 small onion, minced
3 tablespoons parsley, minced
½ pound fat salt pork, sliced into 8 pieces

Dredge the fish in flour.

Mix the crumbled bread, butter, onion, and parsley. Stuff into the cavity of the fish, and fasten with toothpicks or sew up.

Lay 4 slices of salt pork in a baking pan. Lay the salmon on the pork. Put 4 slices of salt pork at intervals on top of the fish.

Preheat oven to 300 degrees.

Bake 15 minutes per pound. Serve with boiled new potatoes. (*6 to 8 servings*)

DRIED LING (LUTEFISK)

This Norwegian dish is still eaten in parts of the Northwest and the Midwest, and this recipe came directly to us in a letter from a resident of that part of the country. It is usually made of salt cod, but in the Northwest it is sometimes made with salt salmon. This recipe is for cod.

It is a mistake to say Norwegians eat herring raw. . . .Cod—yes. . . .[as] for lutefisk, the Norwegians take the dry cod, soak it in a mild lye solution to soften it— then boil the hell out of it and serve it with butter to give you the finest eating fish you ever wanted to eat.

Serve with lefsa, a thin dry pancake.

ALASKAN KING CRAB RÉMOULADE

1 cup mayonnaise
1 teaspoon lemon juice
3 tablespoons minced chives
3 tablespoons minced parsley
Dijon mustard to taste
1 pound king crab meat, fresh, frozen, or canned
olive oil
lettuce leaves

Put the mayonnaise, lemon juice, chives, parsley, and mustard into a mixing bowl; beat with a wire whisk.

Let stand 30 minutes, then add the crab meat. Mix thoroughly, and serve on lettuce leaves that have been brushed with olive oil. (*4 servings*)

ROCKY MOUNTAIN RAINBOW TROUT, CAMP STYLE

The abundance of trout of all species—brooks and rainbows—in the cold, rapid streams of Montana and Idaho has lead to the cultivation of these delicious fish on a commercial scale. Fish from the streams have been transported to twenty-thousand-gallon vertical "silos" where they are carefully fed, bred, and developed for markets all over the country. Controlled, scientific feeding has produced edible protein in quantity at a far cheaper per-pound cost than the cattle ranches; and aquaculture is only beginning.

The following recipe will serve well for almost any small freshwater pan fish such as brook trout, perch, pickerel, and so forth. . . . and you can use bread crumbs or cracker meal in place of cornmeal, and almost any kind of fat or vegetable oil.

2 to 3 pounds freshly caught trout
2 teaspoons salt
pepper
½ cup cornmeal, yellow or white
½ cup flour
2 tablespoons butter
2 tablespoons bacon fat
2 teaspoons chopped parsley
1 lemon, sliced

Eviscerate the fish, clip off the fins and tails but leave heads intact. Wipe them dry with a paper towel, and season well with salt and pepper. Roll them in a mixture of cornmeal and flour until well coated.

Heat the butter and bacon fat in a skillet. Brown the fish for 4 minutes on each side or until golden brown and flesh flakes when fork-tested.

Serve at once, garnished with chopped parsley and lemon slices. (*4 to 6 servings*)

POACHED TROUT WITH SCALLIONS

4 brook trout (about ½ pound each)
1 cup dry white wine
1 cup water mixed with a pinch salt
¾ cup chopped scallions
1 tablespoon butter
3 tablespoons flour
2 cups milk
1 teaspoon salt
½ teaspoon pepper
few grains cayenne
1 egg yolk
paprika

Eviscerate the trout, remove the tails and fins but leave the heads on. Poach them gently in a mixture of the wine and salted water, about 3 minutes on each side.

Meanwhile sauté the scallions in the butter, sprinkle in the flour, and cook 5 minutes. Stir in the milk and seasonings. Remove from the heat and stir in the egg yolk. Do not boil after adding egg yolk.

Place the trout on a warm serving platter, pour the sauce over them, sprinkle with paprika, and serve. (*4 servings*)

MEATS

ROAST VENISON

Let the meat hang until you judge proper to drefs it, then take out the bone; beat the meat with a rolling pin. Lay fome flices of mutton fat that has lain a few hours in a little port wine; fprinkle a little black and Jamaica pepper over it, in finest powder; roll it up tight, and fillet it. Set it in a

ftewpan that will only juft hold it, with fome mutton or beef gravy, not ftrong, half a pint of port, and fome pepper and pimento. Simmer, clofe covered, and as flow as you can, for three or four hours. When quite tender, take off the tape, and fet the meat on a difh, and ftrain the gravy over. Serve with currant jelly fauce.

The foregoing instructions for treating venison were written when most venison in the Colonial markets was poorly handled and "tainted." It was believed that properly hung meat was more tender than meat that wasn't hung. In some parts of England and Europe this is still believed. But in 1824 when Dr. Thomas Cooper wrote his *Treatise on American Medicine* and the proper treatment of food, he said, "Few people like it [venison] when it has much of the haut gout. The sooner it is eaten after killing the better." Here are a few chosen suggestions to follow when you have just bagged a deer:

Gut it as soon as possible following the kill.

Prop open chest cavity to allow air to circulate freely and cool the carcass quickly and evenly.

If the weather is warm, butcher immediately and freeze cuts you are not using.

Trim all the fat from the meat, as fat tends to cling unpleasantly to the roof of the mouth.

Lard with beef fat.

Removing the bones will reduce the wild flavor.

Marinating will tend to break down the tough connecting tissues.

Old and tough animals are best ground into hamburger.

Tender young animals may be cut into small broilable steaks.

In Montana, where venison is still plentiful during the fall months, they roast it this way:

> 6 to 8 pounds venison, leg, loin, or saddle
> 3 cups dry red wine or cider
> 3 tablespoons oil
> 2 onions, sliced
> 3 bay leaves
> 1 teaspoon salt
> 4 slices bacon
> ¼ teaspoon pepper

Place the meat into an earthenware, enamel, or glass bowl, add 2 cups wine, oil, onions, bay leaves, and salt.

Cover the bowl and marinate in the refrigerator 12 hours or longer, turning so that all parts of the meat are exposed to the marinade.

Preheat oven to 325 degrees.

Transfer the meat to a shallow baking pan, drape with bacon slices, and cook about 1½ hours or until meat is like pink lamb. Baste from time to time with some of the marinade.

Turn up the heat to 450 degrees, brown for 15 minutes. Add remaining cup of wine to the roasting pan. Stir. Pour into gravy bowl and serve with the roast.

Serve buffalo-berry jelly, if available. (*6 to 8 servings*)

PEMMICAN

Pemmican was the famous Indian "ration" used on long trips and in winter when meat was scarce. The back fat or tallow of buffalo was eaten the way we eat butter. Lean buffalo meat was cut in thin sheets and hung out to dry into jerky (in bad weather, it was hung at the top of the lodge above the fire). Pemmican was made from these two ingredients, and sometimes wild cherries were added for flavor. The following is a Blackfoot pemmican recipe:

> Dried jerky of 2 cow buffaloes
> 1 large dried bull's hide
> buffalo tallow, melted
> 1 large dried bull's hide cut in 2 oblong pieces, corners rounded and sewn together into a sack to hold meat
> chokecherries

Prepare 2 large fires of quaking aspen; allow to burn down to coals. Lay the first bull's hide flesh side up between these fires. Throw the sheets of dried meat on one of the fires. Allow to heat through, then throw them on the hide. If the first fire begins to smoke use the other. Smoke gives a bitter taste to jerky. After all the meat has been heated and is on the hide, flail it with sticks. Being brittle it will flake easily. Stir and pound it until all is fine.

Put the cooling melted tallow and the meat in a bull's hide trough and stir with a wooden spade until well mixed. Add chokecherries.

Shovel it into one of the sacks, hold open, and ram it down. Make sure all the air is expelled. Pack as tight as possible and sew up the bag. Repeat with other sack.

Put both sacks on ground and ask several women to jump on them. Lay them in the sun to cool and dry.

Pemmican was eaten either dried as it came from the sack, or stewed with water.

MONTANA BUCK STEW

This can be made with venison, elk, or antelope.

    3 pounds venison, cut into 1-inch cubes
      dry red wine
    2 teaspoons salt
    1 teaspoon pepper
      flour
    ½ cup cooking oil
    1 cup chopped carrots
    1 cup chopped onion
    1 cup chopped celery

Place the venison pieces into a shallow glass or other nonmetallic dish, and pour in enough dry red wine to almost cover. Cover the dish and marinate for about 48 hours, turning meat occasionally so that all sides of the meat are exposed to the marinade.

Drain, season with salt ,and pepper, dredge with flour, and brown on all sides in hot oil, using a heavy skillet. Cook to medium rare or pink, remove to warm platter.

Brown vegetables in the cooking oil. Add marinade and enough water to cover. Simmer until vegetables are tender, return the meat to the stew, and heat through. Serve as you would any stew. (*4 to 6 servings*)

CHARCOAL-BROILED ANTELOPE STEAK

These delicate little steaks, comparable in size to medium pork chops, can be pan-broiled, but should not be overcooked.

    4 antelope steaks, ¾ inch thick
      salt
      pepper

Prepare a charcoal fire and allow to burn down to white coals.

Put steaks on rack 6 inches above the fire. Cook 3 to 5 minutes on each side, turn, and cook until the steak is just pink inside, or until droplets of juice come through the top side. Season and serve.

Follow this same recipe for charcoal-broiling venison steak. Cook 5 to 7 minutes on each side. (*4 servings*)

NEVADA BAKED STEAK

This method of cooking steak, almost unknown in the eastern states, is said to be common practice in Reno and the Lake Tahoe area, where a well-done steak is the thing.

    1 porterhouse steak, 2 inches thick
    1 clove garlic, cut in half
    1 teaspoon salt
    ½ cup olive oil
    ½ cup ketchup
    1 tablespoon Worcestershire sauce
    1 lemon, thinly sliced
    2 teaspoons paprika

Preheat oven to 375 degrees.
Slash the edges of the steak to prevent curling, rub thoroughly on both sides with the cut garlic, season with salt, and place into a shallow baking pan.
Mix together the olive oil, ketchup, and Worcestershire, and pour over the steak. Cover with the lemon slices, sprinkle liberally with paprika, and bake about 45 minutes. (*4 to 6 servings*)

OREGON BEEF-FRUIT STEW

Here's northwestern stew that uses the abundance of dried fruits, in a combination of flavors that makes an ordinary stew taste special.

    3 tablespoons beef fat
    2½ pounds stewing beef, cut in 1 inch
      cubes
    3 cups cider
    4 small onions
    ½ cup dried apricots
    ½ cup dried prunes
    1 teaspoon sugar
    1 slice lemon with rind
    ⅛ teaspoon pepper
    3 tablespoons flour
    3 tablespoons butter

Melt beef fat and brown meat cubes on all sides. Add cider. Lower heat.
Peel onions (leeks can be used), and add them to stew.
Wash apricots and prunes, and sprinkle them over the stew.

Add sugar, lemon slice, and pepper.
Simmer 2 hours or until meat is tender.
Mix butter and flour together and stir into stew. Cook several minutes, until thickened, and serve with baked Idaho potatoes or dumplings. (*4 to 6 servings*)

RANCH-BARBECUED BEEF WITH COWBOY SAUCE

The large stock ranches prepare meat this way for the roundup crews. We don't expect that you will have to call upon this recipe very often, but should you find yourself with 1,500 guests on hand some Sunday afternoon, you will now know how to feed them. Serve with Cowboy Sauce and whatever accompanying dishes the season provides: corn on the cob, boiled potatoes, beans, watermelon . . .

      500 pounds beef, butchered into 25-
           pound pieces
       10 pounds salt

Bone and roll the beef. Salt and wrap pieces in cheesecloth.
Dig a pit 5 feet deep, 3 feet wide, and 20 feet long; build up wood fire until coals are within 1½ feet of ground level.
Level off the coals and cover surface with fine, dry sand.
Place beef on sand, cover with sheet metal, and pile dirt over all to hold heat.
Cook for 12 hours. (*1500 servings*)

COWBOY SAUCE

       2 pounds butter
    2½ quarts water
       1 cup vinegar
    1½ tablespoons dry mustard
      ¼ cup sugar
       3 tablespoons salt
       3 tablespoons chili powder
       1 teaspoon cayenne
       2 tablespoons Worcestershire sauce
       2 tablespoons Tabasco sauce
       3 tablespoons pepper
       4 teaspoons paprika
       1 onion, finely chopped
       1 clove garlic

Mix all ingredients and boil 30 minutes. (This should be enough sauce for each 25 pounds of meat.)

CHICKEN FRIED STEAK

A different and economical way to serve round steak or minute steak. Made where the steaks grow and chickens are scarce, it is a very western dish.

       8 thin slices round steak
       1 large egg, beaten
       1 cup bread crumbs
      ½ teaspoon salt
      ¼ teaspoon pepper
       4 tablespoons peanut oil
       2 tablespoons flour
       1 cup water or milk

Dip beef into beaten egg and then into bread crumbs mixed with salt and pepper.
Heat peanut oil and brown steaks over low heat 10-15 minutes on each side. When well browned put on hot platter and cover to keep warm. The steaks may be served without gravy if desired.
Add flour to pan drippings, when light brown, stir in water until it thickens into gravy. Add more water if too thick. Return steaks to pan and simmer gently until ready to serve. (*4 servings*)

IDAHO LUMBER-CAMP HASH

       1 pound cold leftover meat
       3 cold cooked Idaho potatoes, peeled
           and chopped
       1 large onion, sliced
       2 teaspoons salt
      ½ teaspoon pepper
       1 tablespoon melted butter (more if
           meat is lean)
    1½ cups hot water

Preheat oven to 350 degrees.
Grind up the meat, potatoes, and onion together (there should be about twice as much potato as meat), and mix well with seasonings, butter, and hot water.
Grease a baking pan, add the hash, put into the oven, and bake for about 1 hour or until nicely browned, but not dried out. (*4 servings*)

ROAST LAMB, UTAH STYLE

1 leg lamb, 7 to 8 pounds, skinned
  salt
4 tablespoons brown sugar
4 tablespoons flour
2 tablespoons dry mustard
  minted applesauce (see below)

Preheat oven to 350 degrees.
Rub lamb with salt. Make a paste by combining the sugar, flour, and mustard with a little water.
Cover the lamb with the paste, place into an uncovered roasting pan and roast for about 1 hour. Add ½ cup water and turn the heat down to 300 degrees. Cook a total of 30 minutes per pound.
Serve with browned potatoes and hot minted applesauce.

6 medium apples
¼ cup water
½ cup sugar
6 tablespoons chopped fresh mint
  leaves

Core, peel, and quarter apples. Cook until soft in water.
Press through strainer, add sugar, and cook until sugar is dissolved. Chop mint and add to applesauce. (*8 servings*)

SHASHLIK

The Alaskans borrowed this dish from the Russians, from whom Alaska was purchased in the first place. The dish is found throughout America in one guise or another, each ethnic group calling it by a different name. The Armenians call it *shish kebab*, the Greeks *arni souvla*, the French *en brochette*. In some areas beef is substituted for lamb. Essentially, the dish consists of cubes of meat on a skewer, cooked over a grill. Sometimes the meat cubes are alternated on the skewer with small onions, tomato wedges, slices of green pepper, and/or mushroom caps. The Armenians and Greeks also use cubes of eggplant, though usually the latter are cooked on separate skewers because of the difference in cooking time. This is the Russian version.

1 small leg of lamb, trimmed and cut
  into 2-inch cubes
4 lemons
2 medium onions, chopped very fine
2 teaspoons salt
  pepper

Place the meat into a shallow, nonmetallic dish, cover with a marinade made by squeezing the lemons over and mixing with the onions and seasonings.
Cover and marinate overnight or 24 hours, stirring occasionally.
String the meat on skewers and grill over white-hot charcoal coals (or under broiler), 5 minutes on each side. Baste with the marinade.
Serve with scallions, green peppers, and eggplant fried in butter. (*6 to 8 servings*)

ROCKY MOUNTAIN OYSTERS

Whoever made up this name for lamb and calf fries certainly had a sense of humor. In many parts of the West, particularly on ranches, they enjoy a great, if limited, popularity. They are the testicles of the young lambs and calves that are "cut" at branding time, and are often roasted over the branding fire. Those who have eaten them say they taste something like a chicken gizzard, or an uncooked chicken leg. For those who like them, they should be peeled, dipped in egg and bread crumbs and fried until brown. They can also be braised.

SALT PORK
WITH MORMON GRAVY

Salt pork:

1½ pounds salt pork, thinly sliced
1 cup milk
  flour

Soak the salt pork in milk for 2 hours, dry, and dredge with flour. Fry until crisp. Remove to heated platter.

Mormon gravy:

2 tablespoons fat (from the salt pork)
2 cups milk
3 tablespoons flour

Heat the fat in a heavy skillet, stir in the milk. Sift in the flour, stirring constantly until thickened to desired consistency. Pour over the salt pork. Serve with split and buttered biscuits. (*4 servings*)

SEAL ALASKAN

The average reader of this book will probably not find the information that follows of much use when preparing the daily dinner, but we thought it might be interesting to say something about the culinary activities of some of America's newest citizens. These notes came to us in a small cookbook written by Eskimo schoolchildren in Shishmaref, Alaska. We pass them on to you exactly as written.

Seal is one of the most common kinds of food in this part of the country. We have three kinds of seal. The common seal [hair seal], the spotted seal and ribbon seal. We use them for food and skins for clothing and mukluks. There aren't any fur seal up here.

Seal Oil
Seal oil is made from the blubber or fat next to the skin of the seal. The blubber and skin is cut off the seal, cut into strips and stored in seal pokes or tins. If left where warm or during the summer, it renders itself. From this you have the seal oil.

Seal Poke
The inside of the seal together with the head and all, is cut and taken out through the head part of the sealskin. The skin is then turned, cleaned and blown up for drying. This is then used to put the meats, berries, leaves or other foods for storing in winter.

Seal Meat (fresh)
Cut the meat into pieces. Put water in cooking pot, and add seal meat. Add salt to taste. Let boil.

Seals Bare Feet (Seal Flippers)
Put the seals bare feet into a cooking pan. Cover them with blubber and keep in a hot place until the fur comes off. Then it is time to eat the seals bare feet. You can cook them or eat them without cooking.

Cooked Blubber
Old people always want to eat cooked blubber. First take pieces of seal blubber from poke. Put them into a cooking pan and pour hot water over them. Cook until the blubber oil has come out. Then eat the blubber.

Seal Head (Neeyak 'ook)
Skin the seal. Cut the head from the seal. Cut the heads into as small pieces as you can. Put into a pot of water, add salt. Boil plenty. When cooked, eat the meat. Break the skull and eat the inside of it.

POULTRY
AND GAME BIRDS

CREAMED SMOKED TURKEY

In pioneer days game birds were hung in the chimney to smoke. Smoking birds can be a tedious process. The bird has to be soaked in brine for 18 hours, and then smoked for 4½ or 5 hours over a steady, smoky fire. All is not lost, smoked turkey can be bought in good food stores.

4 tablespoons butter
4 tablespoons flour
¾ teaspoon finely chopped onion
3 cups light cream
2¼ cups diced smoked turkey
½ teaspoon salt
⅛ teaspoon pepper
1 tablespoon sauce diable
parsley or watercress

Melt butter, stir in flour until smooth. Add onion and stir.

Add cream gradually, stirring constantly until the sauce has thickened. Add turkey, salt, pepper, and sauce diable. (If sauce diable is not available, use 1 teaspoon meat glaze and 1 teaspoon sherry.)

Serve on toast points, garnished with parsley or watercress. (*4 servings*)

SAGE HEN
OR RUFFED GROUSE,
HUNTER STYLE

    3 or 4 young sage hens or grouse, dressed and cut into serving pieces (breast only—legs are very tough)
    1 cup flour seasoned with 1½ teaspoons salt
    1 teaspoon pepper, and 1 teaspoon sage
    ½ cup butter
    ½ cup cooking oil
    ½ cup chicken broth
    2 tomatoes, peeled, seeded, and cut up
    1 cup sliced mushrooms
    1 green pepper, cut into thin slices
    1 small onion, chopped

Shake the birds in a paper bag with the seasoned flour until well coated.

Melt the butter and oil in a heavy skillet, and heat almost to the smoking point. Brown the birds on all sides.

Add the broth, tomatoes, mushrooms, pepper, and onion. Cover, and simmer 20 minutes or until birds are fork-tender. (*4 to 6 servings*)

PHEASANT, WESTERN STYLE

    1 pheasant, dressed and quartered
    1 cup flour seasoned with 1 teaspoon salt, ½ teaspoon pepper, and a pinch thyme
    3 tablespoons butter
    3 tablespoons cooking oil
    ½ cup dry white wine or chicken broth
    3 tablespoons flour
    1 cup light cream or water

Shake the pheasant pieces in a paper bag with the seasoned flour. Shake off excess flour.

Melt the butter and oil in a heavy skillet, heat almost to the smoking point, and brown quarters well on all sides.

Reduce heat, add the liquid, and continue cooking about 1 hour. (The breasts, being tender meat, will cook first and should be removed from the skillet first. Some discard the legs entirely because they are tough.) Transfer to a hot platter, and keep warm.

Pour off all but 3 tablespoons of fat from the skillet, then stir in the flour, scraping the bottom of the pan. Add the cream and cook, stirring constantly, until sauce thickens. Season to taste and serve with the pheasant, and rice—wild rice, if available. (*4 servings*)

BRAISED CHICKEN
WITH TOMATOES

    ½ cup cooking oil
    1 onion, sliced
    1 clove garlic, minced
    2 tablespoons flour
    1 cup hot water
    6 medium tomatoes, peeled and seeded
    1 green pepper, seeded and cut into strips
    1 cup diced cooked ham
    1 teaspoon dried basil
    1 teaspoon salt
    1 teaspoon freshly ground pepper few dashes Tabasco sauce
    1 roasting chicken, cut into serving portions minced parsley

Using a heavy skillet, heat the oil, stir in the onion and garlic, and then the flour. Cook 3 minutes, then stir in the water. Continue stirring until smooth.

Add the tomatoes, pepper, ham, and seasonings. Cover and simmer 10 minutes over low heat.

Add the chicken parts, and cook uncovered about 30 minutes or until chicken is tender.

Serve chicken with sauce spooned over it, sprinkled with parsley. (*4 to 6 servings*)

VEGETABLES
AND SIDE DISHES

IDAHO POTATO LOAF

    1 tablespoon butter
    ½ cup fine, dry bread crumbs
    4 cups mashed leftover baked potatoes
        mixed with ½ cup milk
    1 cup condensed cream of tomato soup
    2 tablespoons butter
    1 pinch oregano
    4 hard-cooked eggs, quartered

Preheat oven to 375 degrees.
Butter a loaf pan well and dust thickly with the
bread crumbs. Put in the potatoes and bake 25
minutes.
Meanwhile heat the tomato soup, butter, and
oregano a few minutes, and add the eggs.
Transfer the potato loaf onto a heated platter
and surround with the eggs in tomato sauce. (*4
servings*)

MONTANA BAKED CORN

    1 dozen ears fresh corn
    1 cup butter, melted
    1 teaspoon salt
    ¼ teaspoon pepper

Preheat oven to 350 degrees.
Pull corn husks back, but do not break off.
Remove silk from each ear. Return husks to
former position to cover corn. Remove only
the outermost coarse and bruised leaves on top.
Dip each ear in cold water. Twist top of leaves
to secure husks. Lay on cookie sheet, and bake
20 minutes or until tender.
Serve with melted butter, salt and pepper.

BAKED IDAHO POTATOES

The famous Idaho potatoes are stored in long,
low potato barns in the country between the
Rocky Mountains and the Snake River. Their
superior baking qualities cause them to be
shipped nationwide.
It has been said that Idahoans cringe at the
suggestion of defiling their potatoes with
extraneous condiments, but throughout the
Northwest it is customary to serve crumbled
bacon and sour cream with baked potatoes.

    4 Idaho baking potatoes
    3 tablespoons butter, softened
    ⅛ teaspoon paprika
    4 pats butter
    ¼ cup heavy cream

Preheat oven to 350 degrees.
Scrub potatoes and rub with softened butter.
Put in a baking pan and bake until soft when
squeezed.
Remove from oven, cut lengthwise, and allow
steam to escape. Add a pat of butter and a
tablespoon of cream, dust with paprika, and
serve. (*4 servings*)

FRIED APPLES

Core and slice apples, leaving the skins on. Fry
in a hot skillet with a little oil until brown on
both sides. Sprinkle with a little sugar (and
cinnamon, if you wish) just before removing
from pan. Serve hot.
Fried apples are excellent served with pork.

SCALLOPED ASPARAGUS

    4 cups fresh asparagus, cut in 1-inch
        pieces
    1½ cups milk
    2 tablespoons flour
    1 teaspoon salt
    ½ teaspoon pepper
    ½ cup grated American cheese
    1 cup bread crumbs
    2 tablespoons butter

Preheat oven to 325 degrees.
Cook the asparagus in a little water until
tender, then transfer to a buttered baking dish.
Shake the milk, flour, salt, and pepper together
until well blended, and add to the baking dish.
Add half the cheese and half the bread crumbs.
Stir. Add the remaining cheese and half the
remaining bread crumbs and stir again. Dot
with butter, sprinkle the remaining bread
crumbs on top, and bake 30 minutes or until
brown on top. (*4 to 6 servings*)

BACON PEAS

The best way to prepare the fresh peas of the
Northwest is to stew them in barely enough
water to cover and dress them with butter, salt,
and pepper. The recipe below is a good lunch
or supper dish.

    4 slices bacon
    2 cups peas, freshly picked, shelled, and
        cooked
    1 cup heavy cream or cream sauce
    ½ teaspoon salt
    ⅛ teaspoon pepper
    ½ cup bread crumbs

Preheat oven to 350 degrees.
Dice bacon and brown in frying pan. Add
peas, cream, and seasonings. Put all in buttered
baking dish, cover with bread crumbs, and
bake 15 or 20 minutes, until brown. (*4 servings*)

SALADS
AND DRESSINGS

CHICKEN SALAD WITH CREAM DRESSING

Molded salads are popular in the Northwest.
The summers are hot, and the salads can be
made in the cool of the morning and refrigerated. Watercress grows wild on the banks of
western streams.

    2 cups diced cooked chicken
    1 cup chopped celery
    1 cup mayonnaise
    1 package unflavored gelatin, dissolved
        in ¼ cup hot chicken broth
    ½ cup heavy cream, whipped
        crisp lettuce
        capers
        watercress

Mix together the chicken, celery, and mayonnaise.
Mix together the gelatin-broth mixture and
whipped cream, stir into the chicken mixture,
and put in mold. Chill for 3 to 4 hours.
Unmold when ready to serve.
Serve on lettuce, garnished with capers and
watercress. (*4 to 6 servings*)

SOUR CREAM LETTUCE SALAD

    1 head crisp lettuce
    1 cup sour cream
    2 or 3 scallions, chopped
        a little chopped chive
        a little chopped fresh dill
    ½ teaspoon salt
        freshly ground pepper

Remove the leaves from the head of lettuce, wash, dry with a towel, break into bits, and place into a large salad bowl.

Mix the remaining ingredients together, add to the salad, and toss until thoroughly blended. (*2 to 4 servings*)

TONGUE AND SPINACH SALAD

1½ cups julienned cold cooked tongue
1 pound fresh spinach leaves, picked over, washed, drained, and dried
½ cup crisp bacon bits
2 tablespoons prepared horseradish
1 teaspoon dry mustard
1 teaspoon sugar
1 teaspoon salt
½ teaspoon pepper
1 tablespoon vinegar
½ cup olive oil

Mix together all the ingredients, toss, and serve. (*4 servings*)

HOT POTATO SALAD

This hearty dish is found wherever there is German cooking—in the East, Midwest, and in the Great Northwest. It goes well with steak.

6 cups thickly sliced raw potatoes
1 teaspoon salt
1 teaspoon pepper
½ cup water
3 tablespoons bacon fat
1 onion, sliced
2 hard-cooked eggs, sliced
3 tablespoons vinegar mixed with 1 tablespoon sugar
lettuce

Season the potatoes, wet them with the water, and cook very slowly in the bacon fat, about 20 minutes or until tender but not soft. Stir well. Do not brown.

Remove to a salad bowl, add the onion and eggs. Pour the sugared vinegar over all, toss lightly, and serve on lettuce. (*4 servings*)

WYOMING BEAN SALAD

The state of Wyoming grows beans, great varieties of beans—lima, green, pinto, kidney, navy, garbanzo, pole. . . . You name the bean, Wyoming grows it. So, when Wyomingites make bean salad, there is no problem as to which kind of bean to use, because invariably the salad ends up with three or four—or more—varieties mixed together.

2 cups boiled beans, mixed together
2 tablespoons salad dressing, French or Italian
1 teaspoon Worcestershire sauce
½ teaspoon dry mustard
½ teaspoon sugar
½ teaspoon salt
pinch cayenne
1 tablespoon chopped cucumber
1 tablespoon chopped pepper
1 tablespoon chopped onion
lettuce leaves, washed and wiped dry
2 hard cooked eggs, quartered

Mix together the salad dressing, cucumber, pepper, onion, and seasonings, stir in the beans and allow to stand an hour or two.

Put lettuce leaves on 4 plates, spoon on the seasoned beans, and serve garnished with eggs. (*4 servings*)

BREADS
AND BATTERCAKES

SOURDOUGH HOTCAKES WITH BERRY SYRUP

Sourdough:

    2 cups flour
    2 tablespoons sugar
    2 cups warm water

Mix together the flour and sugar, and add enough water to make a thick, rubbery dough. Place into a bowl, cover with a cloth, and let stand in a warm place about 2 days to ferment.

Hotcakes:

    1 egg, beaten
    1 cup milk
    2 tablespoons sugar
    1 teaspoon salt
    1 teaspoon baking soda
    2 cups sourdough
      flour
      cooking oil

Always save one cup of sourdough to start the next batch.
Beat the egg and milk, then stir in the sugar, salt, baking soda, and sourdough. Mix until foamy. Thicken, if too thin, with ½ cup flour. Cook on a hot, greased griddle until bubbles form. Turn and cook on the other side, and serve with butter and red huckleberry or wild cranberry syrup.

Syrup:

    1 cup berries, any kind
      water to cover
    1 cup sugar

Pick over berries and cook in water about ten minutes. Strain through colander and mash well to get as much pulp as possible.
Add sugar and bring to a boil. Serve with hotcakes or waffles. (4 to 6 servings)

ALASKAN SOURDOUGH WAFFLES

The following authentic recipe is a slight modification of that of the old prospectors, who started their sourdough pot with wild yeast and kept it going throughout the year.

    1 cake or package yeast soaked in ¼ cup
      water
    3 cups water
    ½ cup powdered milk
    ¼ cup sugar
    4 cups flour

Mix all the ingredients together and put in a warm place.
The following day, remove one cup of the above, and set aside, covered, in refrigerator for future use as a starter. To the remainder add the following:

    2 teaspoons salt
    ¼ cup melted fat
    2 eggs, beaten
    ½ teaspoon baking soda dissolved in 1
      tablespoon water

Mix well and bake on a hot waffle iron. Turn, cook the other side, and serve with butter and maple syrup, blueberry jam, or Red Huckleberry Syrup* (6 to 8 servings)

ESKIMO SOURDOUGH DOUGHNUTS

The following charming recipe came to us from an Eskimo cookbook put together by the schoolchildren of Shishmaref, Alaska:

1 teaspoon soda into sourdough and as much flour as you need. Sprinkle with little salt, then knead. Take one piece of the dough at a time, roll between hands, then make a hole in the middle with your finger. We melt the seal blubber. After it is melted we put doughnuts in it and cook them in the seal oil.

SPIDER CORN BREAD

A spider is a heavy, cast-iron frying pan with a lid and three 3-inch legs. Carried on covered wagons across the country, it was especially popular in the days of open-hearth cooking when it was set over hot coals, covered, and heated with additional coals on the lid. In the following recipe, use a heavy 9-inch skillet and cook on top of the stove, or in a 350-degree oven.

    ½ cup flour
    1½ cups cornmeal, yellow or white
    2 teaspoons baking powder
    1 teaspoon salt
    1 tablespoon sugar
    2 eggs, beaten
    3 cups milk
    5 tablespoons butter or a mixture of
       butter and bacon fat

Mix together all the dry ingredients.
Mix the eggs and milk together, then stir the dry ingredients into the liquid mixture.
Put the butter into a heavy 12-inch skillet over high heat. When the skillet is good and hot, pour in the batter, cover, turn the heat to low, and cook about 20 minutes or until done. (6 servings)

BUTTERMILK BUCKWHEAT CAKES

    2 cups buckwheat flour
    ½ cup whole wheat flour
    1 teaspoon baking soda
    1 tablespoon sugar
    ½ teaspoon salt
    2 cups buttermilk
    1 tablespoon bacon fat

Mix together and sift all the dry ingredients. Beat in the milk and then the fat until smooth. Cook by tablespoonfuls on a hot, well-oiled griddle until bubbly. Turn and brown on other side.
Serve hot with chokecherry jelly. (4 to 6 servings)

HUNTERS' HOTCAKES

    2 cups packaged pancake mix
    1½ cups beer
    1 egg

Mix all together and brown by the tablespoonfuls on a greased frying pan or griddle hot enough to make a drop of water dance. Flip and brown on other side. (4 to 6 servings)

DESSERTS

SHORTBREAD

    3 cups flour
    1 tablespoon rice flour
    5 tablespoons sugar
    ½ teaspoon baking powder
    1 cup butter

Preheat oven to 325 degrees.
Mix and sift together all the dry ingredients, then cut in the butter. Knead, and roll out on a floured board to a thickness of about ½ inch. Cut into 2-inch squares, pierce with a fork, and place onto a greased baking sheet. Bake about 30 minutes or until golden. (2 dozen cookies)

ESKIMO ICE CREAM

This interesting Eskimo recipe appeared in the cookbook published by the Alaska Crippled Children's Association in Anchorage.

Grate reindeer tallow into small pieces. Add seal oil slowly while beating with hand. After some seal oil has been used, then add a little water while whipping. Continue adding seal oil and water until white and fluffy. Any berries can be added to it.

WASHINGTON STATE PEACH PIE

This dessert is a cross between shortcake and baked Alaska, and is a wonderful way to use the vast harvest of ripe peaches that come to the markets from the orchards in August.

  1 spongecake layer (see Orange Cake*)
  2 egg whites
  ⅓ cup granulated sugar
  6 medium-sized ripe peaches
  1 cup heavy cream
  1 teaspoon confectioners' sugar

Make spongecake as directed in orange cake recipe, halving the recipe to make 1 layer.
Beat egg whites until stiff, then fold in granulated sugar gradually. Preheat oven to 325 degrees.
Put sponge cake layer on an oven-proof baking dish. Peel and slice very ripe peaches and spread over the spongecake in an evenly spaced layer. Cover with meringue.
Bake in oven 15 minutes or until brown.
Serve with cream whipped with confectioners' sugar. (*6 servings*)

OREGON APPLE PIE

  4 or 5 Northwest apples, peeled, cored, and sliced
  1 cup sugar
  ¼ teaspoon cinnamon
  2 tablespoons flour
  ¼ teaspoon salt
  1 tablespoon butter
  2 unbaked pie crusts

Preheat oven to 400 degrees.
Place apple slices into a heavy skillet.
Mix together the sugar, cinnamon, flour, and salt, and sprinkle over the apples. Dot with pieces of butter, and cook, covered, over very low heat until apples begin to soften.
Line a pie pan with unbaked pie crust, spoon in the apples, cover with top crust. Press edges down firmly and perforate top with a fork.
Bake 15 minutes, lower heat to 325 degrees and bake another 30 to 35 minutes, until juice bubbles through holes in crust. (*6 servings*)

WILD BLACKBERRY PIE

This pie is often served at the end of a dinner of baked king salmon. This recipe can also be used with raspberries, cherries, huckleberries, rhubarb, peaches, apricots, or plums, but wild blackberries are especially prized for pie, perhaps because they have to be picked and can't be bought.

  6 cups fresh, ripe wild blackberries, picked over and washed
  1 cup sugar, white or brown
  ¼ teaspoon cinnamon, nutmeg, or ginger
  1 tablespoon flour
  ¼ cup butter
  pastry for a 2-crust pie

Preheat oven to 400 degrees.
Fit bottom pastry into deep pie plate and add the berries. Mix sugar with spice and flour, sprinkle over berries, and dot with butter. Fit second crust over the top and cut steam vents.
Bake 15 minutes, lower heat to 350 degrees, and bake 20 to 30 minutes longer. When filling boils through the vents the pie is done.
Cool and serve with whipped cream. (*6 servings*)

BUTTERMILK RAISIN PIE

This pie comes from Custer, Montana, and though like a sour cream-raisin pie, it is lighter and more flavorful.

  4 tablespoons flour
  3 eggs, separated
  2 cups buttermilk
  1 cup half-and-half
  1 cup brown sugar, firmly packed
  ½ cup raisins
  ⅛ teaspoon salt
  ½ teaspoon cinnamon
  1 baked 9-inch pie shell
  2 egg whites, beaten stiff
  2 tablespoons sugar

Mix flour, egg yolks, buttermilk, half-and-half, brown sugar, raisins, salt, and cinnamon in a saucepan. Bring to a boil over low heat until thickened. Cool. Pour into pie shell.
Preheat oven to 250 degrees.
Whip egg whites with 2 tablespoons sugar to make a meringue. Spread over pie and brown. (*6 servings*)

VENISON MINCE PIE

In the Northwest most game is eaten by those who hunt it, and much of it goes into mince pies and game salamis, particularly if the animal is tough. What cannot be used immediately is cut into family-size portions and frozen in the family freezer. The steaks are usually tender and juicy; all the rest is cooked in stews, roasts, and pot roasts. Roasts are usually marinated.

    2 cup coarsely ground cooked venison
    1 cup vinegar mixed with ½ cup water
    4 cups brown sugar
    4 cups finely chopped apples
    2 cups raisins
    1 teaspoon nutmeg
    2 teaspoons cinnamon
    1 teaspoon salt
    4 uncooked pie crusts

Preheat oven to 400 degrees.
Mix all the ingredients together and spoon into two 9-inch pastry-lined pie pans. Cover with top crusts, crimp edges together, perforate with a fork in several places, slide into the oven, and bake for 10 minutes. Reduce the heat to 250 degrees, and finish baking until done (about 30 minutes more, until filling bubbles through holes in crust). (*12 servings*)

RHUBARB PIE

Also called pieplant pie. As soon as the pink stalks are high enough, rhubarb pies are baked all over the United States.

    3 cups chopped rhubarb
    1 cup sugar
    2 tablespoons flour
    1 egg, lightly beaten
      pastry for a 2-crust, 9-inch pie

Preheat oven to 400 degrees.
Mix together the rhubarb, sugar, flour, and egg; spoon into a 9-inch pie pan lined with pie crust.
Cover with second crust, pinch tightly all around, pierce top with a fork in several places, and bake about 10 minutes. Reduce heat to 350 degrees and cook 20 minutes longer or until done when juice bubbles through vents. (*6 servings*)

GOOSEBERRY CHIFFON PIE

These pretty green berries make a delightful and delicate pie.

    1½ cups ripe gooseberries, picked over
        and rinsed
    1½ cups water
      1 cup sugar
      1 envelope unflavored gelatin,
        dissolved in ¼ cup water
      2 eggs, separated
        baked 9-inch pie shell
      1 cup sweetened whipped cream

Cook gooseberries in water until soft. Strain through sieve to remove skin and seeds. Add sugar, and bring to a boil. Add gelatin. Remove from heat.
Beat egg yolks and add to berry mixture, stirring constantly. Beat egg whites until stiff and fold into mixture. Pour into baked pie shell and refrigerate until congealed. Serve topped with whipped cream. (*6 servings*)

WILD CHOKECHERRY JAM

Trees are scarce in the Big Sky Country, and any tree that produces fruit is precious. Chokecherry trees, thus, assume a far greater importance in Montana than in the eastern states. It takes a lot of chokecherries to make a quart, but many westerners do take the time and trouble to gather them for this interesting jam.

    5 cups chokecherries
    1 cup water
      about 4 cups sugar

Pick over and wash chokecherries. Stew in water until soft, 5 to 10 minutes. Put through strainer. Measure chokecherries—they should measure 4 cups; if not, add equal amount of sugar.
Boil rapidly until the mixture jells (220 to 222 degrees on candy thermometer). Test by spoon: Hold bowl of spoon up sideways. If the juice sheets and two drops hang from it together, the jelly is done. Skim.
Pour into sterilized glasses. (*Approximately 8 eight-ounce glasses*)
Serve with pancakes or with roast venison or venison steaks.

WASHINGTON APPLESAUCE CAKE

In the high mountains of the Northwest and Alaska, allowances should be made in cake recipes. Cake flour should be increased by 1 tablespoon over 3,500 feet, and 1 more tablespoon every 1,500 feet thereafter. Baking soda or baking powder should be decreased by one third per teaspoon over 3,500 feet and proportionately every 1,500 feet. Egg whites do not have to be beaten stiff. Oven temperatures should be increased by 25 percent at 3,500 feet. Breads do not need changes in ingredients, but will rise in less time.

    1 cup applesauce
    1 cup brown sugar, firmly packed
    ½ cup melted butter
    1¾ cups flour
    1 teaspoon baking soda
    ½ teaspoon salt
    1 teaspoon cinnamon
    ½ teaspoon powdered cloves
    1 cup raisins
    1 cup chopped nuts
      whipped cream

Preheat oven to 350 degrees.
Mix together the applesauce, sugar, and butter, and set aside.
Sift into a large bowl the flour, baking soda, salt, cinnamon, and cloves. Add the raisins and nuts, then add the applesauce mixture.
Spoon the batter into a buttered and floured 9-inch-square pan and bake about 40 minutes.
Slice and serve hot or cold, topped with whipped cream. (*8 to 10 servings*)

PEACH ICE CREAM

The last time we had homemade peach ice cream was at a Fourth of July picnic in the wheat lands of Montana. One young woman had been saving the cream from the milk cows all week, and brought two gallons. Husky ranchers took turns at the crank. Most of us had forgotten how to make it, so we guessed. It turned out all right, though there were not quite enough peaches in it.
There are enough peaches in this one.

    6 eggs, separated
    1 pound sugar
    1 quart cream
    8 ripe peaches

Beat egg yolks. Add the sugar, and beat until very light.
Scald the cream and pour it over yolks and sugar gradually.
Peel and mash peaches, add to cream mixture. Beat the egg whites until stiff, then fold into the cream. When well mixed, turn into a freezer container and put in freezer. Turn crank for 5 minutes, then cover with ice and freeze 2 hours or more, as desired. (*12 or more servings*)

IDAHO POTATO DOUGHNUTS

The state of Idaho is so full of potatoes that the natives are hard-put to find ways to eat them. They have even devised a way to make doughnuts from them—and, surprisingly, they are good.

    1½ cups sugar
    3 tablespoons butter
    2 eggs, beaten
    1 cup milk
    2 teaspoons baking powder
    1 teaspoon grated nutmeg
    1 teaspoon cinnamon
    1 teaspoon salt
    1 cup mashed potato
    2½ to 3 cups flour
      lard for frying

Cream 1 cup sugar with 3 tablespoons butter.
Mix together the eggs, milk, and ½ cup sugar, and blend in with the sugar-butter mixture.
Mix together the flour, baking powder, nutmeg, cinnamon, and salt and add to the potatoes. Combine the two mixtures. Mix to a soft dough just enough to roll out.
Roll out on a floured board, cut with a doughnut cutter, and fry a few at a time in 375-degree deep fat on each side until golden. (*about 2 dozen*)

BEVERAGES

OLD-FASHIONED BOILED CAMP COFFEE

People often ask, "Why did coffee always taste so good when it was made over a campfire?" Here's why. Whole eggs, shells included give the coffee that rich flavor that makes getting up in the morning in the open a pleasure. With the pure, fresh water of the mountain streams, coffee reaches its zenith.

    1 cup ground coffee (all-purpose)
    2 eggs
    1½ cups cold water
    12 cups freshly boiled water
    ¼ teaspoon salt

Wash eggs, break shells, and beat slightly.
Put 1 cup cold water and eggs in large coffeepot, mix. Add salt and coffee grounds. Pour boiling water into pot onto coffee grounds, and stir. Cover pot and stuff the spout.
Put over fire or on stove, over direct heat. When the coffee comes to a boil, let simmer 3 minutes.
Pour in ½ cup cold water to settle grounds. Let stand 1 minute, and serve. (*12 servings*)

ROCKY MOUNTAIN FLIP

    1 ounce white creme de menthe
    1 ounce gin
      heavy cream

Shake the gin and creme de menthe with plenty of cracked ice, and strain into a 3-ounce glass. Top with heavy cream and serve with cut straws. (*1 serving*)

BLUE BLAZER

You'll need two large mugs with handles (porcelain, pewter, or silver).

    1½ ounces bourbon, rye, or Canadian
      whiskey
    1½ ounces boiling water
    1 teaspoon sugar
      lemon peel

Pour the whiskey into one mug, and the boiling water, sweetened with sugar, into the other. Ignite the whiskey and, while blazing, mix the two by pouring back and forth several times.
Serve with a twist of lemon peel in a 4-ounce cup or glass. (*1 serving*)

ELDERBERRY CORDIAL

    8 quarts ripe elderberries, stems
      removed
    2 quarts water
      sugar
      spice bag (1 tablespoon allspice, 1
      tablespoon whole cloves, 1 stick
      cinnamon tied in gauze)
      whiskey or brandy

Cover the elderberries with water and cook until mushy. Strain, measure the juice, and for each quart add 2 cups sugar. Add spice bag. Cook until thick.
Remove spice bag. Measure again, and for each quart syrup add 1 pint whiskey or brandy. Bottle; cork tightly. Improves with age. (*6 quarts*)

SOUTHWESTERN
COOKING

SOUPS AND CHOWDERS

Gazpacho
Cream of Artichoke Soup
Southwest Peanut Soup
Sopa de Arroz
Mexican Clam Soup
Cream of Cucumber Soup
Garbanzo Soup

PASTA, EGG, AND CHEESE DISHES

Eggs, Ranch Style
Chilaly
Stuffed Chili Peppers
Eggs Flamenco
Cream Enchiladas

FISH AND SHELLFISH

Red Snapper, Vera Cruz
Red Snapper Steak, Texas Gulf Style
Mexican Pan-Broiled Shrimp
Scallops Ceviche
Shrimp in Beer

MEATS

Chuck Wagon Porterhouse Barbecue
Adobe Steak
Pichola
Indian Stew
Jerky
Arizona Jerky with Eggs
Texas Beef Enchiladas
Chili con Carne
Kid
Roast Wild Pig
Juniper Lamb Stew
Army Jambalaya

POULTRY AND GAME BIRDS

Chicken Mole
New Mexico Chicken
Southwest Stuffed Chicken
Arroz con Pollo
Chicken or Jackrabbit Stew

VEGETABLES AND SIDE DISHES

Arizona Refried Beans
Baked Lima Beans
Deviled Tomatoes
Mexican Rice
Oklahoma Beans
Mexican Corn
Pickled Figs

SALADS AND DRESSINGS

Southwestern Vegetable Salad
Garbanzo Salad
Arizona Avocado Salad
Guacamole
Wagon Train Wild Greens Salad

BREADS AND BATTERCAKES

Squaw Bread
Tortillas
Apache Rolls
Santa Fe French Toast
Pumpkin Piñon Bread
Wild Sage Bread

DESSERTS

Melon with Berries
Arizona Deep-dish Grapefruit Pie
Southwest Bread Pudding
Pecan Pudding, Marmalade Sauce
Mormon Pudding
Almond Custard
Oklahoma Pudding
Flan
Gooseberry Tart
Artillery Pie

BEVERAGES

Southwest Chocolate
Grapefruit Pecos
Tequila con Sangrita
Hailstorms
Toast and Water

SOUTHWESTERN COOKING

General Francisco Vásquez de Coronado traveled over what is now our Southwest between 1540 and 1542. Castaneda, one of his captains, wrote from Gran Quevira (now New Mexico),

These natives are called Querechos *and* Teyas. *They live under tents of tanned buffalo skins and subsist by the chase of these animals. . . . These Indians live on raw meat and drink blood but they do not eat human flesh. Far from being evil, they are very gentle, and very faithful in their friendships.*

The blood of kid is still used in a stew called *capretto.* It is added when the stew is almost done and makes the gravy very light. This dish is also native to the island of Jamaica, West Indies. It is possible that its place of origin is Africa, but it could also have traveled there from Mexico.

Two thousand years before Christ, Basket Makers inhabited the Southwest. They were precursors of the Pueblo Indians. These people took up the practice of corn growing, which freed them from the constant chase for food, and allowed them to perfect their arts. Later the Pueblos continued this custom and had to group together in protected villages to prevent raids on their granaries. By the time of the Spanish conquest they were concentrated in sixty or seventy towns on the Rio Grande.

In *Death Comes to the Archbishop* Willa Cather wrote, "The peach orchards of Oraibi were very old, having been cultivated since the days of the earliest Spanish expeditions, when Coronado's captains gave the Moquis peach seeds brought from Spain." She went on to say, "The early churchmen did a great business of carrying seeds about, though the

Indians and the Mexicans were satisfied with beans and squash and chili, asking nothing more." She should have mentioned corn, as well. She described a Pueblo meal as follows:

Over the fire a pot of beans and dried meat was simmering. The burning piñon logs filled the room with sweet-smelling smoke. Clara, Jacinto's wife, smiled at the priest as he entered. She ladled out the stew, and the Bishop and Jacinto sat down on the floor beside the fire with their bowls. Between them Clara put a basin full of hot corn bread baked with squash seeds—an Indian delicacy comparable to raisin bread among the whites.

When Willa Cather spoke of chili, she meant chili con carne, which was made of jerked meat cut into pieces, not ground meat. All stews were seasoned with chilies. Meat, chicken, and beans, corn, and peppers are still the basis of many southwestern recipes, from chili con carne to enchiladas, tacos, and mole. Masa—made from corn treated with lye or lime, like hominy—is still a staple. It is ground between stones to a paste, from which tortillas are made.

Until 1848 the southwestern states were Mexican territory populated mostly by Indians, and travel was hazardous. Susan Shelby Macoffin, nineteen years old and newly married, traveled the Santa Fe Trail with her husband, who was on his way to help negotiate a treaty of peace in which Mexico ceded Texas and California and all the territory in between to the United States. She wrote on August 8, "The crossing of the Arkansas was an event in my life I have never met before: separating me from my own dear native land. Perhaps I have left for not the first, but the last time." On August 15 she wrote,

We have an abundance of game, fine turkies, one of which we had roasted for dinner today, prairie chicken, hares, and they say we are to have bear meat soon. Three bear were seen this morning by the teamsters and we passed in the road the carcass of one seeming to have been killed yesterday. I must look sharp when I ramble about these woods, or I will get myself into a nice hugging scrape.

At Matamoras, south of Santa Fe, near Corpus Cristi, traders had done a thriving business with the Mexicans since the Battle of New Orleans. French-Creole and southern-American foods were added to the basic Indian-Mexican foods of the region. In Brownsville, a town that grew out of Fort Brown during the Mexican War, a German sea captain named Miller opened a hotel and restaurant, "Viands were tasty and the drinks copious." Two river boat captains named Kenedy and King celebrated King's twenty-sixth birthday there with a large party. Later Richard King and Mifflin Kenedy in partnership bought a ranch with the profits from their boats.

Ranching had been a Mexican way of life ever since the Spaniards introduced cattle to the country in 1521. The tough range cattle that had evolved were known as Texas longhorns. King imported the best bulls, and slowly improved not only the breed, but the beef, gradually replacing the longhorn with the famed Santa Gertrudis breed of cattle. The dining table at the King ranch became famous for the quality of roast beef, which was borne in on huge platters and carved adroitly by Robert Kleberg, King's son-in-law. Richard King some years later also established the first ice plant in Brownsville in 1877. According to Tom Lea, in *The King Ranch*, top hands on trail drives were paid $42.50 per month, cooks $32.50. Their employers furnished them with horses to ride, and with the victuals at the cook's wagon: beans, bacon, rice, coffee, bread, molasses, pickles, fresh vegetables (usually wild green salad), chicken, butter, and milk.

An early diarist, James Bell, on his way from San Antonio to the pueblo of Los Angeles with a cattle drive, wrote,

Evening, killed a beef being in want of fresh meat. It would astonish a regular bred butcher to see with what dispatch three Mexicans can rope, kill, and have beef cut in ropes. [the underlining is Bell's] The beef is first thrown down by means of a rope, then stuck, not struck on the head. The head is turned to one side which holds the beef in the proper position. One side is skinned, the skinned side is allowed to turn up, half the beef is dissected, the entrails taken out, the ribs are left whole and roasted before the fire. The other half and the head is made into ropes and exposed on a line in the sun until jerked.

In Arizona the drying meat was sprinkled liberally with pepper to keep away flies. Fresh-butchered meat is not tough if cooked before rigor mortis sets in.

The original Aztec *barbacoa* was cooked on special occasions. The word derives from *barba a cola*, beard to tail in Spanish. A hole large enough to accommodate the whole animal was dug, and a fire was built and allowed to burn down to coals over porous stones. The hole was lined with roasted maguey cactus leaves, and the carcass was lowered into the hole, covered with more maguey leaves, and then with mud or clay and stones. A fire was built on top and all was left to cook for five to eighteen hours depending on the size of the animal, and served with "drunken sauce," made with pulque, a strong liquor made from the same maguey cactus. Southwesterners learned the barbacoa from the Mexicans for fiestas, but when hurried they often roasted the meat directly over the fire, basting it with a barbecue sauce as it cooked.

The Mormons who settled in Emigrant Valley in Utah, soon had outlying forts as far away as Las Vegas, Nevada. Their customs were an odd combination of Puritanism and polygamy. They drank "church coffee" made of roasted barley, ground and brewed. Bread was baked with a hard, brown crust. Potatoes were boiled unpeeled, or baked. They ate wild mustard, and cooked milkweed like asparagus. Pigweed and watercress were favorites, too. The sego lily was plentiful, and the bulbs were eaten as a vegetable. Starvation in their early years in the valley had taught the Mormons to eat anything that grew. They liked meat well done. It was a Mormon who picked up a rare steak, shot a hole through it, and said, "I've killed it, now you cook it!"

Though the U. S. Cavalry no longer rides out of the gates of the fort in twenty-two-man patrols as we have seen them do in frontier movies, the U. S. Army is still a presence in the Southwest. In the old days the men were paid little but fed well—good plain food, plentiful and rough. They gave descriptive names to some of the army commissary's efforts. One boiled molasses pudding was called "cannon-balls," and a ground meat pudding "bomb-shells" was cooked in shell casings. A sweet apple pudding was called "artillery pie." Working with enormous limitations, the army cooks did their best with what they had, and some of it was pretty good food.

Soon after the Civil War the range laws were changed to permit farmers to homestead the land, and waves of land-hungry people swept over the area until the last rush on the Cherokee Strip in Oklahoma Territory. Despite range wars they came, and with them came New England, Middle Western, and Southern foods. Dumplings, catfish, cane syrup, and many other non-Mexican or Indian foods were added to the already wide choice available.

Today along the Gulf Coast, where the earliest Americans came in, fish and shellfish are prepared in many delicious ways—dishes such as pescado Veracruz, pan-broiled shrimp, ceviche, and shrimp-in-beer. In Nevada imported chefs and local ones make everything from French pink lamb to ranchman's soup. Along the border there is a drink made from tequila, tomato juice, and hot pepper. It is not called a Bloody Mary, it is called *tequila con sangrita*. Whether one derives from the other would only be a guess—tastes have a way of ignoring borders.

The Southwest is changing rapidly. No one can take away its arid beauty, or the glamour of its wide vistas, or its resilient Indians. Modern technology has brought in scores of non-native technicians and oil businessmen, and also what was called in a recent article "phony Texas food." The same article quoted the menus of several debutante parties, and there was not one barbecue in the lot. In many southwestern cities regional favorites have been nudged aside by "American-Continental" cuisine. It is doubtful that they can be displaced for long, for there is something about the combination of flavors of these dishes that fits perfectly with the flamboyance of the Southwest and its people.

SOUPS AND CHOWDERS

GARBANZO SOUP

    2 cups dried garbanzos (chickpeas),
      soaked overnight, or 2 cups canned
      chickpeas
 1½ quarts water
    5 slices bacon, cut into bits
    1 onion, sliced
    1 clove garlic, crushed
 1½ tablespoons tomato paste
    2 teaspoons chili powder

Drain and put the chickpeas and water into a pot, bring to a boil, and reduce to a simmer. Fry the bacon in a skillet over low heat. Add the onion, garlic, tomato paste, and chili powder, stirring. Cook for 5 minutes and stir into the chickpeas.

Cover the pot, and simmer about 1½ hours or until chickpeas are tender but not cracked open (if canned chickpeas are used cook 30 minutes). (*4 servings*)

GAZPACHO

Gazpacho, the Spanish salad-soup, shows up in various sections of the United States: in New York (the melting pot), in international San Francisco, and in the Southwest, where it doubtless came up from Mexico. There is even a very old version called *guspachy* and another called *gispacho* found in Florida.

> 2 cloves garlic, finely chopped
> 3 very ripe fresh tomatoes, peeled, seeded, and chopped
> 2 cucumbers, peeled, seeded, and chopped
> 1 green pepper, seeded and chopped
> 1 onion, peeled and chopped
> ½ cup olive oil
> 2 tablespoons vinegar
> ¼ teaspoon Tabasco sauce
> 1 teaspoon salt
> ½ teaspoon freshly ground pepper
> 2 cups tomato juice, frozen into cubes
> chopped chives

Place the garlic, vegetables, oil, vinegar and seasonings into a blender, and blend thoroughly.
Chill in the refrigerator and serve in chilled bowls with a cube of frozen tomato juice in each, garnished with chopped chives. (*4 to 6 servings*)

SOUTHWEST PEANUT SOUP

Peanuts, or goobers, brought in by Africans, first put their roots into the soil of Virginia and North Carolina. Early Americans knew nothing about protein, but they knew enough to take along these nutritious and versatile plants when they traveled west.

> 1 medium onion, finely chopped
> ½ cup finely chopped celery
> 1 sprig parsley, finely chopped
> 1 bay leaf
> 1 cup cold water
> 1 cup peanut butter (freshly made peanut butter is best)
> 1½ cups milk or light cream
> 1 teaspoon salt
> ½ teaspoon pepper
> 1 tablespoon butter
> 1 tablespoon flour

Put onion, celery, parsley, bay leaf, and water into a saucepan, and simmer gently for 5 minutes or until vegetables are tender.
Add the peanut butter, most of the milk, and the seasonings. Bring to a boil, and simmer 15 minutes longer, stirring.
In a separate pan melt the butter, and stir in the flour, then the rest of the milk. Add this thickener to the soup, stir, and serve. (*4 servings*)

SOPA DE ARROZ

Those who regard soup as a liquid will have some difficulty identifying sopa de arroz as such, but Texans who borrowed this dish from their neighbors south of the border still serve it as a first course.

> 2 tablespoons cooking oil
> 1 cup uncooked rice, washed and drained
> 1 cup chopped tomatoes
> 1 cup cooked shelled shrimp
> 3 cups hot water
> 1 teaspoon salt
> few dashes Tabasco sauce

Put oil into a heavy skillet and heat to a sizzle, add rice, and cook, stirring, to a deep brown color.
Add the remaining ingredients, cover, and cook until rice is tender and liquid is almost absorbed. (*4 servings*)

MEXICAN CLAM SOUP

> 2 dozen fresh cherrystone clams
> 2 cups water
> 1 onion, chopped
> 1 clove garlic, crushed
> 3 tablespoons olive oil
> ½ cup tomato sauce
> chopped parsley
> 1 teaspoon chili powder
> 1 teaspoon salt

Scrub the clams, put them into a pot, add water, and cook until the shells open.
Discard the shells, chop the clams coarsely, add them and all the other ingredients to the broth, and simmer 15 minutes. (*4 servings*)

CREAM OF CUCUMBER SOUP

Here is a soup that is easy to make, yet unusual enough to serve at dinner parties, refreshing for lunch on a hot day.

- 3 cucumbers, peeled, seeded, and chopped
- 3 cups chicken broth
- 1 tablespoon cornstarch dissolved in ½ cup water
- ½ teaspoon Tabasco sauce
- 2 tablespoons dried dill
- 1 cup cream
  chopped parsley

Simmer the cucumbers in the broth until soft. Stir until well mixed. Add the dissolved cornstarch, and simmer 10 minutes, stirring frequently.
Cool, put into a blender, and mix. Add the Tabasco, dill, and cream. Blend a few minutes longer.
Chill well and serve, garnished with chopped parsley, in chilled cups. (*6 servings*)

CREAM OF ARTICHOKE SOUP

A very special soup with a rich flavor— eminently suitable for occasions when something different is in order.

- 1½ tablespoons butter
- 1 tablespoon flour
- ½ teaspoon salt
  pinch cayenne
  pinch nutmeg
- 3 cups water
- 4 cooked artichoke hearts, mashed
- ½ cup cream
- 1 egg yolk, beaten
- 3 tablespoons dry white wine

Using a medium saucepan, melt the butter, stir in the flour and seasonings. Gradually add the water, stirring, and then the artichokes. Cook for 2 minutes.
Mix together the cream, egg yolk, and wine, and slowly add to the soup, stirring constantly. Bring to just under boiling and serve. (*4 servings*)

PASTA, EGG,
AND CHEESE DISHES

EGGS, RANCH STYLE

Eggs rancheros are a standard item throughout the Southwest, but they never seem to appear twice cooked in the same way. The following recipe impressed us as representative. It can be made less spicy by letting up a bit on the *salsa jalapeña*.

- ½ cup minced onion
- ½ clove garlic, minced
- 2 tablespoons bacon fat
- 1 cup tomatoes, peeled, chopped, and drained
- 1 teaspoon green chili sauce (salsa jalapeña)
- ½ teaspoon salt
- 4 tortillas
  cooking oil
- 4 eggs

Sauté the onion and garlic in the bacon fat 2 minutes.
Add the tomatoes, chili sauce, and salt, and continue to cook for 30 minutes, stirring occasionally.
In a separate skillet, fry the tortillas in hot oil until soft, drain, and remove to heated plates, 2 to each plate.
Fry the eggs in the same skillet, place onto the tortillas, spoon the sauce over, and serve. (*2 servings*)

CREAM ENCHILADAS

This recipe shows the evolution of New Mexican cooking from early Spanish days to the present. Early foods, like tortillas, are now prepared with cultured sour cream, longhorn Cheddar cheese and green chilies.

    3 tablespoons chopped onion
    1 tablespoon butter
    1 or 2 (4 oz.) cans green chilies, chopped
    1 (19 oz.) can tomatoes, drained and cut up
    1½ cups sour cream
    1½ cups shredded longhorn or mild Cheddar cheese
    10 thin corn tortillas

Sauté onion in butter until golden. Add chilies and tomatoes and simmer slightly. Stir in sour cream, simmer then add cheese. Blend all thoroughly, and add salt to taste.
Serve each portion on one tortilla, topped with another, and another spoonful of mixture as topping. (5 servings)

CHILALY

This is a kind of Welsh rabbit with Mexican influence. The name could have come from the many Irish-American troops stationed in Brownsville, Texas, during the Mexican War, or it could be an Americanization of a Mexican word.

    1 tablespoon melted butter
    2 tablespoons chopped green pepper
    2 tablespoons chopped onion
    ½ cup chopped tomatoes
    ½ pound Monterey Jack, mozzarella, or mild Cheddar-type cheese, cut into pieces
    ½ teaspoon salt
      few dashes Tabasco sauce
    1 egg beaten into ½ cup milk

Mix together the butter, pepper, onion, and tomatoes, and cook in a saucepan over low heat for 5 minutes.
Add the cheese and seasonings. Cook, stirring, 5 or 6 minutes longer.
Stir in the egg-milk mixture and spoon over toast. (4 to 6 servings)

EGGS FLAMENCO

    4 tablespoons chopped onion
    1 clove garlic, crushed
    2 tablespoons olive oil
    1 cup thinly sliced chorizos (or other sausage)
    1 teaspoon minced parsley
    2 pimentos, minced
    2 tomatoes, peeled and diced
    ½ cup chicken broth
    1 teaspoon salt
    ½ teaspoon pepper
    8 eggs

Sauté the onion and garlic in the oil, add the sausage, and brown.
Add the parsley, pimentos, tomatoes, chicken broth, and seasonings. Simmer 5 minutes.
Preheat oven to 425 degrees.
Spoon this sauce into 4 shirring dishes or pans. Break 2 eggs into each dish, and bake until whites of eggs are set. (4 servings)

STUFFED CHILI PEPPERS

This version of chili peppers stuffed with cheese came from Texas via Montana. Canned green chilies (poblanos) are used for this. One intrepid Montanan we know uses bell peppers in place of green chilies, and skins them by dipping them with tongs in a solution of half lye and half water, then in vinegar to neutralize the lye, and then rinsing them thoroughly in cold water. Lye is such a dangerous caustic that we do not recommend the method. Another method used to skin bell peppers is to shake the peppers in a hot frying pan with a lid, remove, and wrap immediately in a dish towel. They will peel easily. However, green chilies can be found in most supermarkets.

    2 medium onions, diced
    4 jalapeño peppers, diced and seeded
    2 tablespoons cooking oil
    2 cups tomato juice
    1 small can tomato paste
    2 cans green chilies (poblanos)
    3 packages (8 ounces each) cream cheese
    6 eggs, yolks and whites beaten separately
    4 tablespoons flour

First make the sauce: Sauté the onions and jalapeños in oil. Add the tomato juice and tomato paste, and simmer over low heat while peppers are being prepared.

Divide the cheese evenly, one piece for each green chili. Drain chilies, put a piece of cheese on each one, and roll up. Pin each package together with a toothpick.

Preheat oven to 350 degrees.

Mix egg yolks and flour, and fold in the stiffly-beaten egg whites. Cover each pepper well with this batter and fry in hot cooking oil. Baste peppers with cooking oil while frying one side to prevent their turning over. Brown each pepper on both sides, and put into a casserole dish or iron skillet.

Cover with sauce and bake for 45 minutes. Serve with warm tortillas. (*4 servings, as main dish*)

FISH AND SHELLFISH

RED SNAPPER, VERA CRUZ

The Gulf's most delicious and copious fish cooked with an unmistakably Mexican accent, a favorite of Gulf Coast Texans.

    1 red snapper, 2 pounds, sliced thick
      (reserve head and trimmings for
      broth)
 1½ teaspoons salt
  ½ teaspoon pepper
      juice of 1 lemon
    6 tablespoons oil
    2 cloves garlic
    3 small onions, sliced
 2½ cups tomatoes, ground and strained—
      do not blend
  ½ cup olives
  ¼ cup capers
    6 chilies jalapeños en escapeche,
      (pickled) seeded and chopped

Wash sliced fish and set aside. Put head and trimmings in 2 cups of water with ½ teaspoon of salt and ⅛ teaspoon pepper. Bring to a boil, lower heat, and simmer.

Rub fish slices with the remaining salt and pepper, and the lemon juice.

Heat the oil in a frying pan, fry the garlic cloves, and remove.

Sauté the onions until light brown and add the ground tomatoes. Add the fish broth, olives, capers, and chilies, and simmer all together for 30 minutes.

Add the fish slices and simmer another 30 minutes or until the fish is cooked through. Serve with warm tortillas. (*4 servings*)

SHRIMP IN BEER

There is a generally little-known shrimp that grows to enormous proportions in the fresh waters near the Gulf of Mexico after having been hatched in the salt sea waters. Actually a giant prawn, it is fifty percent edible, and has the taste and texture of lobster. These and similar species are now being cultivated in controlled underwater culture pens, where shrimp up to 1 pound each have been grown. The recipe below is a favorite of many Texans. Use it for preparing any kind of shrimp.

    2 pounds fresh shrimp in the shell
    3 cups beer
    1 clove garlic, chopped
    1 teaspoon salt
  ½ teaspoon thyme
    1 teaspoon celery seed
    1 tablespoon minced parsley
      few dashes Tabasco sauce
    2 teaspoons lemon juice
      melted butter

Mix together all the ingredients except melted butter, bring to a boil, then simmer about 4 minutes or until shrimp are pink.

Drain, and serve in a napkin with melted butter on the side. Some Texans spice up the butter with Tabasco or salsa verde. (*4 servings*)

RED SNAPPER STEAK, TEXAS GULF STYLE

2 pounds red snapper steak
salt
pepper
2 tablespoons butter
½ carrot, chopped
1 stalk celery, chopped
2 tablespoons chopped parsley
6 raw shrimp, peeled and chopped
1 cup dry white wine
pinch basil

Preheat oven to 400 degrees.
Wipe the steak (or steaks) with a paper napkin, season to taste with salt and pepper, and place in a well-buttered casserole.
Mix all the other ingredients well and pour over and around the fish.
Bake for 30 minutes or until fish steak flakes with a fork.
Serve in the casserole. (*4 servings*)

MEXICAN PAN-BROILED SHRIMP

24 large shrimp, shelled and deveined, but with tails intact
½ cup lime juice
½ cup coconut oil (or olive oil)
4 cloves garlic, chopped
2 or 3 green chilies, (jalapeños), peeled and chopped, or ½ teaspoon cayenne
3 tablespoons butter
minced parsley

Marinate the shrimp overnight in the lime juice, oil, and seasonings in a shallow glass or porcelain dish.
Remove the shrimp from the marinade, pan-broil in butter for 5 minutes on each side, and serve garnished with minced parsley. (*4 servings*)

SCALLOPS CEVICHE

The Mexican method of preparing raw fish has been adapted somewhere along the line to scallops—and very successfully, too.

2 pounds bay scallops, if available (or sea scallops, cut up)
1 cup lime juice
½ cup olive oil
1 clove garlic, minced
½ cup finely chopped spring onions
¼ cup finely chopped green chilies (jalapeños)
¼ cup chopped parsley
few dashes Tabasco sauce

Soak and chill the scallops in the lime juice (using a glass or porcelain container) for several hours or until they become opaque or "cooked." Stir occasionally so that all surfaces are exposed to the lime acid.
Drain, mix thoroughly with the remaining ingredients, and serve cold, garnished with chopped chives. (*4 to 6 servings*)

MEATS

PICHOLA

1 pound fresh lean pork or beef, cubed
1 onion, chopped
2 cups tomatoes, fresh or canned
1 teaspoon salt
2 tablespoons chili powder
½ cup water
1 can (number 2) hominy

Brown the pork or beef cubes and onion in a heavy skillet.
Add the tomatoes, salt, chili powder, and water. Turn down the heat to a simmer, cover the skillet, and cook about 1 hour or until meat is soft.
Add the hominy, cook 30 minutes longer, and serve in bowls. (*4 servings*)

JERKY

Men out on the range carried these tough, lean strips of dried meat with them whenever they could to chew on when they were hungry. Slices were cut across the grain from the rump of beef or venison, rubbed well with salt and pepper, and hung in the sun until dry and leathery.

Jerked meat, similar in a way to the commercial dried beef (or chipped beef), will last a long time without spoiling. You can even find it offered as a snack in taverns and bars.

Jerky was, and is, a convenient kitchen product. Soaked overnight until soft, it can be cooked in a stew with vegetables like any other meat, or fried with onions and chili.

The Pueblo Indians make jerky in a way that explains the name, the beef is literally "jerked" after it is cut.

Cut a chunk of lean boneless beef into 4-inch cubes. With a very sharp knife slice spiral-like with the grain of the meat, starting at one end, into ¼ inch strips, unrolling into one long piece. Take each strip by its two ends and stretch (actually jerk). Then thread with string by one end and hang strips, not touching, on line. If hung in the hot sun during the day and protected from any dampness at night, the meat will dry in a few days. Jerky may also be dried indoors in a warm, dry place with good air circulation.

Pueblo Indian Cookbook, Recipes from the American Southwest, compiled and edited by Phyllis Hughes.

ARIZONA JERKY WITH EGGS

    1 pound jerky or dried chipped beef, shredded
    6 tablespoons oil
    1 small onion, minced
    1 clove garlic, minced
    ½ teaspoon paprika
    1 teaspoon vinegar
    4 tablespoons chopped cooked tomatoes
    2 eggs, slightly beaten

Both jerky and chipped beef should be pre-soaked in water to cover to remove salt in beef and to soften jerky.

Fry the beef in hot oil with the onion, garlic, paprika, and vinegar until brown.

Add the tomatoes, and cook until almost dry. Stir in the eggs, and cook about 4 minutes or until eggs are creamy.

Serve on tortillas or tostadas. (*4 to 6 servings*)

CHUCK WAGON PORTERHOUSE BARBECUE

Driving across a dry, treeless plain in the Oklahoma Panhandle a few years ago, we came to a general store with a restaurant attached. Written on the blackboard above the counter was "Filet Mignon—$1.25." Scarcely believing what we saw, we ordered it. A large crosscut of tenderloin of beef was served to us. It was grey on the outside and cooked well done, tender, but more like a venison steak and not nearly as rich as the eastern beef we were used to. We wondered what kind of beef it could be, then came to the conclusion that it was grass-fed beef, which has not been fattened on special feeds for the eastern markets. Here's a recipe from the Southwest for grass-fed porterhouse steak, which you could even use for a cornfed one.

    1 porterhouse steak, 2½-inches thick
    2 tablespoons paprika
    2 tablespoons dry mustard
    1 teaspoon salt
    1 teaspoon pepper
    ¼ cup butter, softened
    2 tablespoons salad oil
    1 tablespoon Worcestershire sauce

Preheat broiler to 500 degrees.

Put steak on grate of broiler pan. Mix the paprika, mustard, salt, pepper, butter, oil, and Worcestershire, and rub into meat on both sides. Place meat under broiler, 3 inches from flame.

Broil 5 minutes, turn, brush with sauce, and cook five minutes, turn again, and brush. Continue this until meat is seared.

Reduce heat to 375 degrees, and put steak in oven and bake 15 minutes per pound for rare, 20 for medium. Baste with drippings in the pan. Serve hot. (*4 servings*)

KID

This is a famous border dish. It is not wise to use twelve jalapeño chilies, unless you are a native of Texas, or have a cast-iron tongue.

1 kid, 6 pounds, dressed (dissolve 1 tablespoon salt in blood and reserve)
4 tablespoons lard
3 cups hot water, or to cover
1 teaspoon salt
1 teaspoon oregano
¼ teaspoon pepper
4 to 12 chilies jalapeños en escabeche, seeded and chopped
2 onions, chopped
2 cups fresh or canned tomatoes
2 green peppers, seeded and sliced

Cut the kid into stewing-size pieces, and fry in lard until brown.
Cover with hot water. Add salt, oregano, pepper, chilies, onions, tomatoes, and green peppers. Simmer 1 hour or until the meat is tender.
Five minutes before serving, stir in the blood. Keep hot, but do not boil. (*6 servings*)

ROAST WILD PIG

Though the wild pig or javelina of the Southwest is scarce and wily, southwesterners do not let this fact stop them. Very often they roast a fresh ham as one would wild pig. If you are lucky you can use this recipe on the real thing.

ham of a wild pig, or fresh ham
2 cups red wine
1 cup vinegar
2 large onions, chopped very fine or grated
6 bay leaves
1 teaspoon each of whole and powdered cloves
30 fresh juniper berries
grated rind of half a lemon
⅛ teaspoon ginger
2 cups light cream
butter

Cut off rind of ham. Put the ham in a marinade made from the first 8 ingredients. Let soak several days, turning once or twice a day. Preheat oven to 325 degrees.
Remove the ham from the marinade and brown it in butter. Put in roasting pan and pour over it 1 cup water and 2 cups marinade. Bake ham for 2 hours, pour cream over it, bake 1 hour longer. To serve, skim fat from gravy in pan, and serve with sliced ham. (*12 servings*)

TEXAS BEEF ENCHILADAS

Briefly, enchiladas consist of tortillas, quickly fried in oil, accompanied by a variety of sauces, fillings, toppings, and garnishes. The following recipe for beef enchiladas may be varied by using ground pork. Or use chicken broth instead of beef broth, and chopped chicken in place of the beef, and end up with chicken enchiladas.

4 cups beef broth
6 tablespoons chili powder
½ clove garlic, minced
1 teaspoon cumin
2 tablespoons cornstarch mixed with 1 tablespoon water

Simmer the chili powder, garlic, and cumin in the broth for 2 minutes. Add the cornstarch, cook 2 minutes longer, reserve, and keep hot.

Filling:

1 tablespoon cooking oil
1 onion, chopped
1 clove garlic, minced
2 cups finely chopped cooked meat
½ cup pitted green olives, sliced
½ cup of the reserved sauce
2 cups shredded Monterey Jack or mild Cheddar cheese

Sauté the onion and garlic in the oil, stir in the meat, and brown.
Add the olives, sauce, and 1 cup of the cheese. Cook 2 minutes, set aside, and keep hot.

Enchiladas:

Preheat oven to 400 degrees.

Fry 12 tortillas in oil quickly, dip into the hot sauce, spoon above filling onto each, roll tightly, and place side by side in a square pan. Sprinkle with the remaining cup of cheese and put into oven for 10 minutes.

Spoon the hot sauce over all, and serve. (*4 servings*)

INDIAN STEW

Here is an interesting recipe we found in an old Oklahoma cookbook. Although attributed to the Indians of the region, it seems likely that the use of spareribs was contributed later by white settlers.

    4 sweet potatoes, peeled
    4 tablespoons salt pork, diced
    1 pound country spareribs, cut into
      chunks
    2 onions, diced
    1 green pepper, diced
    2 tablespoons flour
      Kernels from 3 large ears fresh corn,
      or 1 package frozen corn, or 1 can
      whole kernel corn
    1 cup fresh tomatoes, chopped

Put sweet potatoes in pan, cover with water, and bring to a boil. Simmer until tender when pierced with a fork; remove, drain and set aside.

Fry out the salt pork until crisp, remove, and put aside. Brown the spareribs well in the salt-pork fat. Add the onions and green peppers to the meat, and when all are brown add the flour, tomatoes, and the corn. Cook another 50 minutes or until meat is done. Serve with the sweet potatoes and pork cracklings. (*4 servings*)

ARMY JAMBALAYA

"In general, most of the meats served to soldiers consisted of some form of stew or hash. Some of the dishes, such as bombshells, cannon balls, and coffee à la Zoave, are clearly the product of the military while others including jambalaya and estufado, reflect a regional origin."

    1 pound rice (wash and soak 1 hour)
    1 pound ham, cubed
    2 onions
    1 pound sausage, sliced
    2 large tomatoes, chopped
    1 small red pepper, chopped
    1 sprig parsley
    2 cups boiling water
    3 tablespoons butter
    1 teaspoon salt

Fry all but rice and salt in the butter, then add the boiling water. Stir in the rice slowly, cover the pot, and cook slowly. Add salt and serve while hot. Jambalaya can be made with oysters, shrimp, or chicken in place of the sausage. (*8 to 10 servings*)

CHILI CON CARNE

Chili con carne is a North American dish with a Mexican flavor. The ingredients, the condiments, and the amounts of each vary widely from region to region. Whether or not good chili should contain tomatoes is an argument hotly contested by many aficionados.

    4 tablespoons olive oil
    2 cloves garlic, minced
    2 onions, chopped
    2 pounds lean beef, cut into small cubes
      or slivers
    4 tablespoons chili powder
    1 teaspoon oregano
    ½ teaspoon cumin
    ½ teaspoon salt
   10 dried chilies, boiled, seeded, and
      skinned
    2 cups beef broth or water
      pinto or pink beans

Sauté the onion and garlic in the oil, using a large heavy skillet. Add the meat and brown, stirring frequently.

Add all the remaining ingredients except beans, cover, and cook over low heat about 1 hour, or until the meat is tender and chili has thickened. If chili gets too dry, add more water.

Serve in bowls with pinto beans that have been boiled in slightly salted water 1½ to 2 hours. Control the hotness of the chili by adding more or less of the bean juice. (*6 servings*)

JUNIPER LAMB STEW

Lamb is fresh in the summer and so are the corn, spring onions and peppers: "Our Great Spirit also gave us the knowledge to know the different wild greens we eat in the spring, summer and fall." (*Pueblo Indian Cookbook*)

    2 pounds lean lamb, cubed small
    6 ears fresh corn
    6 spring onions with tops, chopped
    3 sweet green peppers, chopped
    1 tablespoon flour
    2 tablespoons lard or cooking oil
    2 teaspoons dried wild celery (⅓ cup
       chopped celery tops may be
       substituted)
    1½ teaspoons salt
    5 dried juniper berries, crushed
    2 teaspoons chili powder
    4 cups water

Mix seasonings and flour to coat meat and brown in hot lard or oil in heavy kettle. Cut corn from cobs and add with other ingredients and water to meat. Cover and simmer for one hour or until meat is tender. (*4 servings*)

ADOBE STEAK

Here is an interesting southwestern version of the Swiss steak that has long been so popular in the East.

    ½ cup flour
    1 tablespoon chili powder
    1 teaspoon salt
    2 pounds round steak, 1 inch thick
    2 tablespoons olive oil
    1 clove garlic, minced
    1 onion, minced
    1 cup tomato sauce
    2 cups water

Mix together the flour, chili powder, and salt. Pound this mixture into the steak on both sides, using the edge of a plate.

Heat the oil in a heavy skillet, and sauté the garlic and onion for a few minutes. Put in the steak and brown well on both sides. Add the tomato sauce and water, cover, and cook over low heat for 1½ hours. (*4 servings*)

POULTRY
AND GAME BIRDS

CHICKEN MOLE

The traditional New Mexican way to make a mole requires considerable time spent over a mortar, grinding and pounding nuts and seeds and chocolate and the pulp from a variety of chilies. Few Texans—and not many New Mexicans—are willing these days to invest such time and effort into making the sauce. Those who wish to do so may follow the recipe below. Otherwise, just use canned mole sauce or mole powder.

    1 fowl, 5 pounds, cut into serving
       portions
    ¼ cup fat, melted
    ½ cup blanched almonds
    1 tablespoon shelled peanuts
    2 teaspoons sesame seed
    ½ teaspoon cloves
    ¼ stick cinnamon
    4 chili peppers, seeds and skin removed
    1 onion, chopped
    1 clove garlic, chopped
    1 ounce unsweetened chocolate,
       chopped
    3 slices dry toast
    1 tomato, chopped

Cover the fowl with water and parboil about 1½ hours or until tender.

Remove, drain, and brown in melted fat. Reserve broth.

Grind together in a mortar the nuts, sesame seed, cloves, cinnamon, peppers, onion, garlic, chocolate, and toast. Add to the broth, and stir until well blended.

Add the browned chicken and tomato, and simmer uncovered for 30 minutes or until sauce is thickened. Serve with rice. (*6 servings*)

NEW MEXICO CHICKEN

Quite obviously, there's the flavor of Old Mexico in this interesting north-of-the-border chicken.

1 teaspoon salt
1 teaspoon pepper
 pinch thyme
 pinch mace
1 fryer, 3 pounds, cut up
1 cup flour
½ cup olive oil
1 onion, chopped
1 clove garlic, minced
1½ teaspoons chili powder
½ cup chicken broth
1 cup dry white wine

Preheat oven to 350 degrees.

Mix together the salt, pepper, thyme, and mace, and sprinkle over the chicken parts. Dredge in flour and brown on all sides in the oil, using a heavy skillet. Transfer to a casserole.

Add the onion, garlic, and chili powder to the skillet, and sauté 5 minutes. Stir in the broth and wine, cook 5 minutes longer, and pour over the chicken.

Bake in the oven for 40 minutes or until tender. (*4 servings*)

ARROZ CON POLLO

Arroz con pollo is eaten wherever Spanish is spoken. It has always been popular in southwestern U.S., where the Mexican influence is strong, and more recently it has been brought into the New York area by incoming Puerto Ricans.

½ cup olive oil
1 large onion, chopped
1 clove garlic, minced
1 frying chicken, cut into serving pieces
1 teaspoon salt
¼ cup tomato sauce
½ cup chopped pimentos
 pinch powdered saffron, or whole saffron soaked in ⅛ cup water
 pinch oregano
1 teaspoon pepper
3 cups chicken broth
1 cup uncooked rice

Sauté the onion and garlic in the oil, using a large heavy skillet. Salt the chicken pieces, add them to the skillet, and brown well on all sides. Put in the tomato sauce, pimentos, saffron, oregano, pepper, and broth. Cover, and cook for 20 minutes.

Put in the rice, stir but do not disturb chicken, cover again, and cook for 30 minutes longer or until all the liquid has been absorbed and the chicken is tender. (*4 servings*)

SOUTHWEST STUFFED CHICKEN

1 roasting chicken, 5 to 6 pounds, dressed
1 pound cooked ham, chopped
8 olives, pitted and chopped
1 hard-cooked egg, chopped
½ cup seedless raisins
1 potato, peeled and finely diced
 chopped cooked giblets
 grated rind of 1 lemon
½ teaspoon salt
 dash Tabasco sauce

Preheat oven to 425 degrees.

Mix together all the ingredients and stuff into the chicken. Truss, and bake about 1½ hours or until brown. Baste from time to time. (*6 servings*)

CHICKEN OR
JACKRABBIT STEW

This stew can be made with hare or chicken and is equally good with both. The lime hominy is the original Indian hominy and is relatively easy to make. (Care should be taken with slaked lime, it can burn the skin.)

    1 jackrabbit (or domestic rabbit or 5
      pound roasting chicken)
    1 large onion, chopped
    1 teaspoon salt
    ⅔ tablespoon chili powder (optional)
  1¼ cups flour
    2 quarts water
    2 large onions
    6 carrots, halved
    2 sweet peppers, halved and seeded
    4 teaspoons salt
    2 cups cooked lime hominy
    ¾ cup melted lard or cooking oil

Cut rabbit (or chicken) into serving size pieces. Dredge with flour. Put lard or oil in large kettle and heat to sizzling. Brown all pieces of meat on all sides, drain and pour off excess oil. Return meat to kettle, add water and simmer two hours, add all vegetables and simmer until carrots are tender.

LIME HOMINY

    1 quart or 4 cups dry white corn kernels
    2 quarts or 8 cups water
    ½ cup slaked lime (available at building
      supply companies)

Dissolve lime in water in large kettle. Add corn and stir well. Boil for 30 minutes or until hulls loosen. Let stand 30 minutes, then wash thoroughly in cold water, working with hands until dark tips of kernels are removed. Rinse again until water is clear. (Always used for posoli.) Posoli is an Indian dish made with pigs feet, tripe and cubed pork or spareribs. (*4 to 6 servings*)

VEGETABLES
AND SIDE DISHES

PICKLED FIGS

    1 gallon water
    1 tablespoon baking soda
    6 pounds fresh figs, stems removed
    3 pounds sugar
    1 pint vinegar
    1 tablespoon cinnamon
    1 tablespoon cloves
    2 lemons, thinly sliced

Bring the water to a boil, dissolve the soda, put in the figs, and let stand 10 minutes.
Remove figs, drain, rinse in cold water.
Place the sugar, vinegar, cinnamon, cloves, and lemons into a separate pot. Add the figs, bring to a boil, and cook until clear.
Remove figs, pack into sterilized jars, boil down the syrup until thick, and add. Seal.
(*about 8 pints*)

MEXICAN RICE

    ¼ cup cooking oil
    1 cup rice
    1 onion, chopped
    1 clove garlic, crushed
    2 cups chicken broth
    1 tablespoon chopped parsley
    1 teaspoon chili powder
    1 teaspoon salt

Heat the oil in a heavy skillet. Add the rice, onion, and garlic, and cook until slightly browned.
Drain off the excess oil, add the remaining ingredients, cover, and simmer over low heat for about 30 minutes. (*4 servings*)

BAKED LIMA BEANS

    2 cups dried lima beans
    1 small onion, chopped
    1 green pepper, chopped
    2 tablespoons butter
    2 cups cooked tomatoes, strained
    ½ teaspoon salt
      few grains cayenne
    1 teaspoon Worcestershire sauce
    1 cup grated American cheese

Soak dried lima beans in water overnight, cook 1 hour or until tender, and drain.

Sauté the onion and pepper in butter until tender. Add the tomatoes, and simmer 10 minutes.

Preheat oven to 350 degrees.

Add the beans and seasonings, place with the cheese in alternate layers into a buttered casserole, and bake 20 to 30 minutes. (*6 servings*)

DEVILED TOMATOES

    2 tablespoons butter
    1 teaspoon confectioners' sugar
    1 teaspoon dry mustard
    1 teaspoon salt
    ⅛ teaspoon pepper
      yolk of 1 hard-cooked egg, mashed
    1 raw egg, beaten
    1½ tablespoons hot vinegar
    3 tomatoes, cut in thick slices
    ¼ cup flour
    ⅛ teaspoon salt
    ⅛ teaspoon pepper
    4 tablespoons butter

To make sauce, melt 2 tablespoons butter over low heat; add sugar, mustard, salt, pepper, egg yolk, raw egg, and vinegar; and stir until the mixture thickens. Set aside.

Dip tomato slices in flour mixed with salt and pepper, and fry in hot butter until brown on both sides. Pour sauce over tomatoes and serve. (*4 servings*)

OKLAHOMA BEANS

Anybody can detect the cowboy influence in this popular dish, which the Oklahomans call their own.

    2 cups kidney or pinto beans, soaked
      overnight
    ½ pound thickly sliced bacon, cut into 1-
      inch bits
    1 large green pepper, seeded and sliced
    2 cups tomatoes, fresh or canned
    1 teaspoon chili powder
    ½ teaspoon cumin seed
      grated cheese

Drain the beans, and cook in enough water to cover about 1 hour or until tender.

Sauté the bacon pieces in a saucepan until crisp. Remove and set aside.

Add the pepper to the bacon fat, and cook until tender, then add the tomatoes. Cook 15 minutes longer.

Add the beans, bacon, chili powder, and cumin to the saucepan. Mix well, cook 15 minutes, and serve in a heated dish, sprinkled with cheese. (*4 to 6 servings*)

MEXICAN CORN

A very famous dish in Mexico, this has become more and more popular in southwestern United States.

    1 tablespoon olive oil
    1 onion, finely minced
    2 cups tomato purée
    2 tablespoons diced celery
    2 tablespoons chili powder
    2 tablespoons butter
    3 cups uncooked corn kernels
    1 teaspoon salt
    ½ teaspoon pepper

Preheat oven to 350 degrees.

In a heavy skillet, heat the oil and sauté the onion until golden.

Add the remaining ingredients, mix well, pour into a buttered casserole, and bake 30 minutes. (*6 servings*)

ARIZONA REFRIED BEANS

This dish has obviously been borrowed from the Mexicans, who serve refried beans with practically every meal. They can be refried and refried over and over again, improving with each cooking, by simply putting them with a bit of bacon fat into a frying pan.

Mexican beans:

> 1 pound dried pinto beans, washed and drained
> 8 cups water
> 1 clove garlic, crushed
>   pinch cumin
> 1 teaspoon salt
> 1 medium onion, chopped
> 5 tablespoons bacon fat
>   mild Cheddar or Monterey Jack cheese, shredded

Put the beans into a large pot with the water, garlic, cumin, and salt. Cover, and cook over low heat 1½ hours.
Add the onion and 3 tablespoons bacon fat, and cook 1½ hours longer or until beans are tender. (Add a little additional water, if necessary, to keep the beans soupy in consistency).

Refried beans:

Heat 2 tablespoons bacon fat in a heavy skillet, add 2 cups Mexican beans and a little of the liquid. Mash well to form a thick paste.
Fry in the skillet, turning to prevent burning. Top with shredded cheese, and serve. (*4 servings*)

SALADS
AND DRESSINGS

GUACAMOLE

> 2 very ripe avocados, peeled and seeded
> 2 tomatoes, peeled and seeded
> 1 onion, finely chopped
> 1 clove garlic, crushed
> 2 tablespoons lemon juice
> 3 tablespoons chopped green chilies
> ½ teaspoon salt

Put all the ingredients into a blender, or mash. Chill in the refrigerator and serve with tortillas as a dip, mixed with mayonnaise as a spread, or with lettuce and tomatoes as a salad.
Guacamole turns brown when exposed to the air, so work quickly and arrange to keep in a tightly closed container until ready for use.

ARIZONA AVOCADO SALAD

> 3 avocados, seeded and peeled
> 1 tablespoon minced onion
> 1 teaspoon chili powder
>   few drops Tabasco Sauce
> 1 teaspoon salt
> 4 medium tomatoes
>   lettuce

Mash the avocados, and mix well with the onion, chili, Tabasco, and salt.
Peel the tomatoes and scoop out most of the pulp. Stuff with the avocado mixture, and serve on lettuce. (*4 servings*)

WAGON TRAIN WILD GREENS SALAD

The only fresh greens available to the people on the trains and the men on the cattle drives were wild. Many a salad like this one was eaten with relish in the Old West after the long dusty day.

  1 bunch tender leaves of lamb's quarter
  1 bunch new plantain leaves
  2 cups tender dandelion leaves, shredded
  1 small onion, chopped fine
  4 slices crisp cooked bacon, crumbled
  ¼ cup vinegar
  ¼ teaspoon salt
  ⅛ teaspoon pepper

Wash greens, drain and dry. Add onion. Add vinegar, salt, and pepper to bacon fat and simmer for two minutes. Pour over washed greens and serve. (*4 servings*)

GARBANZO SALAD

  1 can (16 ounces) garbanzos (chickpeas), rinsed and drained
  1 small onion, minced
  2 tablespoons minced parsley
  2 medium carrots, diced and cooked
  ¼ cup olive oil
  2 tablespoons vinegar
  1 teaspoon salt
  1 teaspoon pepper
    lettuce leaves, washed and dried
  ½ cup sliced olives (ripe or green)
  2 hard-cooked eggs, quartered
    mayonnaise

Mix together the garbanzos, onion, parsley, carrots, oil, vinegar, and seasonings. Chill in the refrigerator.
Place lettuce leaves on 4 salad plates, and spoon the chilled mixture onto each. Garnish with olives and eggs, and serve with mayonnaise on the side. (*4 servings*)

SOUTHWESTERN VEGETABLE SALAD

  1 cucumber, peeled and sliced
  ½ cup cooked peas, drained
  ½ cup cooked diced carrots, drained
  6 stuffed olives, sliced
  ½ green pepper, diced
  ¾ cup mayonnaise
  1 teaspoon chili sauce
  ¼ teaspoon sugar
  ½ teaspoon horseradish
  ½ teaspoon salt
    salad greens
  2 tablespoons olive oil
  1 tomato, quartered
  4 scallions

Mix together gently the cucumber, peas, carrots, olives, pepper, mayonnaise, chili sauce, sugar, horseradish, and salt.
Toss the salad greens with the oil.
Arrange the salad greens onto 4 salad plates, heap the vegetables on top, and serve garnished with tomato and scallions. (*4 servings*)

BREADS
AND BATTERCAKES

TORTILLAS

Tortillas are thin, flat cakes made from masa (a meal made from lime- or lye-treated corn), mixed with water and salt, and molded with the hands. Available packaged in many stores in the Southwest, California, and the large cities, they are used for making enchiladas, tostadas (crisp-fried tortillas), tacos, and other great southwestern dishes or served on the side like bread. They were not borrowed from Mexico, but rather the other way around. When the Spanish came into what is now New Mexico, they found these corn pancakes being made by the cliff-dwelling Pueblo Indians and took them back to Mexico.

    2 cups fine white or blue cornmeal
    1½ cups warm water

Mix meal and water until dough is not sticky. Form into balls about one and three quarters inches in diameter and roll out between waxed paper or pat with hands until about six inches in diameter. Cook on moderately hot stove lid or griddle, turning frequently until flecked with brown. (3 or 4 tortillas)

SQUAW BREAD

This American Indian recipe, in one form or another, shows up in several parts of the United States. Its very simplicity may be the reason why. The ingredients were usually mixed, by Indian and settler alike, right in the flour sack.

    1½ tablespoons lard, melted
    2 cups water
    1 teaspoon salt
    2½ teaspoons baking powder
      approximately 3 cups flour

Melt the lard, add the water mixed with the salt and baking powder.
Pour into the flour sack and mix with as much flour as the liquid will take up to make a soft biscuit dough. Knead a few times. Break off pieces of dough the size of a biscuit and form into 3-inch squares, ¼ inch thick. Perforate each with a fork, and fry in hot fat (370 degrees) until golden brown. Or bake in a Dutch oven with coals underneath it and on top, for 15 to 20 minutes. (12 biscuits)

PUMPKIN PIÑON BREAD

Priscilla Vigil of Tesuque Pueblo writes in The Pueblo Indian Cookbook: "Pumpkin is one of our main foods, too. We fix pumpkin in different delectable ways, as a green vegetable or ripe and roasted."
Here is a recipe with piñon nuts baked into a sweet bread.

    1¾ cups cooked pumpkin
    1½ cups light brown sugar (packed)
     ½ cup butter, melted
      3 eggs, lightly beaten
      3 cups flour
      2 teaspoons baking powder
      1 teaspoon cinnamon
     ½ teaspoon each, nutmeg and salt
      1 cup roasted shelled piñon nuts

Preheat oven to 350 degrees.
Sift flour, baking powder and spices, stir in nuts. Mix together other ingredients, and add flour mixture, blending thoroughly. Pour batter into two oiled loaf pans and bake for about an hour or until the bread tests done. Cool on rack. (2 loaves)

APACHE ROLLS

These rolls were made in the American Southwest before any other recipe in this book. With the exception of the salt, which the Indians did not use, all the ingredients are native.

    1 cup white cornmeal
    1 cup yellow cornmeal
    1 teaspoon salt
    ½ teaspoon cayenne
    1 cup boiling water
    ½ cup heated buffalo fat or ½ cup bacon
       drippings
       green corn husks

Preheat oven to 350 degrees.
Mix together all the dry ingredients, wet down with the water and bacon drippings, and form into small rolls.
Wrap in corn husks and bake in the oven 1 hour. (*about 10 rolls*)

SANTA FE FRENCH TOAST

This unusual puffed-up French toast was made famous by an unknown chef of the Santa Fe Railroad dining car. It has, as might be expected, spread throughout the southwestern part of the nation. The secret of its success is a hot oven and the thickly sliced bread.

    2 eggs, well beaten
    ½ cup light cream
    ½ teaspoon salt
       pinch nutmeg
    3 slices slightly dry bread, ¾ inch thick,
       crusts trimmed, cut in half diagonally

Preheat oven to 400 degrees.
Beat together in a bowl the eggs, cream, salt, and nutmeg.

Soak the bread slices, a few at a time, in the egg mixture.
Fry on both sides in a heavy, oiled skillet.
Transfer at once to a baking sheet, slide into the oven, and allow to puff up for 3 or 4 minutes. Serve with orange-blossom honey or the syrup of your choice. (*2 servings*)

WILD SAGE BREAD

There for the picking, wild sage gives a flavor of the Old West to this bread. Don't close your eyes while baking it or you may find yourself in the Canyon de Chelly.

    1 package dry yeast
    1 cup homemade cottage cheese
    1 egg
    1 tablespoon melted lard
    1 tablespoon sugar
    2 teaspoons crushed dried wild sage
    1 teaspoon salt
    ¼ teaspoon baking soda
    ¼ cup lukewarm water
    2½ cups flour
       butter
       piñon nuts or coarse salt

Mix all dry ingredients together thoroughly. Dissolve yeast in lukewarm water. Beat together egg and cheese until smooth, add melted shortening and yeast.
Combine all ingredients in a large bowl adding flour mixture slowly and beating vigorously after each addition until stiff dough is formed. Cover dough with cloth and let rise in a warm place for an hour or until double in bulk. Punch dough down, knead for one minute and put into a buttered pan or casserole. Cover and let rise for 40 minutes.
Preheat oven to 350 degrees.
Bake for 50 minutes. Brush top with melted butter and sprinkle with crushed, roasted piñons or coarse salt. (*6 to 8 servings*)

DESSERTS

ARIZONA DEEP-DISH GRAPEFRUIT PIE

1 cup grapefruit sections
½ cup orange sections
½ cup pineapple chunks
sugar
unbaked pie shell

Preheat oven to 400 degrees.
Combine all the fruits, sweeten to taste, and arrange in a 3-inch-deep pie pan.
Cover with pastry, and bake 10 minutes. Lower heat to 300 degrees, and cook 30 minutes longer. Serve hot. (*6 servings*)

SOUTHWEST BREAD PUDDING

1 pound brown sugar
1 stick cinnamon
1 clove
1 tablespoon butter
6 slices toast, cubed
3 cups sliced, peeled apples
1 cup raisins
1 cup chopped nuts
½ pound Monterey Jack cheese, sliced

Put the sugar, cinnamon, and clove into a quart of water, and boil down to a syrup. Discard cinnamon and clove.
Preheat oven to 325 degrees.
Butter a casserole and put in a layer of toast, cover with half the apples, sprinkle with raisins and nuts, and lay on the cheese. Repeat layers, using all the ingredients.
Pour the syrup over the pudding and bake for 30 minutes. Serve either hot or cold. (*4 to 6 servings*)

GOOSEBERRY TART

A young New York woman traveling along the Santa Fe Trail by covered wagon was surprised at the quality of the food served. "We enjoyed a fine dinner," she wrote. "It consisted of chicken, rice, and a dessert of wine and gooseberry tart. Jane and I went off as soon as we got here and found enough to make a fine pie."

2 cups gooseberries
⅔ cup sugar
½ cup white wine
1 recipe pie crust
2 tablespoons apricot jam
1 cup heavy cream, whipped

Preheat oven to 375 degrees.
With scissors snip off tops and tails of gooseberries, and wash. Mix sugar and wine in saucepan and bring to a boil. Add berries. Simmer until tender, about 20 minutes. Set aside to cool.
Bake pie shell 15 minutes until light brown. Brush with apricot jam and fill with cooled berries.
Cover with whipped cream and refrigerate until ready to serve. (*6 servings*)

MELON WITH BERRIES

2 ripe cantaloupes or honeydew melons
2 cups strawberries, blackberries, or raspberries, rinsed and capped
2 tablespoons confectioners' sugar
2 ounces tequila

Halve the cantaloupes and remove the seeds. Spoon the berries into the centers, sprinkle with confectioners' sugar and tequila. Chill and serve. (*4 servings*)

OKLAHOMA PUDDING

We have not been able to find out by what right the state of Oklahoma lays claim to this excellent pudding, but we don't blame it for trying.

½ cup brown sugar, firmly packed
1 cup flour
2 teaspoons baking powder
1 teaspoon nutmeg
1 teaspoon cinnamon
¼ teaspoon salt
½ cup milk
2 tablespoons butter, melted
1 cup dates, seeded and chopped
1 cup raisins
1 cup chopped nuts
1 cup brown sugar dissolved in 2 cups boiling water
whipped cream, plain or sweetened

Preheat oven to 350 degrees.
Sift and mix together the dry ingredients, stir in the milk and butter, then add the dates, raisins, and nuts.
Stir in the sweetened boiling water, place into a baking dish, and bake 30 minutes. Serve hot with whipped cream. (*6 servings*)

MORMON PUDDING

2 cups cooked carrots, mashed
1 cup brown sugar, firmly packed
1 tablespoon flour
½ teaspoon salt
¼ teaspoon cinnamon
⅛ teaspoon each cloves, nutmeg, allspice, ginger
1½ cups milk
1 egg, beaten
½ cup seedless raisins (optional)

Preheat oven to 300 degrees.
Put all the ingredients into a bowl, mix well, and pour into a greased 2-quart baking dish.
Bake 1 hour or until a knife inserted in center comes clean.
Serve hot or cold with cream. (*6 servings*)

FLAN

A favorite dessert down in Mexico, the ubiquitous flan seems always to be included on restaurant menus, and is a popular standby in every home south of the border. It was inevitable, therefore, that it would find its way northward into the United States, where it is called baked custard.

¾ cup sugar
3 eggs
3 cups milk
½ teaspoon vanilla

Preheat oven to 350 degrees.
Heat ¼ cup sugar in a small skillet to a light brown syrup. Coat the sides and bottom of a custard dish with this syrup, and cool.
Beat the eggs, add the remaining sugar, then add the milk and vanilla.
Pour the egg mixture into the custard dish, set into a dish of hot water, and bake in the oven about 30 minutes or until knife inserted into center comes out clean. (*4 servings*)

ARTILLERY PIE

Army cooks had to use everything at hand when hungry men sat down to eat. Here is an example of commissary ingenuity which is not exactly top-notch fare, but probably tasted good after morning patrol.

8 pounds bread
1 pound suet
4 dozen apples
2 pounds sugar

Melt suet in frying pan, cut the bread in slices one quarter inch thick, dip each piece into the melted fat and place them in the oven to dry. In the meantime get the apples peeled, boiled, and mashed with the sugar. Cover the bottom of the baking dish with the bread, cover the bread with some of the apples, then add more bread over that, then the apples until all are used; place it in a moderate oven and bake for 20 minutes. This may be made with any kind of fruit. (*sufficient for 22 men*)

PECAN PUDDING, MARMALADE SAUCE

Texas is famous for its pecans and its grapefruit marmalade. This dessert came to us by way of an old cookbook, and it was on a menu that included half an avocado filled with caviar, spiced beef, pickled mangoes, broccoli, carrots, and Mexican salad. Serve this pudding hot.

> 2 tablespoons sugar
> 2 tablespoons butter
> 2 eggs
> 2 tablespoons crumbled cake crumbs (or sweetened bread crumbs)
> 6 tablespoons finely chopped shelled pecans
> 1 cup milk, warmed
> pie crust

Cream the sugar and butter together, beat in the eggs, then add the crumbs and pecans. Stir in the milk.
Preheat oven to 400 degrees.
Line a pudding dish with pie crust, fill with the pecan mixture, and bake for 20 minutes.
Make the following marmalade sauce:

> 1 cup orange or grapefruit marmalade
> ½ cup hot water
> ½ cup white wine
> 2 tablespoons chopped pecans

Mix all the ingredients together, cook down to a thick consistency, and serve over the pudding. (*4 servings*)

ALMOND CUSTARD

> 1 cup raw rice
> 2 cups milk
> 2 egg yolks, well beaten
> ½ teaspoon salt
> ½ cup sugar
> ¼ teaspoon cinnamon
> ½ cup ground roasted almonds

Mix the rice with the milk, place into a double boiler, and cook until rice is soft.
Stir in the remaining ingredients, and cook 15 minutes longer.
Spoon into dessert dishes, cool, and place into the refrigerator.
Serve cold. (*4 to 6 servings*)

BEVERAGES

SOUTHWEST CHOCOLATE

> 2 egg whites, lightly beaten
> 6 tablespoons cocoa
> ½ teaspoon cinnamon
> 6 teaspoons sugar
> 1½ quarts milk

Make a thin paste of egg whites, cocoa, cinnamon, sugar, and ½ cup milk.
Scald the remainder of the milk, and slowly add to the paste, beating with a rotary beater.
Serve at once. (*4 to 6 servings*)

GRAPEFRUIT PECOS

> 2 eggs, separated
> 2 cups grapefruit juice
> 4 teaspoons honey
> ¼ teaspoon salt
> nutmeg

Beat the egg yolks, then stir in the grapefruit juice, honey, and salt.
Beat the egg whites until stiff. Fold into the juice mixture, mix well, and serve in chilled glasses, sprinkled with nutmeg.
Note: This cooling hot-weather drink is improved, to the taste of many, by the addition of 2 ounces of tequila per serving. (*2 servings*)

TEQUILA CON SANGRITA

Sangrita:

- ⅓ cup fresh orange juice
- ¼ cup lime juice
- ½ teaspoon salt
- ⅛ teaspoon pepper
- 1 chili jalapeño en escabeche, chopped and seeded
- 2 teaspoons of liquid from the jalapeño
- 3 tablespoons onion, minced
- 1⅔ cups tomato juice

Put all ingredients except tomato juice in blender for 15 seconds, or mix or shake until smooth. Add tomato juice and refrigerate.
Use as a mixer with an equal amount of tequila: 1 jigger tequila, 1 jigger of the sangrita. Serve in small glasses that have been prepared by wetting the rims and dipping in salt. (*10 servings*)

HAILSTORMS

At Bent's Fort on the Santa Fe Trail there were always balls on the Fourth of July. A party was sent into the mountains to gather wild mint for mint julips. For mixing these, ice was brought from the ice house. They called the drink "hailstorms."

—George B. Grinnell.

We give you his recipe verbatim:

- 1 pint Mason jar per person
- 3 ounces bourbon whiskey per person
- 1 large sprig of mint per person
- 2 tablespoons sugar per person

Into each jar put whiskey, mint, and sugar. Fill with crushed ice. Put cap on jar and let each guest shake his "hailstorm" and sip right out of the jar. Wonderful for picnics.

TOAST AND WATER

The following recipe was taken directly from U.S. Army sources published during the Indian Wars.
This we are sure, was very popular among the men.

Cut a piece of crusty bread, about a ¼ lb. in weight, place it upon a toasting-fork, and hold it about six inches from fire; turn it often, and keep moving it gently until of a light-yellow color, then place it nearer the fire, and when of a good brown chocolate color, put it in a jug and pour over 3 pints of boiling water; cover the jug until cold, then strain it into a clean jug, and it is ready to use. Never leave the toast in it, for in summer it would cause fermentation in a short time. A piece of apple, slowly toasted till it gets quite black and added to the above, makes a very nice and refreshing drink for invalids.

PACIFIC COAST
COOKING

SOUPS AND CHOWDERS

French Onion Soup
California Olive Soup
Chinese Egg Drop Soup
Minestrone
Abalone Chowder
San Francisco Halibut Broth
Cold Avocado Soup
Senegalese Soup

PASTA, EGG, AND CHEESE DISHES

Hangtown Fry
Jack and Beans
Eggs Foo Yong
Fettucini Carbonara
California Macaroni
Chinese Fried Noodles
San Diego Omelet

FISH AND SHELLFISH

Olympia Pan Roast
Cracked Dungeness Crab
Fried Crab Fingers
Baked Portland Salmon
Seattle Salmon Mousse
Cioppino
Tempura
Abalone Steak
Abalone con Chilies
Fried Geoducks
Planked Opakapaka

MEATS

Steak Teriyaki
Puchero (Boiled Dinner)
Monterey Tamale Pie
Chinese Sweet-and-sour Pork
Sautéed Beef with Mustard Sauce
Queen City Cream Schnitzel
Sukiyaki
Charcoal-broiled Leg of Lamb
Planked Steak, Fairmont
Barbecued Spareribs, Chinese Style
The Hawaiian Luau

POULTRY AND GAME BIRDS

California Oven-barbecued Chicken
Curried Breast of Turkey
Pacific Chicken Mousse
Hawaiian Chicken
Chicken Tetrazzini
Chicken Luau

VEGETABLES AND SIDE DISHES

Lentils Mexicanos
Baked Artichokes with Cheese
Hawaiian Yams
Scalloped Tomatoes
Chinese Fried Rice with Pork

SALADS AND DRESSINGS

Caesar Salad
San Fernando Salad
California Fruit Salad
Ensalada de Verdolaga
Crab Louis
Hawaiian Surprise
Avocado Supreme
Green Goddess Dressing
Lorenzo Dressing
Columbian Salad
Chicken Salad, California Style

BREADS AND BATTERCAKES

Sourdough Bread
Tait's French Pancakes
Prune Bread
Garlic Bread
Orange Surprise Biscuits

DESSERTS

California Guava Shortcake
Loganberry Cake with Brown Sugar
    Lemon Sauce
Queen Anne's Cookies
Haupia (Coconut Pudding)
Tropical Figs
Fried Bananas
Hawaiian Sweet
Poached Plums
California Prune Pudding
Six-Citrus Marmalade

BEVERAGES

Champagne Punch
Hawaiian Mai Tai
Sangría
Orange Julep
Cappuccino
Caffè Borgia

PACIFIC COAST COOKING

A year before the Boston Massacre a Franciscan monk, Junipero Serra, who had been born on the island of Majorca, one of the few places in the world where oranges then grew, made his way northwestward from Mexico toward the country called California. He founded his first mission at present-day San Diego. In the years afterward the Franciscans established twenty-one missions as far north as San Francisco, all a day's march apart, like the Pope's castles in Italy. The priests planted gardens, vineyards, groves of orange trees, and tomatoes, which they had learned to eat when the Aztecs had taught the Spaniards that the fruit was not poisonous. The monk's food was that of Mexico's Indians mingled with that of Spain; new to them were tortillas, tamales, tacos made from hand-ground corn, avocados, pumpkins, vanilla, chocolate, sweet potatoes, chili peppers, and buffalo. Beef, olives, rice, sugar, wine, and cinnamon had come from Spain. On the California deserts and coast lived the Digger and acorn-eating Indians. The Digger Indians were so named because they dug for roots in the deserts of southern California; the Miwok, Maidu, Pomo, and Hupa tribes processed acorns to make meal, and were therefore called acorn-eating Indians. There was a long leeching of the bitter tannic acid from the acorn meal, which was then boiled with chunks of game.

Traders and sailors were the first Europeans to settle on the Pacific coast. One of them was a German named John Sutter, who had traveled as far as Alaska and the Sandwich Islands, and had brought with him some of the islanders as servants. Other parties of missionaries and adventurers trickled overland before 1840, and in the next year John Bidwell took wagons overland into the San Joaquin Valley. Bidwell wrote,

It was understood that everyone should have not less than a barrel of flour—more than the usual quantity. This I did because we were told that when we got into the mountains we probably would get out of bread, and to live on meat alone, which I thought would kill me, even if it didn't the others.

Their foods in California were deer, wild cattle, plums, and weeds. It is said the settlers were so hungry for greens that once across the Sierra Nevada, they fell on their knees in the green meadows.

At the end of the Mexican War, John Sutter and James Marshall formed a partnership to start a sawmill forty miles north of Sutter's Fort on the Coloma river. When the mill was finished the tailrace needed deepening. Marshall inspected the work and noticed "numerous bright brass-colored particles the size of wheat grains," which turned out to be gold. By the time the partners decided that the discovery should be kept secret, it was too late. San Franciscans learned of the discovery and closed their places of business, deserted ships in the harbor, and hurried to the gold fields. Even the city's two newspapers had to close down for lack of personnel. After that, precious metals were found all along the Sierra Nevada mountains. Precious too were the talents of the fine cooks attracted to California's mines and restaurants. Gold-rich millionaires hired great chefs to provide the finest cuisine for themselves and their guests, thereby setting a tradition of fine food in San Francisco that still exists.

The dish call hangtown fry got its name from the mining town, which was later called Placerville by less-lawless citizens. It was probably very costly, because it contained fresh eggs and fresh oysters, a luxury to miners tired of sourdough and beans. Such a dish could have cost as much as one hundred dollars.

Bret Harte wrote a story about miners

down from the gold fields in San Francisco, who entered a Chinese restaurant, drunk and hungry. The proprietor protested that he had little food left to prepare, but the miners were insistent. The proprietor retired to the kitchen and dumped into his wok what was left of several dishes he had served earlier to Chinese patrons. He stir-fried the dish and took it steaming to the table. The miners ate with gusto, and put a large bag of gold dust on the table when they rose to leave. One asked the name of the dish. The proprietor thought quickly and said, "Chop suey," which in Chinese means chopped-up everything, or hash. Because of this, Bret Harte thought the dish was of American origin, but a dish of that name has long been known in Hong Kong. The tale is probably apocryphal, but it does attest to the dearth of good food in the mining camps.

In 1851 a Hungarian, Count Augustin Haraszthy, planted a vineyard of wine grapes in Sonoma County. His vines flourished, so much so that ten years later the California legislature commissioned him to return to Europe in order to bring back one hundred different kinds of grape seedlings. (For reasons unknown, the vines of European wine grapes will not grow east of the Rocky Mountains.) The favor was returned to Europe when the wine blight wiped out most of their vineyards in the late 1800s, almost destroying the wine industry there. American roots, immune to the blight, were grafted to the old vines of Europe's famous wine grapes, and the European vines survived.

Wine is used copiously in coastal cooking, in pot roasts, chicken, gravies, and pan juices. Turkey and geese are stuffed with wine flavored dressings, and wines are used in salad dressing and for marinades. Named for the grapes from which they are derived, coast wines combined with the fresh breads, seafood, fruits, vegetables and salad greens, make this one of the finest cuisines in America.

The botanist Luther Burbank moved from Massachusetts to California in 1865, bought a farm in Santa Rosa, and set to work testing, experimenting, strengthening, and improving plants, trees, and vines. An employee spoke of trying to follow Burbank along the rows when Burbank was in his seventies. The employee could not keep up with the old man. A genius in his field, Burbank performed what seemed like miracles in developing disease-resistant strains and new, better, and stronger varieties.

When winter snows cover other parts of the nation, fruit and almond trees are in blossom in the San Joaquin Valley, and the Imperial Valley is harvesting its first vegetable and date and olive crop of the year. In February the temperature in the Imperial Valley can be in the nineties. In summer it can go as high as 125 degrees Fahrenheit, making it possible to harvest three crops a year, with the help of the waters of the Colorado River harnessed for irrigation by the Hoover Dam.

With all this productivity and a plethora of vegetables, the salad has risen to hitherto unreached heights on the Coast. In one California cookbook there are ninty-six salad recipes. One, a magnificent mixture of romaine lettuce, olive oil, croutons, anchovy, egg, and grated Romano cheese, is the Caesar salad. The creamy soft avocado, native to the West Coast, lends its smooth flavor to guacamole and Hollywood salad (grapefruit and avocado), and is eaten by itself and even in sandwiches. Artichoke hearts lend their pungent crispness to other salads. Orange and grapefruit sections are mixed with sweet onions and dressing, and served on escarole. San Francisco's Palace Hotel is famous for several salads, but most particularly for green goddess dressing—avocados and anchovies—named after the movie of that name. In California salads are served before the main course, but not before the soup.

It is hard to find a bad restaurant in San Francisco. The late George Rector said,

"The restaurants out there, ever since I can remember, have been about the best in this or any other section of the land. The French cuisine predominates, yet there are ever so many Italian restaurants. And for the Chinese food—well, I'm told that the best Chinese restaurants in all of China are right in San Francisco!

Rector didn't mention the Japanese, Mexican, Hawaiian, or Greek restaurants, but he did mention the Dungeness crab and the tiny shrimp-like French *écrevisses*.

Then there is the geoduck, a rare giant long-necked clam; the abalone, a monoshelled mollusk with a large edible muscle; the razor clam; the Pacific lobster; the tiny Olympic oyster; and the immense Alaskan king crab. Grunions ("silversides") fling themselves onto the beaches when they spawn, and are picked up by the bucketful, taken home, and fried. And there are the tuna, sardines, and mackerel that lured Portuguese and Italian fishermen to California. The heritage of these men is responsible for cioppino. A fish stew reminiscent of the many fish stews of the Mediterranean, it is made with crab or mixed fishes and plenty of chopped onion, parsley, much fresh basil, and olive oil. All these Pacific delicacies are served with French bread, Italian bread, or native sourdough bread.

The many Chinese, Japanese, Philippine, Vietnamese, Korean and Hawaiian Americans give an Oriental quality to the cities of the Pacific Coast. Though hundreds of miles out in the ocean, the Hawaiian Islands seem very close by. Perhaps they always have been, for when the Tahitians migrated over the sea to Hawaii, they brought many foods with them, and some of the foods carried in the canoes are believed to have been taken to Tahiti by pre-Columbian Americans. Among these were the pig and the sweet potato. Other foods carried were bananas, breadfruit, and taro root for poi. They found hundreds of varieties of fish. For seasonings they used the kakui nut, roasted, and a seaweed called limu-komo. The pineapple was taken to Hawaii many years later.

Perhaps the West Coast was also influenced by the delightful way of life of the Hawaiian Islands, because meals are cooked and eaten outdoors whenever possible. Perhaps the vision of handsome people wearing a minimum of clothing, enjoying luaus under palm trees, was too charming to ignore, and good enough to be imitated. This mixture—Polynesian, Oriental, American (polyglot in its own way)—as well as the climate, the sea, the air, and the automobile have made these the most mobile people on earth, always searching to see, to know, and to taste everything new.

SOUPS AND CHOWDERS

ABALONE CHOWDER

1 pound fresh or frozen abalone meat, trimmed and pounded (see p. 269)
1 quart water
1 pinch thyme
dash of Tabasco sauce
1 teaspoon salt
¼ pound salt pork, diced
1 onion, chopped
3 potatoes, peeled and cubed
2 cups milk or half-and-half
3 tablespoons butter
chopped parsley

Put abalone into a pot with water, season with thyme, Tabasco, and salt. Cover and boil for 1 hour or longer, until it is tender. Remove abalone from broth and chop.

Meanwhile sauté the salt pork and onion in a skillet until crisp and golden.

Put the abalone, salt pork, and onion into the broth, add the potatoes, and simmer 20 minutes or until potatoes are cooked.

Stir in the milk or half-and-half, add the butter, check the seasonings, and serve garnished with chopped parsley. (*4 servings*)

SAN FRANCISCO HALIBUT BROTH

Without a doubt this dish was brought to California by the Italian fishermen and vineyard workers.

>   2 pounds fresh halibut, cleaned, boned, and cut into pieces
>   1 cup dry white wine
>   4 cups water
>   1 teaspoon lemon juice
>   1 clove garlic, chopped
>   1 bay leaf
>   2 tablespoons olive oil
>   1 teaspoon salt
>   ½ teaspoon freshly ground pepper
>   minced parsley
>   Parmesan cheese

Combine all the ingredients except parsley and Parmesan cheese in a heavy pot or kettle, bring to a boil, and simmer gently for 30 minutes. Serve garnished with minced parsley and Parmesan cheese. (*4 servings*)

COLD AVOCADO SOUP

>   2 ripe avocados, peeled, seeded, and mashed
>   2 cups chicken broth
>   1 teaspoon salt
>   1 teaspoon dried tarragon
>   few dashes Tabasco sauce
>   1 tablespoon lemon juice
>   1 cup heavy cream (or sour cream)
>   chopped chives

Put the avocados and chicken broth into a blender, and blend at low speed until smooth, or mash and whip together.
Add the salt, tarragon, Tabasco, and lemon juice. Blend again.
Add the cream, and blend briefly again. Chill and serve in chilled cups, garnished with chives. (*4 to 6 servings*)

CALIFORNIA OLIVE SOUP

We've never found this interesting luncheon soup anywhere but California, but we wouldn't mind helping to spread its acceptance by including the recipe here.

>   1 cup ripe olives, pitted and sliced
>   1 cup green olives, pitted and sliced
>   1 clove garlic, minced
>   1 small onion, minced
>   2 cups chicken broth
>   1 cup light cream
>   1 egg, beaten
>   dash Tabasco sauce
>   minced parsley

Place the olives, garlic, onion, and broth into a saucepan, and simmer 15 minutes.
Mix together the cream, egg, and Tabasco; stir in a little of the hot broth; and return to the soup, stirring constantly without boiling until thickened.
Serve hot or cold garnished with parsley. (*4 servings*)

MINESTRONE

This worldwide favorite soup was introduced to California by the large Italian population attracted to the state by the fishing and grape-growing industries. Minestrone is a rich vegetable soup and varies greatly from region to region—and cook to cook. There are certain standard ingredients—olive oil, onion, garlic, beans, pasta, Parmesan cheese—but in a place like California the vegetable variations can go wild.

>   3 tablespoons olive oil
>   6 scallions, cut into 2-inch pieces
>   1 onion, chopped
>   1 clove garlic, minced
>   ½ cup chopped celery
>   ½ cup chopped string beans
>   1 cup shredded cabbage
>   6 cups warm chicken broth (or beef stock)
>   1 cup chopped tomatoes (or solid-pack canned tomatoes)
>   1 tablespoon chopped parsley
>   1 cup kidney, lima, or chick beans
>   1 bay leaf
>   1 teaspoon chopped fresh thyme or basil
>   2 teaspoons salt
>   1 teaspoon pepper
>   ½ cup raw elbow macaroni or other macaroni (or vermicelli)
>   grated Parmesan cheese

Heat the oil in a large soup pot or marmite and add the scallions, onions, and garlic. Cook over low heat for 5 minutes.

Add the celery, beans, and cabbage, and cook-stir until vegetables are soft.

Add the broth, tomatoes, parsley, beans, bay leaf, thyme or basil, salt, and pepper. Cover and cook 30 minutes.

Add the macaroni and cook 20 minutes longer. Serve with grated Parmesan cheese on top. (*4 to 6 servings*)

CHINESE EGG DROP SOUP

The Chinese were imported to California to help build the first transcontinental railroad. They stayed, and many gravitated to what is now Chinatown in San Francisco, where they introduced a kind of cooking new to this country—a kind of cooking that has since been accepted with astonishing rapidity into the mainstream of American eating. Small surprise considering how inventive and flavorful Chinese cooking can be.

    4 cups chicken broth
    3 water chestnuts, thinly sliced
      pinch ground ginger
    2 tablespoons soy sauce
    1 teaspoon cornstarch mixed with 2
      tablespoons water
    4 eggs
    2 tablespoons dry sherry
    1 tablespoon finely chopped scallions

Mix together the broth, water chestnuts, ginger, and soy sauce, bring to a boil, and then reduce the heat. Stir in the cornstarch mixture. Beat the eggs with the sherry and gradually drip into the hot broth. Stir with a fork to "scramble" the eggs as they congeal.

Serve garnished with scallions. (*4 servings*)

SENEGALESE SOUP

An interesting and versatile soup imported from the Orient—and one not difficult to make. It can be a robust, soul-warming soup to serve on a cold day; or chilled, it becomes a delightful summer soup.

    3 tablespoons butter
    2 tablespoons chopped onion
    4 tablespoons chopped celery
    2 tablespoons flour
    1 teaspoon salt
    1 teaspoon curry powder
    1 cup chicken broth
    3 cups milk, scalded
    1 cup diced cooked chicken
    ½ cup thinly sliced peeled apple

Using a saucepan, melt the butter, add the onion and celery, and cook 5 minutes. Stir in the flour, salt, and curry powder; cook 2 minutes longer; then stir in the broth.

Gradually stir in the milk, add the chicken, and simmer 15 minutes.

Serve hot with apple slices floating on top; or chill and serve cold. (*4 to 6 servings*)

FRENCH ONION SOUP

Born in France, onion soup has turned up all over the United States, first in New Orleans and New York, and then in the restaurants of San Francisco. Its aroma probably spread over the West with the *coureurs du bois*, the fur trappers of the American Fur and Hudson's Bay companies.

    3 tablespoons butter
    1 tablespoon olive oil
    2 large onions, peeled and thinly sliced
    1 teaspoon salt
    3 cups hot chicken broth
    ½ cup dry white wine
    4 slices toasted French bread
    4 tablespoons grated Parmesan cheese

Sauté the onions in butter and oil, using a heavy skillet, until soft but not quite browned. Add salt, hot broth, and wine. Cook over medium heat 5 minutes.

Ladle into 4 oven-proof bowls, top each with a slice of toast, and sprinkle liberally with grated cheese.

Place under the broiler for 5 to 10 minutes or until cheese melts and bubbles. (*4 servings*)

PASTA, EGG,
AND CHEESE DISHES

HANGTOWN FRY

Hangtown, California, was a mining town, a town experiencing a hard time with supplies. Food was scarce—and expensive. A barrel of oysters must have been a rare treat. We can't help but wonder, therefore, what a nice dish like this was doing in a town like that.

      4 slices of bacon
      6 to 8 medium-sized oysters
      1 egg, beaten
      ½ cup bread crumbs
      3 to 4 eggs
      2 tablespoons milk

Cook bacon in skillet until crisp, put on hot plate. Dip oysters in egg, then in bread crumbs. Fry one side until golden, then fry on other side.
Beat the eggs and milk together, and add to the oysters in the pan. Stir eggs around the oysters without disturbing them. When firm, fold like an omelet, and serve with bacon. (*2 servings*)

CALIFORNIA MACARONI

      2 tablespoons butter, softened
      2 cups milk
   1½ cups Monterey Jack cheese, cubed
      2 cups macaroni, uncooked
      ½ teaspoon salt
      ½ teaspoon mustard
      2 tablespoons green chilies, chopped
      2 eggs, beaten
      2 tablespoons butter, melted
      ½ cup bread crumbs

Preheat oven to 350 degrees.
Mix all ingredients except last two together, and put in a 1½-quart casserole. Sprinkle with bread crumbs mixed with butter. Bake 40 to 50 minutes. (*6 servings*)

FETTUCINI CARBONARA

In the mountains of Italy, carbonara or charcoal burners are the poorest of people. They have to make the most of what comes their way, thus the modest ingredients of this flavorful dish, another of our debts to Italian migrants. Usually made with spaghetti, it becomes very special when made with home-made noodles or fettucini, as it is in fine restaurants on both coasts of the U.S.

      3 slices salt pork or bacon, diced
      2 slices prosciutto (Italian ham),
         chopped
      4 tablespoons butter
      2 eggs
      ½ cup Parmesan cheese
      ½ cup Romano cheese
      1 recipe homemade noodles or 1 pound
         of fettucini

Drop the fettucini into a pot of boiling, salted water. Stir gently. Cook until all the fettucini rise to the top of the pot, about 4 minutes. Drain and keep hot.
Cook diced salt pork in frying pan until brown, add the ham, stir. Add butter.
Beat eggs with 2 tablespoons cheese.
Add fettucini to the pork and ham, add the eggs, and toss all together gently. Serve immediately with remaining cheese sprinkled on top. (*4 servings*)

EGGS FOO YONG

Every Chinese restaurant in the country serves this Oriental omelet. Here is a recipe you can make in your own kitchen, now that Chinese ingredients have been made available in local markets.

½ cup cut spring onions
½ cup bean sprouts
½ cup sliced water chestnuts
½ cup chopped shrimp or cooked pork
½ tablespoon peanut oil
2 tablespoons soy sauce
2 tablespoons flour
5 eggs beaten with ½ cup water
½ cup peanut oil
1 cup chicken broth
½ cup soy sauce
4 teaspoons cornstarch blended with 2 tablespoons water

Stir-fry the onions, bean sprouts, water chestnuts and shrimp (or pork) in the ½ tablespoon peanut oil 10 minutes.

Add the soy sauce and flour. Stir well, cool slightly, and blend in with the raw eggs.

Heat ½ cup peanut oil in a heavy skillet, and drop the egg mixture in by large spoonfuls, turning to brown on both sides. Remove and keep warm.

Make a sauce by mixing together the last three ingredients cooking until transparent.

Pour sauce over the omelets, and serve. (*4 servings*)

SAN DIEGO OMELET

4 cups potatoes, peeled and thinly sliced
1 quart water
1 teaspoon salt
⅓ cup cooking oil
¾ cup chopped ham
6 eggs, lightly beaten

Put the potatoes to soak in cold salted water for 1 hour.

Heat oil. Drain potatoes, dry, and fry in hot oil until light brown.

Spread potatoes in a layer, sprinkle with ham, and add the eggs. Reduce heat, and when the bottom is golden brown, place a large plate over the pan, and turn the whole onto the plate. Slide, uncooked side down, into the pan. Brown again and serve. (*6 servings*)

JACK AND BEANS

This seems to be a Californization of an old Mexican recipe, *frijoles con queso*.

½ pound dried kidney beans, soaked overnight, drained
1 tablespoon butter
1 small onion, chopped
½ pound Monterey Jack cheese, chopped
2 tomatoes, chopped
1 dried red chili pepper, grated
½ pimento, finely chopped
¼ cup dry white wine
½ teaspoon salt

Cook the beans in a little water until tender. Drain.

Meanwhile, in a heavy saucepan, melt the butter, add the onion and cheese. Stir until cheese is melted.

Add the beans and the remaining ingredients. Cook over low heat until cheese is smooth and creamy. Serve hot. (*4 to 6 servings*)

CHINESE FRIED NOODLES

These crunchy noodles are served as an appetizer in Chinese restaurants.

1½ quarts water
½ teaspoon salt
½ pound thin noodles
2 cups peanut oil

Boil water, add salt. Cook noodles until they will just bend. Drain.

Heat oil to 375 degrees.

Take up a forkful of noodles, dip into hot fat, and swirl until brown. Drop on brown paper; continue until all are done. (*4 to 6 servings*)

FISH AND SHELLFISH

TEMPURA

The past generation of Americans have become more and more conscious of Oriental cooking. The Japanese method of cooking shrimp, small pieces of fish, and cut-up vegetables in a light cornstarch batter has become increasingly popular. The food is dipped into this batter and then deep-fried in 370-degree oil in the familiar manner.

In Japanese tempura restaurants the cook stands behind the counter where the guests sit, and places the hot pieces of food on each plate as done. Hot sake is served before and during the meal, and a bowl of rice with the meal.

In American homes a fondue pot could be used, or an electric frying pan—each person could fry his or her own.

- 2 eggs, separated
- 1 tablespoon peanut oil
- 1 tablespoon soy sauce
- 1 cup stale beer
- 1 teaspoon dry mustard
- 1 cup cornstarch
- 4 cauliflowerets
- 4 broccoli flowerets
- 8 carrot sticks, 2 inches long, ¼ inch thick
  peanut oil for frying
- 12 shrimp, shelled, deveined
- 4 lemon sole fillets, cut in 4 pieces

Beat the egg yolks with the oil, soy sauce, and beer until well blended.

Mix and sift together the mustard and cornstarch, and beat into the egg yolk mixture. Beat the egg whites until stiff, and fold into the yolk mixture.

Prepare sliced vegetables. Cut no more than ¼ inch thick so that inside will be crisp but cooked when the outside batter has browned. Heat oil to 370 degrees. Using chopsticks, dip 4 shrimp, pieces of fish, and vegetables into batter, and fry each variety in turn. Serve as each is done. (*4 servings*)

CIOPPINO

Cioppino is a sort of Pacific Coast bouillabaisse. A creation with a strong Genovese accent highly seasoned with basil. This rich seafood stew can be found along the California coast and especially in most of San Francisco's waterfront restaurants. The fish differs from season to season and area to area, depending upon the catch. The recipe that follows is authentic, but by no means definitive. If you are making cioppino, feel free to use whatever seafoods you may find available.

- 2 pounds sea bass, halibut, or other firm fish
- 1 Dungeness crab or lobster, cooked
- 1 pound large raw shrimp
- 1 pound squid, cleaned and sliced
- 2 dozen mussels or 1 dozen medium clams and/or oysters
- ½ cup olive oil
- 1 cup chopped onion
- 1 cup chopped green pepper
- 2 cloves garlic, mashed
- 5 medium tomatoes, sliced, or 1 can (number 2) tomatoes
- 2 cups dry red wine
  dash Tabasco sauce
- 1 bay leaf
- ½ cup chopped fresh basil
  pinch thyme
- 2 teaspoons salt
- 1 teaspoon pepper
- ½ cup finely chopped parsley

Clean the fish, and cut into pieces (reserving the head and tail for making stock).

Crack the crab, remove and discard the gills, remove the top shell (reserve for making stock). If you use lobster, crack the claws, if any, remove the tail, and cut into pieces (reserve the body for making stock).

Split the shrimp shells down the back.

Steam the mussels, clams, and/or oysters in a little water until they open. Remove and discard the top shells (reserving the broth).

Place the fish trimmings, crab or lobster shells, and mussel broth into a saucepan. Add 2 cups of water, and boil for 15 minutes. Strain the stock and reserve.

In a saucepan heat the oil, sauté the onion and pepper until soft, then add the garlic, tomatoes, wine and seasonings.

Add the reserved broth and strained stock, and simmer 15 minutes.

Place the fish and shrimp into a large pot, pour in the above sauce, cover, and simmer over low heat for 15 minutes.

Add the crab or lobster and squid and simmer 10 minutes longer. Serve in bowls with the mussels, clams, and/or oysters on top in their shells. Garnish with parsley. (*4 to 6 servings*)

ABALONE STEAK

The single-shelled abalone clings to rocks with a large, strong muscle. This muscle is the edible part, and must be relaxed by gentle pounding, which makes it tender.

    4 abalones
    2 eggs
    ½ teaspoon salt
    ¼ teaspoon pepper
    1½ cups bread crumbs
    6 tablespoons butter
    1 lemon, sliced

Slice the abalone traversely into ½-inch steaks. Lay these on a hard surface and pound gently with a mallet, 100 strokes or until the fibers have completely relaxed.

Beat the eggs, add salt and pepper, and stir. Dip each abalone slice in egg and then in bread crumbs.

Heat 4 tablespoons butter in the frying pan over moderate heat. Sauté the steaks until lightly brown on one side, turn, and brown on the other, about 3-5 minutes in all. If the steaks are cooked too long the fibers tighten up again and the meat will be tough.

Remove to hot platter. Melt remaining butter, and put a spoonful on each steak. Surround with lemon slices. (*4 servings*)

ABALONE CON CHILIES

    4 thin slices fresh abalone, pounded
      (see preceding recipe)
    4 poblano chilies
    1 cup grated Monterey Jack cheese
    1 egg lightly beaten with 1 cup light
      cream
      cracker crumbs
    ½ cup butter
    ½ cup olive oil

Place the abalone slices onto the chilies, and spoon grated cheese onto each.

Roll, and fix with toothpicks. Dip into the cream-egg mixture, then into cracker crumbs. Heat the butter and oil in a heavy skillet, and fry the abalone rolls gently on all sides.

Serve with tortillas. (*4 servings*)

OLYMPIA PAN ROAST

The little Olympia oysters found only in North Pacific waters are about thumbnail size, tangy and succulent. Most often they are removed from the shell, and served with a cocktail sauce. Here is a long-standing Seattle recipe worthy of serious consideration.

    1 quart shucked Olympia oysters
    1 cup ketchup
    1 tablespoon Worcestershire sauce
    4 tablespoons butter
      salt
      pepper
    1 cup light cream
      hot toast

Heat the oysters in their own liquor over low heat. Stir in the ketchup, Worcestershire, butter, and seasonings. Bring almost to a boil, then add the cream. Serve immediately, on toast. (*4 servings*)

FRIED CRAB FINGERS

Crack Dungeness legs, dip them into beaten egg and then into cracker crumbs, and pan-fry them in butter until brown. Or fry them in deep fat.

Serve with melted butter.

PLANKED OPAKAPAKA

The *opakapaka* is a fish found in Hawaiian waters which closely resembles red snapper. Planked opakapaka is one of the important traditional features of a luau.

> 1 opakapaka (or red snapper), 4 to 5 pounds, dressed
> rock salt
> meat of 1 fresh coconut, cut up
> 1 cup water
> 2 tablespoons sherry
> orange sections
> grapefruit sections
> pineapple chunks
> sliced papaya

Rub the fish with rock salt and place into a buttered, shallow baking dish.
Put the coconut meat with 1 cup water into a blender and blend at high speed for 30 seconds. Strain into a bowl, pressing the meat to extract all the milk. Let milk stand 1 hour, until cream has risen to the top. Skim off the cream and pour over the fish.
Preheat oven to 350 degrees.
Bake fish 20 minutes, spoon on the sherry, and cook 25 minutes longer or until it flakes when fork-tested.
Remove to a heated plank, surround with the fruit, and serve. (*4 to 6 servings*)

CRACKED DUNGENESS CRAB

The Pacific Dungeness crab, with a body six to eight inches across, is the "largest" of the crab family found in American waters. (The so-called Alaska king crab, measuring often four feet and sometimes even six feet across, is almost all leg and claw, the body being small and without appreciable meat.)
The Dungeness can be served in any way the eastern blue-claw crab can be served, but because of its size the most popular way is usually just cracked, brushed with butter, and broiled briefly under heat or over coals. You eat it hot or cold with melted butter, barbecue sauce, or mayonnaise.

SEATTLE SALMON MOUSSE

> 1 pound fresh salmon, cooked, boned, and flaked
> 1 envelope unflavored gelatin softened in ½ cup warm water
> ½ cup chopped celery
> ¼ cup vinegar
> 1 teaspoon dry mustard
> ½ teaspoon salt
> few grains cayenne
> 1 tablespoon minced onion
> ½ cup unsweetened whipped cream
> lettuce leaves
> parsley or watercress

Put all the ingredients except the last three into a blender, and blend at high speed about 1 minute or until smooth.
Fold in the whipped cream, pour into a mold, and chill until firm.
Unmold and serve on lettuce leaves. Decorate with parsley or watercress. (*4 to 6 servings*)

BAKED PORTLAND SALMON

> 3-pound salmon, dressed, head and tail removed
> 1 teaspoon salt
> ½ teaspoon pepper
> flour
> cooking oil
> 2 tablespoons butter, melted
> 1 cup strained, chopped tomatoes
> 1 onion, minced
> 1 clove garlic, minced
> 2 teaspoons Worcestershire sauce
> ½ cup cream

Preheat oven to 350 degrees.
Wipe the fish dry, season with salt and pepper, dust with flour, and place into a well-oiled baking pan. Cook 10 minutes.
Mix together the butter, tomatoes, onion, garlic, and Worcestershire. Add this mixture to the pan, and cook 30 minutes longer.
Remove the fish carefully to a heated platter. Stir the cream into the sauce, pour into a gravy boat, and serve separately. (*4 servings*)

FRIED GEODUCKS

As far as we have been able to learn, geoducks (pronounced gwee-ducks) are found in the United States only along the shores of Puget Sound in Washington. The name seems to be of Chinook Indian origin. The geoduck is a clam, one of the largest, averaging six pounds in weight—sometimes as much as ten pounds. The two-foot-long neck, which makes the clam resemble a duck, squirts water at low tide, betraying its hiding place in the sand.

If you are able to catch a geoduck—and there is considerable likelihood that you will not—you will find the meat (only partially enclosed in the shell) deliciously tender.

Slice the muscle, season with salt and pepper, and dip it into a mixture of beaten egg and milk and then flour. Deep-fat fry it in 370-degree oil for 4 or 5 minutes, and serve as you would any other clam. Chop the neck and make geoduck chowder. Six pounds of luscious meat from the sea, and only the shell wasted!

MEATS

PUCHERO (BOILED DINNER)

This is one of the rare early California Spanish dishes, most of the old Spanish recipes having been lost with the influx of gringos to southern California.

We never knew anyone who dried tomatoes, and we have no idea what kohl leaves are. It is possible that kohl was a local name for some fragrant herb or garden vegetable. We assume that a "hard" apple and pear meant not quite ripe.

- 1 veal knucklebone that has dried in the sun
- 2 pounds veal
- 2 pounds beef
- 3 ears corn
- 3 sweet potatoes, peeled
- 1 cup garbanzo beans
- 2 onions
- 3 dried tomatoes
- 2 jalapeño chili peppers
- 1 pound string beans, tied in bunches
- 1 bundle of kohl leaves
- 3 small zucchini, unpeeled
- 1 hard apple
- 1 hard pear
- 2 teaspoons salt
- ½ teaspoon pepper

Cover knucklebone and meats with cold water in a pot big enough to hold all the above. Bring to a boil, skim.

Place all the vegetables and fruits in the pot in the order given. Simmer the dinner over low heat for 3 hours. Do not stir. Serve vegetables on one platter, sliced meat on another, and the broth in soup plates or a tureen.

Serve with tortillas or sourdough bread. (*12 servings*)

MONTEREY TAMALE PIE

Southern California belonged to Mexico until 1848-49, and though it was quickly inundated by Americans in search of gold, many Mexican influences remained.

- 1 pound salt pork, finely chopped
- 1 large onion, finely chopped
- 1 clove garlic, finely chopped
- 2 tablespoons butter
- ¼ cup olive oil
- 1 can (1 pound) tomatoes
- 1 can (1 pound) corn, whole kernel or cream style
- 2 cups yellow cornmeal
- 1 cup milk
- 3 tablespoons chili powder
- 1 cup ripe olives
- 3 eggs, beaten

Preheat oven to 350 degrees.

Fry salt pork in a large iron skillet or other large shallow pan until brown.

Add onion, garlic, butter, and olive oil, then tomatoes and corn. Cook 15 minutes.

Combine cornmeal and milk, and add to mixture; stir. Add eggs, olives and chili powder; stir again.

Put the pan into oven and bake 1 hour. Serve hot in skillet. (*8 servings*)

PLANKED STEAK, FAIRMONT

This once-glamourous restaurant steak seems to be disappearing from today's menus. Planks, once for sale in many restaurant-supply stores, are no longer in evidence, though they can be found with a little searching. Of course an enterprising cook, with the help of the local lumberyard, can produce his own plank.

> 4½ pounds sirloin or porterhouse steak, about 2½ inches thick, excess fat removed and edges slashed
> ½ cup butter
> 4 cups mashed potatoes
> salt
> freshly ground pepper
> 2 teaspoons minced parsley
> juice of ½ lemon
> buttered cooked carrots, sautéed mushrooms, broiled tomatoes, buttered green beans, or other seasonal vegetables

Season a 1-inch-thick plank of hickory, oak, or pine as follows: Soak overnight in cold water, dry, rub with oil, and place into a preheated 350-degree oven for an hour.

Place the steak on a broiler rack and slide into a preheated 550-degree broiler close to the heat; broil 15 minutes on each side or until medium done, and transfer to the warmed plank.

Brush the edges of the plank with butter, and decorate with a border of mashed potatoes forced through a pastry bag.

Reset the oven to 400 degrees, slide in the plank, and brown the potatoes, taking care not to overcook the steak.

Remove the plank, season the steak well with salt and pepper, and spread with a maître d'hôtel sauce made by creaming 3 tablespoons butter with minced parsley, and seasoning with lemon juice, salt, and pepper.

Garnish with bouquets of hot seasonal vegetables. (*8 servings*)

BARBECUED SPARERIBS, CHINESE STYLE

The Cantonese method of marinating and basting pork spareribs produces morsels of superb tenderness and succulence.

> 4 pounds spareribs or 3 pounds loin ribs, separated
> 3 tablespoons heavy soy sauce
> 5 tablespoons light soy sauce
> 2 tablespoons sugar
> 2 tablespoons honey
> 3 tablespoons applesauce (or crushed pineapple)
> 3 tablespoons sake, sherry, or gin
> 2 cloves garlic, crushed
> 1 teaspoon salt

Trim excess fat from ribs and place them into a shallow dish. Mix together the remaining ingredients, pour over the ribs, cover, and allow to stand about 2 hours, stirring occasionally. Grill over white-hot charcoals or under the broiler until crusty on the outside and juicy inside, brushing from time to time with the marinade. (*4 servings*)

CHINESE STYLE SWEET-AND-SOUR PORK

> 2 cups cold cooked lean pork, cubed
> 4 tablespoons soy sauce
> 3 tablespoons brown sugar
> ½ cup vinegar
> 1 cup chicken consommé
> 2 green peppers, seeded and cut into 1-inch squares
> 1 cup canned pineapple chunks, drained
> 2 carrots, julienned
> 2 teaspoons cornstarch
> ½ cup flour
> 4 tablespoons water
> 1 egg
> peanut oil for deep frying

Toss the pork in 3 tablespoons soy sauce, and marinate for 2 hours, stirring from time to time.

To make the sauce, put the sugar, vinegar, and consommé into a small saucepan with 1 tablespoon soy sauce. Bring to a boil, and cook until reduced to about half. Add the peppers, pineapple, and carrots. Cook about 5 minutes. Make a paste with the cornstarch and a little cold water, stir into the sauce, and cook a minute or so, until sauce is thickened and translucent. Set aside.

Prepare the meat: Combine the flour, water, and egg, and beat until smooth. Add the pork and its marinade to this batter, and stir until well coated.

Fry, a few pieces at a time, in deep fat at 370 degrees until golden.

Serve in a bowl with the hot sauce poured on top. (*4 servings*)

SAUTÉED BEEF WITH MUSTARD SAUCE

  2 tablespoons butter
  2 cups tender beef slices or cubes (flank steak would be good)
  ½ cup heavy cream or sour cream
  ½ teaspoon dry mustard
      juice of ½ lemon
  ¼ teaspoon salt
  ⅛ teaspoon pepper

Sauté beef in butter, transfer to warm platter. To the butter remaining in the pan add the cream, mustard, lemon juice, salt, and pepper; stir.

Return meat to sauce, and serve on toast or noodles. (*4 servings*)

STEAK TERIYAKI

This Hawaiian creation is admirably suitable for backyard cook-outs, but if the weather is not accommodating and you can't wait, use the oven broiler.

  1 1-pound can pineapple chunks
  ½ cup soy sauce
  1 clove garlic, minced
  ½ teaspoon powdered ginger
  1 pound sirloin steak, cut into ¾-inch cubes
      wooden skewers

Drain the juice from the pineapple and put it into a bowl with the soy sauce, garlic and ginger.

Add the beef cubes, cover and marinate about 1 hour.

Thread the beef cubes and pineapple chunks alternately onto skewers and grill 4 inches away from white hot charcoals about 10 minutes. Brush with the marinade, turn and repeat. (*about 20 skewers*)

SUKIYAKI

The Japanese, relative latecomers to these shores, first settled in Hawaii and California. Their contribution to American cuisine is considerable and undisputed, the following being one of the best-known of their dishes.

  2 pounds lean beef, pork, or chicken, very thinly sliced
  2 tablespoons sesame oil
  2 large onions, very thinly sliced
  3 green onions (tops included), chopped
  ½ cup mushrooms, chopped
  ½ cup bamboo sprouts
  ½ cup soy sauce
  2 tablespoons sugar

Cook meat in sesame oil on a hot griddle about 5 minutes, turning often.

Add onions, mushrooms, and bamboo sprouts, keeping each separate.

Add soy sauce and sugar to meat, and continue cooking until tender.

Serve with hot rice. (*6 servings*)

CHARCOAL-BROILED LEG OF LAMB

This method of cooking leg of lamb should prove a welcome change from the usual oven-roasted version.

  1 leg of lamb
  ½ cup olive oil containing ½ teaspoon rosemary and 1 clove garlic, minced
      salt
      freshly ground pepper
  2 tablespoons lemon juice

Remove the bone from the leg of lamb, and butterfly it (that is, split it so that it lies flat). Remove the fell and rub both sides with the oil mixture.

Broil cut side down, as you would a steak, over white-hot coals 15 or 20 minutes, depending upon thickness.

Turn and repeat on the other side. Lamb should be pinkish on the inside and crispy brown on the outside.

Remove to a heated platter and season to taste. Carve slices diagonally, and serve with remaining seasoned oil, to which 2 tablespoons of lemon juice have been added. (*6 to 8 servings*)

QUEEN CITY
CREAM SCHNITZEL

An enterprising Austrian cook must have introduced westerners to this dish, found in the state of Washington. It is known in Vienna as veal cutlet à la Sacher. Queen City is Seattle.

    2 tablespoons butter
    1 cup sliced onions
    ¼ cup flour
    1 teaspoon salt
    ¼ teaspoon paprika
      dash cayenne
    1 veal cutlet, 1 inch thick
    1 cup sour cream

Melt butter, add onions, and sauté until light brown. Mix flour and seasonings, and dredge cutlet in this mixture.

Push onions to side of pan and brown cutlet on both sides. Lower heat, spoon the onions onto the cutlet, and add the sour cream. Cover. Cook over *very* low heat for 1 hour, until cutlet is tender. Turn once during cooking and spoon onions back onto the cutlet. (*2 servings*)

THE HAWAIIAN LUAU

The Hawaiian luau is an all-day ceremonial feast characterized by an abundance and variety of food and a relaxed, informal atmosphere. Once the luau had a religious significance, but today it might mark the celebration of a birthday or wedding—or it might be simply an excuse to get together with friends. From early in the morning preparations for the event are made. A pit, or *imu*, is dug into the ground and lined with lava rocks. A wood fire is built on top and kept burning until the rocks have reached a degree of intense heat.

Meanwhile the pig or *kalua*, is prepared for cooking. This indispensable feature of all luaus is eviscerated (the head is left intact), rubbed with Hawaiian rock salt, slashed with crisscross cuts, stuffed with hot stones from the *imu*, and firmly trussed with wire. The fire is cleared away, the hot rocks are covered with wet ti leaves and banana palms, and the pig is laid in the pit. More leaves go on top and the whole is covered tightly with wet gunnysacks and earth.

A 150-pound pig requires 6 hours to cook, so preliminary food is passed around while the celebrants wait—meat or fish on skewers; fresh fruit; and *lomi lomi*, a salad of salmon, tomatoes, and green onions. The pig, when it is finally done, is served in slices. It might be accompanied by yams, sweet potatoes, breadfruit and/or bananas baked in the *imu*; by chicken cooked with taro leaves in coconut milk; coconut duckling in pineapple shells; or whole planked *opakapaka*, a fish resembling the red snapper. And of course there is always poi, the Hawaiian equivalent of rice or potatoes. Poi, made by pounding taro root into a heavy paste, can be quite thick in consistency (onefinger poi), or thin and runny (five-finger poi). Not only the poi, but the entire meal, is eaten with the fingers.

The repast might be topped off finally with *haupia* (coconut pudding), passion-fruit pie, and an assortment of fruits. A sort of punch, with or without rum, is drunk throughout the feast, accompanying all the courses.

POULTRY
AND GAME BIRDS

CURRIED BREAST OF TURKEY

2 tablespoons butter
2 onions, sliced
8 slices turkey breast, ½ inch thick
2 teaspoons curry powder
1 cup yogurt
1 tablespoon tomato purée
1 clove garlic, chopped
½ teaspoon powdered ginger
1 cup water
1 teaspoon salt
⅛ teaspoon cayenne pepper (optional)

Sauté onions in butter in frying pan until golden. Push onions aside, add the turkey, sauté on both sides until golden. Add curry, yogurt, and tomato purée. Mix well, and cook for 10 minutes or until mixture starts to get dry.
Add garlic, ginger, water, salt, and cayenne. Cook slowly until sauce is thickened. Serve with rice. (*4 servings*)

HAWAIIAN CHICKEN

2 young chickens, cut into serving pieces
2 cups chicken broth
2 cups chopped raw spinach
meat of 1 coconut, grated
1 cup milk
salt
pepper

Put the chicken parts into a heavy pot, cover with broth (add a little water if necessary), and simmer until tender.
Add the spinach and cook a few minutes longer.
Meanwhile heat the grated coconut in milk, drain off the liquid, and squeeze out the pulp in a cheesecloth bag. Discard the pulp.
Add the coconut milk to the chicken, bring to a boil, season to taste, and serve on rice. (*4 to 6 servings*)

PACIFIC CHICKEN MOUSSE

1 envelope unflavored gelatin, softened in ½ cup warm water
1 cup chicken broth
1 cup mayonnaise
1 cup ground cooked chicken
1 tablespoon minced onion
2 tablespoons minced celery
2 pimentos, chopped
lettuce
½ cup pineapple chunks
1 cup mayonnaise

Place the softened gelatin, broth, mayonnaise, chicken, onion, celery, and pimento into a blender, and blend at medium speed for about 1 minute.
Spoon into a 4-cup ring mold, cover, and refrigerate overnight.
Unmold onto a chilled platter, surround with lettuce and pineapple, and fill center of ring with mayonnaise. (*4 servings*)

CALIFORNIA OVEN-BARBECUED CHICKEN

2 frying chickens, disjointed
1 teaspoon salt
6 tablespoons flour
6 tablespoons bacon fat or lard
1 cup butter
¼ cup tart wine
the rind of 1 orange, grated

Preheat oven to 325 degrees.
Roll chicken pieces in the salted flour, and fry in hot fat until brown.
Melt the butter, add the wine and orange rind, dip each piece of browned chicken in this mixture, and put in a baking pan. Bake 40 minutes to 1 hour, depending on the size of the chicken, covered for moist chicken and uncovered for crisp chicken. (*8 servings*)

CHICKEN TETRAZZINI

It has not been definitively recorded whether this pasta dish was made for the great Italian-American coloratura or merely named for her. It appears to have originated in the early 1900s in San Francisco, where Tetrazzini spent a great deal of time at the Opera House.

    5 tablespoons flour
    3 tablespoons butter, melted
 1½ cups chicken broth
    1 cup light cream
    ½ pound thin spaghetti
       nutmeg
    1 tablespoon sherry
    2 cups diced or sliced cooked chicken
    ½ cup grated Parmesan cheese

First, make velouté sauce: Stir flour into melted butter, season with a little salt and pepper. Blend well, and slowly stir in chicken broth. Bring to a boil, cook 2 minutes, and add 1 cup light cream.
Second, cook the spaghetti in salted water until just *al dente*. Drain.
Preheat oven to 400 degrees.
Stir a few grains nutmeg and 1 tablespoon sherry into the sauce.
Put the spaghetti into a shallow baking dish. Pour in half the sauce, and add the cooked chicken. Add the remaining sauce.

Sprinkle with the Parmesan cheese and bake 5 or 10 minutes in the oven or until browned. (*4 servings*)

CHICKEN LUAU

    1 cup finely chopped onion
    1 cup finely chopped celery
    1 cup cooking oil
 1½ cups chicken broth
    ½ cup tomato purée
    1 tablespoon curry powder
       salt
       pepper
    1 broiler, 3 pounds, quartered
    ¼ pound chopped macadamia nuts or
       peanuts
    1 ripe fresh pineapple, peeled and
       sliced

Sauté the onion and celery in ½ cup oil until golden. Add the broth, purée, and curry; simmer 30 minutes. Season to taste with salt and pepper, remove from heat, and set aside. Rub the chicken parts with the remaining oil, season with salt and pepper, and cook under a hot broiler about 30 minutes on each side, basting frequently with the curry mixture.
Serve with rice, chopped peanuts or macadamia nuts, and pineapple slices with the sauce on the side. (*4 servings*)

VEGETABLES
AND SIDE DISHES

CHINESE FRIED RICE WITH PORK

    ½ cup peanut oil (or other cooking oil)
    4 cups cooked rice
    2 cups cooked lean pork, finely
       chopped
    2 tablespoons soy sauce
    2 eggs, lightly beaten
    ¼ cup finely chopped scallions

Heat the oil in a heavy skillet to the smoking point, add the rice, and stir-fry about 6 minutes.
Add the pork, cook 5 minutes longer, then stir in the soy sauce. Turn up the heat, and drip the beaten eggs gradually into the hot mixture, stirring vigorously so that the eggs cook and blend in with the rice.
Sprinkle in the scallions and serve. (*4 servings*)

BAKED ARTICHOKES WITH CHEESE

4 fresh artichokes
1 teaspoon salt
4 tablespoons chopped onion
1 tablespoon chopped parsley
2 tablespoons grated Monterey Jack cheese
1 cup dry bread crumbs
¼ cup cooking oil

Put the artichokes into a saucepan, cover with water, add salt, and cook uncovered 20 to 30 minutes or until leaves will pull out. Drain, cut off the stalks and tips of the artichokes, and press open the centers. Remove the spiny chokes.
Preheat oven to 325 degrees.
Mix together the onion, parsley, cheese, and bread crumbs with salt and pepper to taste. Spoon this mixture into the centers of the artichokes, sprinkle with oil, and place into a shallow baking pan. Pour a little water into the bottom of the pan and bake 25 to 30 minutes. (*4 servings*)

HAWAIIAN YAMS

2 tablespoons butter
3 tablespoons brown sugar
2 tablespoons light cream
4 slices pineapple (fresh or canned)
2 cups mashed cooked yams (or sweet potatoes)
¼ cup milk
2 tablespoons melted butter
½ teaspoon salt
¼ teaspoon pepper

Put the butter and sugar into a small saucepan, and blend over low heat. Add the cream, stirring, and then the pineapple slices, one at a time, turning so that they will glaze on both sides.
Remove the pineapple slices to 4 heated plates. Add the yams, milk, butter, and seasonings to the saucepan. Heat and beat until fluffy. Spoon the hot yams onto the pineapple slices and serve. (*4 servings*)

SCALLOPED TOMATOES

4 fresh tomatoes, peeled, seeded, and cut up
2 cups bread crumbs
3 tablespoons butter
¼ cup minced onion
1 teaspoon sugar
1 teaspoon salt
½ teaspoon pepper
few grains cayenne

Preheat oven to 350 degrees.
Drain tomatoes, and put them with the bread crumbs into a buttered baking dish. Dot with butter; sprinkle with onion, sugar, and seasonings.
Bake 30 minutes or until brown on top. (*4 servings*)

LENTILS MEXICANOS

2 cups lentils
2 quarts beef broth
½ cup olive oil
1 thick slice ham, chopped (about 1 cup)
3 medium onions, sliced
2 cloves garlic, chopped
1 cup tomato purée
1 teaspoon coriander, minced
2 tablespoons chili powder
1 teaspoon salt
⅛ teaspoon cayenne pepper
½ cup grated Monterey Jack cheese

Wash and pick over lentils. Cover with broth, and bring to a boil. Simmer slowly until done, 40 minutes to 1 hour.
Preheat oven to 300 degrees.
Heat olive oil. Fry the ham, onions, and garlic until lightly browned. Add the tomato purée, coriander, chili powder, salt, and pepper. Stir well for a few minutes. Add lentils and mix well.
Put all in a large oven casserole, sprinkle with cheese, and bake in the oven 15 or 20 minutes or until the cheese melts. Serve with tortillas. (*8 to 10 servings*)

SALADS
AND DRESSINGS

CAESAR SALAD

To the best of our knowledge, it has never been firmly established where the first Caesar salad was made. There are reports that Tijuana, Mexico, is its point of origin, and others that Hollywood should get the credit. Tijuana gets our vote because there was a well-known restaurant there during Prohibition times named Caesar's.

Caesar salad is not difficult to make, but there are a rather large number of ingredients that go into it and a certain procedural order is necessary to make it come out right.

```
2 heads romaine or mixed salad greens,
    washed thoroughly, dried, and chilled
1 clove garlic, minced, in ½ cup olive
    oil
    juice of 1 lemon
1 teaspoon salt
½ teaspoon dry mustard
8 anchovy fillets, chopped (optional)
½ cup grated Parmesan cheese
1 egg, raw or slightly coddled
    freshly ground pepper
    Worcestershire sauce
1 cup French bread croutons, previously
    sautéed in ¼ cup olive oil mixed with
    1 clove garlic, minced
```

1. Rub the salad bowl with a cut clove of garlic.
2. Break the salad greens into bite-size pieces, and place into the bowl.
3. Add the olive oil. Toss well so that all greens are well coated.
4. Sprinkle with lemon juice, salt, and mustard. Toss.
5. Add the anchovy fillets and cheese. Toss.
6. Break the egg into the bowl and toss again.
7. Sprinkle with freshly ground pepper, add a few drops Worcestershire sauce, and throw in the croutons.
8. Toss well, check for seasoning, and serve. (*4 to 6 servings*)

CRAB LOUIS

This elegant dish originated in San Francisco at an early date, but is now available around the world. Originally made with Dungeness crab, it is equally good made with the back-fin meat of the blue-claw crab of the East.

```
1 cup mayonnaise
½ cup unsweetened whipped cream
½ cup chili sauce
2 tablespoons lemon juice
¼ cup chopped green pepper
1 tablespoon grated onion
½ teaspoon salt
    dash Tabasco sauce
3 cups cooked lump crab meat
    lettuce
    ripe olives
```

Blend the mayonnaise with the whipped cream, chili sauce, lemon juice, pepper, grated onion, and seasonings.

Add the crab meat, toss well, and serve on lettuce. Garnish with ripe olives. (*4 servings*)

CALIFORNIA FRUIT SALAD

This salad, of course, features most of the fruits for which California is noted. It is served always as a first course, as are all salads in California (but not before the soup).

```
    lettuce leaves
8 ripe apricots, halved and pitted
2 oranges, peeled and sliced
12 cooked prunes, drained and pitted
    juice of ½ lemon
4 tablespoons mayonnaise or olive oil
```

Wash and dry the lettuce leaves and place onto 4 plates.

Arrange the 3 fruits on the lettuce, sprinkle with lemon juice, and top with mayonnaise or olive oil. (*4 servings*)

ENSALADA DE VERDOLAGA (PURSLANE SALAD)

Purslane, known to early Californians as verdolaga, grows in lawns and along the irrigation ditches in southern California and in the Southwest. Other wild greens, like young pokeberry shoots, chicory, wild garlic, wild mustard, and watercress, can be used in salads in the spring when they are young and tender. Dandelion greens can be cut until they are six or eight inches high. Be sure you know what greens you are eating—don't take chances. Many domestic greens, such as radish, turnip, and beet tops, are eaten in salads too.

    2 pounds verdolaga
    4 tablespoons olive oil
    1 tablespoon vinegar
    ½ teaspoon salt
    1 medium onion, sliced

Wash verdolaga well, drain, and dry. Put oil, vinegar, and salt in salad bowl, and mix with wooden spoon. Add onion and verdolaga, toss. Chill until ready to serve. (8 servings)

HAWAIIAN SURPRISE

    4 tomatoes
    1 cup chopped pineapple
    2 tablespoons mayonnaise
    1 tablespoon capers
    2 tablespoons chopped macadamia nuts
      or other nuts
    1 teaspoon salt
      lettuce

Remove the skin from the tomatoes by dipping into boiling water, slice off the tops, and scoop out the center portions. Chill.
Mix together the remaining ingredients. Stuff into the tomato shells, and serve on lettuce. (4 servings)

AVOCADO SUPREME

Split ripe avocados lengthwise and remove the pits. Fill the cavities with French dressing made of 2 parts olive oil to 1 part lemon juice, and a little salt, pepper, and paprika.

GREEN GODDESS DRESSING

This dressing was created at the Palace Hotel in San Francisco in honor of George Arliss, for his performance in *The Green Goddess*. Its fame has long outlasted that of the movie.

    2 tablespoons chopped chives
    1 clove garlic, minced
    ¼ cup finely chopped parsley
    ½ teaspoon celery salt
    ½ teaspoon salt
    1 teaspoon sugar
    2 tablespoons chopped anchovies
    2 tablespoons tarragon vinegar
    ¾ cup salad dressing or mayonnaise
    2 tablespoons gin
    ½ cup sour cream
    1 tablespoon lemon juice

Mix together all the dry ingredients, then stir in the remaining ingredients. Or put everything into a blender and mix at high speed. Serve on salad greens or as a dressing for seafood. (approximately 2 cups)

LORENZO DRESSING

    ½ cup French dressing
    2 tablespoons chili sauce
    2 tablespoons chopped watercress
    1 teaspoon finely chopped pimento
    1 teaspoon finely chopped chives or
      onion

Blend all the ingredients together, and serve on a mixed green salad.

CHICKEN SALAD, CALIFORNIA STYLE

    1 large head lettuce, washed, dried, and
      torn into bits
    1 cup cubed cooked chicken
    1 orange, peeled and sectioned
    1 apple, cored, peeled, and cubed
    ½ cup chopped celery
    ½ cup toasted almonds
    5 to 6 tablespoons French dressing

Mix all the ingredients together, toss well, chill, and serve. (4 servings)

SAN FERNANDO SALAD

    1 clove garlic, cut
    8 large lettuce leaves, washed and
      thoroughly dried
    1 stalk celery, chopped
    1 bunch watercress, coarsely chopped
    2 cups chopped, seeded ripe olives
    3 tablespoons olive oil
    1 tablespoon wine vinegar
    1 teaspoon salt
      freshly ground pepper
    2 peeled tomatoes, sliced

Rub a salad bowl well with cut garlic, and put
in the lettuce leaves, celery, watercress, olives,
olive oil, vinegar, and seasonings. Toss vigorously.
Add the tomato slices. Mix well but carefully,
so that tomato slices will not be broken. (*4
servings*)

COLUMBIAN SALAD

      sections of 2 seedless oranges
    2 large tomatoes, peeled and cut into
      bits
      crisp romaine lettuce
  1½ tablespoons vinegar
    4 tablespoons olive (or other) oil
    2 tablespoons orange juice
   ½ tablespoon minced parsley
    1 teaspoon confectioners' sugar
   ¼ teaspoon salt

Arrange the oranges and tomatoes on a bed of
washed and dried romaine lettuce leaves.
Mix together the remaining ingredients, and
pour over the salad. (*4 servings*)

BREADS
AND BATTERCAKES

SOURDOUGH BREAD

This is a specialty of the West Coast and
Alaska that came with the settlers, and is now
made by commercial bakeries. A light, pleasant
bread, its slightly sour taste goes well with
salads, and makes superior sandwiches. Make
starter in the following way:

    4 tablespoons sugar
    2 cups flour
    2 cups lukewarm water

Mix together all the ingredients, and let stand
in warm place 2 to 3 days to ferment. Store in
the refrigerator until ready to use. Always
leave 1 cup starter to start the next batch of
pancakes or bread. (To speed the starter, ½
teaspoon of yeast can be used, and reduce the
sugar to 3 tablespoons.)

    2 cups starter
    2 cups lukewarm water
    1 tablespoon salt
    3 tablespoons butter, melted
    2 tablespoons sugar
    6 cups flour

Mix starter, water, salt, butter, sugar, and flour
in large mixing bowl.
Knead 12 to 15 minutes, until smooth and
satiny. Put in a greased bowl, and cover with
cloth. Let rise until double in bulk, about 1½
to 2 hours. Push down, knead again briefly, let
rest 10 minutes, shape into 2 round loaves, and
put on a greased cookie sheet (or put into 2
well-greased loaf pans), allowing space for
expansion. Let rise until double.
Preheat oven to 375 degrees for 10 minutes.
Bake 40 to 50 minutes, until brown and loaf
sounds hollow when tapped. (*2 loaves*)

ORANGE SURPRISE BISCUITS

2 cups flour
5 teaspoons baking powder
1 teaspoon salt
2 tablespoons shortening
½ cup milk (or more)
1 orange
16 small cubes sugar

Preheat oven to 375 degrees.
Sift the dry ingredients together, cut in shortening with a knife, and add enough milk to make a soft dough.
Roll out on a floured board to a thickness of about ¾ inch, and cut with a round cutter into 16 biscuits.
Place the biscuits into a greased pan, and grate orange rind over each.
Squeeze the orange, dip the lumps of sugar into the juice and quickly press into the center of each biscuit. Bake about 20 minutes or until done. (*6 to 8 servings*)

TAIT'S FRENCH PANCAKES

These pancakes, unusual in that they are oven-baked rather than griddle-cooked, originated in Tait's Old Restaurant Down Town in San Francisco.

2 eggs, beaten
1 cup flour
2 cups milk
  butter
  Six-Citrus Marmalade*
  confectioners' sugar

Preheat oven to 375 degrees.
Mix together the eggs and flour, then gradually add the milk, beating all the time.
Butter 4 oven-proof saucers, spoon a quarter of the batter into each, and bake 8 to 10 minutes or until golden.
Remove from oven, put a dab of marmalade onto each pancake, roll up, and serve dusted with confectioners' sugar. (*4 servings*)

PRUNE BREAD

Californians and Oregonians produce so many prunes that they are sometimes hard-put to find uses for them. One of their more successful efforts is this excellent bread.

1 cup flour
½ cup whole-wheat flour
½ teaspoon baking soda
½ teaspoon baking powder
½ teaspoon salt
½ cup sugar
1 egg, lightly beaten
2 tablespoons butter, melted
½ cup milk
½ cup chopped cooked prunes
½ cup prune juice

Preheat oven to 375 degrees.
Sift together all the dry ingredients.
Mix together the egg, butter, milk, prunes, and juice. Add the dry mixture, and blend in an electric mixer.
Spoon into a buttered 9-by-5-inch loaf pan, and bake about 40 minutes to 1 hour.

GARLIC BREAD

1 large clove garlic, minced (or to taste)
½ cup butter
1 long loaf French, Italian, or sourdough bread

Preheat oven to 450 degrees.
Cream together the garlic and butter.
Slice the loaf lengthwise and spread with the garlic butter.
Put the loaf together again, wrap in foil, and bake 15 minutes.
Slice the loaf crosswise and serve.

DESSERTS

QUEEN ANNE'S COOKIES

From an old clipping:

Over a hundred years ago my great-great-grandmother went from New Jersey to Indiana as a bride. Later my own mother carried these prize recipes across the plains in a covered wagon to a prairie homestead in the Middle West. Then still later I myself brought them to California, and now once again they find a place with my three married daughters. . . .

The recipe below is the only one we have.

    ½ cup butter, softened
    ½ cup sugar
    2 egg yolks
    ⅓ cup sour cream
    ½ teaspoon baking soda
    2 cups flour
      caraway seeds

Preheat oven to 350 degrees.
Cream butter, add sugar, beat until light.
Beat the egg yolks with the sour cream, in which the soda has been dissolved. Add the flour gradually, adding enough to allow the dough to be rolled out.
Roll thin, cut into pleasing shapes, and sprinkle with caraway seeds. Bake 20 minutes. (*2 dozen cookies*)

TROPICAL FIGS

    8 fresh figs, peeled and cut in half
    ½ cup rum
    ¼ cup brown sugar, firmly packed
      juice of 1 lime
      freshly grated coconut
      fresh mint, chopped

Mix together the figs, rum, sugar, and lime juice.
Serve topped with coconut and mint. (*4 servings*)

FRIED BANANAS

    4 bananas, peeled and halved
      lengthwise
    4 tablespoons butter
    1 cup brown sugar, firmly packed
    1 cup orange juice
    1 teaspoon grated orange rind
    ½ cup sour cream mixed with ½ cup
      confectioners' sugar

Fry the bananas quickly in the butter (1 minute on each side), using a heavy skillet.
Mix together the sugar, orange juice, and grated rind, and pour over the bananas. Cook and turn the bananas, spooning the syrup over them as they cook.
Serve hot, topped with the sweetened sour cream. (*4 servings*)

HAUPIA (COCONUT PUDDING)

This dessert is as common in Hawaii as rice pudding in New York. It is said that no luau would be considered complete without it.

    3 cups grated fresh coconut
    1 cup boiling water
    3 tablespoons cornstarch
    1½ tablespoons sugar

Pour the boiling water over the coconut, and allow to stand about 20 minutes. Strain through a double thickness of poi cloth (or cheesecloth), squeezing out as much milk as possible.
Combine the cornstarch and sugar. Add enough of the coconut milk to make a smooth paste.
Heat the remaining milk to boiling, and slowly stir in the cornstarch paste. Continue boiling until pudding thickens.
Pour into an 8-inch square cake pan and allow to cool. Cut into 2-inch squares. Serve Hawaiian style on ti leaves, or on small paper doilies. (*6 to 8 servings*)

CALIFORNIA
GUAVA SHORTCAKE

Shortcake went west with the settlers, and stayed. Many new fruits were added to its repertoire—loganberries, youngberries, and oranges—and many old ones kept, like strawberries and huckleberries.

        2 cups flour
        2 tablespoons sugar
        1 tablespoon shortening
        1 tablespoon baking powder
        ½ teaspoon salt
        ¾ cup milk
        4 to 6 ripe guavas
          sugar
          whipped cream

Preheat oven to 450 degrees.
Combine the first 6 ingredients, and work into a biscuitlike dough, using a floured board.
Form into 2 one-inch-thick round cakes, and bake.
Remove blossom ends from guavas, peel, and cut in half. Scoop out the pulpy centers, and force through a wide-mesh wire sieve. Sweeten this pulp to taste.
Spoon half the guava paste onto one of the cakes, cover with the other, and top with the remaining guava. Top with whipped cream. (*4 servings*)

SIX-CITRUS MARMALADE

There are marmalades made with one citrus fruit, with two citrus fruits, and even three citrus fruits. The recipe below is made with nearly every citrus fruit that grows. Where was it found? In California, of course.

        1 medium grapefruit
        1 lemon
        2 oranges
        2 limes
        5 kumquats
        2 tangerines
        1½ quarts water
        6 cups sugar

Halve the fruits, slice as thinly as possible, discarding seeds. Put into a large pot with the water, and allow to stand overnight.

Put the pot over medium heat, and simmer 40 minutes or until peel is tender.
Add the sugar and cook, covered, at a fast boil to the jelly stage (jelly thermometer should read 220 degrees).
Cool, put into sterilized jars, and seal. (*15 pints*)

POACHED PLUMS

        1 cup water
        1½ cups sugar
          pinch salt
        ½ teaspoon vanilla extract
        18 fresh plums, split, pits removed

Heat the water in a saucepan, dissolve the sugar, and stir in the salt and vanilla. Bring to a boil, add the plum halves, and poach until tender. A few pieces of lemon zest can be used instead of vanilla for flavor.
Cool in the syrup, and serve hot or cold. (*4 servings*)

CALIFORNIA PRUNE PUDDING

This is a West Coast version of a dessert called prune whip in the South, in which the egg whites are incorporated into the prune mixture before baking (and the result is equally good).

        3 cups dried prunes, washed and pitted
        1 cup sugar
        2 eggs, separated
        2 tablespoons cornstarch
          few drops lemon extract
          dash grated nutmeg
        1 tablespoon sugar

Preheat oven to 325 degrees.
Soak prunes overnight in water to cover, simmer until tender, cool, and drain, reserving a cup of the juice for later use.
Cut up the prunes, mix well with sugar, well-beaten egg yolks, cornstarch, lemon extract, and nutmeg.
Spoon into a buttered pudding dish. Beat the egg whites with a tablespoon of sugar until stiff, and spread over top.
Place in the oven, and cook until meringue is golden, then fold into the pudding. Bake 6 to 8 minutes longer. (*4 servings*)

HAWAIIAN SWEET

Anything with pineapple in it is called
Hawaiian—whether this is truly Hawaiian we
don't know. But it's a lovely dessert for a
summer party, and the fruits can be varied
according to the season.

- 1 cup cubed fresh pineapple
- 1 large apple, peeled, seeded, and
  cubed
- 1 orange, peeled and sliced
- 1 banana, peeled and sliced
- 1 cup Bing cherries, seeded
- 1 dozen marshmallows, quartered
- 1 cup heavy cream
- 1 teaspoon vanilla
- 2 tablespoons sugar
- 1 envelope unflavored gelatin, softened
  in ½ cup warm water

Cut a good slice off the side of a ripe pineapple.
Scoop out meat, and cut into cubes.
Mix all the ingredients together and spoon
back into pineapple shell or individual molds.
Chill. Serve cold. (*4 servings*)

LOGANBERRY CAKE

Loganberries were developed in the 1880s by
Judge Logan, a botanist, from the Pacific
Coast dewberry and the European raspberry.
It is a large, lush, seedy berry that tastes
something like a raspberry, but warmer and
smoother. Closer to a black raspberry or black
currant with a freshness that lifts it out of the
ordinary, it is often used in jams and cakes.

- ½ cup butter
- 1 cup sugar
- 3 eggs, lightly beaten
- 1½ cups cake flour
- ¼ teaspoon salt
- 1 teaspoon baking powder
- ¼ teaspoon baking soda
- ½ teaspoon cinnamon
- ½ teaspoon nutmeg
- 1½ cups ripe loganberries, fresh or
  canned, with juice

Preheat oven to 325 degrees.
Cream the butter, add the sugar gradually.
Add the eggs, beat well.
Sift the flour, salt, baking powder, baking
soda, and spices together, and add to the egg
mixture.
Stir in the loganberries and juice to make a
thick batter. Spoon into a 13 x 9 x 2½ buttered
baking pan, and place into the oven. Bake for 1
hour or until straw inserted comes out clean.
Serve as is, or with Brown Sugar Lemon
Sauce:

- 1½ cups brown sugar, firmly packed
- 2 cups water
- ¼ cup lemon juice
- 2 tablespoons butter
- 3 tablespoons cornstarch stirred into ¼
  cup water

Mix sugar and water. Bring to a boil, simmer 5
minutes. Add lemon juice and butter.
Mix cornstarch to a paste with water, and stir
into sauce. Simmer until thick. Serve hot.

BEVERAGES

SANGRÌA ·

It is only in recent years that this refreshing
Spanish punch has been formalized and sold
commercially. When mixing sangria at home,
one has the option of making it more lethal—or
less lethal—by controlling the amount of
Cointreau and cognac.

- 1 bottle red wine, dry or sweet,
  according to taste
  juice and peel of ½ lemon
  juice and peel of 1 orange
- 4 ounces Cointreau
- 4 ounces cognac

Mix all the ingredients together in a 1½ quart
pitcher, and let stand a few hours.
Fill with ice cubes, stir until chilled, and serve.
(*6 servings*)

CHAMPAGNE PUNCH

We tested several white sparkling wines and champagnes for a family wedding, and the one we liked best was from California. It had been customary at weddings to serve the very best French champagne. What to do? We served the one we liked.

    2 teaspoons sugar
    1 cup lemon juice
    1 lemon, thinly sliced
    1 orange, thinly sliced
    1 cup diced pineapple
    2 bottles champagne, chilled

Dissolve the sugar in the lemon juice, and pour into a punch bowl over a large block of ice. Add the fruit. Pour in the champagne, and stir well. (*about 20 servings*)

HAWAIIAN MAI TAI

This delightful drink is native to the island of Hawaii. It is a sipping drink like a mint julep and is served in the same circumstances—on special occasions and for special guests. Recently it has grown in popularity on the mainland.

    4 teaspoons sugar
    4 teaspoons water
      finely crushed ice
    4 jiggers heavy black rum
    4 jiggers light rum
      juice of 2 limes

Put 1 teaspoon sugar and 1 teaspoon water into each of 4 Old Fashioned glasses. Fill the glasses with ice, and pour a jigger of black rum and a jigger of light rum into each, add lime juice, and stir. (*4 servings*)

ORANGE JULEP

    1 quart fresh orange juice
      juice of 6 limes
    1 cup sugar
    ½ cup chopped mint leaves
    2 cups club soda
    8 sprigs fresh mint

Mix together the juices, sugar, and chopped mint. Chill.
Half fill 8 glasses with ice, add the prepared juice, and fill with club soda. Serve, garnished with a mint sprig in each glass. (*8 servings*)

CAPPUCCINO

    2 ounces very hot Italian-roast coffee
    1 ounce brandy,
    1 tablespoon heavy cream
      cinnamon
      nutmeg
    1 lump sugar

Pour the coffee and brandy into a 4-ounce demitasse or glass, top with cream, and sprinkle with cinnamon and nutmeg. Serve with a lump of sugar on the side. (*1 serving*)

CAFFÈ BORGIA

    1½ ounces very hot Italian-roast coffee
    1½ ounces very hot chocolate
     1 tablespoon sweetened whipped
       cream
       grated orange peel

Pour the coffee and chocolate into a 4-ounce demitasse or glass, stir, top with whipped cream, and sprinkle with grated orange peel. (*1 serving*)

ACKNOWLEDGMENTS

It has been our purpose in this book to write an in-depth report on cooking in every section of the United States. By in depth we mean the cooking not only of the present day, but down through the years: the roots, the evolution, and development. We began with the native cooking of America and worked through the years of colonization, westward migration, immigration, and integration of the tastes of many different cultures into new and regional cuisine.

The fulfillment of our goals necessitated a great deal of research, and although we have visited at one time or another most of the fifty states, we could be there only in the present, although much was to be learned from the past. The New York Public Library and the libraries of Hackensack, Leonia, and Englewood, New Jersey, gave us considerable help as did our Congressman, Henry Helstoski; the National Park Service; The Library of Congress; Harold L. Peterson, Chief Curator, U. S. Department of Interior, the Museum of New Mexico in Santa Fe, to all of whom we are grateful.

We consulted old cookbooks long out of print with interesting, if not always usable, recipes:

The Accomplished Cook (1664), published in England (Boston edition 1712).

American Cookery (1796), Amelia Simmons, one of the first cookbooks to be published in America. Hudson and Goodwin, Hartford, Connecticut (1963 Limited Edition, West Virginia Pulp and Paper Company).

The Compleat Housewife, E. Smith, collected from the Fifth London Edition, published by William Parks (Williamsburg, 1742).

Fanny Farmer Cookbook (1896), 1939 Edition, Little, Brown & Company, Boston.

Mary Johnson Bailey Lincoln's Cookbook (1884).

Miss Parlea's New Cook Book (1884).

Mrs. Beeton's Book of Household Management (1861), Isabella Beeton, 1915 Edition, Ward Locke and Co., Ltd.

Old Time Cookery (1824), Monroe Aurandote, Jr., taken from *A Treatise on Domestic Cooking and Practical Systems of Domestic Cooking* by Thomas Cooper, M.D., and from *The Art of Preserving All Kinds of Animal and Vegetable Sustenances for Many Years*, published in 1824 by George Gertz, Reading, Pennsylvania.

Practical Cooking and Dinner Giving (1888), Mrs. Mary F. Henderson, Harper and Bros., New York.

The Virginia Housewife (1824).

Friends, knowing that we were doing this book, sent us favorite recipes. We have included many of these anonymously, by permission.

A valuable source of help came from small cookbooks privately produced by church groups, women's clubs, and societies that have recorded historic and regional dishes popular in their areas. Some outstanding examples:

From the Galleys of Nantucket (1969), First Congregational Church of Nantucket Island.

Maine Coastal Cooking (1963), Courier-Gazette, Inc., Rockland, Maine.

A Tour of Cape Cod Kitchens (1937), Episcopal Church, Harwich Port, Massachusetts.

The Bedingfield Inn Cook Book (1966), Stewart County Historical Commission, Lumpkin, Georgia.

Centennial Cookbook (undated), Memorial Episcopal Church of Baltimore.

Charleston Receipts (1950), Junior League of Charleston, South Carolina.

Coastal Carolina Cooking (1958), Women's Auxiliary, Ocean View Memorial Hospital, Myrtle Beach, South Carolina, published by Myrtle Beach Printcraft, Inc.

Eighteenth Century Hostesses Are Twentieth Century Cooks (1966), Tryon Palace Commission, New Bern, North Carolina.

A Few Recipes from Maryland (undated), St. Johns Episcopal Church, Bethesda, Maryland.

Mountain Measures, A Collection of West Virginia Recipes (1974), Junior League of Charleston, West Virginia.

Some Favorite Recipes (1929), Marianna (Florida) Woman's Club.

A Tryon Palace Trifle or Eighteenth Century Cookery (1960), Tryon Palace Commission, New Bern, North Carolina.

The Women's Exchange Cookbook (1964), Women's Exchange of Memphis, Tennessee.

A Collection of Favorite Recipes of Parents of East Junior High School Students (1972), Parent Teacher's Association, Great Falls, Montana.

Eskimo Cookbook (1952), Alaska Crippled Children's Association.

Out of Alaska Kitchens (1961), Easter Seal Society foɪ Alaska Crippled Children and Adults.

Treasured Armenian Recipes (1949), Detroit Women's Chapter of the Armenian General Benevolent Union.

Then there were the many cookbooks, contemporary and vintage, from more standard publishing channels:

America Cooks (1940), the Browns, originally published by W. W. Norton, republished by Bantam Books, New York.

The Art of Irish Cooking (1965), Monica Sheridan, Doubleday & Company, Inc., Garden City.

The Art of Spanish Cooking (1963), Betty Wason, Doubleday & Company, Inc., Garden City.

At Home on the Range (1939), George Rector, sponsored by Gas Exhibits, Inc., The Rector Publishing Co., N. Y.

California Cookbook (1946), Genevieve Callahan, M. Barrows & Company, Inc., Clifton, N. J.

The Cookbook of the United Nations (1964), Barbara Kraus, United Nations Association of the U. S. A., Inc., New York.

Elena's Secrets of Mexican Cooking (1964), Prentice-Hall, Inc., Englewood Cliffs.

The Encyclopedia of Cooking (1951), edited by Ruth Berolzheimer, Director of Culinary Arts Institute, Consolidated Book Publishers, Chicago:
"Body Building Dishes for Children,"
"500 Delicious Salad Recipes,"
"250 Delicious Soup Recipes,"
"250 Ways to Prepare Poultry and Game Birds."

Farm Journal's Country Cookbook (1959, 1972), compiled by the Food Editors of *Farm Journal*, edited by Nell B. Nichol, Doubleday & Company, Inc., New York.

Father Was a Gourmet (1965), Carol Truax, Doubleday & Company, Inc., New York.

Favorite Recipes of California Wine Makers (1963), Wine Advisory Board, San Francisco.

The First Ladies' Cook Book (1959), Parents Magazine Press, New York.

Florida Fish Recipes (1966), U. S. Dept. of the Interior.

Ford Treasury of Favorite Recipes from Famous Eating Places, Vol. 3, compiled and tested by Nancy Kennedy, Golden Press, New York.

Heirloom Treasure (undated), Bureau of Commercial Fisheries, U. S. Dept. of the Interior.

The Home Book of Greek Cookery (1963), Joyce M. Stubbs, Faber & Faber Ltd., London.

James Beard's American Cookery (1972), James Beard, Little, Brown & Company, Boston.

Meta Given's Modern Encyclopedia of Cooking (1953), S. G. Ferguson Associates, Chicago.

The Mexican Cookbook (1971), George and Ingar Wallace, Nitty Gritty Productions, Concord, Calif.

My Yesterday, Your Today (1973), Inez Wendell Alfors, Piedmont Bible College Press, Winston-Salem, North Carolina.

Nebraska Pioneer Cookbook (1974), compiled by Kay Graber, University of Nebraska Press, Lincoln.

The New York Times Cook Book (1961), edited by Craig Claiborne, Harper & Row, New York.

New York World's Fair Cookbook (1939), Crosby Gaige, Doubleday, Doran, and Co., New York.

Of Cabbages and Kings (1938), William Rhode, Stackpole Sons.

The Picayune Creole Cookbook, Second Edition, originally published 1901, republished 1971 by Dover Publications, Inc., New York.

Pillsbury's Fifth 100 Grand National Recipes (1954), adapted for use by Ann Pillsbury, Pillsbury Mills, Inc., Minneapolis.

Plantation Cookery of Old Louisiana (1938), Eleanore Ott, published by Harmonson, New Orleans.

Pueblo Indian Cookbook (1972), edited and compiled by Phyllis Hughes, Museum of New Mexico Press, Santa Fe.

The Smorgasbord Cookbook (1949), Ann Olsen Coombs, Hill & Wang Paperback Library, New York.

The South Pacific Cookbook (1970), Victor Bennett, Prentice-Hall, Inc., Englewood Cliffs.

The Southern Cookbook (1951), Marion Brown, Pocket Books, Inc., New York.

200 Years of Charleston Cooking (1930), Natalie Scott, published by Jonathan Cape and Harrison Smith.

200 Years of New Orleans Cooking (1931), Blanche S. Rhett, published by Jonathan Cape and Harrison Smith.

Washington Cookbook (1972), Mary Clifford, E. P. Dutton & Co., Inc., New York.

Where to Dine in '39 (1939), Diana Ashley, Crown Publishers, Inc., New York.

In addition to the aforementioned cookbooks, we quoted from the following selected list of novels, references, and historical books:

Adventures in Good Eating (1951), Duncan Hines Adventures in Good Eating, Inc., Bowling Green, Kentucky.

The Adventures of Huckleberry Finn (1896), Mark Twain, 1906 Edition, Harpers Library, New York.

The American Heritage Reader (1956), Dell Publishing Co., Inc., New York.

The American Past (1957), Roger Butterfield, Simon and Schuster, Inc., New York.

Blackfoot Lodge Tales (1962), George Bird Grinnell (1849-1938), University of Nebraska Press, Lincoln.

Death Comes for the Archbishop (1926), Willa Cather, Alfred A. Knopf, Inc., New York.

Democracy in America (1956), Alexis de Tocqueville, edited by Richard D. Heffner, The New American Library, Grossman Publishers, Inc., New York.

Diary of America (1957), edited by Josef and Dorothy Berger, Simon and Schuster, Inc., New York.

Domestic Life in Virginia in the Seventeenth Century (1957), Annie Lash Jester, The Virginia 350th Anniversary Celebration Corp., Garrett & Massie, Inc., Richmond.

The Flowing Stream (1939), Florence Kelly, E. P. Dutton & Co., Inc., New York.

The Food Book (1971), James Trager, Grossman Publishers, Inc., New York.

The Golden Age of American Anthropology (1960), Margaret Mead and Ruth L. Bunzel, George Braziller, Inc., New York.

The Great Events by Famous Historians, (Vol. XV (1905), Editor-in-Chief, Rossiter Johnson. Limited Members Edition, National Alumni, No. 343 (1918), registered in the name of Helen Brokenbrough Hawkins:
"The Louisiana Purchase" (A.D. 1803), Henry S. Randell, L.L.D.,
"The Lewis and Clark Expedition" (A.D. 1804), James Davey Butler and Robert Southey.

The King Ranch, 2 Vols. (1957), Tom Lea, Little, Brown & Company, Boston.

"Recipes from Antoine's Kitchen," (1948), Clementine Paddleford, *This Week* Magazine, New York.

Red-Flannel Hash and Shoo-Fly Pie: American Regional Foods and Festivals (1965), Lila Perl, World Publishing Co., New York.

Regional Geography of Anglo-America (1964, 1974), C. Langdon White, Edwin J. Fescue, Tom L. McKnight, Prentice-Hall, Inc., Englewood Cliffs.

So Big (1924), Edna Ferber, Doubledey & Company, Inc., New York.

The Story of an Old Farm (1889), Andrew D. Mellick, *Unionist Gazette*, Somerville, N. J.

Tales of the Frontier (1970), selected and retold by Everett Dick, University of Nebraska Press, Lincoln.

Territory of Treasures (1972), Bob and Kathryn Wright, The Old Army Press, Fort Collins, Colorado.

Under Their Vine and Fig Tree (1965), Julian Ursyn Niemcewicz, translated and edited by Metchie J. E. Budka, the N. J. Historical Society, Grassman Publishing Co., Elizabeth, N. J.

Finally, we thank our editor, Carol Cartaino, for countless hours of dedicated and creative work of fine-tooth-combing our manuscript.

INDEX

CONVERSION TABLE FOR OVEN TEMPERATURES

FAHRENHEIT DEGREES	CENTIGRADE DEGREES	OVEN TEMPERATURE
225	105	
250	120	VERY SLOW
275	135	
285	140	
300	150	SLOW
325	165	
350	175	
375	190	MODERATE
400	205	
425	220	
450	230	HOT
475	245	
500	260	VERY HOT

MEASUREMENT CONVERSION TABLES

AMERICAN MEASUREMENTS			APPROXIMATE METRIC MEASUREMENTS
FLUID			
DASH	=	LESS THAN 1/8 TEASPOON	
3 TEASPOONS	=	1 TABLESPOON	150 MILLILITERS
1 TABLESPOON	=	1/16 CUP	160 MILLILITERS
6-1/2 TABLESPOONS	=		1 DECILITER
16 TABLESPOONS	=	1 CUP	2-1/2 DECILITERS
1 CUP	=	8 OUNCES	2-1/2 DECILITERS
16 OUNCES	=	1 PINT	5 DECILITERS
2 PINTS	=	1 QUART	10 DECILITERS (1 LITER)
1 QUART	=	4 CUPS	10 DECILITERS (1 LITER)
4 QUARTS	=	1 GALLON	4 LITERS
DRY			
DASH	=	LESS THAN 1/8 TEASPOON	
1 OUNCE	=		28 GRAMS
3-1/2 OUNCES	=		100 GRAMS
1 POUND	=		450 GRAMS

TABLE OF EQUIVALENTS

FOOD—1 CUP	APPROXIMATE METRIC MEASUREMENTS
BREAD CRUMBS	450 GRAMS
BUTTER, MARGARINE	226 GRAMS
CHEESE, GRATED	113 GRAMS
COCONUT, FLAKED	100 GRAMS
CORN MEAL	140 GRAMS
CORNSTARCH	130 GRAMS
FLOUR, ALL–PURPOSE (sifted)	110 GRAMS
CAKE (sifted)	90 GRAMS
WHOLE WHEAT	120 GRAMS
LENTILS, PEAS, BEANS	225 GRAMS
RICE	225 GRAMS
SALAD OR COOKING OIL	225 GRAMS
SUGAR, GRANULATED	180 GRAMS
CONFECTIONERS' (sifted)	90 GRAMS
BROWN (packed)	190 GRAMS